BEETHOVEN'S
FRENCH PIANO

BEETHOVEN'S FRENCH PIANO

A Tale of Ambition and Frustration

TOM BEGHIN

THE UNIVERSITY OF CHICAGO PRESS
CHICAGO AND LONDON

The University of Chicago Press, Chicago 60637
The University of Chicago Press, Ltd., London
© 2022 by The University of Chicago
Published 2022
Printed in the United States of America

31 30 29 28 27 26 25 24 23 22   1 2 3 4 5

ISBN-13: 978-0-226-81835-1 (cloth)
ISBN-13: 978-0-226-81836-8 (e-book)
DOI: https://doi.org/10.7208/chicago/9780226818368.001.0001

This book has been supported by the General Publications
Fund of the American Musicological Society, funded
in part by the National Endowment for the Humanities
and the Andrew W. Mellon Foundation.

Library of Congress Cataloging-in-Publication Data

Names: Beghin, Tom, 1967– author.
Title: Beethoven's French piano : a tale of ambition and frustration /
Tom Beghin.
Description: Chicago : The University of Chicago Press, 2022. |
Includes bibliographical references and index.
Identifiers: LCCN 2021047928 | ISBN 9780226818351 (cloth) |
ISBN 9780226818368 (e-book)
Subjects: LCSH: Beethoven, Ludwig van, 1770–1827. Sonatas, piano. |
Piano music—19th century—History and criticism. | Piano—
Performance—History—19th century. | Maison Erard (Firm)
Classification: LCC ML410.B42 B439 2022 | DDC 780.92—dc23
LC record available at https://lccn.loc.gov/2021047928

to

Malcolm Bilson
mentor and friend

CONTENTS

Plates

Tables

ABBREVIATIONS

AmZ *Allgemeine musikalische Zeitung.* 1798–1806. Leipzig: Breitkopf & Härtel.

Bw Brandenburg, Sieghard, ed. 1996–98. *Ludwig van Beethoven: Briefwechsel Gesamtausgabe.* 8 vols. Munich: G. Henle.

EL&D Adelson, Robert, Alain Roudier, Jenny Nex, Laure Barthel and Michel Foussard, eds. 2015. *The History of the Erard Piano and Harp in Letters and Documents 1785–1959.* 2 vols. Cambridge: Cambridge University Press.

Kh Köhler, Karl-Heinz, Dagmar Beck, Grita Herre, with Günter Brosche, Renate Bormann, eds. 1972–2001. *Ludwig van Beethovens Konversationshefte.* 11 vols. Leipzig: VEB Deutscher Verlag für Musik.

WvZ Dorfmüller, Kurt, Norbert Gertsch, and Julia Ronge. 2014. *Ludwig van Beethoven: Thematisch-bibliographisches Werkverzeichnis.* 2 vols. Munich: G. Henle Verlag.

PREFACE

The Orpheus Institute for Advanced Studies & Research in Music, located in the city of Ghent in Belgium, is a special place. Performers, composers, and scholars gather there from all parts of the world to discuss questions of artistic research in music. In January 2015 I joined the institute to direct a research cluster and immediately began working on a project around Beethoven's French piano, made in Paris by Erard Frères in 1803. The structure of the institute is flexible: researchers can follow wherever they feel their research is leading them. This meant that my team just kept growing. Initially hand-picked to cover certain areas of expertise, it gradually expanded to include doctoral students who joined the institute's docARTES program in affiliation with the University of Leuven.

Not knowing where our research would take us next led us to develop a remarkable methodology. The project taught us patience, as the drive to seek out new expertise for the team also meant bringing each new member up to speed. Further patience was required as we familiarized ourselves with new bodies of repertoire. The greatest accomplishment—which was also the generator of all subsequent research—was the making of a replica of Beethoven's Erard. After it was finished in November 2016, it took a central place in a basement room of the institute. It was there that many of the hypotheses pursued throughout this book emerged, as enthusiastic practicing was followed by lively conversation with team members. The suggestion, "Let's go down to the basement," often resulted in new lines of investigation and further sub-projects. There was frustration, too, when a team member left to resume their life elsewhere and questions arose that required that particular person's expertise.

The larger research group that I direct at the Orpheus Institute is called "Declassifying the Classics: Rhetoric, Technology, and Performance, 1750–1850." During the time of our Beethoven Erard research, it included the following members:

Robin Blanton, associate researcher, organologist
Prach Boondiskulchok, doctoral researcher, pianist, composer
Song Hui Chon, visiting associate researcher, music perception and cognition researcher
Robert Giglio, associate researcher, museum scientist
Camilla Köhnken, postdoctoral researcher, pianist
Chris Maene, associate researcher, piano maker, and owner of Pianos Maene
Luca Montebugnoli, doctoral researcher, pianist
Ellie Nimeroski, doctoral researcher, violinist
Michael Pecak, associate researcher, pianist
Charles Shrader, visiting doctoral researcher, musicologist
Tilman Skowroneck, associate researcher, keyboardist, musicologist
Eleanor Smith, associate researcher, organologist
Thomas Wulfrank, associate researcher, acoustics engineer
Sanae Zanane, doctoral researcher, pianist

When I employ the collective "we" in this book it is to acknowledge the collaborative origin of the research that has informed it. Sometimes I refer to a team member by their first name: doing otherwise would feel unnatural. This collaborative spirit also explains the book's unusual structure. Twelve chapters follow my expanding and cumulative inquiries as a performing musician and researcher; they are interspersed with four "vignettes." These short interventions represent contexts or voices from outside—some of them, indeed, were either written by or co-written with associate researchers, whose authorships are acknowledged accordingly.

In addition, Michael helped me with the first part of chapter 10; Eleanor provided the organological research for chapter 4, which Robin in turn helped me write; Bobby created and helped interpret all data relating to our piano action experiments; Song Hui analyzed all acoustical data and produced corresponding graphs; Prach transcribed all the musical examples; Sanae assisted me with illustrations.

Originating from the same context of collaboration, individual essays by Hester Bell Jordan, Robin Blanton, Camilla Köhnken, Luca Montebugnoli, Michael Pecak, Charles Shrader, Tilman Skowroneck, and Eleanor Smith have made it into *Keyboard Perspectives* 13, the 2021 yearbook of the Westfield Center for Historical Keyboard Studies. This publication also includes essays by Erin Helyard, Jeanne Roudet, and Frédéric de La Grandville, who joined us during our 2018 Orpheus Summer Academy.

A lot of what I describe needs to be seen or heard. Therefore, *I ask the reader to consult the following website*, for it documents this book's research in a more direct way than prose ever could:

www.BeethovenErard.com

The website also features an eighty-minute lecture-documentary with the same title as this book, a bonus video on the "Lure of *una corda*," and a complete performance of Beethoven's Sonata Op. 53, along with a video-lecture featuring my analysis of this piece. Last but not least, a double CD on the Evil Penguin Records label (EPRC 0036) is commercially available: it features both the instrument and the repertoire that are central to this book.

All translations are ours. I especially thank Tilman for his advice on all matters German; Michael's Polish heritage led us to the remarkable Elsner passage in vignette 2. Original-language quotations may be found on the website, as well as a PDF document with a translation of Louis Adam's 1804–5 method. To convert the republican French calendar, I have used the "Tableau de concordance des calendriers républicain et grégorien" from Raymond Monnier, *Le Faubourg Saint-Antoine (1789–1815)* (Paris: Société des Études Robespierristes, 1981).

Parallel Tales

I'm holding a piece of wood: a thin piece of plywood, 21 × 7 cm. On November 24, 2015, one exactly like it was given to each of around eighty guests, including our sponsors. The front, stained to give the appearance of age, shows the imprint of an inscription: "Erard Frères~Rue du Mail N.° 37. à Paris 1803." We had photographed the original a couple of months before on a piano that Ludwig van Beethoven once owned. The reverse side explains: "It is said of Beethoven that he transcended the instruments of his day, yet his Erard [. . .] bears striking fingerprints of its famous owner. A more complex story is waiting to be told." This was how the piano maker Chris Maene and I officially revealed our plan to make a replica of this unique instrument.

Five years after this special event, the wooden plaque remains charged with significance: a handshake between craftsmen separated by more than two centuries, it also symbolizes my hope as a pianist-researcher that we could unlock the aspirations and memories of the piano's erstwhile owner. Above all, it represents the beginning of a multiyear research project that brought together artisanship and artistry, combining the building of an exceptional historical piano with experimental playing upon it under the umbrella of artistic research.

Players and builders of pianos interacted far more in Beethoven's day than they do today. It would be entirely normal, for example, when ordering a new piano, to discuss the choice of wood for the case, the number and sequence of stops, and types of leather for the hammers. By contrast, the closest a modern pianist gets to physically meeting anyone involved in the actual making of their instrument would be when they travel to Hamburg, to select one Steinway D concert grand out of a number of finished pianos in the company's showroom. For a pianist, even this would be an extraordinary privilege, probably the result of being invited to join an official delegation, say, of a concert venue wishing to upgrade its showcase piano. Even so, the chances are that on such a visit one would only meet a person in charge of sales.

It is also true, today as in the past, that once a piano is made, there's not much about it that can be changed. Today, after the purchase of an instrument, one relies on the services of a piano technician—a person unrelated to the creation of the instrument itself, but capable of adjusting its feel and character according to the desires of the customer. Back in Beethoven's day, however, there would have been no such separation between the roles of the maker and technician: in many cases—and certainly in the case of a customer as valued as Beethoven—they would have been one and the same person. So why not express one's desires from the very start? But there are limits to historicizing this builder–player relationship. When it comes down to technical details, we simply don't know how Beethoven really interacted with a particular builder such as, for instance, Nannette Streicher *née* Stein, and the way that I have interacted with piano makers and technicians over the years may not be typical of all historically informed pianists.

Beethoven's Erard makes for a complex study: how do we make the case that Beethoven interacted with its maker if the Parisian Erard brothers and Beethoven, resident of Vienna, never even met? Conversely, are Chris Maene's and my interactions when building a replica of Beethoven's Erard in any way reflective of what might have taken place if Beethoven had crossed paths with either Sébastien or Jean-Baptiste Erard? Beethoven's French piano encapsulates a panoply of human–object interactions, defying the boundaries of sociocultural, political, and economic behavior.

This book is about a single object: an 1803 Erard Frères *piano en forme de clavecin* with the serial number 133. (The Paris-based firm had been producing such "wing-shaped" or grand pianos since 1797, of which Beethoven's was the one hundred and thirty-third.) Just as the building of Beethoven's Erard as a modern-day, newly functioning replica has become part of what we studied, my own persona as a professional performer on historical keyboards informs every page in this book. This and the following chapters follow a string of questions that have been triggered by my own artistic aspirations as I started living with our replica of Beethoven's Erard, which we inaugurated on November 14, 2016, or just short of one year after our official announcement. In this sense, this book may be read as a logbook of some sort—from the declaration of intent through the first years of ownership—making up for the lack of such a record by Beethoven, but reflective of a relationship between one owner and another, linked across history through the parallel lives of an identical object.

As a modern-day performer on historical keyboards, I often find myself arguing that "if it was good enough for them, it ought to be good enough for me." "It" in this statement refers to the instrument I choose to play, but can also be interpreted as a metonym for materiality in general. "Them" is a reference to my historical counterparts—first and foremost, the keyboardist-composers whose scores I play, but also those who used their scores for the first time—a description I prefer to "their listeners," honoring a historically much more active context of performance: especially in a private genre like solo piano music, there was no listening without playing, and often it was the same person doing both. "Good enough" taps into a pre-Romantic tradition of music as a rhetorical art and the expectation that through musicking there should also be some act of communication or social interaction. "Me" refers to my identity as an artist-researcher, and the expectation that similar embodied knowledge to that of my historical counterparts will yield artistic insight relevant to modern-day performance. "Ought to," finally, reflects a healthy dose of self-doubt—and acknowledges an inevitable degree of subjectivity in any transferral from past to present.

It this case, however, I had doubts about the veracity of my statement to an extent I hadn't experienced with any other instrument documented to have belonged to a distinguished composer of the past. Was Beethoven's Erard indeed good enough for him? If so, why did he have it technically revised—twice? This question had been staring us in the face ever since Chris Maene and I measured and documented the preserved Erard in Linz and compared it with an unaltered 1805 Erard in the collection of the Musical Instrument Museum in Brussels: these were no minor revisions, and exactly how and why they had been undertaken became the topic of heated debate among members of my research team. Furthermore, the revisions were irreversible, so they had to be understood not only from a technical point of view, but also from a broader biographical or cultural perspective. Was it Beethoven's disavowal of the French emperor (captured in the well-known story of the composer crossing out the dedication of his "Eroica" Symphony in 1804) that finally made him give in to the frustration he felt with his French piano and decide to act upon it so invasively?

The Latour-school sociologist Adeleine Akrich has introduced a concept she calls "de-scription," which helps shine a light on Beethoven's act of instrumental revision. Her example is a lighting kit designed in France and adjusted to circumstances in Senegal. De-scription, or the undoing of the object's original inscription, stems from "the lack of a relationship [. . .] between designers and users" or from an inevitable discrepancy "between the world inscribed in the object and the world described by its displacement."[1] It could be argued that Beethoven's Erard had been displaced from its designer. It could also be argued that it had been appropriated by its new habitat. Early on, my research colleagues and I christened Beethoven's attempts to "improve" his Erard as *viennicizing*, as they so clearly were efforts to adjust French technology to Viennese standards. But does that mean that, during the years before the revisions, Beethoven had already interacted with his piano from a more general perspective of appropriation, trying to force not only his technique but also his artistic expectations and wishes onto it? The research that my colleagues and I have undertaken has led me to conclude decisively that this was not the case, but that instead his original intention was to embrace the instrument's Frenchness. To go further, he had wanted an Erard piano precisely *because* of its Frenchness.

We know that after the revisions Beethoven quickly started losing interest in his Erard. If it weren't for the instrument's displacement to Vienna, one might imagine at least two different scenarios. For instance, if Beethoven had been in a position to interact with Sébastien Erard directly, perhaps the latter might have convinced him that the specific design of the piano was there for a reason, and Beethoven's French adventures might have lasted longer (even though the words *liberté*, *égalité*, and *fraternité* sounded more and more hollow after 1804). A different, rather attractive scenario would be that Erard might have listened carefully to Beethoven's concerns or wishes and, unlike his Viennese colleague, would have succeeded in making technical adjustments of a more constructive nature, allowing for a positive process of viennicization of the French piano.

Beethoven knew what he was doing when he ordered a French piece of technology, and for at least a year and a half he enthusiastically used it as a tool for his own experimentation and creation. But an inner prompting to undertake adaptation and adjustment grew, as initial excitement gradually yielded to frustration and failure. Interestingly, even when reduced to ultimate thingness, when the Erard no longer served any of his pianistic or compositional needs, Beethoven never quite abandoned it—a fact testified to by its continued existence until the present day.[2] (Haydn's Erard, by contrast, was not so lucky: its emptied case ended up as a flour bin in an attic of a distant cousin in Rohrau, as reported by a witness in 1843, never to be heard of again.)[3]

The psychology is familiar to anyone starting to use a new piece of technology. After willingly adjusting one's behavior to the new thing, which one instinctively decides to love, there is inevitably a period of frustration as one runs up against the formerly routine tasks that the new object makes difficult. Why, we ask, can we not have both the advantages of the new, and the ease and familiarity of the old? Following this line of reasoning, Beethoven wanted to make an already superb piano better still.

The superb replica Maene ended up building was of Beethoven's piano as it had left the Erard Frères Paris workshop, before the revisions. Both for Beethoven and for me, then, our French pianos were not only new, but also novel: we had never seen or played anything like them before. But also our frame of reference is remarkably similar. Both our pianistic backgrounds are definitely Viennese. In my case this meant that after growing up practicing on modern pianos like anyone else, in my early twenties I began performing exclusively on historical keyboards, starting with what is commonly considered a classical fortepiano: a model from the 1790s, with a so-called Viennese action and a five-octave keyboard. For his part, Beethoven came from Bonn to Vienna in 1792 at the age of twenty-one with a lifelong experience already of playing German- and Viennese-style pianos, clavichords, and organs; eleven years later, at the age of thirty-two, he acquired the Erard, which would have been the first foreign-made piano he had owned. Despite the differences in our circumstances, Beethoven and I approached our French pianos not only with similar curiosity and wonder, but also with comparable embodied knowledge.

The following chapters are not about Beethoven's music per se. I'll end up discussing three piano sonatas more extensively—his Op. 53 ("Waldstein"), Op. 54, and Op. 57 ("Appassionata")—but that's because these works tell a compelling story of a composer who interacted with his instrument over a number of years, starting with the sketches for Op. 53 (in November 1803) through the publication of Op. 57 (in May 1806). In all likelihood, the sonatas were conceived as a trilogy to celebrate the acquisition of a new piano. I look for questions in their scores, which I reorient to my own engagement with the instrument. The challenge here is to pretend we do *not* know the results of Beethoven's own artistic research.

One recent author on Beethoven's Erard acknowledges that "few pianists today have access to any kind of period piano, let alone a five-and-a-half-octave Erard," but still maintains that "even if modern pianos preclude playing Beethoven's piano music 'with limits' in the strict sense, engaging critically with the instruments of his day can help us to recognize and appreciate where those limits were once drawn, inviting richer and more nuanced interpretations."[4] This makes it seem as if modern pianos, unlike period pianos, are *without* limits or, indeed, transcend the idea of being limited altogether. The suggestion for modern-day pianists, furthermore, to consult with "period instruments" so as to at least reconnect with the idea of a limit ends up feeding a belief that instruments in their standardized modern manifestations allow musicians to achieve anything, if only they put their minds to it.

This book, on the contrary, aims to put technology back into music (and musicking). It does so without giving in to any expectation of using the modern instrument as a frame of reference. I prefer to think of Beethoven's French piano's "affordances" (a term coined more than thirty years ago by the psychologist James Gibson) and "dependences" (a term developed by the archaeologist Ian Hodder during this past decade)—both concepts that point more directly to a mutual interaction between human and thing.[5] By here telling the story of my living with its replica *as my only instrument* during several years, I hope to gain insight into a pianist-composer's experiences with his Erard No. 133 some two centuries ago.

London, even if this is arguably clearer in retrospect for second-generation Broadwood in 1817 than for first-generation Erard in 1803. It also helps that, already in 1802, Beethoven was claiming in a letter to Zmeskall that "the entire swarm of piano makers besieges me and wants to serve me—for free; every one of them wants to make me a piano the way I want it."[11] Even if we take such a statement literally, the significant part of the letter shows that Beethoven was willing to pay a builder who actually mattered to him—the then fifty-year old Anton Walter—but on two conditions. We don't know whether the request ever reached Walter, but the chances are he wouldn't have been impressed. A certain hierarchy had to be respected—Walter was Imperial Instrument Maker, after all—meaning that Beethoven, a talented thirty-one-year-old, had to accept his place.

Speaking of hierarchy, there was also Beethoven's position with respect to Haydn, who at this time would have been the only other owner of an Erard grand piano in Vienna. There are stories of a falling-out between teacher and pupil, but these anecdotes (from Czerny, Ries, Schindler, and others), some of them recorded well after Beethoven's death, were, as James Webster has demonstrated, part of an emerging Beethoven biography.[12] Even if we accept that Haydn faded into retirement around 1803, it may not be wise to give in to the temptation to fill his vacated spot in history immediately. As we see Beethoven becoming the new dominant presence in the Austrian capital, the temptation is to also imagine him a gravitational force for Erard and Broadwood, who aim to strengthen by association their dominant positions within their own geographical regions. However, it is wrong to assume that Beethoven was already an international celebrity in his early thirties. As far as France was concerned, this was not the case: Beethoven *was* known in certain Parisian circles already, and this burgeoning reputation will inevitably be part of our Erard story, but his fame was very much less than that of Haydn, who was then celebrating his biggest international successes with *The Creation* and *The Seasons*.[13]

Then, in 2005, came a bombshell. A crucial piece of evidence from the Erard archives had been recovered by the pianist and Erard scholar, Alain Roudier, and Maria Rose–van Epenhuysen was the first to disseminate it. In Erard's sales books, we find an entry dated 18 Thermidor An 11 (August 6, 1803) that reads: "M. Bethowen [*sic*], harpsichordist in Vienna [*claviciniste à Vienne; sic*], owes 1500 livres for the sale of wing-shaped piano No. 133."[14]

It turns out that Beethoven's Erard had *not* been a gift, but that in fact he had *ordered* one. But before we cry foul (and with Rose–van Epenhuysen start asking whether it was Beethoven who ended up spreading the false rumor of a gift), we must pause and have a closer look at the mechanics of bookkeeping. The lefthand side of the page is the column of *doit*, or the amount owed, and shows the value of Beethoven's piano. On the right side, however, under the heading *avoir* (where the figures are meant to reconcile the invoiced amount with the actual payment), we find no corresponding amount (i.e., the account has not been balanced) but instead a pen flourish, almost certainly meaning that payment has been waived. Still, Rose–van Epenhuysen concluded that Beethoven, even if he did not pay for it, still ordered the piano, and that "at the very least, the transaction with Erard was considered a purchase by the Erard firm at the time when they shipped the instrument." But semantics do matter, and therefore vignette 3 will reveal some particulars of accounting practice in Erard's *livres de ventes*, with this specific document as its point of entry.

Our findings may be anticipated as follows. Beethoven—or someone in Beethoven's circle—took the initiative: a piano was ordered. But someone else again—presumably in Paris—convinced the Erard brothers that acknowledging the rising *claveciniste à Vienne* would be a very good idea, indeed. Thus, even if the initiative of a gift hadn't come from Erard, the instrument may still have felt like a gift to Beethoven, and that's what he presumably told Georg Griesinger, who told Gottfried Härtel in Leipzig in a letter of December 14, 1803: "The brothers Erard of Paris have made Beethoven a present of a mahogany piano (as they did earlier to Haydn)." Reversing the position maintained by Newman, that the Erard was an "unsolicited gift," while not jumping to the same conclusion as Rose–van Epenhuysen, one can assume that, at the very least, Beethoven's Erard was a *solicited* gift. Even if Beethoven had felt entitlement all along and gambled that someone might step up and either help him pay for it or get the payment waived altogether, there's still that initial element of *wanting* an Erard. The question arises, then, of whom in particular Beethoven ought to have thanked. Ries's letter of October 22, 1803, contains an intriguing hint: "Beethoven owes [Louis] Adam a courtesy on account of the Paris piano." The plot thickens—and it is in c. 1800 Paris that more clues are to be found.

Why did Beethoven want a French piano? By owning one, was he when, the piano did end up with brother Johann sometime between April 2, 1826, and January 19, 1827—so, barely but crucially, still *within* Beethoven's lifetime, at his initiative.

Clearly, it felt hard for Beethoven to give up on his Erard. When he finally gave it away, he must have known that it was in good hands: brotherly tensions aside, it was Johann who attended to the ailing Beethoven in Vienna, taking precious time away from his business at his Linz pharmacy. But this was not the case for all those Viennese instruments on Newman's list. In a city overpopulated with makers and instruments, it was easy for Beethoven to have any Viennese piano exchanged for the next competitive model and for them to disappear into the anonymity of a secondhand market. Where, then, did the reluctance to part with his Erard come from?

Points of reference would have to be his Broadwood and the Graf: they too survived the ages—why? The easy answer is that they just happened to be in Beethoven's possession at the time of his death. Their transition into iconic status as Beethoven-owned pianos would have been smooth and uncontestable, since the late composer was also their most recent user. Immediately after Beethoven's death, the Graf made it back to Conrad Graf, who remained the actual owner. Any preserving of it, while making the object's association with Beethoven known, would have been Graf's initiative. The Broadwood, for its part, simply became part of the late Beethoven's estate. It was initially sold to the music publisher C. A. Spina, who passed it along to Franz Liszt in 1836. Having kept it in his library for many years, Liszt bequeathed the instrument to the Hungarian National Museum in Budapest, where it entered the collection in 1887.[22] Unlike the Graf, the association of Broadwood with Beethoven had been firmly advertised on the actual piano from the start, by an inked inscription (see above) and by a special "BEETHOVEN" plaque above the keyboard.

While the Erard has remained unaltered since Johann van Beethoven donated it to his brother, the Broadwood fell victim, if you will, to the authenticity movement of the second half of the twentieth century, focused on "bringing back its voice which once could be heard in Beethoven's own music room" (to quote David Winston, as the latest of the Broadwood's restorers, in 1992).[23] Today's museum science (which carefully weighs "conservation" against "restoration") would certainly condemn these various restoration attempts, which, furthermore, have remained startlingly undocumented (with the exception of Winston's, although a promised "detailed restoration report" has not been published).[24] There is an element of déjà vu here. We might compare our own emotions, triggered by such tampering with an important historical artifact, with Beethoven's feelings when he received his Broadwood from London and blurted out, "[T]hey all like to tune it and spoil it, but they shall not touch it"—"they" referring to his Viennese builder friends, eager to offer their help. The experience with his Erard must have weighed on him, the regret about ill-guided revisions provoking a deeply felt reaction, even many years later.[25]

Entanglement

Erard's is the piano that entangled Beethoven the longest of all. If entanglement is the sum of human-thing (HT) dependences, then what is the pattern here? We propose the following as a starting point:

HT. Beethoven wants a French piano. He wants to try something different—something that will allow him to be exceptional and original. He turns to French technology for inspiration. But originality comes at a price, as he continues writing and publishing music for a Viennese/German market. (His business network does not change overnight with the acquisition of a new instrument.) If the instrument provides Beethoven with the opportunity of doing something new, then Beethoven's dependence on it also turns into a liability. To illustrate the latter point *a contrario*: Karl von Lichnowsky, dedicatee of Beethoven's Sonata in A-flat Major, Op. 26, of 1800–1801, which is when Beethoven's "wanting" may have started, ended up buying an Erard *piano en forme de clavecin*, too—but he's the exception confirming the rule in a large market of German/Austrian piano owners.

HH. Beethoven is intrigued by the style of his French colleagues, including Daniel Steibelt (who visited Vienna in 1800) and Louis Adam (in charge of educating a next generation of pianists at the new Paris Conservatoire). He wants to liaise with them, and through these connections (whether amiable or confrontational), he wants France to notice him. He wonders, furthermore, why his old teacher already has a French piano and he himself doesn't. The lure of Paris—its politics and its artistic life—is powerful. Partaking in this highly competitive international network, through the ownership of a Parisian piano, is an ambition that is hard to give up on, even as usership and maintenance of the piano become problematic. (The Lichnowsky connection provides an example of how emotions can spill over from HT to HH, or from an object that connects two people to a falling-out with the object in turn affecting the human relationship: Beethoven's connection with Lichnowsky ended abruptly when the Prince asked Beethoven to perform for some French officers presumably on the Prince's own Erard in October 1806—at a time when Beethoven's enthusiasm for both French politics and his French instrument had dramatically waned. Beethoven refused to play and walked away in anger.)[26]

TT. Pinpointing its *una corda* device as a particular point of interest, Beethoven explores and exploits other features of his French piano—or what I think of as "sub-things": individual parts that contribute to the instrument's overall thingness. All of these may be combined to create new possibilities. Ultimately, Beethoven is not capable of embracing his French piano entirely. Long familiarity with Viennese pianos leads him to complain about its heavy touch and to miss the articulatory precision he's used to. Perhaps unavoidably giving in to local custom, he engages a Viennese builder to undertake a series of technical revisions, creating some kind of hybrid between French and Viennese technology.

TH. Any piano needs a player. If that player happens to be Beethoven, this might seem like hitting the jackpot in terms of prestige. Technologically speaking, however, ownership by Beethoven almost guaranteed an intense focus on customization, to the possible detriment of the piano's engineered identity. There is a risk also that such a piano will no longer attract the attention of the modern scholar. As we collectively adopt the instrument as a "Beethoven piano," we may no longer recognize the specifically French qualities that came along with its original design—those musical-technological and sociocultural inscriptions that not only attracted Beethoven to start with, but also elicited characteristic responses from him at least during the first few months of his ownership.

Keeping these various dependences and dependencies apart is hard— who or which depends on which or whom?—but this kind of messiness is precisely what a theory of entanglement thrives on. Furthermore, our suggested associations straddle an extended timeline, making it hard to keep track of what "thing" exactly we're talking about: the piano as it left Erard's workshop, the revised version, or our replica? Table 1.1 attempts to create some order. The first column presents our version of the piano's behavioral chain. Each activity shapes a certain context or referential framework for defining or naming our "thing" (second column). This definition is always from the perspective of the particular human who engages with it most prominently (third column). The fourth column, finally, describes the kind of dependence/dependency that these consecutive thing-human relationships encapsulate—with active and passive voices used only for linguistic convenience, since the agencies reflect bi-directional relationships. Even so, active and passive voices are clearly reversed between human and thing as we move from wanting and awaiting to using and revising, when it is the piano that both inspires and frustrates. My schematic representation suggests different ways of naming the piano, to reflect its respective position (numbered) in the behavioral chain. Thus, in his November 1802 letter to Nikolaus Zmeskall (discussed in detail in vignette 1), Beethoven referred to it loosely as "a piano in mahogany with the *una corda* stop" (2) before realizing that what he really wanted was not some Viennese imitation but an authentic Erard Frères *piano en forme de clavecin* (1). These represent two early poles in the piano's thingness, Beethoven's artistic aspirations (themselves presumably inspired by Haydn's Erard piano) leading to his ordering a specific type of instrument. When it comes to technological identity, we may distinguish not only between original (3) and revised (4) but also between old (Beethoven's Erard, corresponding with 1–7) and new (our replica, 8). Together, the original piano, the original after revisions, and the facsimile of the original represent three versions of the instrument, with various degrees of similarity among them. For example, the "old original" and "old revised" pianos are less similar to each other than the "new replica" and "old original," which—passage of time notwithstanding—are practically identical. As an actual thing, "old original" does not exist anymore. While one might be attracted to the idea of restoring the old instrument back to its original condition, from a practical point of view, this would be almost impossible: the revisions are too extensive to undo. In

more developed industrial prowess), it may have been the Erard, more than the Broadwood later in his life, that for a period encapsulated Beethoven's artistic vision and boldness.

A Tanglegram

A single piano may be the focus, but in the end this book is just as much about humans as it is about things. Inspired by Hodder, I end this first chapter by offering a "tanglegram" of the many human–thing connections that we are about to identify and explore (fig. 1.1). Connecting lines suggest dependences and dependencies. Squares denote things; ovals are used for humans. The diamonds at the bottom are for concepts or what Hodder would call "ideas about things":[34] they lead to greater abstractions like "Frenchness" and "viennicization," but only through their connection with specific things such as action parts or pedal components. To acknowledge

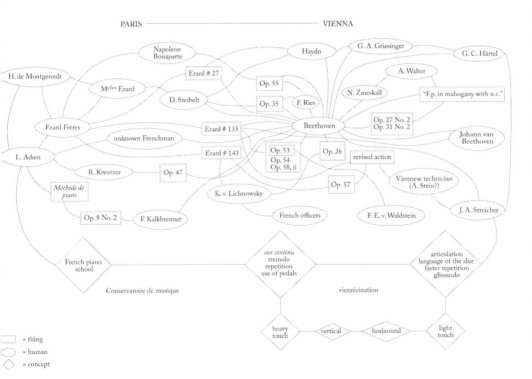

FIGURE 1.1 Tanglegram of Beethoven's Erard.

a geographical dimension, I have placed anything gravitating toward Paris on the lefthand side, and anything belonging to Vienna on the right. Finally, the Paris Conservatoire is represented as a single institution, and its relevance through the shipment from Paris will become clear as chapters and vignettes unfold.

Central in this tanglegram remains Beethoven, as the human whose emotions matter the most. One such emotion stands out in the trail of documents: Beethoven's attachment to the instrument and his inability to sell it because it is "a souvenir [*Andenken*] such as nobody here has honored me with." In this private note, countering Streicher's blunt advice to sell the instrument (which certainly is one way of discarding it), Beethoven leaves us with yet another possible definition of our "thing"—as a memento, representative of something in the past.[35]

In his Heiligenstadt Testament of October 6, 1802, Beethoven confessed to his brothers the onset of his deafness, opening up to them and famously giving them a glimpse into his emotional life. The document (a suicide note that thankfully served a self-therapeutic purpose only) was instructed "to be read and executed after my death," which is when it was found among Beethoven's papers. As a leave-taking if only in style, in Maynard Solomon's words, "Beethoven here metaphorically enacted his own death in order that he might live again."[36]

This book proposes to associate that "living again" with the order of his Erard, as an object that embodies new opportunity and ambition. If Beethoven had intended to relocate to Paris, Paris instead came to him. That someone had convinced Erard Frères to waive the payment must have boosted Beethoven's confidence and raised new hope for the future. Pursuing the career of a pianist-celebrity was no longer an option, but the Erard piano directed him toward a higher path as a pianist-composer. At this career-defining moment, Beethoven sat down at the most innovative and prestigious piece of composition-aiding hardware in all Europe at that time—at *his* French piano.

The Letter

by Tilman Skowroneck

Count Nikolaus Zmeskall von Domanovecz (1759–1833) was a Hungarian official living in Vienna, an exceptionally well-connected music lover and a good amateur cellist who also took a special interest in the piano.[1] He regularly assisted in negotiations between piano buyers and the piano builder Anton Walter.[2] In 1800, he was involved in the purchase of a new piano for Anna Brunswick, the mother of Josephine Deym (who may well have been Beethoven's "immortal beloved"). Letters went back and forth from Buda, where Anna lived, to Vienna, where Josephine and her husband worked on obtaining the piano. The passages about Zmeskall's involvement spell out what it was that made him a tough negotiator. He possessed a very keen ear—Josephine writes that he was picky, *"difficile dans son choix"*—and he was especially good at selecting the very best instruments, at closing deals and negotiating transport.[3]

Zmeskall was also, as we know, one of Beethoven's rather few close friends, a relationship underpinned by Beethoven's constant teasing and punning, preserved in countless notes and letters. Sometime in November 1802—the exact date is unknown—Beethoven wrote to Zmeskall about ordering a piano by Walter:

My dear Z[meskall], you may in any case present my matter to Walter in a strong dose, first of all because he deserves it anyway, and besides, ever since they started believing that I am at odds with Walter, the entire swarm of *Klawier* makers besieges me and wants to serve me—for free; every one of them wants to make me a *Klawier* the way I want it; Reicha, for example, has been implored by the [builder] who made his *Klawier* to persuade me to allow him to make me a *piano forte*. And he is, after all, one of the worthier ones and I have seen some good instruments by him—therefore you can tell [Walter] that I will pay him 30 *Dukaten* although I can have it for free from all the others, but I will only give 30 *Dukaten* on the condition that it is of mahogany [*Mahaghoni; sic*], and I also want to have the stop with one string [*den Zug mit einer Saite*],—if he does not agree, tell him that I will choose one of the other [builders], to whom I will point this out, and whom I will also take to Haydn to have him see this [*dieses*]—today, an unknown Frenchman comes to visit me around noon and Mr. R[eicha] and I will have the pleasure of me having to demonstrate my art on the *piano* by Jakesch—note well—if you would like to come too we would entertain ourselves well, because afterwards we would go out to eat together, Reicha, our miserable baron [i.e., Zmeskall], and the Frenchman. You would not need to put on your black jacket because we will be among men.[4]

In this letter, Beethoven mentions a number of people:

- Anton Walter, the famous piano builder. Beethoven offers him 30 ducats for a mahogany piano with an *una corda* stop.
- The composer Anton Reicha, Beethoven's friend from Bonn. Reicha had just arrived in Vienna after living for two years in Paris.[5]
- An unknown piano builder who made Reicha's piano.
- Joseph Haydn.
- An unknown visiting Frenchman.
- Johann Jakesch, another piano builder. Beethoven apparently had a Jakesch piano at his disposal at the time.

On Mahogany Pianos with the *una corda*: Walter and Erard

A number of things in this letter remain rather obscure, but one thing that is clear is Beethoven's claim that he is famous enough for the Vien-

Five years later we meet a somewhat more relaxed Beethoven in our second document, a letter to Andreas Streicher from between July and September 1796. Here he seems most concerned about the impression he makes as a composer, intrinsically linked to the way others perform his works, and especially the question of how to play the piano well and according to its proper nature. He writes about one of Streicher's pupils, likely the young Elisabeth von Kissow (later Bernhard), whom he had heard perform an Adagio, most probably from his new Piano Trio, Op. 1 No. 1:

> Your young pupil, dear St[reicher], apart from moving me to tears when she played my *adagio*, has astonished me [. . .] For the first time I dared to listen to my trio in performance, and this will really make me compose more for the *Klavier* than before [. . .] Until now, the way of treating the *Klavier* [*die Art das Klavier zu spielen*] is certainly still the most uncultivated of all instruments. Often one believes one hears only a harp, and I am glad that you are one of the few who understand that, if one can feel, one can also sing on the *Klavier*. I hope the time will come, when the harp and the *Klavier* are two totally different instruments.[16]

Compared to Junker's article, Beethoven is more outspoken here in his criticism of the habits of other pianists. The quality or character of the instrument itself is not mentioned, but it is a silent presence in his reflections about good and bad keyboard players, as Beethoven is directing his remarks to the pianist-husband of Nannette Streicher, one of the outstanding piano builders of Vienna, expecting the dual implication to be silently understood and relished by the other man. Should a player attempt to "sing" rather than "harp about," the piano must be able to match this attempt—which clearly was not always the case. The qualities he is now expecting from pianos differ fundamentally from his considerations when, as a self-conscious young performer, he rejected an unknown instrument for public performance largely because it was unfamiliar (if we can believe Junker on this point). Beyond the banter about other players, we see a negotiation going on about the option to choose between "harping" and "singing" kinds of pianos, where the singing kind is seen as better, but underrepresented. So somewhere hidden between the lines of this letter is a quest for a better piano.

We learn about another facet of this quest in November 1796, when Beethoven visited Pressburg (Bratislava) to play a concert on a new fortepiano by Geschwister Stein, which he afterward helped to sell. On November 19, two days after receiving the instrument, he wrote to Andreas Streicher:

> I received your *forte piano* the day before yesterday. It is really marvelous, anybody else would like to have it for his own, and I—you may laugh, but I would have to lie, if I didn't tell you that it is too good for me, and why?—Because it deprives me of the freedom to create my own tone. Anyway, this shall not prevent you from making all your fortepianos in the same way, there will not be found many others with similar whims.[17]

As in his encounter with Junker, Beethoven's idiosyncratic approach to piano playing receives attention here, but this time Beethoven ties the topic to the question that provided the background for his previous letter to Streicher—that is, the question of what a piano does and does not do well. The other pianists and their preferences get a friendly pass this time, but they are still seen in contrast to Beethoven's own "whims." Of course, we also see a good dose of sugarcoated criticism here. To Beethoven's taste, the Stein piano apparently possessed too outspoken a personality of its own, but surely also too narrow an expressive range.

To get a step closer to understanding what would have brought Beethoven in 1802 to contemplate new and different expressive stops (in the Walter, mentioned earlier), and ultimately new piano models (his new Erard), the passage about "the freedom to create my own tone" is central. This is not about otherwise quite important technical details, such as the responsiveness, reliability, or mere sturdiness of a piano's action. Nor is it about the overall loudness of the Viennese piano (or at least, for Beethoven, not yet). Beethoven was interested in the *malleability* of the tone: the possibility to shape and create a true *Beethoven* at the keyboard, instead of having to pick and choose between louder and softer Stein (or Jakesch, or Walter) tones.

CHAPTER TWO

The Psychology of Waiting

The idea of rebuilding Beethoven's French piano arose quite spontaneously during a dinner in Ghent one evening in the fall of 2014. I wasn't wearing a suit and tie, but not for the same reasons Beethoven expressed in his spontaneous invitation to his friend Zmeskall. As we leaned back in our seats after the meal, the director of a leading research institute, who was soon to be my employer, asked me, "So, what instrument would you like Chris to build?" He was speaking of the eminent piano builder Chris Maene, who was seated at the table with us. It had been my past collaborations with Maene that had triggered the institute's interest in establishing a research cluster dedicated to historical piano performance. Ghent is located a mere 20 kilometers from Ruiselede (the home of the Maene workshop), so there seemed an irresistible logic to the plan. Still, the director's query caught me off guard. Chris and I had recently inaugurated a newly built replica of Beethoven's 1817 Broadwood piano, and I was only beginning to realize the full potential of the artistic research questions opened up by that extraordinary instrument. Now circumstances were encouraging me to come up with another project—and fast. In that career-defining moment I blurted out, "Why not make Beethoven's Erard?"

For fifteen years or so I had been teaching an upper-level undergraduate course entitled "Fortepianos and Their Music." I had stolen the title from a 1995 book by Katalin Komlós, which had inspired a new approach to teaching a piano repertoire class, focusing on developmental changes in the instrument itself and giving equal weight to the roles of the builder and the player-composer. Teaching the course had allowed me to keep my finger on the pulse of the newest scholarship in the history of the piano. When it came to Beethoven, one of the key figures of the course, the most exciting additions had been those made by Maria Rose and Tilman Skowroneck.[1] They had come to the topic of Beethoven's "French piano" from different perspectives: Rose from her expertise on the French school of pianos and pianism, and Skowroneck from his deconstructionist work on Beethoven the pianist. While Rose's 2006 dissertation provided the tools to start recognizing "Frenchness" in Beethoven's music, Skowroneck's 2010 book invited new Erard-based ways of looking at Beethoven pieces such as his Piano Sonatas, Op. 53, 54, and 57 (together the core solo repertoire of 1803–5), but also at accompanied piano music, like the Cello Sonata, Op. 69; the "Ghost" Trio, Op. 70 No. 1; and the Fourth Piano Concerto, Op. 58. Something was in the air, and the time felt ripe to go to the next level, the construction of an accurate replica of Beethoven's Erard piano—not only because the original is now unplayable, but also because the hands-on artistic research we were doing deserved the same optimally functioning tool that Beethoven had when he initially received his Erard and embarked on his pianistic and compositional experiments.

There was even a precedent. Our project to build a replica of Beethoven's Erard may have been a first, but the making in modern times of a new Erard *piano en forme de clavecin* was not. The British-French historical keyboard maker, Christopher Clarke, had finished one in 2011. Copied after an 1802 original in the Paris Musée de la musique, it was identical to Beethoven's—that is, identical to Beethoven's at the point when it left the Erard workshop. Technically, this makes the Paris piano even more authentic than the one in Linz, which, as we have seen, encapsulates revisions made under Beethoven's ownership in Vienna. The mandate given to Clarke's project, "to approach the original as closely as possible," had a national heritage ring to it from the start, coming as it did from France's most important instrument collection. (The Musée de la musqiue is part of the newly vamped City of Music, which also includes a 2,400-seat concert hall and the relocated Conservatoire national supérieur de musique et de danse.) The team around Clarke took their task to heart. In an open letter to the

replicate an instrument crucial to the rediscovery and reappraisal of turn-of-the-nineteenth-century French repertoire would be a much tougher sell, even for a French institution as well established as the Musée de la musique. Piano students next door, attending the modern-day premises of the Conservatoire, need not worry: they will not be asked quite yet to replace their Beethoven or Mozart sonatas with those of Boieldieu or de Montgeroult.

What about Haydn? The CD booklet continues by suggesting that "works written by Haydn" may again be heard "as they originally sounded."[6] Haydn received his instrument as a gift in early 1801, when he was still at the height of his powers, having recently finished his oratorio *The Seasons*, Hob. XXI:3. But as far as his piano works go, his thirteen *Part Songs*, Hob. XXVc (1796–99), had been the last involving the keyboard, and no more would follow. The Erard firm could not have known that, of course—for his part, Haydn expressed his intention of actually using their instrument, a pragmatic reflex that kept defining Haydn "the rhetorical man" even at the advanced age of sixty-nine. On May 20, 1801, he wrote the following thank-you note to Erard, here newly translated from the original German:

Monsieur!

It was not only a long-lingering indisposition but also the excess of business that prevented me from sending you more promptly my overdue thanks for the wonderful *forte piano* you have shipped to me! I received it in relative good condition except for one hammer, which was torn off but which has already been repaired. I also regret that in the tenor register the soundboard has warped itself almost up to the strings, which causes some rattling [*schnurren*] when one plays loudly. I do hope that after some time it will settle back in its usual position. But as far as everything else is concerned, I must admit to your praise that this *forte piano*, from its outward as well as its inner beauties, is the greatest masterpiece I have ever seen or heard. Many *Cavaliers* wish to know what the price of such an instrument would be, which is why I ask you to let me know.

Meanwhile I express to you my deepest thanks for this costly gift, and as far as my powers allow, I shall not fail to show my gratitude to you. I remain with utmost respect,

Your most obedient servant,

Joseph Haydn[7]

This letter addressed to Erard Frères as a singular *Monsieur* (an easily forgivable oversight, were it not for Haydn's usual sensitivity to matters like this)[8] contains more red flags, and we will return to them in chapter 6. For now, suffice it to point out that Haydn's praise of the instrument is not unreserved: he cannot help but mention his disappointment about a technical issue, a warp in the soundboard that causes an occasional rattle of strings against wood. Haydn's precise diagnosis implies that he has already consulted with a local technician, who must have explained that warping most likely occurred during the long transportation by boat and that his only hope was that with time the soundboard would again "settle in its usual position." While annoying to Haydn, the issue would have been outright embarrassing for Sébastien Erard. How was he to respond, beyond admitting that, yes, there might have been a construction fault, as in not waiting long enough for the soundboard to dry before its ribs were attached, or for the ribbed soundboard and piano case to adopt the same humidity conditions before they were glued together? Recalling the instrument to his workshop to rectify the issue was hardly an option.[9]

Be all this as it may, Haydn finishes the letter with utmost politeness. In good rhetorical tradition, he shows both business-mindedness ("many *Cavaliers* wish to know [. . .] the price of such an instrument") and a sense of reciprocity—a promise to, "as far as my powers allow [. . .] not fail to show my gratitude to you," presumably, as H. C. Robbins Landon specifies, "in the form of a composition."[10] The composition, however, never happened—at least not in the form of a keyboard work.

This leaves Beethoven—waiting.

We know that he must have tried Haydn's Erard at least once. When, in his November 1802 letter to Zmeskall, he mentions the prospect of "taking [another builder] to Haydn to have him see this," the implication is that Beethoven himself had seen it, presumably more than once. What would he have played? We may imagine Beethoven for the first time sitting down at the piano, freshly unpacked in his old teacher's living room in Gumpendorf, an invigorating thirty-minute walk from downtown Vienna.

"Erard Frères—Rue du Mail No. 37 à Paris 1800." This is what Beethoven would have read on the nameplate above the keyboard. Paris, French. Let's think. Remember Daniel Steibelt about a year earlier? (The notorious competition between the twenty-nine-year-old Beethoven and the thirty-

four-year-old composer and pianist Steibelt will be discussed in chapter 6.)
There's some joking around, some exchanging of anecdote—anything to
dissipate tension between the older and the younger man (their relationship
at this point was known to be strained). A third person may be in the room:
someone who had also been present at the salon of Count von Fries, during
that memorable encounter between Beethoven and the cocky would-be
Frenchman. Even though he was born in Berlin, Steibelt had refused to
speak any German, even to Beethoven. What a snob. (Stronger words may
have been used.) And yes, those silly tremolo effects! Beethoven starts playing something like example 2.1, a drumroll-like *tremulando*, swelling om-
inously and impressively from *piano* to *forte*, leading up to a double bang,
fortissimo. This is where Steibelt's wife Catherine would have joined in
(could it get more ridiculous?), striking her tambourine with military-like
speed and precision.[11]

But playing the effect now on an actual French piano (rather than
the Viennese or the possibly borrowed English piano that Steibelt would
have used at the Count's), the tremolo strikes Beethoven as surprisingly
effective—and authentic. In the third movement of the Sonata in A-flat
Major, Op. 26 (whose sketching Beethoven ended by March 1801, about
when Haydn's piano would have made it to Vienna), the effect becomes
the first instance in Beethoven's scores where he notates the use of pedal
(which, as we shall establish in chapter 7, is essential for a tremolo). The
notation that Beethoven uses is not quite "Ped." yet (which will make its
first appearance in his "Tempest" Sonata, Op. 31 No. 2), but is less opera-
tionally specific still: *senza sordini* (without dampers), to be put into effect
by either foot or knee. The undamped tremolo is to be contrasted with a

EXAMPLE 2.1 Beethoven, Sonata in A-flat Major, Op. 26, third movement, mm. 31–32.

razor-sharp upper blow to be played *con sordini* (with dampers). Contrary to the Viennese piano, however, the blow on the French piano would no longer be exclusively sharp: instead, it would have produced a halo of lingering resonance, very much like the jangle of the little cymbals on Mrs. Steibelt's tambourine.[12]

Could Beethoven's first acquaintance with Haydn's Erard have been the starting point for his interest in French pianism? Or did it begin with his antagonistic encounter with Steibelt? Acknowledging ambiguity and the work of the unconscious in this process seems important: to put it another way, there is waiting, and there is *waiting*. Explaining the rhetorical figure of *distinctio* (the purposeful play between different meanings of the same word), Quintilian gives the following example: "When Proculeius reproached his son with waiting for his death, and the son replied that he was not waiting for it, the former retorted, Well then, I ask you to wait for it."[13] I would suggest that something similarly forceful happens when we argue that Beethoven "waited" for his French piano: we *want* him to wait, if only because we *know* he eventually received one. The trap of teleology opens up, of course, albeit within a relatively short time frame: we're talking about three and a half years, between March or April 1800, or the time between the back-to-back encounters with Steibelt, and October 1803, when Beethoven's own Erard made it to Vienna. But in November 1802, when Beethoven asked Zmeskall to approach Anton Walter about the prospect of making a mahogany piano with an *una corda* stop, Beethoven may still have been projecting two French qualities onto *any* piano: first, *solidity*, and, second, although by no means less important, *variety* of sound. The square, boxy design of the Erard would already have made it appear sturdier than local models, but the mahogany casing would have imbued it with particular robustness (even if this was a visual impression only, since we're talking about a mahogany veneer: the actual case would have been of oak). Meanwhile, the *una corda* stop would have greatly expanded the instrument's sonic range. Combined with the triple stringing throughout the keyboard, the stop could produce not just *una corda* but *due corde* and *tre corde* as well. As we know from vignette 1, all three of these are possible on Haydn's piano precisely thanks to that triple stringing through the entire keyboard, while a Viennese piano typically featured triple stringing only from the middle register up and double stringing from the middle down, making it harder to incorporate an *una corda* stop.

Still, commissioning the "French" piano that Beethoven had in mind not from Sébastien Erard in Paris but from Anton Walter in Vienna made a lot of sense. Having the most exclusive local builder copy a foreign design, and with the exact model at hand, no less, offered the best of both worlds. In the case of an almost certain problem—the annoying rattle in Haydn's instrument being the perfect case in point—the maker himself would be on hand to fix it. When exactly the plan changed, we do not know. But some time between November 1802 (the letter to Zmeskall) and August 6, 1803 (the date of the Erard accountant's note), Beethoven decided to bite the bullet and order a piano from Paris, too—completely identical to his old teacher's, except (surely) for that annoying rattle. (In this sense, there's a second chance for Erard Frères as well: what are the odds that the second piano they send to Vienna would develop the same problem?)

What, then, are the musical signals that Beethoven is "awaiting" his French piano that we can read in his "Moonlight" and "Tempest" Sonatas, the sonatas that Lubimov recorded on the Clarke Erard? I propose two possibilities, one from each sonata. I present them here while alternately testing them on a Walter fortepiano and the finished Maene/Erard, fully aware that I may be cheating and that Beethoven would not have had that option: he may have visited Haydn's instrument several times (the tone of Beethoven's letter suggests no fear in inviting himself to his old teacher's house), but I find it hard to imagine that Beethoven would consistently have gone back and forth during a multiweek process of composition. The first movement of "Moonlight," carrying the well-known directive, "This whole piece must be played most delicately and without damper [*senza sordino*]" (see ex. 2.2, top), sounds appropriately pristine when using the Erard's *una corda* in combination with the damper pedal—the latter to be pressed by one's left foot. (We will have to remind ourselves several times throughout this book, but the Erard pedals from left to right are: [1] *peau de buffle*, [2] damper, [3] *céleste*, and [4] *una corda*.) Not delicate enough? We can literally put a veil over our sounds by also using the *céleste*, to be pressed by either one's right foot, which would need to be turned sideways, or one's left, which would need to be similarly maneuvered. (At this stage of our experimentation, we're exploring all options. As we shall see, while there is historical precedent for pressing down adjacent pedals with a single foot, pressing down the two middle pedals [2 and 3] with a single foot would not be recommended.) Once we discover the affordances of multistop pedaling, why not go for the superlative *delicatissimamente* and push down *all four pedals together*? Both feet now firmly locked in position (inside-out, awkward but possible), there is no easy letting go. Nor would Beethoven want us to: "the whole piece" (meaning "movement")[14] is to be played "without damper"—the singular noun arguably hinting at a single collective damper-raising stop, although "dampers" in plural (*sordini*) would have been technically more exact (as Beethoven had himself indicated in example 2.1). Blurring harmonies while keeping the collective dampers up all the time is not an option, but clearly the modus operandi for Beethoven's fantasizing is in true C. P. E. Bach tradition: "The undamped register of the pianoforte is the most pleasing and if one knows how to apply the necessary caution in the face of its reverberations, the most delightful for improvising [*Fantasiren*]."[15]

On his recording, Lubimov does use the Erard's distinctive *una corda*, but "changes pedal" (in the modern sense, in reference to a modern pianist's constant use of the damper pedal) with every new harmony (again, in modern conventional fashion). From a foot-coordinating point of view, this solution is understandable and its execution even impressive, since the damper pedal, as the second on the left, must be played with one's left foot, especially in combination with the right foot operating any of the two pedals at the right. Selecting the *una corda* as single right-side stop allows Lubimov to leave his right foot pushed down all the time, while continuing to operate his left foot in familiar ways, telling the brain to essentially keep doing the same left as what is normally done right, but at a higher level of self-consciousness. This is the equivalent, if you will, of driving a continental European car in England, while consciously reminding oneself to drive on the left. But what if Beethoven, with his suggested coloristic options at the outset of the "Moonlight" Sonata, is not just swapping left and right, but stirring things up altogether, and from a sound-expressive point of view exploring a different set of gears, their number doubling from two to four? In this sense, Beethoven's blanket *senza sordino* makes sense: just leave your *left foot* down all the way (once pressed, one needs to think of it no longer), while freeing up one's more versatile *right foot* for the additional effect and nuance, to be handled as desire or need arises. (To be sure, this advice holds for a right-handed or -footed pianist, but in all likelihood this would have included Beethoven, who is shown in contemporary images holding pipe or pen in his right hand.)[16] As the Adagio movement progresses, Beethoven adds more and more subtle dynamic indications, such as *messa di voce* hairpins, *crescendo* and *decrescendo, pianissimo* and *piano*—reflective, perhaps, of various uses of the *céleste* and *una corda* stops with one's right foot.

It is important to remember that Beethoven would have pursued these proposed explorations not at his own Erard quite yet, but already on his Viennese Walter—the fortepiano at which Carl Czerny remembered himself auditioning for Beethoven as a ten-year-old.[17] This fortepiano would have had the usual two knee-levers: right for raising the dampers and left for *céleste* or moderator. That Beethoven was interested in different sonic possibilities in his piano at a time when he started confiding in friends about the onset of his hearing loss adds an intriguing dimension. On July 1, 1801, he reassured Carl Amenda (but surely mostly himself) that "my [hearing] difficulty affects me least in my playing and composing, however all the more in my social interactions."[18] During this time of leading up to and through the start of his ownership of an Erard, it is clear, as Robin Wallace writes, "that Beethoven was suffering, that he was acutely self-conscious." But what is less clear, he continues, is "the extent to which his condition bothered him musically." It is telling indeed (and, in Wallace's words, "so strongly counterintuitive") that, in the face of increased physical hardship, Beethoven showed attraction precisely to unknown acoustic sonorities, triggered by his acquaintance with Haydn's new Erard.[19]

What we're dealing with, then, is a fascinating example of imagined hearing—the sounds emanating from Haydn's Erard (not the actual ones, but those stuck in Beethoven's memory) fusing with those on his Walter (still his instrument of composition). The "Moonlight" experiment, then, represents some hybrid version of two acoustical realities. This may explain why, whenever I test my sound effects at our Maene/Erard replica (after my much longer experience of living with the "Moonlight" Sonata on a Walter instrument), I always feel unsatisfied by the actual results. Yes, the buff stop (if one decides to add it, too) turns the Erard into a harp of some sort, effectively cutting its usual resonance, but even so, the single

French strings still resonate significantly longer than a Walter's bi- and tri-chords, and its hammers are too self-important and heavy (each requiring a full, *stoss*-action blow) to allow for the light and dreamy treatment that my previous overly eager and fantastical paragraphs evoked. To save my (and possibly Beethoven's) vision, I would have to qualify the circumstances: the Erard should be moved to a bigger space with more resonant acoustics—perhaps like the grand salon at Count von Fries's residence where Beethoven had heard Steibelt get away with his effects. Is there, then, a "perfect instrument" for Beethoven's "Moonlight" Sonata? Josephine Deym, née Brunswick, proclaimed the Walter piano belonging to the dedicatee of the sonata, Countess Julie Guicciardi, as the "best" known to her in Vienna in 1803.[20] At this point in Beethoven's career, was the customer always right? Or are we witnessing a turning point, and is Beethoven starting to look beyond Vienna? His Erard obsession may indeed have taken hold, as he fantasized and idealized French timbral possibilities on his own Viennese instrument.

My second example similarly represents a sonic world somewhere between those of an Erard and a Walter (ex. 2.2, bottom). This second group of the first movement of the "Tempest" Sonata is widely discussed in the Beethoven literature because of its baffling status within the movement's sonata form: it may be interpreted as "a first theme that-never-quite-was" but at the same time it sets in motion a modulatory transition to the second key area.[21] The formal ambiguity extends itself to the non-committal rumble of a tremolo. Within this tremolo, triplet figures shift the good or the metrically strong of three between the higher and lower notes, creating an isorhythmic pattern that, because of its clearer hammer attacks, the player is made more consciously aware of on the Viennese fortepiano than on the Erard. One may distinguish between a forceful arpeggio x and a yearning turn-figure y (to be played *forte* and *piano*, respectively), but on the Erard the tremolo middle voice remains much more the driving motor of a single wash of sound that starts with a bang but then just dies out. The question becomes: is Beethoven's notation of *piano* descriptive (as in, "it happens anyway") or prescriptive (as in, "make it happen")? On a Walter, it's most definitely the former: the sounds of the tremolo (of course, to be played without dampers) have sufficiently tapered off to make y respond

EXAMPLE 2.2 Beethoven, Sonata in C-sharp Minor, Op. 27 No. 2, first movement, mm. 1–5 (*top*); Sonata in D Minor, Op. 31 No. 3, first movement, mm. 21–25 (*bottom*).

to *x* in a natural and smooth manner. On a more resonant Erard, however, where sounds neither materialize nor decay as crisply as on a Viennese fortepiano, there's more effort involved: one has to carve out some sonic room for *y* to tag on to *x* (again: all while keeping the dampers raised). On the Erard, in other words, there's more intentionality on the part of the player—precisely how I imagine Beethoven to have listened to his Walter, imbuing it with powers it does not normally have.[22] In his rendition, as most pianists do, Lubimov makes sure to separate the *x* arpeggio from the *y* response, while using pedal sparingly only and making sure that the inner voices do not intrude, but this may be to miss the point of Beethoven's exercise, which is to foreground a tremolo exactly at the climax of a structural conundrum, where dramatic effect and motivic content should not be in contradiction with one another.

So, was Beethoven awaiting his Erard? Proculeius was not on hand to insist he do so. Yet wait he did, consciously or unconsciously. Something was in the air—beckoning, making him restless—and it was neatly encapsulated by Haydn's French piano, the Erard. Paris was thriving; musicians were traveling. And in the mind of a musician whose surrounding social world was rapidly shrinking, the prospect of hopefully one day owning his own Erard seems to have taken on tremendous power of compensation. When it arrived, the instrument would trigger the boldest plan of all: to relocate and reboot his life and career in Paris.

* * *

Unlike Beethoven, our team did eventually make it to Paris, to witness the very instrument that Christopher Clarke and his team had built. On October 10, 2016, four of us listened with great interest to presentations by Thierry Maniguet, Christopher Clarke, Stéphane Vaidelich, and Matthieu Vion on the historical context and the making of their 1802 facsimile, and we responded to our French colleagues with presentations on our soon-to-be-completed 1803 Erard.[23] We inaugurated our instrument five weeks later at the Orpheus Institute. By no means, however, did this inauguration erase the memory of first playing Clarke's magnificent instrument at the Musée de la musique, which pleasantly surprised me by its accurate and springy action and especially its superbly light-sounding, silky, and bell-like treble register. Discovering its Frenchness through the performance of Caprice, Op. 24 No. 3 (1795), by Daniel Steibelt and the Violin Sonata in A Minor, Op. 2 No. 3, by Hélène de Montgeroult (1800) felt priceless, even as I had to overcome my Viennese-trained prejudices against "silly" tremolos and "pointless" repetitions, the latter often involving the most basic types of melodic fragmentation and the most consonant of harmonies. These prejudices, understandably, had been strongest when practicing those works in advance, on a Viennese Walter fortepiano, with the sound from the Lubimov CD as my only guide. Clearly, when it came to French taste and pianism in the early 1800s, I had some serious unlearning and relearning to do. Like Beethoven, I couldn't wait to start experimenting with an instrument of my own.

CHAPTER THREE

Malleability of Tone

How does one set about describing the behavior of a piano action? Typically, when writing on the history of the piano, an author resorts to a technical drawing at this point. Each constituent element of a specific type of action is carefully numbered, for easy identification. From key descent to hammer blow, each component's role is explained, relying on the reader to reconstruct a chain of cause and effect.[1] By contrast, the description by a pianist of how their fingers and the piano's action parts work in tandem is visceral. This description is usually given while sitting at the piano, when none of those moving parts can be seen at all. Quite literally, one has to take the pianist's word for it, as they resort to metaphors to describe their tactile experience. Consider, for example, the following report by Georg Griesinger to Gottfried Härtel, written on December 14, 1803. No more than two months into Beethoven's ownership of the Erard, Beethoven was clearly enthusiastic about his new piano:

> [Beethoven] is so enchanted with [his *Fortepiano* in mahogany from the Erard brothers in Paris] that he regards all the pianos manufactured here as rubbish [*Quark*] by comparison. Because you run a thriving business in instruments, it will [not] be uninteresting for you to hear that also before Beethoven has always criticized the tone [*den Ton*] of the local instruments for being woody [*hölzern*], and that they create the habit of a small, weak touch [*kleines schwaches Spiel*]. Beethoven being Beetho-

ven might be right, but how many players are there like him? Even by
Beethoven's admission the keyboard action of the Parisian piano is not as
supple and elastic as that of Viennese pianos. But that is a trifle to a master
like Beethoven.[2]

The French "keyboard action" (*Tastatur*, a term somewhere between "keyboard" and "action") is here described in terms of what it is *not*, namely
"not as supple and elastic as that of Viennese pianos [*nicht so geschmeidig
und elastisch wie die der Wiener Fortepiano*]." Similarly, there are no an-
tonyms to "small" and "weak" (which are the terms used by Beethoven to
describe a Viennese touch), but one assumes the French touch for him to
be "big" and "heavy" in comparison.

When Beethoven deems the French instrument not "as supple and elastic," however, it is not immediately clear what he means. Were those words
even his? That Beethoven admits to this statement may in fact indicate
that they came from Griesinger, as the interlocutor of a recorded dialogue.
Griesinger may have offered this comment not only as a long-time listener
of Beethoven at the piano, but also as someone used to hearing Viennese
playing—that is, *of many tones together* forming nicely punctuated musical
phrases and eloquently executed musical periods. "But, dear Beethoven, is
not the Walter more supple and elastic?" "Yes," Ludwig admits, but "go
on, try," he says, as he invites Georg to play a single tone on the Erard:
"Is the sound not much less wooden than the one produced on a Viennese
fortepiano?" Beethoven, in this imagined scenario, reduces the definition
of tone (*Ton*) to the experience of *a single strike*, regardless of musical or
rhetorical context. If anything, Beethoven may have retorted to Griesinger
that the French sound, by itself and produced by a single strike, is in fact
more supple and elastic than that of the Viennese. On his mind may have
been exactly the thought, discussed in vignette 1, of creating his *own*, malleable tone.

I do not purport to give a decisive answer to the perceptual conundrum that Beethoven himself was unable to avoid: in a pianist's description of how a piano action behaves, which is the predominant factor—
the feeling through one's fingers or the corresponding sensation received
through one's ears? Nor do I wish to challenge Beethoven's or Griesinger's

choice of words as they described their experiences either as a player or as a listener. This chapter, on the contrary, aims to provide a scientific-empirical dimension to the comparison of two historical piano actions. Say, very hypothetically, that Griesinger had the option of looking *inside the piano*: what might he have observed as Beethoven played a single tone, first on his new Erard, then on his old Walter? A single tone, indeed, is all we're interested in here, and then mostly the mechanics of it: sound will be acknowledged, of course, but will not be analyzed. This singular focus—indeed, unveiling the single strike of a piano key as a complex conglomerate of events—may provide a solid basis for further comparisons between Viennese and French actions during the remainder of this book. Did the Erard meet Beethoven's expectations? Is a single French strike inherently more malleable than a Viennese one? And what might this mean?

Making Three Action Models

A single strike of the key and movement of the hammer occurs at hundredths of a second—five, six, or seven at the most—in any case too fast to truly comprehend with the naked eye. Of course, one can easily take out an action and understand the basics of how it works, but to slow down time and watch the mechanical parts move in synchronicity, at times testing logic and demanding explanation, can only be achieved through technology. First, we need a camera capable of capturing, say, at least one thousand images in a second, or one image every millisecond. Second, it needs to be positioned with a clear view of the entire mechanism, so as to capture the complex series of events from finger to string contact. To squeeze a camera into the case of a *piano en forme de clavecin* would be difficult, so we had to create a cross-section of the piano—an action model that is true to its subject, in all its parts capable of the exact same kind of performance as in the real conditions, and viewable in its entirety.

To a piano builder like Chris Maene, replicating a small part of the instrument would not be a problem. But what exactly should the action model look like, and how should we film and measure any experiments we had in mind? Here I solicited the help of my former student, Robert (Bobby)

Giglio, who had experience exactly in this domain.[3] Together, we considered the option of going to a highly equipped lab (such as the one at the Centre for Interdisciplinary Research in Music Media and Technology in Montreal, where we had worked before) to experiment, but quickly decided to improvise our own version of it on the top floor of the Orpheus Institute. This choice came with positives and negatives. On the positive side, the setup was eminently flexible. Bobby was able to explore and vet new questions or hypotheses by simply walking down the stairs and conferring with the research team. But prioritizing flexibility had an impact on what equipment was available to us. First and foremost, we needed a camera that satisfied our needs while also being cost-effective. Having worked with a complex and expensive 3D-motion-capture system before, we knew we had to look for something different: an elegant solution that could achieve reasonably high frame rates while retaining sufficient spatial resolution for the image to be clear.[4] After searching for available cameras on the market, Bobby zeroed in on a new model, made by a start-up company in the United Kingdom. Simple, small, and portable, the fps1000 model could achieve one thousand frames per second with good enough image quality. In spite of several developmental issues, which were dealt with in collaboration with its engineer/inventor, Graham Rowan, the camera in the end did what we needed it to do—film the detail of not just one but two action models, French and Viennese, respectively.

What did we want the models to look like? Whatever design we wanted for our Erard, we'd need the same for a fortepiano by Walter, for exact comparison. Back in 2013, Chris, Bobby, and I had already made and worked with a model with interchangeable Viennese actions.[5] That experience was now to inform the building of a prototype action model of the Erard—strikingly, again with interchangeable actions, to represent the piano both as Beethoven had initially received it and in its later, revised state. So, with the French model split into two, we needed three action models, with two of those to be accommodated within a single case. This chapter may be based on a single strike only, but what other questions might come up, we wondered, as we compared first the French with the Viennese piano, but then also the original Erard and the revised version? What kind of musical effects, articulations, little fragments from phrases might we be interested in? What else might we want to observe and analyze? Most pressingly, *how many notes should our action model have?* My mind was racing through passages in Beethoven pieces that I might want to submit to scientific experiment. Bobby kept thinking that, the more notes we had, the more difficult it would be to actually see what was going on in an array of hammers. And between us stood Chris, as the one who would have to build the contraption. His prime concern was with the feasibility of the engineering. There were exciting possibilities, yes, but also structural boundaries that we had to be made aware of.

Even if we were interested in observing the action alone, the surrounding structure should be as real and as complete as possible, which meant constructing a piece of soundboard of the actual length corresponding to a specific key or pitch, along with accurately tensioned courses of strings. But there was a limit to guaranteeing the structural health of a model that also needed to provide optimal visibility: two large windows had to be cut on either side to expose the entire mechanism, from beginning to end of the key lever (or from the pianist's finger all the way to the point where the key lever lifts the damper) and especially the part where the "action" happens (from hopper to string contact). It had also been agreed that any view of the pivot point of the key would have to be sacrificed, unless we were to replace wood with plexiglass, which seemed an unreasonable request to make of a historical piano builder. To include more keys would also mean increasing the need for structural anchoring, which in turn would mean a decrease in visibility.

A final compromise was found in the range of a fourth from c^1 to f^1, with chromatic tones in between, for a total of six keys. This made for one note fewer than the five-note diatonic slurred figure from the fifth bar of the "Waldstein" Sonata that I had hoped for (sol, fa, mi, re, do, to be played in a single right hand) but I decided that a model with six keys would be versatile enough to test a scaled-down version of this figure (fa, mi, re, do), as well as a tremolo (do/mi, a major third), an appoggiatura (including several options for a minor second), repeated intervals (such as the bouncy do/mi thirds at the beginning of Op. 53), and so on.

A few weeks later, the models—Erard and Walter—were ready. Side by side, they revealed a whole array of investigative paths (fig. 3.1). Like

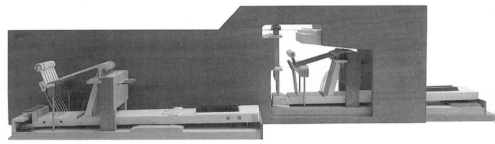

FIGURE 3.1 Action models in customized cases of pianos by Anton Walter (Vienna, c. 1800; *top*) and Erard Frères (Paris, 1803), along with interchangeable revised action (*bottom*), built by Chris Maene (Ruiselede, 2016). Photo by Piet Meersschaut.

Griesinger and Beethoven, we were ready to compare. For now, this comparison is between Walter and the original Erard; the revised Erard will be discussed later in the book. Plate 1 offers a view of all three.

French vs. Viennese Hammer Strike

In any piano action, energy has to be transferred from the player's finger to a hammer, which is propelled to strike a set of strings. What happens in between finger strike and string contact has been the subject of much scrutiny during the last three centuries of piano building.[6] A multitude of innovative solutions have been employed. But all told, they are variations on two basic principles: those that *push* the hammer toward the strings and those that *pull* the hammer toward the strings. The two specimens we are examining represent these two categories: the Erard is a pushing mechanism, or *Stossmechanik*, while the Walter is a pulling mechanism, or *Prellmechanik*. One could argue that the German *Prellmechanik*, highlighting the activity of *prellen*, to flip, focuses on a mechanical aspect that the Germans (and later Austrians) would have taken particular pride in: that explosive moment when the hammer is caught by the escapement lever and is made to *flip*, or "move with a small quick motion," toward the strings.[7] The French action, for its part, has an engineering beauty to it, the *pilote* (the French equivalent for the English "hopper") both guiding and catapulting the hammer into free flight.

Through figure 3.2 we may familiarize ourselves with the various components of the respective model actions. We're looking not at a technical drawing, but at a frozen single frame of our high-speed camera. Black-on-white little circles, printed, cut out, and stuck on selected points of the action to facilitate measurement during motion-capturing, also help name these components. In the Walter action (top), we recognize, from right to left and working our way to the top, the key front, key rear, escapement lever, *Kapsel* or "little fork" in which the hammer is made to pivot, hammer shank, hammer-head base, and hammer-head tip. The same markers in the Erard (bottom) correspond to the key front, mid-key lever, key rear, hopper (*pilote*), hammer hinge, hammer shank, hammer-head base, and hammer-head tip. One's experience of spatial direction when naming these parts—flowing for Walter versus staggered for Erard—reveals a fundamental difference already: whereas the Walter hammer is pointed toward the player, that of the Erard is turned the other way.

With the camera received and tested, the model built and marked, the lights positioned and adjusted, we are ready to sit down and play. But how? New questions arise. How high exactly should the elbow be with respect to the keyboard? Which finger should I use? How loud or soft should I play? For how long should I hold the key? Remarkably, under carefully prepared scientific-experimental conditions, the simplest thing like "just" trying out a single tone (as we've imagined Beethoven asking Griesinger to do) takes on complex proportions. We're attempting to measure them, but how are we to generate a specifically *French* versus a *Viennese* strike? Somehow, in our focus on re-creating technological environments for our experiments, we had begun neglecting the human side. Just as there are French and Viennese hammers, there must be French and Viennese fingers to operate them.

Rather than dismiss this human factor (and, say, replace our nerve-operated finger by an actuator responding to a sensor), we decided that our definition of a strike must be cultural as well as mechanical.[8] We're interested in these pianos not as automatons, but as machines operated by human

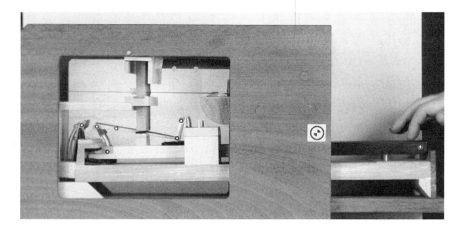

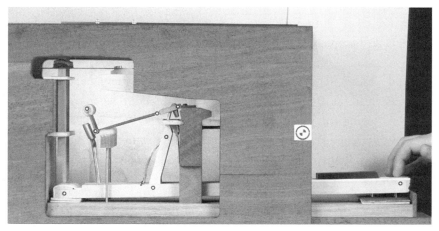

FIGURE 3.2 Action models of Walter (*top*) and Erard (*bottom*), with marks for slow-motion tracking.

beings. *Beings* (plural, as in a different person playing either action), since it normally takes years of training to master each type of instrument. So, to establish some combined level of cultural-scientific objectivity, we searched for guidelines. We found them in two authorities: (1) Andreas Streicher in Vienna, the husband of Vienna's prominent piano builder, Nannette Streicher, and author in 1801 of *Kurze Bemerkungen über das Spielen, Stimmen und Erhalten der Fortepiano, welche von Nannette Streicher geborne Stein in Wien verfertiget werden* (Brief Remarks on the Playing, Tuning, and Maintenance of Fortepianos Made in Vienna by Nannette Streicher, *née* Stein);

(2) Louis Adam, piano professor at the Paris Conservatoire and author of this institute's official *Méthode de piano* in 1804–5 (republican Year XIII). Table 3.1 assembles their respective guidelines on how to sit, how to use one's arms and fingers, and how to bend that finger before striking that single tone.

At first sight, one is struck more by what connects the two piano pedagogues than what separates them: one's elbows need to be higher than the keyboard by one Viennese *Zoll* for Streicher (equal to 26.3 mm or 1.035 inch) or by an unspecified "little" for Adam; arms, close to one's body, must always be relaxed; shoulders are mentioned by Adam, but only as a hinge for anything below: "The forearm alone must act; the part from the shoulder to the elbow must remain motionless." Most crucially, when it comes to the actual generating of movement in the key, both French and Viennese honors go to *fingers alone*.

No surprise, then, that the section on "finger" is the longest in table 3.1. But it is also here that we come across some crucial differences between Streicher and Adam. About the need to avoid any contact with the nail, or about keeping the fingers nicely curved, they both agree, although Streicher alone stresses that "the finger should touch the key only with its fleshy pad [*mit seinem vordern, fleischigten Theile*]." Streicher also specifies that one must "draw back [the fingers] far enough to be in line with a naturally held thumb." But from this perfect lateral line of attack, it is Adam who specifies the need to "*lift* the fingers a little *above* the keyboard" just before striking, and he is quite specific also about what it means for fingers to strike: "One will make them fall *perpendicularly and successively* [*perpendiculairement et successivement*] on the indicated keys" (emphases mine). Streicher, from his side, does not explicitly ask to rest one's fingers on the keys before striking, but he warns against touching the key "before the moment in which the sound should be heard, for even the slightest weight [of the finger] will push the key down somewhat, causing the beak of the hammer to begin forcing backward the pivoted escapement," which is testimony of what for him must be the ideal prestriking position: the finger *ever so slightly* hovering above the key, as close as possible, if not *quasi* touching it, ever so conscious of the weight of the key, without actually depressing it.

Streicher's warning not to let the weight of the finger interfere with any flipping potential of the Viennese action speaks to his mechanical insight,

TABLE 3.1 Comparison of Streicher and Adam on arm, hand, and finger technique

	Streicher (1801) / de Silva (2008)	Adam (1804–5) / Beghin with Jensen-Large (2021)
Seat	It is necessary to adjust the seat of the player so that with his arm hanging naturally close to his body, his **elbow** is at least *a good inch* [*Zoll* = 26.3 mm] higher than the keyboard. (p. 45)	It is necessary, when [people] are sitting, that the **elbows** be a little higher than the level of the keyboard [. . .]: the body [. . .] at a distance, where the **elbows** may be carried more forward than backward so that the hands have the liberty to cross one another freely. (p. 7)
Arm	The **arm** should rest *against* their body, without being pressed against it. (p. 45)	All movement of the **arms** that is not absolutely necessary is detrimental to execution [. . .] [T]he forearm alone must act; the part from the shoulder to the elbow must remain motionless. (p. 8)
Hand	The **hand** should rest naturally, in the same way it has developed on the arm. Do not bend the wrist either up or down. (p. 45)	It is necessary that [. . .] the **hands** be slightly inclined toward the keys from the top of the forearm to the knuckles of the fingers; neither raise nor lower the wrist too much. (p. 7)
Finger	The **fingers** must be curved while playing, i.e., one must draw them back far enough to be in line with a naturally held thumb. (p. 45) The **finger** should touch the key only with its fleshy pad, and never with the fingernail. (p. 47)	[B]end [the **fingers**] at the first knuckle and curl them very slightly at the second, so that the hand takes a rounded form [. . .] It is necessary that each finger move independently from the others, that is to say, when one of them lifts, the others should not move [. . .] [O]ne should avoid playing the keyboard with nails. (pp. 7–8)

Streicher (1801) / de Silva (2008)	Adam (1804–5) / Beghin with Jensen-Large (2021)
The **finger** must not be held far above the keys before the stroke, since a finger *falling from too great a height* makes a small noise during the attack, robbing the tone somewhat of its purity. (p. 47) One should try as much as possible to strike the keys at their front edge, because, as in the case of a lever, only limited strength is needed to produce a healthy tone. (p. 47) A key must not be touched before the moment in which the sound should be heard, for even the slightest weight [of the **finger**] will push the key down somewhat, causing the beak of the hammer to begin forcing backward the pivoted escapement [*Tangente*]. (p. 47)	It is [. . .] necessary to place the **fingers** in the middle of the white keys in order to avoid disturbing the hands when one wants to use the black keys. (p. 7) When placing the right hand [. . .] in order to strike the five notes: *ut, re, mi, fa,* and *sol* successively [. . .] it is necessary that all **fingers** are placed at the same time on the surface of the keys that one will have to make sound, so that they are ready *to strike*; then one will lift the fingers a little above the keyboard, but without extending them [. . .] and one will make them fall perpendicularly and successively on the indicated keys. (p. 8) Never allow the **little finger** or the **thumb** to drop below the level of the keyboard because, in this case, the other fingers could become trained to leave the position prescribed in the preceding section. (p. 8)

| Finger/hand | When individual notes are connected, be they fast or slow, strong or weak, *only the fingers* should be moving, without raising the [entire] **hand** for the attack and letting it fall again. Only in the case of staccato notes or full chords may the hands be raised somewhat. (p. 47) |

TABLE 3.1 *Continued*

	Streicher (1801) / de Silva (2008)	Adam (1804–5) / Beghin with Jensen-Large (2021)
Fingers/hand/arm	The **arm** must support the **hand**, the hand its **fingers**. The calmer the arm and hand, the surer the motion of the fingers, the greater the dexterity, and the more beautiful the tone. (p. 45)	
Other keywords	One should endeavor to produce individual tones through a quick and elastic bounce, and full-voiced chords by a quick thrust [of the hand], rather than through hard hitting or unnecessary pressing into the keyboard.[1] (p. 49)	

Notes: 1 On p. 59 Streicher uses in this connection the phrase "nervous gripping [*ein nervöses Anprellen*]."

both as a builder (or the next best thing, as the partner of a builder, both in life and in business) and as a pianist. Of the two authors, he alone fuses the human-physical with the machine-technical, and when he describes an integrated system of "arm supporting the hand and hand supporting its fingers," we may detect an analogy with the two-way connection of the Viennese piano action, its key holding the *Kapsel* and the *Kapsel* pivoting the hammer. From his side, pursuing technical precision on all matters anatomical (arguably more so than Streicher), Adam does not digress into any action-technical terminology—at least not relating to components that are not directly visible to the pianist. Emphasis on human mechanics shows in Adam's recommendation as to where to place the finger on the key, namely, "in the middle of the white keys in order to avoid disturbing the hands when one wants to use the black keys." (Adam means the middle of the portion from the front of the white keys to where the black keys start.) This differs from Streicher's technology-oriented view that as much as possible one should "try to strike the keys at their front edge, because, as in the case of a lever, only limited strength is needed to produce a healthy tone." But then Adam gives peculiar additional advice, for the hands "to be slightly inclined toward the keys from the top of the forearm to the knuckles of the fingers," as if to give an extra edge—or, indeed, higher leverage—to the fingers' downward strikes and to compensate for the French action's larger key dip and heavier hammers.

These clarifications and omissions on either side end up painting two significantly different approaches. On the French keyboard, it is considered wise to lift your finger higher than the key so as to create a head start of movement before initial impact with the key. On the Viennese keyboard, by contrast, it's all about absolute economy of movement—both by carefully positioning one's finger at the front of the key and by anticipating key contact in the fleshy pad of the finger.

We're ready to describe what happens, frame by frame. The photos shown as plate 2 capture the moment when my index finger is just about to descend: they're drawn from slow-motion video clips that may be followed along on the website. First, a Viennese strike, by the second finger of the right hand, to be held down sufficiently for the strings to speak. ("Think of it as a single quarter note, in *allegro* time.") I aim for a normal strike, the definition of which has been agreed on in advance. For the record, Bobby spells it out before I play: "As if you approached the piano for the first time; without thinking of any particular muscle movement, simply activate the mechanism and produce a tone—not too soft, not too loud." Then, the countdown: "Ready? . . . Recording."

The fleshy pad of my finger, correctly curved, has barely touched the key when the escapement lever starts swinging the hammer upward. In the hammer's ascent, one observes a gradual increase in speed, and when the hammer hits the strings, it almost feels like the energy of the upward motion is cut off too soon. On its descent, the hammer is almost instantaneously caught and immobilized by the back-check: the efficiency is stunning. (The back-check is that leather-covered wooden nub designed to create contact with a falling hammer.) When the finger releases the key, the hammer beak slides down the face of the escapement lever, which, pressured by a spring in the back, then resumes its initial position above the beak of the hammer, ready to be engaged again. While the back-check did a superb job catching the downward-falling hammer, the escapement rocks back and forth no fewer than three times before standstill. Finally, watch how the fleshy pad of my finger, once down onto the key-bed and no longer pushing, still wants to keep caressing the key. The distance traveled by the finger is relatively short, and it makes sense to visualize it as part of a curving line toward the player's body, arguably mirroring the curving motion that has been initialized by the escapement. This curve, at its turn, is transferred to the hammer, which hits strings from a tilted position rather than straight on.

Second, a French strike. The lift of my finger, by a significant 3–4 mm, displays perpendicular determination. In shape and proportion, it's the human equivalent of Erard's *pilote* (hopper), fleshy-pad awareness yielding to a straight and long line down. Different from the *prell*-action, where it seemed important for the finger to feel the friction of the escapement before descending, the focus here is on accumulating energy by lifting the finger. The *pilote* drives the hammer-hinge, hammer-shank, and hammer-head into action. In contrast to the Walter action, where the movement of the back of the key may be said to mirror that of the hammer (one curving motion leading to another, enlarged), here it is the hammer that travels the farthest of all moving components: it is truly being *catapulted* toward the strings. Impact with the strings is strong and results in a clear backlash: hammer-shank and -head visibly shake on their way down. The backcheck, individually mounted on the key itself rather than being part of a rail that is independent of the key, proves its efficiency when catching the hammer on its downward trajectory, but after the key is released, it takes a bounce or three by the hammer before stability of the overall system is restored. One final moment warrants our attention. Watch the felt padding under the front key. It is designed to smoothen the impact when the front key hits that bottom plate of the action, or key-bed. Reacting to the impact, the felt first compresses, then decompresses again, and it takes a few milliseconds for key and finger to settle on a default down position. This is what is known as after-touch. The Walter has an entirely different system to stop the key on its way down. On a Viennese piano, a stop rail blocks the rear end of the key quite abruptly and as far away as possible from my finger pad: there's nothing to feel under the key. The thin piece of cloth glued onto the stop rail is designed to eliminate mechanical noise rather than to soften the blow of my finger.

Analyzing the Results

Bobby tested me in three series of five equal single strikes on each of the model actions, in three dynamic ranges: normal, *piano* ("With a slow and gentle finger movement, make the strings speak with minimal excitation"), and *forte* ("With a vigorous finger strike, excite the strings with a sudden burst of energy"). This order is drawn from real life, as we imagined Beethoven inviting a student or colleague to try out the action of his new piano, then to explore its softer range, and finally, to test its explosive potential.

But I'm submitting myself to science. Playing a single tone during a social encounter is one thing. Doing so five times in a row, in highly planned and controlled circumstances, is quite another. So many thoughts ran through my head. As I write this chapter, joining Bobby in his role of observer, I must distance myself from those inner thoughts, or even the memory of them. No more second-guessing. Thirty single strikes, each played with utmost concentration, have become analyzable data, ready to be presented in graphs. To show my commitment to objectivity, from here onward I will refer to the person sitting at those action models as *the pianist*.

When first introducing the marked action components in the photographs of figure 3.2, I appealed to you, the reader, to imagine them *in action*. You may, in addition, have checked out the slow-motion video on the website. In fact, what we have been looking at has been the second in a *normal* strike series, on Walter and Erard pianos, respectively. There's significance here: we found that, for both actions, the first strikes were exploratory at best. It was only at the second strike that idiomatic behavior kicked in—finger and action collaborating in remarkable ways for the remainder of the sequence.

The graphs in plate 2 track the movement for each of the marked components of figure 3.2. Each component has been given a different color. The x-axis indicates time (in milliseconds, or ms), while the y-axis tracks vertical distance (up or down, in centimeters).[9] We define an *entire* strike as beginning with finger descent and ending with key release. This means that, for the time-axis, point zero has been set at the beginning of finger descent. For the y-axis, zero means complete rest, which for the Erard was easy to establish, but for the Walter, because of Streicher's recommended finger contact, required some judgment on the analyst's part.

The graph of an entire strike on Walter shows that everything happens not only immediately but also in synchronicity: what each component is supposed to do, they're doing *all together*. The Erard, in contrast, espouses individuality: respective motions appear *out of phase* with one another, and they start happening only much later, 64 ms into the graph. This timing, of course, reflects finger movement: while in the Walter strike, there is no loss of time before the setting in motion of the various action components (because the finger is already in touch with the key), in the Erard strike, because the finger starts from above, there's a lapse of 64 ms before any action component starts to move.

Both actions share the same goal: that singular hammer strike, rising high above everything else. Strictly speaking, this highest peak as we see it on the graphs represents not the point where the hammer hits the strings, but the point just after contact (one or two frames later), where the hammer has created maximum compression to the strings, just before it starts descending again. To establish the exact moment of contact, we cannot read the graph, but must consult the logged video file. On the Walter action model, hammer–string contact occurs at 54 ms, which is much sooner than the 129 ms on Erard. Even when leveling the playing field to finger–key contact also on Erard (which is at 64 ms into the sequence), it takes 65 ms for the Erard hammer to make contact with the strings—still making Erard a significant 11 ms *slower to respond in sound* than Walter.[10]

Though taking more time to reach its goal, the Erard hammer *moves at a faster speed* than the one in Walter. Taking into account that the latter travels only 3.4 cm toward the strings compared to the 5.2 cm for Erard, one calculates a substantially faster average speed for Erard than for Walter: 90 cm/s as compared to 62 cm/s. We can make further calculations from the video data: in this particular *normal* strike, the Walter's hammer maximum speed is 146.1 cm/s or 5.26 km/h versus Erard's 202.9 cm/s or 7.30 km/h. For the fastest speeds across the board, we must go to the *forte* strikes: 226.1 cm/s or 8.14 km/h for Walter versus 384.7 cm/s or 13.85 km/h for Erard. The Walter maximum speed occurs at the final stage of contact between escapement lever and hammer, while for the Erard it is reached just at the moment when the hopper starts losing contact with the hammer butt and sends the hammer into free flight.

The key dip (or the depth of movement for a key) is noticeably lower for Erard than Walter. A Walter key reaches a depth of 4.33 mm. In Erard, the key sinks all the way to 7.45 mm, or almost 75 percent farther than Walter.[11] Comparing the green line (the lowest, for the key front) between Walter and Erard, one observes a longer, more or less parallel line with a rather decisive curve at the end for Walter, and a shorter, overall more slanting line, with a less decisive final curve for Erard. The moment of key release, therefore, is more identifiable in Walter than Erard.

Figure 3.3 isolates these two key-front lines, showing much more detail in the distance axis (y-axis). Observe the little bump as the Walter hammer hits the lowest point: we're witnessing the boxwood key front slightly bending under finger pressure, in reaction to the abrupt stoppage at the back of the key. In contrast, as we saw already, the felt padding under the Erard key absorbs the impact of the finger as smoothly as possible: it compresses and decompresses—and we can now count exactly how many times. This is a vibrato of some sort—comparable, in fact, to a *Bebung* on the clavichord, with two important distinctions: first, the experience remains tactile only (on a hammer-operated piano, there's no sonic effect, of course); second, it is entirely unintentional (something that I can vouch for, as the subject of the experiment). Intriguingly, we see a feverish kind of shaking in the Walter key, too—something that I have not at all been aware of as a player. While the Erard key reacts to the felt landing as a single, remarkably steady piece of wood, the much more bendable Walter key lever responds strongly to the abrupt rear-key impact. It takes a releasing finger to allow the Walter lever to find its inner stability again and then ascend along with the rising finger. The ascent of the Walter key is more decisive and straightforward than Erard's, which happens more gradually and, at least initially, more reluctantly.

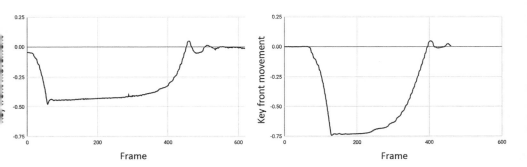

FIGURE 3.3 Key-front behavior for Walter (*left*) and Erard (*right*).

It may be useful here to compare down-weight and up-weight: the former is what is needed to press down the key (and is measured up to the final point before escapement), while the latter corresponds to the maximum weight on a slowly ascending key (encapsulating the upward force of the key). For a key to be light, we want the down to be low and the up to be high, and that's indeed what we find in our Walter key, which has a down-weight of 22 grams and an up-weight of 8 g, as compared to 32 g down and 5 g up for Erard. If *Kapsel* and hammer had not been mounted onto the key itself, the Walter key could have been lighter still. But although this would have been of help going down (if extreme lightness is indeed what one wants), when going up the additional weight in the back helps the front in what is essentially a seesaw movement. By contrast, an Erard hammer hangs in its own, independent rail; otherwise, an Erard key would have been even heavier to press down. To summarize:

1. Sound is produced sooner by a Walter action than one by Erard.
2. The Erard action is faster and thus potentially louder, while Walter is more explosive.
3. After-touch is highly relevant for Erard and not at all for Walter. (I define "after-touch" here in the widest possible sense, applying to any awareness of the key after the initial strike and through the release.)
4. An Erard key is significantly heavier than Walter, both down and up.

But now, a question: why does the pianist hold their sound significantly longer when playing Walter than Erard? This tendency is corroborated by the four other strikes. There's an aesthetic undertone to this question: English-style pianos are known to lend themselves better to longer tones than Viennese ones. Why, then, does exactly the *opposite* happen in this particular experiment?

Attack, sound, release: that's how one would reasonably describe the threefold process of a strike. But during a Walter strike, attack and sound are so closely linked that as a result sound starts to dominate, both as it is produced and when being clipped. Where's touch? Arguably in the fleshy pad of one's finger. In Erard, however, as the finger first settles down and then withdraws, there's touch, more touch, there's sound somewhere along the way, and then there's even more touch. The pianist receives an overdose of touch—or is it sound? Sound becomes a tactile as well as aural experience.

But in terms of the length of the played note, there's awkwardness in both mechanisms. When asked to play a quarter-note tone, the pianist is expected to make three consecutive decisions: down, hold, up. But on a Viennese-style piano it is much more natural to focus only on down and up, without worrying much about the middle: that's why one usually says that Viennese fortepianos *articulate* very well. I'd say that the exigencies of the experiments (the pressure to get them right) raised the subject's neurological consciousness, resulting in the production of an atypically long tone. An Erard strike, for its part, takes longer to initialize. Rather than a complete down, hold, and up, I would argue that the graphs in plate 2 show only the down of what might have developed into a much longer French tone. The middle—the part attesting to the French piano's reputation to *sing* very well—never really happens, and would in any case have required a length of sound much beyond the experiment's stipulated quarter note. Finally, there was also the technical reason for cutting down on length: a mere half-second longer would have resulted in many more gigabytes of raw video data to process.

Fingerspitzengefühl

In the following chapters we will have many opportunities to extol the French instrument's capacity to *spin* sound (*filer le son*) in a quasi-continuous fashion. Here, however, we remain interested in the very beginning of finger and key contact—well before escapement or maximum hammer speed; in fact, well before any sound at all. We now zoom in on that proverbial moment of *Fingerspitzengefühl*, when the initial feeling of resistance in one's finger provokes a split-second decision on how to proceed. Does the pianist's finger know whether to strike the key in the Viennese manner or *à la française*? An answer may be found when analyzing the learning curve that we observed earlier between the first and second strike. What does the pianist do better in the second strike? What adjustment is made?

Figure 3.4 features four graphs, extracted from Walter runs nos. 1 and 2, and the same for Erard. They magnify what we saw in plate 2 already, now displaying the first 15 or 30 ms after finger/key contact instead of the

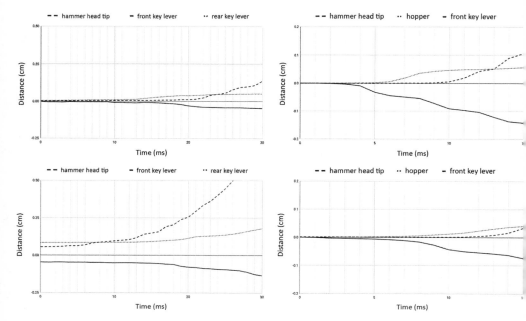

FIGURE 3.4 Beginning of strike for Walter (*left*) and Erard (*right*): comparison of first (*top*) and second (*bottom*) runs.

600 ms before. (To account for a finger starting at standstill, we needed just a bit more time for Walter to observe any meaningful beginning of movement.) The graphs also drastically reduce the number of markers, keeping only three strategic points of weight that a pianist's finger needs to deal with: the front of the key (where the finger makes its initial contact); one point in the back of the key that connects most directly with the hammer (Bobby chose the rear of the key lever for Walter and the hopper for Erard); and the tip of the hammer (as the ultimate beneficiary of all exerted power or movement).

When we compare Walter run no. 1 with Walter run no. 2, one difference jumps out immediately—demonstrating a process of learning clearly, if not spectacularly. The pianist starts no. 1 (left, top) by holding their finger on or right above the key, exactly as Streicher would want them to: as a result, the mechanical parts in the graph are shown at a perfect standstill. We see some minuscule movement at around 9 ms, but front and rear key, mirroring one another, only clearly start moving at 14 ms, preceding the hammer at 21 ms. Kickoff, then—lever triggering hammer—happens within 7 ms.

Notably (and this is true for nos. 3–5 as well), Walter run no. 2 (left, bottom) *ignores* Streicher's advice, and starts, quite sensitively, with the key slightly depressed, exactly at the point where the escapement holds the hammer-beak, allowing the pianist to eliminate what to engineers is known as lost motion. (This is why in the graph the three components start slightly below or above zero.) As a result, *the three mechanical points start moving almost together.* Even more, if we are pressed to name one, it is *the hammer* that takes the lead. This demonstrates remarkable efficiency. If no. 1 reflects the technique of a gifted amateur, then no. 2 bears the mark of the professional.

How, then, are the Walter strikes different from those of Erard? While in Walter, the three points of departure are designed to take place more or less simultaneously (with no. 2 being more successful than no. 1), there's a sequence in Erard, each point of departure remaining clearly distinguishable from the other. In Erard no. 1 (right, top), we see the front key develop movement at 3 ms, then the hopper at 6 ms, and finally the hammer at 10 ms. If 3 ms is impressive enough for finger-in-motion to overcome the initial weight of an altogether heavier Erard key, then, by the second run (right, bottom), the pianist *does even better.* Timings now read 1 ms, 5 ms, and 11 ms—a slightly expanded sequence from Erard no. 1, but a clearly paced sequence nonetheless. Engineers speak of lost motion, but in this design those pockets of time between events are far from "lost." On the contrary, they're essential. One finds them in each of my five Erard runs, revealing that *while the exact timing may vary,* all *Erard strikes entail an essential sequence of tactile events.* If it is a sign of professionalism to flip that Walter hammer as quickly as possible, it takes a different level of skill to explore the endless variety in the sequential tactility of a single Erard strike.

Conclusion

The conundrum that we hinted at previously flares up again. It is one thing to argue that in 1803 Beethoven was looking for new challenges and that he found them in his new piano. (I do argue this, and I do think that Beethoven believed he had finally found the piano that gave him that "freedom to create [his] own tone.") But it is quite another to claim that *tone* can be explained in terms of *sound* alone. Onset of deafness, on the contrary, makes it entirely logical that on his French piano Beethoven embraced a perception of sound hitherto unknown to him—one that was inextricably linked with *touch*.

Beethoven described the Viennese tone as "woody," and one assumes that he meant that it was woodier than the French. But then, he might just as well have been comparing the design of a Viennese hammer with that of a French one: the former is pointed, smaller, and with fewer leather coverings (our action model has three), while the latter is round, bigger, and has no fewer than four layers of leather that are bound to create an altogether bouncier contact with the strings. The association of tool and sound is entirely warranted, of course. But we're left in the dark as to how Beethoven would have described the French tone by comparison. Leathery? Kneadable? Elastic?

I don't think "leathery" would have come up in Beethoven's mind. We have a long history behind us of piano hammers with softer coverings. Leathery means something to us, but only because it implies something different than felt-like. But I doubt that "felt-like" is a term that a modern-day pianist would use to describe the tone of their beloved Steinway grand (until felt is replaced by something else, that is). Modern pianists would describe the tone of a piano as "round," "full," or "expressive"—all to be understood within the same paradigm of "felt." Beethoven uses "woody" because it suggests something well known to him—but also something old-fashioned. The quantity and softness of leather used on an Erard hammer—as well as an action that thrives on much less explosive contact of it with the strings—would have struck Beethoven as entirely new and different.

I would say that "kneadable" captures the difference in tactility between Erard and Walter very well, even if "elastic" is the term used by both Beethoven and Streicher. In order to play "individual tones" with a certain emphasis, Streicher recommends "a quick and elastic bounce [*ein elastisches Anschnellen*]" over "hard hitting or unnecessary pressing into the keyboard" (see table 3.1, under "other keywords").[12] Elastic for Streicher, however, does not mean those explosive Viennese hammers (although, as it turns out, their key levers *are* surprisingly bendable), but the fleshy pads of one's fingers. On a Viennese fortepiano, in other words, human flesh has the potential of taking away the harsh edges of woodiness. And as we saw at the outset, Beethoven used *elastisch* exactly in reference to the Viennese action.

Is the answer, then, in the interaction of human and thing? Our experiment has made it abundantly clear that a French single strike generates a rich tactile experience—there's just no comparison with a Viennese strike. But embracing French tactility also means yielding to *mechanical* principles that are inherent in the French instrument. Caught up in his enthusiasm for something new, Beethoven may not have realized that his enchantment (causing him to call all other pianos "rubbish" by comparison) also meant giving up a significant degree of human control of the kind he'd been used to before, and *of the kind he'd crave again*, after using his Erard and living the dream of its malleable tone.

CHAPTER FOUR

The Lure of
una corda

Dear young artists! [. . .] A lofty allegory paints the image of Apollo, who's sent down from heaven to bring happiness on earth: at the sounds of his lyre everything stirs; everything's moved; everything gets better and more perfect.

> —From a ministerial speech given at the Distribution of
> Awards for pupils of the Paris Conservatoire,
> shared in German translation with the readers of *AmZ*
> on March 18, 1801 (3, no. 25:432–33)

When Beethoven saw Haydn's Erard for the first time, he may well have been envious. The grand piano No. 28 was *orné*, meaning that its case was not only mahogany-veneered, but also lavishly ornamented—a fitting tribute to the sixty-nine-year-old composer who by 1801 had reached pan-European stardom. But Viennese builders, too, had a tradition of adding bronze embellishments and using expensive mahogany by special request of their aristocratic customers. Beethoven would have known and played such instruments, including those built by Anton Walter. So, teacher-pupil psychology aside, what would have attracted Beethoven to Haydn's instrument? What in particular about this piano would have made him decide that he wanted one, too? In his 1802 letter to Zmeskall, Beethoven stresses the *una corda*. But what in Erard's realization of this technology triggered Beethoven's enthusiasm to the extent that he would insist on taking local builders to go and see "it"—*dieses*, "this thing," this particular piece of technology?

At first glance, several features of Haydn's piano would have attracted Beethoven's attention: the four hook-shaped, iron gap spacers jutting out from the instrument's soundboard, for instance, or the four shiny brass rods thrusting down from beneath the keyboard. These projections would not have existed on any of the familiar Viennese instruments, which had knee-levers or hand stops at the most, and certainly no pedals to be operated with one's foot. On closer inspection, Beethoven's admiration for Sébastien Erard's technical vision and the technological sophistication of the French machine would only have grown. Beethoven, then still a fit thirty-year-old, might have stolen a moment while the old man was out of the room to crawl under the piano, tracing the direction of the pedal rods with his eyes. Studying the various levers crisscrossing the belly of the instrument (fig. 4.1), he would have been intrigued by one structure in particular, at the far right: the register with one string. The device was still to receive its proper name.

Two Registers in One

The principle of the fourth pedal is simple: the keyboard is made to shift to the side, causing the hammers to strike not three strings, but either two strings or just one. The term *una corda* is thus a synecdoche in that it comprises the intermediary *due corde* and arguably also *tre corde* (as the default, when not pressing down the pedal). The apparatus requires two mechanical components: a lever to initiate the shift and a spring to return the keyboard to its original position, both contained within the case of the piano, out of sight to Beethoven but made visible to us in the drawing of figure 4.1. But what Beethoven would have noticed on the instrument's underside is *an additional spring* with an entirely distinct function: rather than to exert force, it is designed to provide resistance—something he had felt in his foot while trying out the piano. Next to Haydn's Erard, in the same room, may have been his Longman & Broderip, an instrument Haydn brought home after his second London trip in 1794–95.[1] It, too, would have had an *una corda*, similarly operated with the foot. Yet there would have been a crucial mechanical difference in executing the transition between one, two, or three

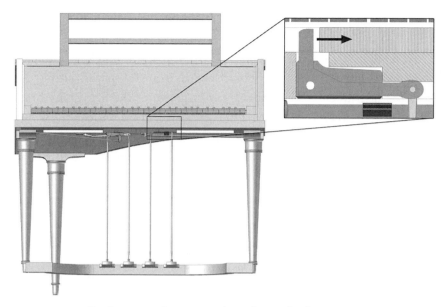

FIGURE 4.1 Tracing *una corda* on an Erard grand. Drawing by Gregoir Basyn.

strings. The English system included a hand-operated latch at the far end of the keyboard, as shown on a 1798 Longman, Clementi & Co. model (fig. 4.2). Raise it, and the keyboard is allowed to slide further, resulting in *una corda*; lower it, and the shift of the keyboard stops at *due corde*. The interpretive decision for the pianist, then (since this is also the perspective that would have come most naturally to Beethoven), is about the degree of contrast one deems appropriate for a particular section, movement, or piece: down means *less* and up means *more* contrast. In his pianos Erard replaced the latch with a spring (fig. 4.3). As the pianist's foot depresses the pedal, it meets the spring at the halfway point: *due corde*. Pushed further— with renewed and heightened pressure—the pedal reaches its lowest point: *una corda*.

From an engineering point of view, the English standard and the French adaptation are two realizations of the same principle. Yet, by the addition of a single spring, Erard upgrades what some scholars have interpreted as a device not even intended for the pianist but rather for the piano technician, allowing him to tune the unison strings of a piano without the nuisance of external mutes. Evidence of this practice may be found on a manufacturer-approved leaflet with directions for "tuning and keeping the grand piano

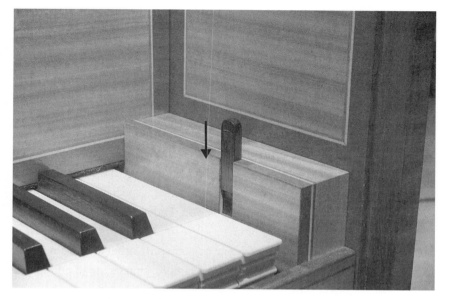

FIGURE 4.2 Latch to control keyboard shift in a 1798 Longman, Clementi & Co. piano. Photo by Jeremy Tusz.

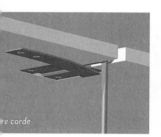

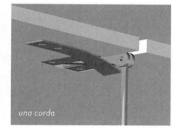

re corde *due corde* *una corda*

FIGURE 4.3 Out-of-case spring in three positions. Drawings by Gregoir Basyn.

forte in order," securely glued behind the name boards of Broadwood grands between 1787 and 1792, which is where a technician would find it: "First, draw up the small Piece of wood which is fixed upon the Block, on the treble Side of the Keys [i.e., our latch], and putting down the left Pedal, the Hammers will strike on one Unison, which tune as you do the Harpsichord; then turn down the said Piece of Wood, and putting down again the left Pedal, the Hammers will strike on two Unisons, which tune; and lastly, by letting the Pedal go, you may tune the third Unison to the other two."[2] The French innovation now explicitly makes this pedal a coloristic device that effectively enlarges the pianist's toolbox. Sébastien Erard explained to a customer in 1797 that "the fourth pedal" is one "with which one can play 1, 2 or 3 strings at will [*à volonté*]; playing only one string makes an admirable effect in the pianos [i.e., those moments when playing in the dynamic register of *piano*], especially in cantabile passages."[3]

Creating admirable effects is one thing, but being able to do so *at will* is quite another. It is this flexibility that the English models lack. If the English pianist wants to take control over their default softer shade (produced either by two strings or by one), they had better take note of the latch's position before embarking on their performance, especially since a piano tuner may have left it in the wrong position. Indeed, personal experience has taught me that it helps to annotate a score to indicate my preferred latch position during a passage, movement, or piece, for otherwise I am apt to forget this crucial step. A penciled ↑, for example, signals me to pull up the latch before launching into a particular piece, movement, or section—this private annotation ensuring I will re-create that special *una corda* sonority that I have practiced and enjoyed. But to what extent did the technology encourage such careful planning? Having grown up with pedaled *una corda* pianos, we're unwittingly prey to anachronism as we assess not only the limitations of an English piano, but also the affordances of the Erard. One thing is certain: penciled-in annotations as specific as mine, beyond the occasional fingering or where to use the damper pedal, are yet to be discovered in historically owned scores.

Still, Sébastien Erard clearly did not hide his enthusiasm for his *quatrième pédale*, so it is worthwhile exploring its potential. Not only does the fourth pedal allow the performer to pursue different options in the heat of the moment; it also enables yet another effect, distinct from the *una corda*—that of the *swell*. Already popularized through the square piano, including those manufactured by Erard Frères, the swell was a stop designed to either dramatically increase or decrease the volume of sound. On square pianos, the flap of the lid immediately to the player's right was separately hinged, and the stop would move it up or down—an erratic operation imperfectly controlled by one's leg muscles alone. Such a swell, or *jalousie*, may well have added charm to an amateur's performance, even if the bobbing lid had a comical effect.[4]

In contrast, the *una corda* pedal on an Erard grand lets the pianist readily adjust and control the volume. By coordinating foot with spring, the pianist can smoothly transition through various levels of loudness. They can go back and forth between playing on three versus two strings, or on two versus one; or they can anticipate the force-resisting spring and by a single swoop accomplish a complete decay from loudest to softest (three to one); or, by a purposeful release, achieve a grand swell from softest to loudest (one to three). Paradoxically, the latter direction, producing loudness, requires the least physical effort, the former, producing softness, the most.

There is good reason to believe that for Erard the *una corda* stop would have constituted a device for varying volume just as much as for providing different strata of color. The position of the pedal—as the rightmost of four—is one important indication, for the exact same position had been reserved on square pianos (both English and French) for the swell. While this makes practical sense for this type of instrument—since the operating rod needs to be as close as possible to the right-side lid—there is no such restriction for the grand piano. One might speculate as to why Erard did not take advantage of the technical differences between the two designs to reshuffle the pedals, most important, bringing the damper pedal on the grand to the extreme right, as on English instruments, rather than keeping it second from the left. But this is hindsight talking: the fact remains that Erard's grand kept the privileged position of the fourth pedal, also the position most easily accessible to the right-footed pianist, for the swell.

To bring some perspective, figure 4.4 (which is drawn to scale) compares our Erard setup with two representative examples from English pianos— a 1798 Longman, Clementi & Co. (which has the same design as Haydn's 1795 Longman & Broderip would have had) and an 1805 John Broadwood (representative of Broadwood models in the early 1800s)—and a Viennese fortepiano by Walter from the same period.[5] The Longman, Clementi & Co. has one pedal protruding from each of the keyboard's two front legs at a distance of 75 cm. The left pedal lifts the dampers, and the right shifts the keyboard. Since pressing both at the same time would have raised questions of impropriety even for trouser-wearing men, there must have been a compelling musical reason for fanning out one's legs. Around 1800, however, Broadwood and his colleagues situated the pedals at the piano's center between the instrument's front legs, some 40 cm apart. Although that spread still exceeds a natural resting position, it does put each pedal comfortably within reach, especially considering that one's feet may be turned sideways from a heel-supported position.

Conceptually, however, it seems jarring to associate such a sideways application of one's feet with two pedals that project straight out toward the player but are still shaped to mirror the contours of a human foot. By contrast, the Erard pedals project no such inhibition. Less hominoid in their design, they also do not hide their functionality: visibly attached to each piece of wood is a metal rod that openly connects with the keyboard on top, while the Broadwood still maintains the earlier design of a leg within which a rod is enclosed. "Use me in whichever way or combination you want," the message seems to be from these four identical rectangles. The outer pedals (measured from their midpoints) are 28.5 cm apart, significantly less than the two Broadwood pedals, and much closer to what may be an ergonomically acceptable width between two resting feet. But it's not just pedals nos. 1 and 4 we're interested in: we're looking for the best position to play all four pedals—and here it helps that the distance between the middle of pedals nos. 1 and 2, on the one hand, and the middle of pedals nos. 3 and 4, on the other, is about 20 cm, which corresponds to a comfortable, yet keenly focused position of the heels, as their perfect vantage point to navigate any combination of pedals. If Leonardo da Vinci were to draw the geometry of a man sitting at a four-pedaled keyboard, that's where the vertical axis would be: in between those knees and heels, between pedals nos. 2 and 3, as the cradle of symmetry. (A horizontal axis of hands and keyboard will be evoked later on in this book; on the topic of historical pedal use, I should stress that, contrary to modern piano practice, the default is for one's complete feet to be resting on the floor: they are to be shifted over one or more pedals only when needed.)

By way of comparison, finally, imagine sitting at a Viennese fortepiano with knee-levers like those depicted in figure 4.4. One's knees would be some 26.5 cm apart, which is less than the distance between pedals nos. 1 and 4 on the Erard, but more than the span of three of them. The stress on the body, however, must be judged from the perspective of heels being raised rather than foot tips digging into the floor. While this movement is not uncomfortable—from experience, I know it to be way friendlier on the back than that of pedals—it is also impossible to maintain such a knees-up

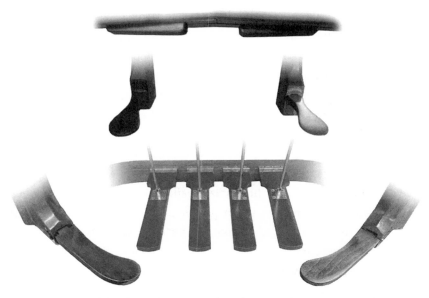

FIGURE 4.4 Pedal and knee-lever setups for (*from top to bottom*) Anton Walter (1800), Longman, Clementi & Co. (1798), John Broadwood & Son (1805), and Erard Frères (1803). Assembled on scale by Gregoir Basyn.

position for too long. Like those first-generation English pedals, Viennese knee-levers are designed to be optional only.

Institutionalizing Pedals

Michael Latcham has observed that from 1800 onward, Erard's square pianos "usually had the same selection of stops, except for the *una corda*, as in his grand pianos."[6] But if we are right in establishing a kinship between *una corda* and swell, we may safely ignore that "except for" clause. Whether sitting down at a square or a grand piano, the French pianist would expect the same kinds of stops. In the new pianos *en forme de clavecin*, which were in production between 1797 and 1808, the company standardized not just the selection of stops, but also their sequence.

It cannot be a coincidence that Erard rolled out its new pianos exactly at the time the Paris Conservatoire embarked on its new educational platform, which ultimately would regularize and professionalize the performing musician's *métier*. It is impossible to know whether manufacturing influenced pedagogy or the other way round, but the standardization of Erard's pedals allowed a clear discussion of the use of pedals in the Conservatoire's manual authored by Louis Adam for the piano department. Just as there was one official textbook, there could be only one order of pedals, and the young and aspiring performer had to learn their way through them: (1) *jeu de luth* or *jeu de harpe*, by which a soft leather strip is pressed against the strings, cutting their resonance considerably but also changing the color of the sound; (2) the *grande pédale*, by which the dampers are collectively lifted off the strings; (3) *jeu céleste*, by fortepianists nowadays commonly called "the moderator," by which small leather strips are slid in between the strings and the hammers; and (4) our *una corda* (for the grand piano) or the swell (for the square). Like Beethoven, we will explore the potential of all, but for now we continue focusing on (4)—"*dieses*," the one pedal that Beethoven explicitly coveted.

Louis Adam gives the *una corda* pedal due attention in his manual. He first dismisses the *jalousie* on the square piano as "sort of useless" because it "only serves to lift the lid"; clearly, he did not approve of the lid's Muppet-like theatrics. Once he proceeds to the fourth pedal on the grand piano, however, his tone changes as he begins to describe the dynamic qualities of swell and decay it enables. Initially he says the pedal "may only be used to create *piano, crescendo* and *diminuendo.*"[7] Intriguingly, these three options—that is, *piano*, on the one hand, and *crescendo/diminuendo*, on the other—correspond to the two-in-one register that we have been describing so far. But he then goes on to explain how the fourth pedal, by "playing one string only," can also lend a *pianissimo* effect. In prose suggestive of an imprecise memory, perhaps of Erard explaining the technology to him, he describes the mechanics thus:

> This fourth pedal shifts the keyboard to the right, imperceptibly moving the hammers away from the strings, until only one string is left under [*sic*] the hammer, and it is with this pedal that one creates *pianissimo* perfectly.[8]

Referring to the string as *under* rather than *over* the hammer may be no more than a slip of the pen. But it could be that Adam assumed that the interior action would mirror the downward thrust of the fingers on the keys. Perhaps what we should be asking, therefore, is whether this inaccuracy is an inadvertent hint of something else. In a method book targeted at an emerging community of professionals, *things* are increasingly described as *effects*. The specified effect here is the *pianissimo*, which one "creates perfectly" by using the fourth pedal. The pianist is no longer merely playing but employing a tool to make a special sound: the English verb "create" does not do justice to the idea of formation that inheres in the phrase *faire le Pianissimo*. At the same time, this formative act takes place mostly out of sight: while it is clear that the keyboard "shifts to the right," no one actually sees the hammers "moving away from the strings."

As Adam notes, the effect is realized "imperceptibly," and maybe *not* seeing is the point. Effects are for the pleasure of an audience, and it speaks to the genius of the piano maker that the pianist has the technological means to realize them. Paradoxically, however, ignorance of technology leads to appropriation: the player appropriates the effects handed to them by the builder, and by either deliberately or unconsciously hiding the technological cause of the effect, it is the player rather than the builder who becomes the magician, sharing their technological naïveté (which may or may not be feigned) with the listener. In 1834, Charles Chaulieu, co-editor with Henry Lemoine of the Parisian journal *Le pianiste* (both had studied with Adam), reminisced about an encounter with Daniel Steibelt:

> "Go sit at the back of the room," [Steibelt] says to me one day at his home, "close your eyes, and listen." Then he played the great adagio of his Op. 64, where he employed the pedals so well, the usage of which was little known before him.[9]

Steibelt published his Grand Sonata in G Major, Op. 64, in 1805, and he relocated from Paris to St. Petersburg in 1808. This impromptu performance would then have taken place at a time when Chaulieu was at the height of his career as a student at the Conservatoire. He was a *premier prix* winner at eighteen years of age (in 1806) and a teaching assistant to Louis Adam. In 1806–7 he was practicing a difficult concerto by Dussek, who, like Steibelt, was a known champion of the pedals and had returned to Paris in 1807 (the topic later of his own Op. 64 Sonata, "Le Retour à Paris").[10] So, more than anyone else, Chaulieu would have known how to appreciate Steibelt's pedaling, and chances are he would have recognized and admired a few of his tricks. But also for Steibelt, that extraordinary Adagio from Op. 64 must have set a new personal benchmark, and playing it for a talented young colleague like Chaulieu must have been a special test. In the published version Steibelt ended up meticulously notating all possible pedal uses—including *la pédale qui fait toucher une corde* (the pedal that makes strike one string).

Of the four pedals, it is this fourth that comes with the most diverse dynamic effects. In his *Méthode*, Adam names *pianissimo*, *piano*, *crescendo*, and *diminuendo*. Add *forte* and all possible levels and gradations are represented: three strings = *forte*; two strings = *piano*; one string = *pianissimo*; pedal going up = *crescendo*; pedal going down = *decrescendo*. All of these may be realized by deft foot coordination on a single pedal. But the spring— that mark of ingenuity by the consummate engineer Erard—preserves the identity of two distinct stops: the one is color-oriented, the spring ensuring that the pianist develops a marked, three-stage muscle-memory for it; the other allows for swelling and tapering off, if the pianist manages to move their foot all the way up or down in one decisive sweep. With Adam's directions, a professional pianist may now learn to incorporate their foot movement into their performance with the intent of controlling color *and* volume to an extent never heard before. Beneath the foot of a highly trained musician, the fourth pedal becomes the ultimate in magic wands.

The Erard Spring

In 1993, the French sociologist Bruno Latour published a delightful essay entitled *La clé de Berlin*. The peculiarity of this "Berlin key" is that it has not one but two bits, one at each end. The key appears reversible, but this assumption doesn't take note of the slightly larger middle groove on one end of the key. Slowly, through the imagined step-by-step research of a determined archaeologist, Latour unravels in detail the key's purpose through its own prism as an object. No fewer than eight drawings are interleaved within his prose, arguably more in the manner of a technical manual than of a scholarly essay. Through trial and error, Latour's archaeologist discovers that, between 8:00 p.m. and 8:00 a.m., she can slide her key through the keyhole of the apartment building's front door only if, once inside, she bolts the door behind her. During the daytime, however, she's not able to bolt the front door, which has to remain open. It is the concierge of the building who, with his own version of a caretaker's key, has the sole power to bolt the lock in the evening (and keep the door closed at night) and to unbolt the lock in the morning (and keep the door open during the day). "In Berlin, this steel key performs mechanically the same function as is performed electronically in Paris by the door codes," Latour concludes.[11]

Beethoven would have looked at Erard's *due corde* spring with the same kind of wonder as Latour's imaginary archaeologist felt as she looked at her key. What is this object? What is it used for? Why is one spring on top of another—the first outside, the second inside the piano? Just as Latour investigated the details of a Prussian locksmith's design in order to understand the Berlin key's role as an agent of human behavior, Beethoven might have analyzed the inner workings of his new pedal to figure out exactly how the spring affects the movement of the hands or feet of the pianist and with what precise sonic effect. From an anthropological point of view, he might already have known the answer: the French loved their *sons filés* and there's nothing more irresistible than a little swell to make a tremolo more striking still. But, as the new owner of and composer on an Erard piano, what could *Beethoven* do to justify the spring as an intermediary presence between two extreme voices of the piano—not just as a declamatory technique, but with an intent and ingenuity that would make its engineer proud?

The second movement of Beethoven's Fourth Piano Concerto, which he began sketching in 1804 or possibly earlier, in 1803, provides a fascinating answer.[12] It reinforces one of this book's core arguments: that Beethoven was interested in his *piano en forme de clavecin* not just as a single and unified tool to produce music (the results of which may be analyzed and explained in terms of stylistic development or change), but also as a sum of technologies that afforded many distinct experiments and trials. In this case, it is the pianist's interaction with a particular sub-thing that encapsulates the musical drama, which takes the form of the enactment of a well-known mythical story.

Above an empty staff, amid some early sketches for the first movement of his Fourth Piano Concerto, Op. 58, Beethoven scribbled down the following words (fig. 4.5): "*2da parte solament[e] / fin al trillo / mit vielen 16 tel / triolen / bis zum Triller auf der / cadenz nach E mo[ll]* [Second part only / end with trill / with many 16th notes / triplets / until the trill on a cadence

FIGURE 4.5 Words scribbled by Beethoven amid sketches for the first movement of
Op. 58. Autograph 19e, fol. 33v. Printed with permission of the Staatsbibliothek zu Berlin.

to E minor]."[13] This memo, almost certainly meant to lock in for further
elaboration a quick-and-dirty improvisation, raises a number of points.
First, as Beethoven sketched the first movement, his mind was already on
the second—an indication that favors musicologist Owen Jander's hypothesis that the second movement, Andante con moto, had "generative" power
for the whole work.[14] Second, these initial thoughts match the finished
results with remarkable accuracy, confirming yet another speculation by
Jander on the movement's origins as a single solo piece.[15] Third, Beethoven
anticipated what indeed became a "second part," beginning in m. 47 of the
finished slow movement, which is the moment when the pianist starts over
on the tonic of the home key of E minor, alone—that is, only minimally
accompanied by a few *pizzicato* tones in the strings. These bars go to the
heart of a dramatic narrative that Jander, through a trilogy of publications
(1985, 1995, 2009), has proposed not just for this movement but also for the
overall concerto: "that crucial moment when Orpheus breaks his vow."

I refer, of course, to the myth of Orpheus and Eurydice, immortalized
by Ovid (*Metamorphoses* X.1–85) and Virgil (*Georgics* IV.453–558), which
Beethoven would furthermore have known through Gluck's 1762 *Orfeo
ed Euridice* (libretto by Ranieri Calzabigi) and August Friedrich Kanne's
Orpheus, eine grosse Oper in zwey Aufzügen (which would be performed in
Vienna in 1807)—to select just four possible sources among many more.

Drawing from these texts, Jander proposed an almost note-by-note tex-
tual underlay for the entire Andante con moto. I here focus on that second
part only, which figure 4.6 represents as a miniature solo piece, resetting
measure 47 of the finished Andante to measure 1, as well as cutting eight
bars toward the end (where the orchestra takes over). I opt, furthermore,
for a singular fragment from Virgil (IV.485–503), featuring Orpheus's un-
successful attempt to rescue his beloved Eurydice from the underworld.[16]
That this unabridged piece of poetry fits every detail in Beethoven's score
is itself testimony to Jander's astonishing discovery, to which I here add
another: like Orpheus on his best behavior in a world dominated by the
gods, Beethoven at first submits himself entirely to the mechanical rules of
his new Erard piano; but just as Orpheus breaks an oath, Beethoven also
ignores a clear directive, with inevitable consequences. That inevitability
hinges on the behavior of a single technological component—the spring
that separates two different soundscapes, produced by triple and single
strings, respectively. The two registers cannot be mixed, and transitioning
between them requires gentle footwork to create a convincing fade-in or
fade-out from one side to the other. While the triple-strung soundscape
represents the piano at its most complete, full-surfaced hammers generating strong vibrations worthy of the instrument's sturdy design, the latter
is evocative of a lyre or harp, where hammers, reduced to only a tiny and
fragile version of themselves, are capable of much less vibrational impact,
but create sounds that have an all the more intimate emotional effect. From
a technical point of view, it requires meticulous alignment of the hammers
to make sure that, in shifted position, they strike only one string without
brushing any adjacent ones, either of the same key (which would be unfortunate but not dramatic) or of the next (which would be outright painful,
since two adjacent tones would get mixed). *Una corda* playing, in other
words, keeps the pianist on guard, as they hope for the best (those delight-
fully pure sounds of individually resonating strings), but fear the worst
(that a perfect alignment of hammers may have been compromised since
the last time they tried, or that some mechanical buzz, thump, or click—
unavoidable noises in the action that in normal circumstances remain reasonably in the background—may suddenly become highly distracting).
When the *una corda* playing is successful, the single-string sounds are comparable to those emanating from a lyre or a harp, plucked by the flesh of

one's fingertips. We know that Beethoven was attracted to the Erard's *una corda* from the beginning. Imbuing it with Orphic song, he's now about to release its mythic power.

Orpheus's Lyre

Figure 4.6 has been transcribed from the first edition by the Kunst- und Industrie-Comptoir in Vienna. This 1808 print features Beethoven's first single-string directive, *nota bene* in French: "*Dan[s] tout cet Andante on tient levée la Pédale, qui ne fait sonner qu'une corde.*" The semantic error of directing the pianist to "leave up" the pedal may be excused in a city where most pianos still had knee-levers (which needed to be "left up" rather than "pushed down"). Beethoven, of course, meant: "*Dans tout cet Andante, on tient mise la Pédale qui ne fait sonner qu'une corde,*" or "In this whole Andante, one *leaves down* the pedal that causes only one string to sound." (We remember the same linguistic sloppiness from Adam, when it came to describing a technology-driven procedure.) The next line reads: "*Au signe Ped: on lève outre cela les étouffoirs* [at the sign Ped: one furthermore raises the dampers]." Three more French indications follow later on in the score: "*2 et puis 3 cordes*" (m. 9), "*à 3 cordes*" (m. 10), and "*2 et puis 1 corde*" (m. 15).

Beethoven's "second part" starts where "Ped." or damper-less playing begins; damper-less in this context also means lyre-like. If in the first part Orpheus called out to the Furies, pleading with them to open the gate of Hades, then this second is a leap forward, featuring Orpheus on his journey back to the overworld, under strict orders from Proserpina not to look back at his beloved Eurydice. The ascent is treacherous, and Orpheus must undertake it as if alone: he has no choice but to trust that Eurydice is closely following behind. Like Orpheus with his lyre, the pianist finds himself alone with his instrument, as the orchestra takes a back seat. The strings contribute only three single *pizzicato* tones—that is, they pluck rather than bow their sounds, gently marking the beginning of each of Orpheus's songful chords and bringing into focus the association of a musician's hand strumming a keyboard or a lyre. (The effect is superbly visual if violinists and violists also put their instruments down on their lap, exactly like a lyre-guitar: see below.)

Thus, plucking his own keyboard-lyre, Orpheus makes his way back

And now, retracing his steps, he evaded all mischance,
and Eurydice, regained, approached the upper air,
she following behind (since Proserpine had ordained it),

when a sudden madness seized the incautious lover,
one to be forgiven, if the spirits knew how to forgive:
he stopped, and forgetful, alas, on the edge of light,
his will conquered, he looked back, now, at his Eurydice.

In that instant, all his effort was wasted, and his pact
with the cruel tyrant was broken, and three times a crash
was heard by the waters of Avernus. "Orpheus," she cried,
"what madness has destroyed my wretched self, and you?

See, the cruel Fates recall me, and sleep hides my swimming eyes,
Farewell, now: I am taken, wrapped round by vast night,
stretching out to you, alas, hands no longer yours."

She spoke, and suddenly fled,
far from his eyes, like smoke
vanishing in thin air, and never
saw him more,

though he grasped in vain at shadows,
and longed to speak further:

nor did Charon, the ferryman of Orcus,
let him cross the barrier of that marsh again.

FIGURE 4.6 Andante con moto, second part, from Beethoven's Fourth Piano Concerto,
Op. 58, arranged from the first edition (Vienna: Bureau des arts et d'industrie, 1808), with
annotations.

to the living and out of the underworld. Initially, his demeanor is calm and composed. Strumming simple chords, he plays natural pitches only—with the exception, first, of a leading tone D♯ in mm. 1–2 (strengthening a grounding presence of tonic E), and a G♯ in m. 3 (an omen of the pitch for Eurydice's cries later on). He treads from the one root-position chord to the next, safely securing his grip by means of an appoggiatura in m. 3. With the arrival on the 6/4 dominant in m. 5 (double appoggiatura, double safety), a certain cadence seems within grasp.

But he hesitates. He gives in to chromaticism and an intricate four-voice texture that spirals downward (mm. 6–8). Also, his singing falters: syncopations escalate into outright panic. He stops and looks back. This is where the trilling starts, on a dominant chord—is he still hoping for a happy ending? In normal circumstances, that's exactly what a trill would imply: imagine this first trill with a suffix, resolving into a final, tonic E-minor chord. Here, however, we're looking at a desperate man. Stuck on dissonant tones, the trilling just continues, culminating from the seventh to the ninth, which is about the harshest dissonant imaginable (m. 9). All this happens in a single bar under a fermata: quite literally a timeout. On that ninth, however ("then and there"; the Latin word is *ibidem*), the spring releases. "Two and then three strings" is no longer to be read as a directive, in contrast to the French lines at the outset. It is a factual statement, not addressing the collective human "one" (as the two lines from the outset) but simply recording what has been announced as inevitable. Once released, the spring wants to unwind all the way. Twice, the keyboard jolts under the pianist's fingers and eyes. The earth of the underworld shakes; all hell breaks loose. We hear three crashes (the chromatic flurries in the left hand), and we hear Eurydice cry, "Orpheus!" (G♯–A, by left hand crossing over right; mm. 11–12), but these cries are hardly audible above all the noise. Orpheus tries to revert the tide ("two and then one string"), but to no avail.

Eurydice, meanwhile, speaks in the key of G major, first in despair ("see, the cruel Fates recall me"), then with regret ("farewell now"), and finally, underlining her fainting words with rhetorical gesture ("stretching out to you, alas, hands no longer yours"). Her words are in G major only by melodic contour: there is no harmonic support. Still, the contrast of her D♮ against all the D♯s before is striking—as is the physical gesture in one's right hand of a diatonic G-major fifth (serene and relaxed) versus the chromatic diminished fifth in one's left hand before (frantic and panic-stricken). Forever separated from his beloved, Orpheus is left alone with his lyre. No more singing; only empty strumming of chords—sadly, exactly those harmonies that in m. 5 could have brokered the desired cadence, if only he had kept his head. With one last appoggiatura, also the final gesture of the piece, he attempts to grasp Eurydice, but she's nothing but a shadow. In my performance, I here consciously touch the resolving key E in my right hand several times, making it move silently only, before striking that final single string after all, but ever so softly: the point is in the trying rather than in actual sound. "Charon, the ferryman of Orcus, did not let him cross the barrier of that marsh again."

Dominating the drama is the order *not to let go* of the *una corda* pedal, or never to allow the spring to relax. We speak of a *deus ex machina*, originally a god who was suspended above the stage toward the end of a Greek tragedy by means of a pulley-operated crane (μηχανή, or machine). Here, it is the machine itself—that spring, also a pulley of some sort—that controls the drama. Nobody—no god, no lyre, no human—can challenge it. By looking back, Orpheus gives in to human desire: the urge to turn around is simply too strong. The release of one's foot is also instinctive, certainly after an extended time of listening to such soft shades and feeling a desire to return to the instrument's "normal" voice. But this change comes with immediate regret over sounds that are suddenly much louder. When, after all the noise and drama, our Orphic pianist tries to turn back the tide, it is too late: we cannot go back to the single string anymore and pretend that nothing has happened. Remember Beethoven's words: "*2da parte solamente*," or in inaccurate Italian, perhaps "the second part *alone*." (The German "*der zweite Teil allein*" is indeed ambiguous with "*nur der Zweite Teil*.") Linguistic glitch or not, the pianist, like Orpheus, is left . . . alone, and the orchestra can only watch this whole scene play out with deepest sympathy.

We have so far focused on areas of the piano operated by the pianist from the waist down: from the spring, down the rod, toward the pianist's foot. But there's an above-the-waist story to be told as well. The first spring release is also a signal for the pianist's fingers to get more active—delicate cantilena yielding to long and loud trills, more intense movement complementing louder sound. I remember performing the concerto some five years ago using a replica of an 1808 fortepiano by Nannette Streicher, the choice of which was in line with what Beethoven might have used for his own first performance, at the Lobkowitz palace in Vienna, in March 1807.[17] Whatever sound I produced on this Viennese instrument, it never felt quite enough. The orchestra's sounds still in my ears, I felt I should do more: faster, louder—to the point of my arm getting tense and incapacitating me altogether. My experience at the Erard, however, is entirely different. It is true that the Streicher firm adopted the *una corda* design on their instruments from 1805 onward—in imitation of Beethoven's Erard—but Erard's *una corda* has a much more distinctive character than its Viennese imitator. Accordingly, when moving out of *una corda*, the swell is much more overwhelming: you're engulfed by a tsunami of vibrations. From a tactile point of view, the experience of playing an Erard is also different. The French action has a way of locking one's finger movement into firm rhythmic patterns. (The reasons have to do with the instrument's heavier touch as well as its efficient, if slower repetition.) Beethoven seems to verbalize exactly this principle when in his initial sketch he mentions "triplets." Taking my cue from the sextuplets in mm. 10 and 11, I play the long trill as double triplets (3 × 2), the main note always on the "good" (strong) part of the triple sub-beat. There's one exception: Beethoven requires an extra pair of notes on the last beat of m. 13. At this moment of what may be interpreted as human resistance, I play four pairs instead of three: I deliberately slow down the pace. The spring, however, has other plans.

Unlike the Berlin key, Erard's spring does not have a locking mechanism: in principle, the foot is always capable of either pushing or releasing it in either direction, either halfway or all the way. Still, like the concierge in charge of the behavior of the Berlin apartment dwellers, Beethoven imbues the spring with what Akrich and Latour call a "program of action": "If you start releasing the spring, it will want to go all the way: there can be no halfway."[18]

There is one notational detail in figure 4.6 we have not addressed yet. We have called "*2, et puis 3 cordes*" a statement rather than a directive— describing rather than prescribing. Underneath, in m. 9 of the score, however, Beethoven clarifies, "*crescendo sino al Fortiss:* [*crescendo* to *fortissimo*]." (The same occurs, in reverse, in m. 15.) Why describe the sonic effect of something that is bound to happen anyway? Am I not, like Orpheus, supposed to simply undergo the consequences? I would suggest that Beethoven switches gears altogether, from descriptive to prescriptive notation, and that this clarification is addressed to those buyers of his score who did not yet have a piano with an *una corda* stop—which, in May 1808 (when the concerto was published by the Kunst- und Industrie-Comptoir in Vienna), would have been anyone with a Viennese model older than, say, two or three years.[19] This notation, then, is a reminder of what, during the winter months of 1803–4, was a special relationship: that of Beethoven with his precious, newly acquired keyboard-lyre.

Beethoven as Orpheus

Upon hearing he was to receive the gift of a Broadwood piano fifteen years later, Beethoven would promise Thomas Broadwood (the younger of "John Broadwood & Sons") to treat the English piano as an "altar where I'll place the most beautiful offerings of my spirit to the divine Apollo."[20] (Beethoven communicated in French, not English.) We're used to lofty images when it comes to the aged composer, when the Beethoven myth had taken hold and prompted such prestigious gifts in the first place. But his self-identification as some kind of high priest to the God of Music may have been, for Beethoven, more than a figure of speech. A famous and much-analyzed portrait by Willibrord Joseph Mähler in 1804–5 (see plate 3) had portrayed him as Apollo's pupil or son—or indeed, as Orpheus. It was the eighty-two-year-old Mähler who referred to the Greek *tholos* as "Apollo's temple." But when, in the same conversation in 1860 with Beethoven biographer Alexander Wheelock Thayer, Mähler described Beethoven "at nearly full length, sitting; the left hand [resting] upon a lyre, the right [. . .] extended, as if, in a moment of musical enthusiasm, he was beating time,"[21] the painter's words lose credibility, since beating time would never have looked so brutish or pedantic. His imperfect memory gave credence to the hypothesis, entertained by various scholars, that it was Beethoven rather than Mähler who had masterminded the details of the portrait's scenery—in which musical imagery is but a small part of the story.

In recent literature, details of the Mähler painting have been both over- and under-interpreted. Jander is an example of the former. He relates numerous iconographical details to specific moments in the score of

Beethoven's Fourth Concerto. At the other extreme is the art historian Alessandra Comini, who emphasizes allegory as the painter's neo-classicist strategy to create what in essence remains a conventional portrait of an early nineteenth-century musician holding "the age-old symbol of music and attribute of Apollo, the lyre." Somewhere in the middle is the political-historical reading by the English studies scholar John Clubbe: "If we knew nothing from other sources about Beethoven's political views during these years, this portrait alone could tell us much about them," he promises.[22] And he delivers, first contextualizing Beethoven's hairstyle, which was short *à la Tite*, named after Titus, son of Brutus, played by the actor Talma on the Parisian stage in the 1790s; the short hairstyle was reminiscent of male antique busts and became sensationally fashionable among French revolutionaries. The two relatively young "liberty trees" positioned in an otherwise open meadow behind Beethoven's outstretched hand (the planting of young evergreens signaled novelty or birth and was another well-known revolutionary gesture), and the dying oak tree at Beethoven's back (its loose branch representing "a past that has no future," or the end of the monarchy) are further visual signals. The blue cloak, the white collar, the red lining that shows from beneath Beethoven's cloak—all have revolutionary significance, echoing the tricolor flag of the French republic. Particularly striking among the colors is that singular dash of red, not just structurally important (as it helps separate the dark colors between cloak and tree), but easily interpreted as a little flame that is about to "ignite the moribund Tree of Absolutism."[23] The reference here is to another heroic figure, much on Beethoven's mind as he was composing his "Eroica" Symphony: Prometheus, who in defiance of the gods gave fire to mankind.

Beethoven knew and loved his Roman classics, just as he developed a keen interest in the figure of Napoleon Bonaparte. Clubbe convincingly suggests that the double liberty trees represent Napoleon and Beethoven, one positioned slightly in front of but diagonally linked to the other. Napoleon had done in 1799 what Lucius Junius Brutus had done some 2,300 years before: in 506 BCE, Brutus had unseated the Tarquin dynasty and had become first consul of a new Roman republic. For his part, recovering from a deep personal crisis, Beethoven is not so much, as Jander suggests, "about to leap forward," but the image of rebirth suggested by the painting is very strong. Sitting on what may be the stump of a tree, Beethoven seems poised to step out of his dark cloak and join the landscape around him. The direction is from the gloom of the lower right corner of the picture toward the sunlit clouds in the upper left, or from darkness to light. Despite his excruciating regret at the onset of hearing loss, Beethoven had never relinquished his ambitions: he may have toyed with the idea of suicide, but by the time of his 1802 Heiligenstadt Testament, this thought had developed into a rhetorical foil for his deeply felt confidence as an artist. Throughout the skillfully composed text, couched in the form of a letter to his two brothers, he uses the term *Künstler* twice, and the term *Kunst* three times. In this carefully composed portrait—one he would treasure until the end of his life, guarding it as carefully as his Heiligenstadt letter—we see him exuding ambition, emerging from his struggles stronger than ever, as a reborn "first consul," his right hand triumphantly leading the way to an illuminated land of artistic freedom.[24]

And the lyre? There's a French connection there, too, as observed by Jander.[25] The *AmZ* of August 1801 published a feature on the lyre-guitar, an instrument that was all the rage in France: "Paris has hardly with the greatest zeal chased the newest [. . .] when it now rushes off to the oldest, from the times of Greek and Roman art."[26] This lyre has a fingerboard and six strings that are tuned E/A/d/g/b/e¹, just like a guitar. E minor is the safest key to play, and it comes as no surprise, then, that Beethoven chooses it for Orpheus at that crucial moment in the underworld, where any misstep could be fatal. It seems very likely, too, that the printed image of the lyre-guitar served as a model for Mähler's painting (see plate 4, left). But Beethoven's self-identification with Orpheus would not have been through this oldest of instruments, but instead through his own newest acquisition from Paris. Those rods streaming down like four parallel strings (juxtaposed as plate 4, right) bear a strong resemblance to a lyre—a visual association that would soon be standardized in French, German, and English pianos by the making of an actual pedal-*lyre* fixture.

It may well have been just after Beethoven's Erard had arrived from Paris that he and Mähler met, in late 1803. After being introduced to Beethoven in his rooms at the Theater an der Wien, Mähler remembers Beethoven playing the finale of his "Eroica" Symphony—or rather, a "theme, variations and a fugue" (most likely his Op. 35 Variations for Piano, on the same Prometheus theme as the symphony finale), whereupon he continued improvising for two hours.[27] Mähler especially recalls the sight of Beethoven's fingers, seemingly "glid[ing] right and left over the keys."[28] But Beethoven's unsuspected magic wands may have been those pedal rods below—each standing for a different color or voice, allowing Beethoven to fully orchestrate himself at the piano.

Instead of an attribute in a musician's portrait, Beethoven's lyre becomes the window onto a revolutionary soundscape. Let's give the four pedal rods the same dominating position as the lyre strings in Mähler's painting and from this low-frontal perspective look at the overall appearance of the French piano (see plate 5). Old-regime harpsichords had all kinds of mythical scenes, often set in landscapes and painted on the undersides of their lids. Freed from such lavish ornament, the Erard piano speaks for itself. The four-rod lyre, symbol of purity and classicism, proudly opens up to a man-made machine that combines nature's best woods with various kinds of iron.

Looming behind the keyboard is a soundboard in spruce—a second one, to complement the one at the heart of the piano, both encased in a box made out of oak, beautified on the outside by a veneer of mahogany. Like that of the pedal rods, the sight would have been curious to Beethoven. (It can be seen from a standing position, as in the second photo of plate 5.) A permanent companion to the actual soundboard below, together enveloping the strings in between, the upper board is to be taken out only when the piano needs tuning.[29] Clubbe has wondered why the two "full-grown, healthy," c. ten-year-old spruce trees in the painting look as though they were planted in the 1790s already, suggesting, "Their fulsome appearance appears to bode well for the future hopes of liberty."[30] In some grander universe of humans and things, this rings true for their potential second lives as soundboards, too.

Sporting a sober, capital-like ornament at the top, three columnar legs elegantly support what in a continued spirit of metaphor may be called an Apollonian temple to music. Finally, imagine a hand with five capable and inspired fingers leading the way to a new world of color and sound. The pianist leans their body to the right. With their foot they push down the most enticing and mysterious pedal of all.

Two Visitors in Paris

with Robin Blanton, Michael Pecak,
and Tilman Skowroneck

We might be justified in calling the composer Johann Friedrich Reichardt (1752–1814) the German Charles Burney: an avid traveler, he was a keen observer, and prolific with his pen. Between November 1802 and April 1803, he attended concerts and plays in the French capital, joined high-society salons, and observed the habits of the Parisian bourgeoisie, publishing his impressions in a kind of epistolary travel diary, one of several forays he made into the genre.

When Reichardt visited Erard Frères (the firm and the brothers) in 1802, it was his second visit to Paris. His first, in 1792, had made him an ardent republican, which cost him his job as Kapellmeister for King Frederick William II. When he returned to Paris ten years later, however, he became disillusioned with postrevolutionary society: he went back to Germany an outspoken opponent of Napoleon, which cost him his home, near Halle, when French forces occupied that city in 1806.[1]

His report of the premises at 37 rue du Mail gives us a glimpse into a historical workshop that, on the one hand, is all too rare, but, on the other, might feel instantly familiar to any of us who have toured a workshop or factory in our own day. The manufacture of grand pianos had reached a new high that year at forty-eight; sales likewise reached an all-time high, at thirty-seven. It was the sheer scale of production and distribution that, combined with the perfect merchandise, seems to have impressed the German composer. We present Reichardt's report here in a new translation:

Paris, November 22, 1802.

There are things that even the best workers in our parts undertake on
only a small scale, but are done here on a much grander one—this I
observe yet again at the establishment of the Erard brothers, who are
currently making fortepianos and harps as perfect as any to be found.
And in such astonishing numbers! This despite their high price, which
exceeds even that of the English builders. Everything from small square
pianos [*Fortepiano's in Clavierformat*] for forty *Louis [d'or] neuf* (what we
call *Carolinen*, at six and a half *Thaler* each) to the largest, most tastefully
decorated grand pianos that range from a hundred up to two hundred
Louis neuf. To every country in Europe, wherever water transport makes
it practical to do so, they send their instruments in large quantities.

No surprise, then, that the establishment occupies nearly two entire,
sizeable houses in one of the best neighborhoods in Paris. Everything
needed to complete even the most ornate instruments, down to the smallest detail, is manufactured in-house and on a grand scale. Not only do the
instrument makers proper, the carpenters, the turners, the locksmiths and
the metalworkers have their own completely fitted-out workshop; but the
bronze worker, the painter, the varnisher, the ebonist and the enameler,
the gilder, the wire-drawer, and goodness knows who else also work on-
site in spacious, well-equipped workshops.

There are large vestibules and halls entirely full of finished cases in
mahogany; other rooms full of instruments being assembled by the various workers, overseen by the master himself; yet more rooms full of
instruments upon which the master is still putting the finishing touches.
Large and elegantly decorated salons are filled with completed instruments awaiting only their *Liebhaber* or their shipping crates. There are
workers busily packing instruments day in and day out. Sheds ring the
courtyards, stacked high with all kinds of expensive lumber.

A fully fitted-out office with a bookkeeper and a clerk handles the correspondence and the bills in the English fashion. An adjoining cashier's
office makes the payments and calculates expenses and revenues.

Alongside it all, this good and cultivated family resides in a manner
befitting respectable burghers of an affluent and luxury-seeking nation.
Each brother has his own apartment, beautifully furnished, and one of
the brothers, a connoisseur of paintings, has an exquisite small gallery in

his rooms. Their excellent sister also lives in the same house, along with her charming daughters, and runs the household; they reside in a very pleasant and elegant apartment whose main room also serves as a daily gathering place for the entire company. And a large, completely empty apartment stands at the ready to receive the frequent distinguished guests who visit this rare establishment to select instruments, and for use on holidays, when the family (who still keep the old, nearly extinct customs of French hospitality) entertain larger companies.

I spent a most pleasant Sunday with this excellent family at just such a domestic party, celebrating the marriage of the eldest daughter to the painter Bonnemaison, a most accomplished and charming man. To my delight I met many more good German artists there as well, such as our outstanding cellist Romberg, whose great talent we all know at home, but who has perfected his art even further here; the accomplished piano teachers and composers Adam, Wiederkehr, Pfeffinger, and others besides.

The young ladies of the house are themselves very interesting singers and pianists [*Sängerinnen und Clavierspielerinnen*] and have established their own music business, which has found a room also in this artful house. All this will give you an idea of the scope of this big establishment. Of the excellence of instruments it is hard to give you an idea with words. But they have everything that can make such an instrument brilliant and agreeable, and in their touch and grateful lightness, with which they follow the player, they are far to be favored over the English instruments.

The brothers also have a sizeable establishment in London, where the older brother, whom I've unfortunately missed here, is staying at the moment.[2]

A second, as yet relatively unknown historical account of the Erard family dates from just a few years after Reichardt's. It comes from the pen of Józef Elsner (1769–1854), the Silesian-Polish musician and pedagogue who founded the Warsaw Conservatory and the Polish National Opera, and is primarily remembered today as the composition teacher of Frédéric Chopin. During a tour of Europe in 1805 to gather ideas for improving musical education in Warsaw, Elsner stopped in Paris. He visited Erard Frères with the specific assignment of buying a piano, and wrote the following account in Polish twenty years after the event. We present it in a new translation as well:

> When I was in Paris, I received a request from Duchess Sapieżyna to select and purchase for her a piano from the firm Erard and Company; she sent me 5,000 zł for this purpose. Handing this sum to Mr. Erard, I was to withhold 500 zł for myself, according to their custom as he explained it to me, but which I did not want to accept and did not accept. He then invited me to his home in the country for several days, where I had the pleasure of meeting his family and Steibelt. During this occasion, while speaking about piano construction and his workshop, he asked if these [i.e., his] instruments would gain traction and be marketable in Warsaw. Also, what pianos do we [Poles] typically use? I responded that, most often, we import from abroad and mainly from Vienna since generally the building and manufacturing of musical instruments is still at a low level in our homeland. He then declared that he would gladly send one piano, like the one I had purchased for the Duchess Sapieżyna, to Warsaw as a trial so long as I would be kind enough to receive it on consignment. "Very good," I replied, "if in this way I may be of service to you." Upon hearing this, Erard added that perhaps he might even be able to establish a piano warehouse in our homeland. "Undoubtedly," I said, "however, I am not familiar with such business and, hence, I am unable to advise further." "In any case," Erard concluded, "for this upcoming summer I will send you a piano."
>
> Having returned to Warsaw I related these details to Messrs. [Fryderyk] Mosqua, [E. T. A.] Hoffmann, and Wobser, the directors of the newly founded Music Society; the price of the piano seemed to them too high, but they reassured me that, if the sent piano meets my description, then they will buy it for the Society. I immediately wrote to Erard, reporting to him everything, and waiving the discount. Shortly thereafter, the piano arrived in Warsaw in proper and whole condition through the mediation of the Exchange office, which charged me 60 thaler for the transport. At this time, the Music Society was opened and consecrated in a new home bought and renovated for this purpose and paid for by investors as well as His Majesty, who also deigned to offer several thou-

sand thaler. The day of its opening and dedication was August 3, 1806, the birthday of His Majesty.

The outward appearance of the newly imported and there-accommodated piano impressed everyone exceptionally and generally, as did its tone, which was sonorous and grand. But the touch of the keyboard, because of its hardness, did not suit the tastes of the ladies, none of whom wanted to show off on this instrument, not even the famous [Maria] Szymanowska. Only her rival, Ms. Wołowska—today the wife of attorney Franciszek Wołowski living in Paris—performed on it Steibelt's Concerto in E Major to the audience's delight. Resolved, I would wait to the year 1807 to retrieve the transport costs as well as the 4,600 zł owed to Erard.[3]

Like Reichardt before him, Elsner describes being fêted by the extended Erard family, this time at the country home in Sèvres. He mentions meeting a famous musician: this time, Daniel Steibelt. And he recalls being quizzed by "Mr. Erard" at quite some length on the possibility of opening up a market for Erard pianos in Poland. Did Elsner think the Erard instruments would sell there? What pianos were already on the Polish market? Would he care for a piano to test: a free sample, as it were? yes? Then perhaps he might be interested in an Erard warehouse! At which point Elsner interrupts the sales pitch, although not before it has been decided that he shall receive a piano before the summer. One begins to suspect that this is typical Erard hospitality: generous, but never turning down the opportunity to do business or establish a foothold in a new market. The same entrepreneurial spirit may have led the Erard brothers to embrace the idea of placing their product in the hands of a promising pianist-composer in Vienna—despite the risks associated with exposing their French design to the competitive and hostile piano-building environment in Vienna.

CHAPTER FIVE

The Perfect Instrument

A recent photograph of the old piano workshop of Erard Frères shows me strolling around a quiet place, free of traffic of any kind (fig. 5.1). When Reichardt visited the same premises, however, quite a different scene met his gaze: his report takes us back to a busy shop that he found both strikingly modern and quite different in scope and organization from any establishment in his native Germany.[1] Perhaps it was possible, amid the prosperous, organized bustle, for Reichardt to forget for a moment the years of disarray that had preceded it. The peril and chaos of postrevolutionary Paris, particularly the brief reign of Robespierre and the Committee of Public Safety in 1793–94, had not left the Erard family untouched. Still, the Erard Frères firm had survived, even thrived. The inventor Sébastien (1752–1831), the younger and more famous of the two brothers, would become the face of the firm to future generations. He was gifted with mechanical ingenuity, was able to envisage a musical instrument as an integrated system rather than just a set of parts, and had a powerful drive to succeed. But perhaps just as important, he had his older brother, Jean-Baptiste (1749–1826), as a business partner.

At least since the early nineteenth century, historians have lionized Sébastien and left Jean-Baptiste in the shadows. Yet the brothers themselves signed their instruments "Erard Frères," and very probably their partnership was responsible for their enduring success. A trove of preserved company documents, published in translation by Adelson and

FIGURE 5.1   Visiting the old Erard Frères premises in the rue du Mail, Paris, February 21, 2018.

colleagues (2015), along with third-party accounts such as Reichardt's and Józef Elsner's, lead us to believe that Jean-Baptiste's role in the Erard Frères partnership was more essential than has previously been acknowledged. In the process of exploring these documents, we are able to see more clearly the Paris workshop at the apex of a production process that had launched in 1797. Joining Reichardt on a tour of the assembly line for *pianos en forme de clavecin*, we cannot help becoming convinced of their perfection, exactly as the business owners intended. It would be only a matter of time before word of these sublime instruments got out, reaching places as far afield as Vienna.

A Tale of Two Brothers

Jean-Baptiste and Sébastien Erard were born in Strasbourg, the second and third, respectively, of five children.[2] Their father was a cabinetmaker of Swiss origin. Jean-Baptiste may have been apprenticed to him; Sébastien, however, was sent to school to study engineering, and as far as we know, he was the only Erard brother to display a particular talent for invention. In a highly romanticized entry in his *Biographie universelle des musiciens* (1837), François-Joseph Fétis gushes about the young Sébastien as a prodigy in the "constructive and mechanical arts."[3] Fétis mentions Sébastien's "inventive mind that would suggest to himself the resolution of problems he would propose," as well as his extraordinary perseverance, which led him at age thirteen to climb the steeple of Strasbourg Cathedral, then the tallest building in the world. He also reports that the young Sébastien garnered special praise for his talent for *exécution*, an essential complement to *invention*. After working in his father's workshop, he had acquired *la main* (literally, "the hand"), which Fétis explains as "the ability to handle tools."[4]

Sébastien the prodigy moved to Paris, aged sixteen, and began to work there as a harpsichord builder. He quickly landed an aristocratic patroness, the Duchesse de Villeroi, for whom he built a pianoforte in 1777. Later, in 1787, he built a transposing piano for Queen Marie Antoinette. After a conflict with the Parisian guild of fan makers, which included musical instrument makers, he applied for and received a royal privilege from Louis XVI in 1785 that permitted him "to make, to have made and to sell in the city and in the surroundings of Paris and everywhere where he chooses, fortepianos and to use, either himself or by his workers, the wood, the iron and all the other materials necessary for the improvement and the embellishment of the aforementioned instrument, without which, for the same reason, he could be troubled or worried by the guardians, the guilds and members of the community of artisans, for whatever reason and under whatever pretext."[5] As Adelson and colleagues note, the privilege was "a precious document," carefully guarded by the Erard firm for nearly two hundred years until the company finally closed in the twentieth century.[6]

Biographical details of Jean-Baptiste are scantier. We know that by 1781, he was working with Sébastien in Paris in a workshop and salesroom on the rue du Mail, and that the brothers established a formal business partnership in 1788.[7] This was also the year in which they began signing their instruments jointly.[8] Fétis, who lavishes attention on Sébastien, spends just a few words on Jean-Baptiste, calling him "a tireless worker, a man of integrity and loyalty" who "shared in Sébastien's labors, successes, and setbacks."[9] Historians up to the present have tended to follow Fétis's lead, regarding Sébastien as the owner and director of Erard Frères and assigning Jean-Baptiste a supporting role.[10]

To bring Jean-Baptiste into sharper focus, we must turn to the primary sources. One of the richest is the collected outgoing business correspondence of Erard Frères, painstakingly transcribed and preserved in the so-called "letter copybook" of the Erard Frères firm, which contains letters to customers and dealers across Europe during the years 1791–97. As Robert Adelson characterizes, "The details of workshop life are so vividly described that in reading the letters one can almost smell the sawdust on the floor in the Erard workshop."[11]

The letters in the copybook (mostly transcribed in the hand of Jean-Baptiste) are unsigned. The early letters, however, evince two quite distinct authorial voices. Sébastien writes with a certain *joie de vivre* ("I put my entire trust in you [. . .] to send me about 600 livres of good ordinary wine, which is not expensive considering that I drink a lot of it")[12] but also shows quick irritability and pride ("I am surprised Monsieur that you are complaining about the price of a piano that I sent you [. . .] Someone came to see this instrument with a music teacher who deemed it very good").[13] Jean-Baptiste is more dutiful, observing the courtesies on behalf of his brother ("M. [Sébastien] Erard has the honor of wishing a good evening to Monsieur Baron")[14] and generally preferring to recount plain facts ("I have the honor of notifying you that the piano that M. [Louis] Adam was responsible for selecting left on 27 March").[15] Up to and including the year 1791, Sébastien's voice is the more prominent, and the contrast between the two aligns neatly with the conventional narrative that casts Sébastien as a genius and Jean-Baptiste as a bit player. As we are about to see, however, there is more to the story.

The Worst of Times

Beginning in 1792 and for about the next four years, Sébastien spent a great deal of his time in London and left the running of the Erard Frères business in Paris to Jean-Baptiste. Sébastien had established an address in London as early as 1786, apparently for a harp salesroom, so he was clearly interested in doing business in the metropolis.[16] Perhaps he also wanted the opportunity to examine pianos by London builders, particularly grand pianos, which were rarer in Paris. At any rate, we know that at least part of his time in London was spent in devising both new harp and new piano mechanisms, as in 1794, he was granted a patent for "Certain Improvements in the Construction of Harps and Piano-fortes, both Large and Small, and which Improvements may also be applied to all Kinds of Instruments where Keys are used."[17]

But Sébastien's extended London sojourns also coincided with the rule of the Committee of Public Safety and the height of *la Terreur*. Was he, as a well-to-do tradesman in the luxury sector with an array of aristocratic patrons, making himself scarce for political reasons? That seems plausible, if difficult to substantiate. If we search for evidence of his political leanings in the letter copybook, we search in vain. He mentions the Revolution in a letter to Henri Jean Rigel on December 7, 1791 ("Do not think Monsieur that the price of my pianos has diminished since this revolution"), but only in passing, as if referring to a shared ordeal.[18] Further references are sparse and veiled. Two letters in September 1792 allude to the Paris massacres earlier that month, but only obliquely, as "the unfortunate Circumstance" and "the unhappy Events."[19] Still, it is quite possible that Sébastien had incurred ill will among his fellow citizens during his quarrel with the fan-makers' guild in the early 1780s. And in September 1793, one *citoyen* Laurent (certainly a pseudonym) took it upon himself to "denounce" to the revolutionary authorities "an emigrant who left fifteen months ago to go and find the other emigrants in London": namely, one "*herard, fabriquent densetrument de musique* [*sic*] [Erard, maker of musical instruments]." The denunciation prompted a police search of the Erard premises.[20]

Whether Sébastien went to London for business or for political reasons, spending so much time abroad could have been risky either way. In the wake of the Revolution, people from all walks of life emigrated from France in waves: some fleeing the guillotine, others simply trying to escape the privations of political upheaval and war. The Republic, however, regarded all émigrés as royalist sympathizers and conspirators against France. A series of laws provided for émigré property to be confiscated and sold. Émigrés from France could not return under pain of death; even their family members risked execution. In other words, Sébastien Erard may have found himself caught between Scylla and Charybdis. If suspected of royalist leanings, he could hardly stay in Paris safely; if suspected of permanently emigrating, he risked losing his business, his property, even his life. Luckily for him, and for the continuation of the business, his brother Jean-Baptiste was at rue du Mail when the police knocked on their door.

The Best of Times

With the dissolution of the Committee of Public Safety in 1795, the political situation in France stabilized a little. The painter Henri-Pierre Danloux, in England, recorded in his journal as early as August 1796 that Sébastien now planned to travel back to Paris.[21] We find no confirmation in the letter copybook that he did return, however, until February 10, 1797.[22] With Jean-Baptiste at the helm, perhaps Sébastien saw no pressing need to hurry home.

The year of his return, 1797, proved pivotal in the history of Erard Frères, and is also a significant year for the research represented by this book. In that year, Erard Frères began producing a new grand piano model that employed a variant of the English action. This model remained in production until 1808. In all of the company documents these instruments are named "harpsichord-shaped pianos" (*pianos en forme de clavecin*). Although it is important to remember that Erard Frères also used this name to refer to the few grands they built prior to 1797, the brothers clearly marked out their 1797 design as a unified model by assigning these instruments a brand-new set of serial numbers.

Setting up a new production line must have been a costly move and would not have been undertaken lightly. But Sébastien was enormously enthusiastic about the merits of the new model. He waxed proud about its beautiful tone and decoration, and even ventured to claim that he had "perfected" the keyboard. For instance, in a letter to Madame de St. Victor on April 4, 1797, he wrote, "The keyboard is perfect [*Le clavier est parfait*]."[23] A resident of Le Mans, Madame could not inspect the instruments in person, but his claim convinced her, as she became the very first person to buy one of the new pianos. Two weeks later, on April 18, he wrote to M. Haiyout in Tournai "in Flanders" that this piano "has been perfected to such a point that it is enjoying a complete success. We can assure you that nothing has been made that approaches its merit, the most famous artists. agree about this and shower it with the greatest compliments."[24]

The introduction of the 1797 model, while perhaps bold, went hand in hand with an overall shift in company strategy for production and sales. Evidence of this shift comes from yet another trove of documents: the Erard Frères sales books, or *livres de ventes*, which provide an invaluable complement to the letter copybook. One early volume covers the two-year period between December 1, 1790, and December 5, 1792, when Erard Frères was still a fledgling business.[25] It reveals a pattern of sales fairly typical for a small manufacturer, including a relatively high number of secondhand instruments, some English-made instruments, and a few special commissions, including *pianos organisés* for which Erard Frères also made the organ pipes.

During the course of the 1790s, under the management of Jean-Baptiste, this sales pattern changed completely. The sales book for the period July 31, 1799, to September 30, 1802, records no sales of instruments by other piano builders, nor any special commissions like the earlier organ-ized pianos, which combine piano and organ as a single instrument.[26] Erard Frères was streamlining its business, allowing it to make pianos—and harps—in much larger numbers. Erard instruments were beginning to flood into the Parisian market, and the European market as well.

Production and sales figures for the new *pianos en forme de clavecin* clearly reflect this forward push (fig. 5.2). Erard Frères built just five grands in 1797 and sold only three, according to the relevant sales book. They fully doubled their production of grands the next year and held steady at that higher level for a few years, building ten grands in 1798, nine in 1799, and eleven in 1800, for a total of thirty-five. Of these, they had sold virtually all: thirty-four, with two additional resales. After the turn of the century, the number of grands manufactured more than tripled in 1801 and 1802 before dropping slightly in the following years. Square piano production over the same period was even higher, for obvious reasons: grands were more expensive instruments, and the luxury market in France after the Revolution was limited. For comparison, Erard Frères built 245 square pianos in 1797 and had produced 1,066 by the end of 1800.

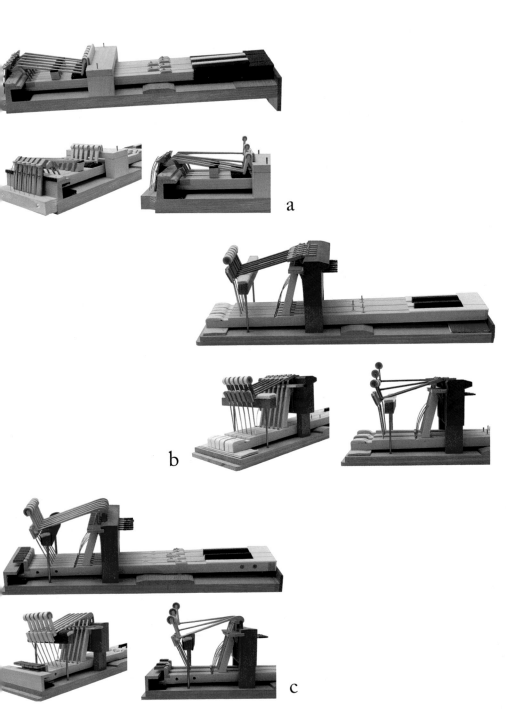

PLATE 1 Action models of (a) Anton Walter, c. 1800; (b) Erard Frères, 1803, original; and (c) revised, built by Chris Maene (Ruiselede, 2016). Photos by Piet Meersschaut.

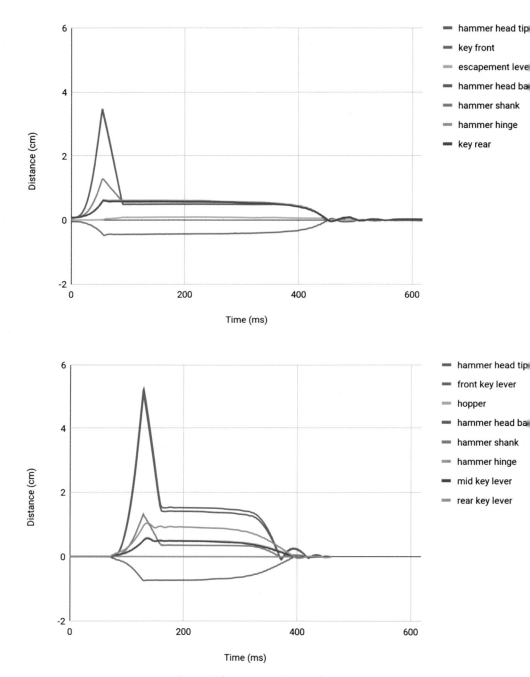

PLATE 2 Entire strike on Walter (*top*) and Erard (*bottom*) action models.

PLATE 3 Willibrord Joseph Mähler, Beethoven in a park landscape, oil on canvas, 1804/5. Reproduced with permission of Wien Museum.

PLATE 4 Illustration of a lyre-guitar, *AmZ* 3, no. 47 (August 19, 1801): 789 (*left*). Pedals of Beethoven Erard replica (*right*).

PLATE 5 Replica of
Beethoven's Erard.
Photos by Pieter Peeters.

PLATE 6 The 1808
Amsterdam Erard.
Reproduced with
permission of the
Rijksmuseum,
Amsterdam.

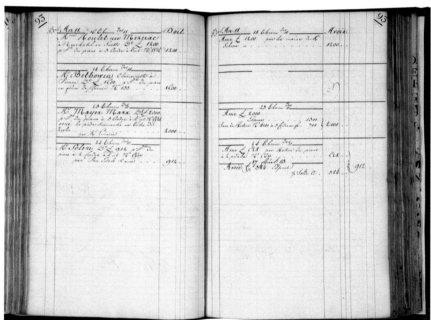

PLATE 7 Folio 93 from Erard's *Livres de ventes*, 1802–6, with a record of Beethoven's
piano. Inv. E.2009.5.101. Musée de la musique, Paris. Reproduced with permission of the
Cité de la musique–Philharmonie de Paris.

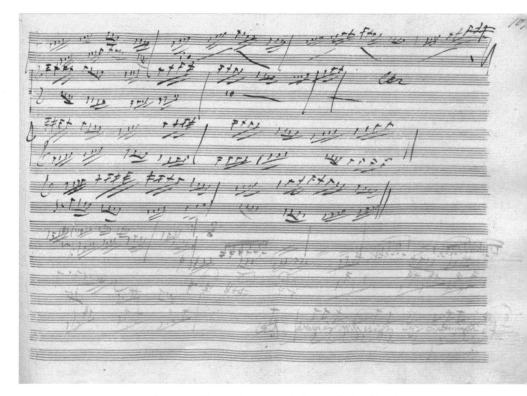

PLATE 8 Page 107 from Landsberg 6 (Beethoven's "Eroica" Sketchbook). Notierungs-buch E 90. Reproduced with permission of Biblioteka Jagiellońska, Cracow.

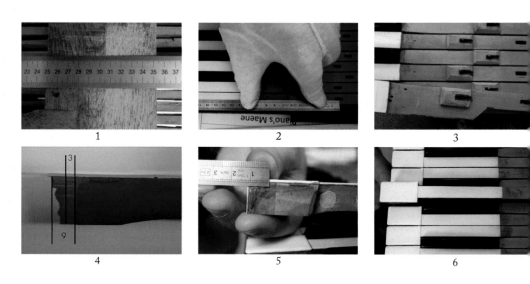

PLATE 9   Marks of revision in the action of Beethoven's Erard (*left and above*); Nos. 4, 11a, 14b, 15b, and 17 are of the Brussels 1805 Erard.

PLATE 10   Our replica next to Beethoven's piano, Linz, April 10, 2019. Photo by Steven Maes.

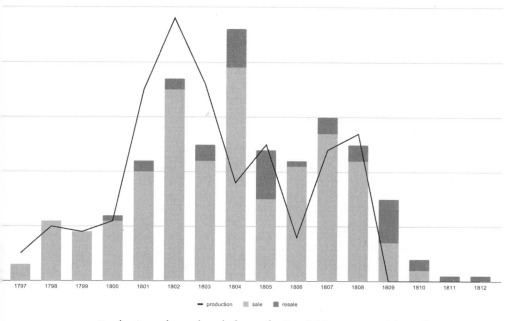

FIGURE 5.2 Production, sales, and resale figures for Erard Frères 1797-model grand pianos. Production figures from Maniguet (2009, 86); sales and resale figures gathered from Erard Frères sales books.

A Letter from Paris

When Reichardt tells us that "the older brother, whom I've unfortunately missed" is presently in London, he must have been mixing up the ages of the two brothers. Visiting the "large establishment of the Erard brothers" on that November day in 1802, he would in fact have been met by the older brother, Jean-Baptiste. Judging from his account, Reichardt was led by Jean-Baptiste along the same path that a piano would have followed through the shop, from case construction to final voicing and shipping. Walking through "spacious, well-equipped workshops," he marveled at the many artisans gathered under one roof. After touring the shop floor, he was shown the business offices, impressive in their own right and organized "in the English fashion." Invited back on Sunday, Reichardt joined a "domestic party" in the elegant family apartments next door to the workshops, where the Erards introduced him to some of their musical acquaintances: his countryman the cellist Bernhard Romberg, as well as "the accomplished piano teachers and composers [Louis] Adam, [Guillaume Melchior] Widerkehr,[27] [Philippe-Jacques] Pfeffinger, and others besides." (Like the Erards, Adam, Widerkehr, and Pfeffinger were Alsatian; Adam and Widerkehr, furthermore, were colleagues at the Conservatoire, the latter teaching solfège.) Reichardt left thoroughly impressed with the size, scope, and success of the Erard enterprise. His published report testifies to instruments being built in "astonishing" numbers, commanding "high prices," and being shipped in "large quantities" all over Europe. And in what was surely an echo of the Erards' own words, he avowed that the pianos were "as perfect [*vollkommen*] as any to be found."

But although Reichardt transmits a vivid picture of the physical and organizational contours of the Erard business—its spaces for manufacture, business, and representation—when it comes to any technical details about the instruments he admired, his account is rather scanty. The lack is explained, perhaps, by the fact that Reichardt, to his great regret, missed seeing Sébastien, the builder and inventor.

A challenge, then! Let us take the tour again, trying to reconstruct what Sébastien might have told us. We can focus in on the technical details of the firm's new flagship grand piano—the model Beethoven would receive in 1803. Let us imagine it passing on its way from one room to the next, still anonymous and interchangeable with its many siblings at different stages of construction.

A Model of Perfection

In 1797, there were two major schools of piano building: the English and the Viennese. The key difference between the two schools lay in their hammer actions. The English action was in essence the same as the earliest known piano actions by Bartolomeo Cristofori. It pushed the hammers up, while the Viennese action flipped them. Viennese pianos had a shallower touch, brighter tone, and faster repetition; English pianos had a deeper touch, a longer sustain, and a full but also darker tone.

Erard Frères built English-style actions. Sébastien had trained in Strasbourg at the workshop of Johann Heinrich Silbermann, whose uncle Gottfried, in the mid-eighteenth century, had built the earliest known Cristofori-type actions in Germany. As we have seen, Sébastien's time in

London also gave him a chance to become acquainted with the work of the builders there.

In France, English-built pianos dominated the market, making them the natural point of comparison for French pianists and customers of Erard Frères. Consider a letter from Erard Frères to Madame Lavau-Mestru in Tours on April 29, 1797. The brothers were writing to inform her that they had finished some repair work on a piano of hers. It is clear that she must have drawn some unfavorable comparison between Erard and English pianos, because their letter includes the following rejoinder: "The English pianos you mentioned, Madame, are even less sturdy than ours. All our artists attest to this fact; they even judge [our pianos] to be far superior in all ways."[28] Just a week or so earlier, the reader may recall, the Erards had also claimed to Monsieur Haiyout that their pianos were favored by "the most famous artists." Perhaps no surprise, then, that Adam, when he laid out the lineage of the piano at the outset of his *Méthode*, constructed the same dichotomy between English and French:

> It is scarcely fifty years ago that the first Piano was constructed in Saxony by an organ maker called Silbermann; this instrument still exists with the grandson of the inventor in Strasbourg. If the English have improved it since then, the French can take pride in having brought it to its highest degree of perfection [*à son plus haut degré de perfection*].[29]

Just as Erard Frères was leading a burgeoning French piano-making industry, Adam had become the main representative of an emerging national institution. His method endorsed Erard's new grand piano model, just as much as its defined pianism as taught at Adam's Conservatoire—not least (as we have seen) through Adam's instruction in the correct use of the four pedals. It is notable that Adam does not even mention the Viennese school: for him, the competition is between the English and the French. When the Erards declared, therefore, that the 1797 model had reached a "hitherto unknown level of perfection," it is clear that their baseline was English pianos.[30]

The notion that English pianos were the ones to beat was a baseline that all Erard Frères customers would have shared—and in fact, not just for pianos. No matter that France's First Republic formally prohibited the

import of goods from its rival across the Channel: the country was wean-
ing itself off a wave of Anglomania. Predilection for all things English had
shaped French furniture, fashion, philosophy and more during the mid- to
late eighteenth century, and English wares remained all the rage among
the Parisian bourgeoisie. As Reichardt wrote from Paris in another letter,
dated January 15, 1803, "No matter how frequent and how strict the prom-
ulgation of laws and prohibitions against the import of English goods, they
are adhered to only so much as will not disturb the proper flow of trade
[. . .] You will scarcely see any youth with the least pretension to fashion
who does not have English products somewhere about his body."[31] Being
better than *English* pianos made Erard Frères pianos even more desirable.
The 1797 model, in other words, was not perfect in a vacuum: it was *more
perfect* than the fashionable English piano.

What, then, were the characteristics of Erard Frères' *pianos en forme de
clavecin*? Table 5.1 lists ten such extant pianos with verifiable serial numbers, spanning the years 1801–8.[32] In addition to Beethoven's 1803 piano
in Linz, our investigations focused on the 1805 piano in Brussels and the
1808 piano in Amsterdam. All three are shown in the table in bold. Plate 6
shows the Amsterdam Erard in full splendor; various details of the Brussels instrument may be seen in plate 9, to be discussed in chapter 11. The
1805 Brussels piano was a particularly valuable source, as we were able to
remove its baseboard and examine its internal structure. The 1808 Amsterdam piano, meanwhile, is the best preserved of the surviving instruments;
its hammer action, in particular, is still in original condition. Based on our
team's examinations of these instruments, and drawing on previously published observations by other organologists, we present here a composite
picture of the Erard 1797 model in factory condition—Beethoven's No. 133
as it would have left the workshop.[33] Through the remainder of this chapter, we have represented this model by drawings made of the 1805 Brussels
instrument, extracted from the computer-assisted design (CAD) plans that
were used during the construction of our Erard replica.

But for comparison, in order to demonstrate how Sébastien Erard systematically set about outdoing his English colleagues, we need to also construct a generic model of an English piano. We decided to do so through
newly made CAD drawings of selected aspects of an unrestored, c. 1800
Thomas Tomkison (FF–c⁴, serial no. 185) in the collection of Chris Maene.[34]

TABLE 5.1 Extant Erard Frères 1797-model grand pianos with verifiable serial number (the instruments that we examined are in bold)

Serial number	Date	First Purchaser (as per *livres de ventes*)	Decoration	Current Location
55	1801	M. Fournier pour Livourne	orné	Musée de la musique, Paris
86	1802	Mlle Coulon (par Steibelt)	[none]	Musée de la musique, Paris
107	1802	M. Mackau	orné	Feller Collection, Hamburg
133	**1803**	**M. Bethowen [*sic*]**	**[none]**	**Oberöster-reichisches Landesmuseum, Linz**
136	1803	César Barre à Lisbonne	églomisé	Private collection, United States
143	1803	M. Breitkoff et Härtel à Leipzig [*sic*]	églomisé	Raduň Castle, Czech Republic
176	**1805**	**M. Deorlor à Louvain**	**[none]**	**Musical Instruments Museum, Brussels**
198	1805	Fouché, ministre de la police Mme Hulot (par Steibelt)	églomisé	Private collection, Germany
234	**1808**	**Louis Bonaparte, roi de Hollande (par Hermann)**	**églomisé**	**Rijksmuseum, Amsterdam**
249	1808	Mme Edmond de Périgord, Princesse de Courlande (par Dussek)	orné	Château de Valançay, France

With great clarity these help visualize our findings from three other English grand pianos that were accessible to us: a 1793 John Broadwood (Musical Instrument Museum, Edinburgh); a 1798 Longman, Clementi & Co. (Chris Maene Collection, Ruiselede, Belgium); and an 1805 Broadwood & Son (Tilman Skowroneck Collection, Olsfors, Sweden).

Hammer Action, Keyboard, and Dampers

We begin at the acoustical heart of the piano: with the hammer-heads and their contact with the strings. (The various parts represented in figure 5.3 are discussed row by row; English design is on the left, and Erard on the right.) Generally speaking, English hammers are built up of relatively more leather around a smaller wooden center, while an Erard hammer has a relatively larger wooden core and proportionately less leathering (see row 1). There is also a significant difference regarding the way the leather is applied. On English hammers, the softer, fluffier flesh side faces out. On Erard hammers, the outermost layer of leather has the harder, smoother skin side facing out. Together, these changes give the Erard piano a brighter tone. The Erard hammers, with their firmer cores, also produce a more marked variation in timbre over the dynamic range from soft to loud. *Forte* strikes sound sharper, while *piano* strikes are relatively more veiled. By contrast, English hammers produce what is often referred to as a "muffled" timbre even in loud playing.[35]

The hammer-shanks in the 1797 model grands (shown in row 2) are about 15 percent longer than in contemporary English instruments: they measure 128 and 130 mm respectively in the 1805 Brussels and the 1808 Amsterdam Erards, compared to 112 mm in the 1793 Edinburgh Broadwood and 110 mm in the 1798 Ruiselede Longman, Clementi & Co. A hammer-shank is a lever that is set into motion by an activator, in this case a hopper. Mounted on the key, the hopper pushes up on the butt of the hammer. When the hammer-shank is longer, more effort is required to raise the hammer-head, but the payoff is correspondingly greater: imagine pressing a stapler closer to or farther away from its hinge. At least in theory, playing *forte* becomes easier with a longer hammer-shank; conversely, playing *piano* becomes harder.

The longer lever is, in a sense, made even longer by the way the Erard hammers are mounted on the hammer-rail, with the result that the hopper strikes the hammer very close to its fulcrum point. English hammer-butts are shaped like square blocks, and the hammers are strung on long axle wires in groups of ten or more, secured in a comb-shaped rail. After the hopper strikes the hammer-butt, it escapes forward (toward the player) and fetches up against the hammer-shank, which in the Tomkison has leather

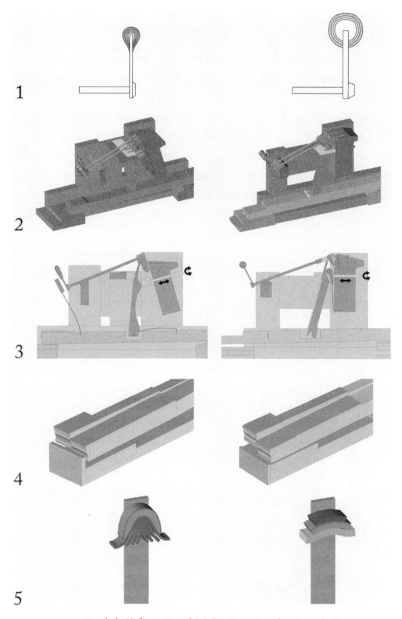

FIGURE 5.3 English (*left*) vs. Erard (*right*). Drawings by Gregoir Basyn.

Row 1: hammer-head for key c[1]

Row 2: hammer mounting

Row 3: intersection of the action, for view of hopper padding and regulating screws

Row 4: two top keys, untouched and pressed down

Row 5: bass damper (key C)

padding at the point of contact (although this is not a universal English feature). The hopper then prevents the hammer from falling all the way back to resting position until the key has been released completely. In the Erard 1797 model, however, the hammer-butts are forked. Each butt has its own wire axle and is hinged to the hammer-rail individually. When the key is depressed, the hoppers strike teardrop-shaped blocks mounted between the forks of the butt. The hopper strikes the teardrop, slides up along its surface, and escapes forward (toward the player) into the empty space between the forks. As a result, the hammer can fall all the way back to its resting position even before the finger leaves the key. This should serve to shorten repetition time in comparison to the usual English action. There is also less risk of the hammer bouncing as it comes to rest.

Meanwhile, the Erard hoppers are themselves guided by a wooden comb covered in soft leather (shown by the brighter color in the drawing). In English pianos, the fingers of this comb face the hammer-rail, thus trapping the hoppers between the comb and the rail. Erard, from its side, reversed the orientation of the comb, mounting it directly on the hammer-rail with the fingers facing out. When it comes to maintenance or repair, there's considerable advantage here: hammers may be attended to individually, either to adjust their lateral position with respect to the strings (by loosening and tightening the screws that hold the hammer-flanges onto the hammer-rail) or to take out a hammer altogether. On an English piano, lateral adjustment can only be achieved by bending the hammer-shanks, and one would have to take out a whole series of hammers, even if only one needed repair.

In the Erard 1797 model, so-called set-off pads regulate the point where the hopper escapes (row 3, with added arrows to indicate movement). These pads are leather-covered blocks mounted on strong springs. The position of each set-off pad can be adjusted by turning a screw that passes through the hammer-rail. By contrast, English pianos simply pad the end of the screw and have it engage the hoppers directly. What's the advantage for Erard? Again, it must be found in maintenance or repair. Their bearing surface being larger, the Erard pads are less susceptible to wear and tear. By contrast, the leathered English screws tend to wear irregularly, making regulation less precise over time.

The key levers of the Erard 1797 model are balanced quite close to their midpoints. In both the 1805 Brussels and the 1808 Amsterdam pianos, the balance point measures at 219 mm from the front of key levers that are 490 mm long. The key dip is regulated in typical English fashion by strips of felted cloth under the fronts of the keys (row 4). From chapter 2, we also remember that there's no over-rail above the rear of the key levers to limit their upward travel.

We measured both touch depth and touch weight in the 1808 Amsterdam Erard. At an even 25 g across the whole compass, its touch weight is almost identical to the 1793 Edinburgh Broadwood and a little lighter than the 1798 Ruiselede Longman, Clementi & Co. Its touch depth ranges from 7.9 mm at FF to 7.3 mm at c⁴, which is unmistakably deeper than both of our English reference pianos: 5.1–6.8 mm for the 1793 Broadwood and 5.4–6.8 mm for the 1798 Longman, Clementi & Co. Despite their deeper touch, however, the Erard key levers and action are so carefully balanced that there is very little lost motion from the moment the player begins to depress the key to the moment the hammer begins to strike.

The hammer action and keyboard of the Erard 1797 model thus exhibit significant refinements to the normal English action. In summary, they are designed to give the best possible repetition that Erard Frères could achieve at the time, and to offer improved reliability and ease of regulation, maintenance, and repair. They are intended to appeal to a national taste for timbral variety, not between registers (as would be the case for Viennese pianos, treble and tenor, for example, sounding distinctly different), but among the different levels of dynamics in otherwise coherent registers across the keyboard, just like the English instruments; this preference has deep roots in a centuries-long tradition of French harpsichord and organ music.

The principle of an English damper (shown in row 5) may be described as follows: a leather-clad wooden top clamps together several layers of cloth loosely glued together so as to retain a certain degree of fluffiness. When brought down, these pieces of cloth brush the strings, tapering their vibrations rather than immediately stopping them. (The English loved their after-ring.) Erard makes these "feather duster"-like dampers—as they're referred to in the literature, usually in contrast with Viennese wedge-shaped dampers—more efficient by first adjusting the cloth layers' angle, no longer folding them sharply but spreading them more widely, and then by leaving it to the bottom layer alone to create a now much firmer contact with the strings. As a corrective to the long bass strings, furthermore, which on English pianos tend to just keep on vibrating, the first twenty-one bass dampers (from FF to c♯) are made significantly heavier by two layers of a lead and tin alloy (of c. 1 mm each). Thus, the Erard model not only increases a degree of dampening efficiency across the board, but also creates more homogeneity in the way sound is stopped between longer and shorter strings.

Pedals

As we well know by now, the 1797-model pianos had four pedals. Consider how the Erard brothers explained their use to Madame de St. Victor, the first to buy a piano of this model. They do so twice, once in an initial letter of April 4, 1797—luring her in, as it were—and once again in their final letter to her, on June 27, 1797, to instruct her in the use of her brand-new piano. Just the day before, the piano had been crated, "weighing 430 pounds," and it "will be delivered to you in ten days." Once again, the Erards stress, "We have attended to every detail to achieve the greatest perfection in this instrument, as you soon will be able to see." Still, they wanted to remind her:

> The 1ˢᵗ pedal is for the mute [*la sourdine*]
> The 2ⁿᵈ is for the forte [*le forté*]
> The 3ʳᵈ is for the stop of leather [*Buffle*; short for what in a previous
>   letter was called *jeux de Buffles*]
> The 4ᵗʰ allows one to play one, two, or three chords at will [*Fait jouer
>   une, deux, ou 3 cordes à volonté*]; but should not be used for difficult
>   passages, nor for the forte [*[ni] pour les difficultés, ni pour le forté*],
>   because it would cause a bad effect and would put the instrument
>   out of order [*discorderait lInstrument (sic)*]. Normally one adds the
>   2nd or the 4th pedal, which produces a very pretty effect [*un très bel
>   effet*], as do pedals 2 and 3 for the cantabile.[36]

Remarkable here is the Erards' own advice as to how various pedals may be combined. Striking, furthermore, in regard to the fourth pedal, is the addition of what sounds like a warning: "It should not be used for difficult passages, nor for the forte." That this "would cause a bad effect" seems subsidiary to the more serious consequence that this "would put the instrument out of order."

How do these various pedals function from a technical point of view? Figure 5.4 shows how the mute pedal brings a batten covered in soft leather to bear on the strings at a point just behind the nut (the strip of wood glued to the wrest plank across which the strings run). Depressing the pedal causes the batten to slide sideways up a series of triangular, ramp-like guides on the wrest plank, bringing it into contact with all the strings simultaneously. Because the batten is close to the nut, it damps the strings, but only slightly, producing a muted sound, in effect not unlike a harpsichord buff stop. In terms of engineering, the mute is the most complex of the four pedals, and its application to the curved and split bridge of a grand piano, while also negotiating the metal gap spacers, is a prime example of the ingenuity that went into the design of the 1797 model. Erard Frères called it a *sourdine*; Adam used both *jeu de Luth* (lute stop) and *jeu de Harpe* (harp stop). The former connects with the tradition of a harpsichord buff stop, while the latter evokes the other major area of expertise of Erard Frères.[37]

The *forté* pedal raises the dampers from the strings and keeps them raised until it is released—like the right pedal (or "the pedal") on a modern piano. Adam calls it "*la grande pédale*."

The *buffle*, which Adam calls "*jeu céleste*," creates a different kind of mute effect by inserting small pieces of leather between the hammers and the strings. Whereas the *sourdine* changes the vibration profile of a string,

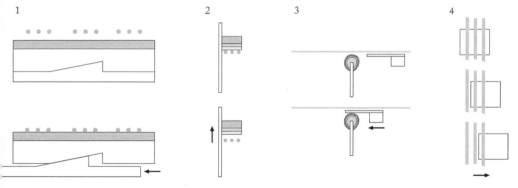

FIGURE 5.4 Four pedals on Erard: (1) "mute" (*front view*); (2) "forte" (*front view*); (3) "stop of leather" (*side view*); (4) "one, two, or three chords" (*top view*). Drawings by Gregoir Basyn.

the *buffle* affects the hammer strike, leaving the string free to vibrate and not curtailing its sustain, and thus producing quite a different sound.

The final stop is the shift—the one pedal, intriguingly, for which Erard does not have a one-word name. Adam pragmatically calls it *"la quatrième pédale"*; Steibelt says that "one calls it (who knows why) *Pédale céleste*," but that a better name would be *"Pédale du Pianissimo."*[38]

Case Bracing, Bentside, Soundboard

Internal bracing is something all pianos need, so that the case does not warp or collapse under the immense tension of the strings (fig. 5.5). Both the Erard 1797 model and its English counterparts use two sets of braces: one at the level of the baseboard, and one at the level of the soundboard. Whereas Broadwood braces are set perpendicular to the spine, however, Erard braces splay out nearly perpendicularly from the bentside (row 1).

In addition to the two main sets of braces, Broadwood pianos pack in a number of small extra struts between the levels. Broadwoods of this period have struts that run from the soundboard braces down to the baseboard, and from the belly rail to the first perpendicular baseboard brace. The effect is one of accumulated add-ons: an old structure shored up again and again over the years. The Erard 1797 model is much more streamlined inside, using only two diagonal braces at soundboard level for additional structural strength. Tension between these braces and the bentside is achieved through the use of wedges. It is as if Erard Frères swept away the accrued bric-a-brac of an English piano and made a clean start: a strategy that seems to have paid off, since despite their lighter bracing, the Erard pianos seem less inclined over time to twist than Broadwood pianos.

Another innovation introduced in the Erard 1797 model is a laminated bentside (as shown in row 2; the bentside is the curved side of the piano). While English bentsides were made from a single plank, Erard's were assembled from three layers of oak. The ever ingenious engineer Sébastien may have realized that laminating the bentside would increase both the strength and stability of this crucial structural element of the case. In any event, laminated bentsides are now common practice in modern piano cases, which must withstand much higher string tension than historical fortepianos.

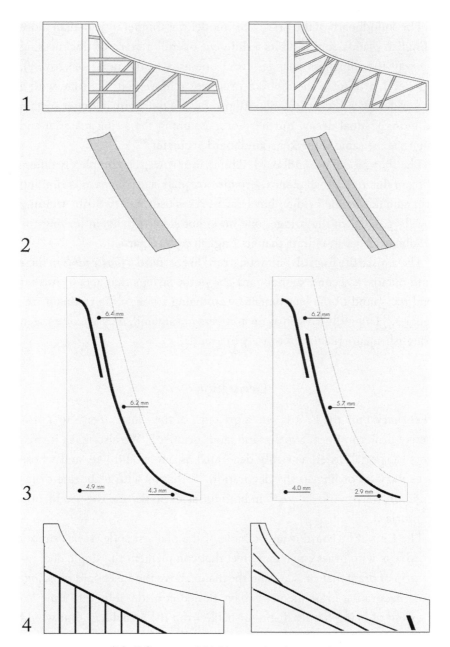

FIGURE 5.5 English (*left*) vs. Erard (*right*). Drawings by Gregoir Basyn.

Row 1: case bracing

Row 2: single-plank and laminated bentside

Row 3: selected thicknesses in soundboard

Row 4: ribbing of soundboard

The soundboard of the Erard 1797 model was thinner overall than those in English pianos, and exhibits a different overall pattern of thicknessing (the way the thickness changes from one area to the next; see row 3). In general, a thinner soundboard produces a more bell-like tone with a quicker decay; a thicker soundboard produces a tone with a longer sustain and more gradual decay. Furthermore, assuming the string material and gauge are the same, a thicker soundboard is quieter.[39]

The 1797 model's soundboard ribbing, too (row 4), is completely different from that of English pianos. Broadwood pianos use many ribs running perpendicular to the bridge, but Erard Frères uses just two ribs running roughly parallel to the bridge, one on either side of it, again leaving the soundboard freer to vibrate than its English counterparts.

Also unlike the English builders, Erard Frères used a *fausse table* in their grand pianos: a second soundboard above the strings that acts to further blend the sound of the instrument by softening some of the resonant frequencies.[40] Unkindly known as dust-covers in England, they are often seen in English square pianos, but rarely in grands.

Decoration

In February 1797 the Erards sent a price list of their instruments to a prospective dealer in Bern, Switzerland, and specified, "We also make instruments to special order, as richly decorated as one would like, and whose prices vary according to the decoration."[41] Pianos with elaborate ornamentation were marked "*orné*" in both the sales books and the production inventories.

The Linz 1803 Erard is an example of the plainest style. It has simply turned legs with brass collars and feet that complement the single decorative strip of brass that runs around the piano above the baseboard molding. These decorative brass elements have dulled considerably with time, to the extent of being hardly distinguishable from the actual legs, but would have been striking against the mahogany veneer when the instrument was new—just as our replica is now. The Brussels 1805 Erard has identical leg decorations, but lacks the additional brass molding.

The surviving *orné* instruments exhibit a variety of decorative elements. These include fluted and gilded legs or legs with highly decorated capitals;

brass molding inlaid into the veneer panels around the case; ormolu (gilded bronze) mounts on the legs and/or in the panels of the case decoration; and (the most expensive option) reverse-painted glass (*verre églomisé*) decoration in the keywell (the area of the piano surrounding the keyboard). One element that unites all of the *orné* instruments is use of higher quality veneer with a more highly figured grain.

Around 1808, the Erards introduced the option of a pedal lyre, as opposed to a semicircular stretcher. The lyre was also available for square pianos; in fact, the first mention in the sales books, on October 5, 1808, of a "*Ped: en lÿre*" piano refers to a square. The 1808 Amsterdam piano has a pedal lyre decorated with brassware and ormolu. The lyre must have been an option and not standard, however, given that another 1808 Erard grand (at Château de Valençay, France) retains the simpler half-moon stretcher.

Even the simpler instruments were veneered in mahogany, an expensive, exotic hardwood that had to be imported from the Americas. Mahogany was immensely popular in Britain throughout the 1700s; it was not until after 1750 that it gained popularity in France, where it was firmly associated with English fashions. But owing perhaps to the wood's general popularity and its increasing depletion in the colonies, perhaps also to trade restrictions and naval struggles between Britain and France during this period,[42] a number of letters in the Erard Frères copybook refer to difficulties in sourcing affordable mahogany. On March 17, 1797, for example, they requested from Ferdinand Staes the favor of "asking in Brussels or in the surrounding region if there is some mahogany wood for sale"; on April 15 of the same year, they wrote to M. Estoriac, a different dealer in Bordeaux, that they were "being offered mahogany wood at a price four times higher than before."[43] Yet, given the popularity of all things English, their use of mahogany was clearly an important selling point for the Erards. They mention it multiple times to Madame de St. Victor, and also Reichardt must have been impressed, as he noted "large vestibules and halls entirely full of finished cases in mahogany" at the Erards' establishment.

* * *

Had the younger brother been present, there's no knowing how different Reichardt's report would have been. It might well have turned out several pages longer: almost every aspect of the 1797 Erard model deserves elab-

oration on what exactly would have made it better than its English counterparts. Instead, Reichardt skips from describing the facilities in which a
production line happens, to a Sunday afternoon party where he heard the
two Erard nieces sing and play. "It's hard to give you an idea with words,"
he says about their performance, but clearly it confirmed what the tour
earlier that week had established already: that Erard's pianos "are far to be
favored over the English instruments."

It's starting to sound like a sales pitch. Also Adam's summary of the
piano's history at the outset of his method sounded familiar: "A German
invention was copied by the English and perfected by the French." From
a historiographical point of view, this version of the facts sounds naïve,
if not blatantly patriotic. But whenever Erard Frères in those early years
called their model of a grand piano "perfect," their mindset would have
been anything but naïve. Surviving the Revolution unscathed, as an Alsatian family, with ties both to the local aristocracy and to French émigrés
in London, may have been nothing short of a miracle. But their actions in
running a family company that would only grow stronger demonstrated
level-headedness and knowledge. Their 1797 model was the flagship of a
business that would have made Adam Smith (1723–90), the father of modern economics, proud.

What Reichardt described in 1802 was the perfect enactment of Smith's
doctrine of division of labor. Dividing labor revolved around two basic
principles: first, the increase of productivity per worker when specialized
tasks are being divided among many; second, an expanding market or demand for the manufactured commodity that exactly enables this kind of
increased labor specialization.[44] It is against this economic backdrop that
Erard Frères' concept of perfection is to be understood. The process of
both solidifying and fine-tuning it is evident in the letters sent to prospective clients. A fully formed version may be extracted from a letter of
July 16, 1797, a good three months after their first sale:

> We have taken our harpsichord-shaped pianos to a hitherto-unknown
> level of perfection: their solidity [*solidité*], tone [*harmonie*] & beauty
> [*Beauté*] astonish the most famous artists; this instrument adds to its dis-
> tinguished merit the argument [*L'argument*] that it can be placed in even
> the most magnificent salon [*dans un salon le plus magnifique*].[45]

In this sales pitch it's no longer clear who's speaking: the engineer, who had kept a close eye on the manufacturing of every detail of an English piece of technology, or the manager, who has translated this know-how to efficiently run workshops, each with their own specialty; the business-owner who oversees the accounting of the larger enterprise "in the English fashion," or the communications officer who constantly reaches out to clients, dealers, and musicians eulogizing the latest must-have commodity? Sébastien and Jean-Baptiste are wearing many hats, and as the production of their pianos continues year after year, boundaries between making and marketing fade.

A model is only perfect until the next, more perfect model comes along. For Erard Frères, this next happened in 1810, when after a hiatus of one year (no grand pianos were produced in 1809), a new model (*nouveau modèle*) was launched to replace the old (*ancien modèle*). Up to that point, 256 such old-model grand pianos had been produced.[46] While this number paled against the 4,209 square pianos manufactured during the same period (1797–1808), the attention that this book devotes to one 1797 model in particular is testimony to a fortuitous and powerful brotherhood that combined technical vision with business acumen.

CHAPTER SIX

An Unlikely Competitor

Germans hate piano stops.
Beethoven is German.
Ergo: Beethoven hates piano stops.

I present this syllogism only partly tongue-in-cheek. It reflects deeply rooted beliefs about classical music, including a distrust of anything deemed distracting to what is considered its essence. If Bach's forty-eight preludes and fugues constitute the Old Testament, then Beethoven's thirty-two piano sonatas constitute the New, and in this Bible of piano playing there is little room for tricks or effects created by stops. Not that on the modern piano we would have many to choose from. Of the two that are available, pianists today use the damper pedal constantly: no longer a device for occasional color change, "the pedal" has become a concept of its own, and pedaling (as a gerund in reference to the singular pedal) an essential part of producing sound altogether. Ironically, playing *without* the pedal has become the effect. Meanwhile, the so-called soft pedal is a very much reduced and compromised version of what the *una corda* once was.[1]

Having performed Beethoven on many types of historical pianos, I feel tempted to discount the proposition in the syllogism at once. Viennese-style pianos had all kinds of stops—why would Beethoven have ignored them? On the contrary, his request for a Walter piano with a one-string stop shows a clear desire to experiment with new sounds and effects. This book,

however, constructs a singular window onto a very specific period in Beethoven's career, and this means that, just as we must refrain from making
sweeping projections onto the modern piano, we must also resist teleolog-
ical argument *within* our own given time frame. If Beethoven's 1803 Erard
represents the newest piano, there may actually be value in accepting the
argument's major premise that, indeed, Germans hated piano stops.

We can read as much in a 1798 *AmZ* review of a rather eccentric new
piano method, written by Johann Peter Milchmeyer and published in
Dresden, then still the heart of clavichord country.[2] The title, *Die wahre
Art, das Pianoforte zu spielen*, was itself provocative, for it put forward
the new pianoforte as the heir to the esteemed old clavichord of the great
C. P. E. Bach. The reviewer ("K.," possibly Justin Heinrich Knecht)
spurns Milchmeyer's preference for "small, square pianofortes" with many
stops and registers, in contrast to Milchmeyer who praises these modifi-
cations [*Veränderungen*] for "having such great effect and always winning
more applause."[3] Not impressed, K. proclaims, "We, Germans, prefer
to stay with our *Stein* instruments, on which one can do *anything*, without stops."[4] It is true that Stein fortepianos normally had only damper-
lifting knee-levers—right and left, with identical functions—whereas the
newer Walter and Streicher *née* Stein instruments from Vienna would typically have had a moderator or celestial-stop knee-lever on the left and a
damper-lifting one on the right. The collective "we" (Austrians notwithstanding) assumes agreement from the entire readership of the Leipzig-
based *AmZ*, which would then have included the twenty-seven-year-old
Beethoven.[5] However, the presumptuous criticism is directed not so much
against "the author" (whom the reviewer calls by name only once), but
rather against the one person whom Milchmeyer in his method had cham-
pioned: Daniel Steibelt, "the man who has shown the world how to use
stops!"[6] Imagine that. The reviewer rests his case. Who, with a proper
mindset, would ever wish to play like Steibelt, widely known for his arrogance, "foolish behavior,"[7] and—when it comes to actually playing the
piano—charlatanry?

The irony amid all this nationalistic posturing is that both Milchmeyer
and Steibelt were Germans, too. What made them easy targets for ridicule in
a journal like *AmZ* was their adopted foreignness. Born the son of a watch-
maker in Frankfurt-am-Main and having been active as a court *mechani-*

cus in Mainz, Munich, and Dresden, Milchmeyer (1750–1813) introduced his method by proudly alluding to his "eighteen-year sojourn in Paris and Lyon," as though this were his true claim to authority.[8] For his part, Steibelt (1765–1823), born and raised in Berlin, took adoptive foreignness as far as renouncing the German language altogether. As an adult he spoke French exclusively, albeit "very badly," as another German reviewer remarked in 1800—notably, in a section of the *AmZ* reserved for critiques of concerts given by "foreign virtuosos [*fremden Virtuosen*]."[9]

Steibelt's rejection of his German origins began early. His father, Johann Gottlieb Steibelt, had been a Prussian military man until shortly after he married, when he turned to building clavichords and fortepianos. Owing to some "youthful indiscretions," the younger Steibelt was forced by his father to enlist in the Prussian army, but soon deserted. Once he fled Prussia, he broke off all relations with his family.[10] But if it is true that an "inclination to the French way of life" began defining him as a person to the point where he tried shedding his German identity altogether, it would be incorrect to ascribe this entirely to a desire to break with his youth. His mother, Maria Couriol, was a French Huguenot; despite this, every effort was made to ban French from the Steibelt household and to ensure that only German was spoken. For the rebellious eldest son, this deliberate suppression may have worked as reverse psychology, creating a desire to return to his mother's roots.[11] By enthusiastically embracing English and French pianism, Steibelt may unconsciously have been keeping at bay his childhood memories of the German-style instruments produced in his father's workshop.

In chapter 2, I speculated about a visit Beethoven may have made to Haydn's house, where the newly arrived Erard would have displayed its full splendor, despite an unfortunate warp and occasional rattle. I further imagined that playing the instrument might well have prompted Beethoven to reminisce about an encounter with Steibelt that had taken place exactly one year earlier. The mere mention of Steibelt would have sparked sympathetic banter between the two composers, however strained their relations were otherwise at this time. The presence of the Erard, however, might have infused the atmosphere with even greater tension. "It is easy to speculate that Erard's gift of a piano to Haydn, the instrument on which Beethoven felt far superior, evoked in Beethoven an acute sense of envy,"

Maria Rose–van Epenhuysen writes.[12] She reminds us that the piano came precisely at the time when Haydn began receiving one French accolade after another, including his election as a Foreign Associate of the Académie des beaux-arts on December 26, 1801. Privately, Beethoven may well have felt more entitled than Haydn to own such an instrument. The superiority of his piano sonatas (which Beethoven believed to be "better than those of Haydn"), or simply the fact Haydn was no longer composing for the piano, justified him in this feeling.[13] But if we are looking for a person who triggered Beethoven's interest in the French piano not so much as a trophy but as an actual working tool, then I suggest that we look to the man whose memory was suddenly evoked in Haydn's living room.

Haydn's Wallet

The Erards' gift to Haydn has long been widely acknowledged as a gesture of respect, if not reverence, and the sincerity of feeling that lay behind it has been taken for granted. Word of the exquisite piano spread quickly in the musical community of the time. On April 15, 1801, Haydn's agent and biographer, Georg August Griesinger, wrote of its arrival in a letter to Gottfried Christoph Härtel in Leipzig, "The Erard *Frères* in Paris sent [Haydn] a beautiful grand piano in English design as a gift, in mahogany and ornamented with bronze." (As we know, some two and a half years later he would write a similar message about Beethoven's piano, and make an explicit connection to this earlier moment: "as they did earlier to Haydn.") The subsequent paragraph in Griesinger's letter, however (one usually left unquoted in the literature), suggests that Haydn himself had a more equivocal response, and not without reason:

> The news that a Demoiselle Erard has illegally copied the *Creation*, has made him more indifferent to the French compliment [*gleichgültiger gegen die französische Artigkeit*]. As long as a similar dirty trick [*ein ähnlicher Streich*] is not played against him in Germany, he still hopes to gradually sell his one thousand copies.[14]

Here we have a privileged glimpse into Haydn's mind: he receives a magnificent piano, yet is unable to muster enthusiasm for it because he asso-

ciates the name Erard with a "dirty trick." The "Demoiselle" to whom
Griesinger refers must have been either or both of the sisters Marie
Françoise Marcoux (1777–1851) and Catherine Barbe Marcoux (1779–
1813), who were the daughters of Catherine Barbe Erard, the younger sister of Sébastien and Jean-Baptiste. The two sisters had started running the
family's young publishing business at 37 rue du Mail under the appellation
"Demoiselles Erard," adopting their uncles' name for both familial and
commercial reasons.[15] So far, so good: but what made their publication of
Haydn's *Creation* illegal?

The year before Haydn received his honorary Erard, Daniel Steibelt
had picked up an Artaria edition of the *Creation*, which he brought back
from Vienna to Paris. From a French correspondent to the *AmZ*, we know
him to have immediately embarked on preparing French translations with
Vicomte de Ségur, in August 1800. The report is less definite about whether
Steibelt already harbored concrete plans to perform or publish the work,
going only so far as to say, "He wants to have it translated and arranged in
such a way that *it may be performed* in the big opera theater."[16] What does
seem clear, however, is that he wanted to be ready, should the opportunity
later arise.

That same August many Parisian music lovers still held out hope that
other arrangements for an oratorio performance would be solidified.
Haydn's former student, the publisher Ignace Pleyel, would personally
convince the composer to come and direct his masterwork in Paris, as well
as to endorse a French translation and edition, to be published by Pleyel.
But such a Pleyel-Haydn co-production was not to be; logistical problems
interfered. Pleyel was denied a passport to travel to Vienna from Dresden,
where he had gone on business, and as a consequence it took too long for
him to receive his own copy of the Artaria score. As late as May 4, 1801,
Haydn would inquire, "*Je voudrais bien savoir [. . .] si tu as, oui ou non, reçu
par Artaria l'exemplaire de ma Création* [I would like to know [. . .] whether,
yes or no, you have received from Artaria the copy of my *Creation*]."[17]

In the meantime, Steibelt apparently took advantage of Pleyel's absence to prepare his own premiere of the oratorio, which took place on
Christmas Eve, 1800.[18] One week later, on December 31, 1800, a notice
about the performance appeared in the *Wiener Zeitung* that would have

left Haydn incredulous, at the very least: "The composer Steibelt has performed Haydn's grand oratorio *The Creation* in the Theater of the Republic. Ségur the Younger has translated the text in French. Garat and Demoiselle Barbier Walbonne sang the main vocal parts. The orchestra consisted of 250 musicians. Entry tickets had been doubled."[19] If these brief facts did not infuriate Haydn already, then a follow-up report in the *AmZ* of March 11, 1801, most certainly would have. The Paris correspondent quotes Steibelt as claiming that "Haydn had *instructed* him to perform this work in the big opera house." The latent sarcasm in the emphasis on instructing (*beauftragen*) grows into outright skepticism with the next thought: "Whether it is true that Haydn had also asked him to make changes to this excellent work, to rewrite so many passages and to transpose complete pieces in different keys—of that we cannot be easily convinced."[20]

One can only imagine Haydn's emotions over these various months, having no choice but to follow the Parisian developments from afar. It is hard to say what would have angered him more: that Steibelt took liberties with his score, the fact of the performance, or the false claim of Haydn's endorsement. Then, on top of all this—presumably some time in late March or early April 1801—Haydn receives the news of an illegal edition by a certain Demoiselle Erard. This chain of events injures and insults Haydn not once, but over and over again, and with every new development Steibelt gets closer to where it would hurt the most: the composer's wallet.

And so we come to the "one thousand copies," mentioned by Griesinger. For the edition of his *Creation*, Haydn had embarked on his own publishing venture, by February 1800 convincing four hundred of his friends and contacts to subscribe to a first printing of the full score, of which he printed no fewer than one thousand copies.[21] But as Haydn needed six hundred more customers to sell through his stock, his audacious business model was suddenly undermined by the "dirty trick" that had taken place in Paris. Griesinger had shared this bad news with Haydn's patron and librettist, Baron van Swieten. Here is what Griesinger writes to Härtel on April 3, 1801:

> I told Baron van Swieten that Haydn's *Creation* had been illegally copied in France and added that this calamity [*dieses Unheil*] would not befall a

proactive publisher. He answered that one initially had counted on a sale of 1,000 copies from which Haydn would be left with a net profit of 2,000 ducats. No publisher would ever have given as much.[22]

Had Haydn been naïve? By a "proactive publisher," Griesinger may well have meant his addressee, owner of the firm Breitkopf & Härtel, with whom Haydn would later that year (on July 21, 1801) indeed sign a contract for his sequel oratorio to the *Creation*, the *Seasons*, for a flat fee of one thousand ducats. Lessons learned, van Swieten would provide not only German and English texts (as he had done with the *Creation*), but a French version as well.[23] Still, one thousand ducats represented only half the profit that in early April 1801 Haydn must still have considered an achievable goal.

Based on Griesinger's accounts, we know that tensions were running high when Haydn's Erard arrived, presumably between April 3 and 15, 1801, the dates of the two Griesinger letters. By this time, Haydn had probably put two and two together, and recognized Steibelt's role in the skullduggery, for it was *Steibelt's* arrangement in French and *Steibelt's* piano reduction (much more profitable than the full score) that Demoiselles Erard had published. If the piano's reception was fraught with ambiguity, then we might well ask why Erard Frères chose to bestow it on Haydn in the first place. Was the gesture simply altruistic, or were other motives at play? Potential clues may be found in the firm's ledgers (see fig. 6.1). The timing of the shipment (November 2, 1800) seems significant in that it took place just as Steibelt and Erard were cementing their joint business venture. The oratorio was set to premier in tandem with the release of the French score. On December 19, 1800, an advertisement, believed to have been penned by Steibelt, reminded the French public that "the authentic keyboard arrangement by Steibelt with text by J.-A. Ségur will be found on the day of the big performance at the Demoiselles Erard, rue du Mail No. 37, *as the only owners of the work*."[24] Had Steibelt truly convinced the Erards that he had Haydn's endorsement, or had they conveniently taken him at his word? Had the Erards considered the ethically suspect nature of their dealings and so tried to defuse a potentially volatile situation by sending Haydn a piano? Or had they lost themselves in the Haydn mania, too, and did their gift reflect genuine admiration of the famous master in anticipation of Steibelt's much hyped performance? After all, Steibelt was

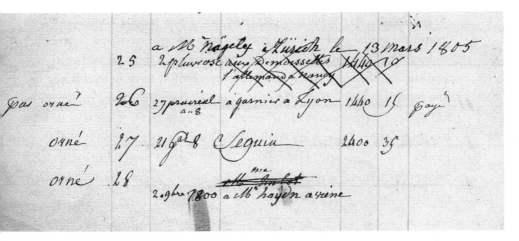

FIGURE 6.1 Entry in the Erard ledger books of Haydn's instrument: "*orné / 28 / 2. 9ᵇʳᵉ 1800 / a Mʳ haydn a viene.*" Reproduced with permission of Fonds Gaveau-Erard-Pleyel, owned by Groupe AXA and deposited at the Domaine royal de Randan.

an emerging patron of Erard Frères, endorsing their pianos and partnering in business, so the Erard family may have felt no choice but to ignore his reputation and move forward with the project. It may well have been this complex mixture of excitement and concern that prompted what in the ledger looks like an impromptu decision: the name of another client, "*Mᵐᵉ Hulot,*" has been crossed out and replaced (in Jean-Baptiste's hand) by "*Mʳ haydn à viene* [*sic*]." A sudden cancellation, in other words, resulted in a spontaneous gift.

For his part, Haydn seems to have vented his ire privately only, and wisely took some time before formally acknowledging the Erards' gift. He waited until May 20 to compose his "overdue" thanks: the letter is given in full in chapter 2. At first sight, his gentlemanly reply seems standard enough. Yet—what gentleman inquires about the value of a gift? Slyly veiling his own financial concerns with those of prospective customers, Haydn writes: "Many *Cavaliers* wish to know what the price of such an instrument would be, which is why I ask you to let me know." Another peek at the Erard ledger informs us that piano No. 27, like Haydn's an "*orné*" (decorated) model, had a price tag of 2,400 livres. In 1800, that sum would have been the equivalent of 171 imperial ducats—not insignificant, but amounting to only 14.2 percent of Haydn's projected loss of 1,200 ducats for those 600 remaining copies. And that's only talking retail value. For Erard, the actual cost of making such a piano would have been lower still and a fraction of what they were set to make from their pirated edition.[25] For Haydn, the unsolicited gift of a piano would have been a bitter reminder of his loss. "If you want to compensate me for your piracy, give me a sales commission already," one hears Haydn think. As it was, he was hardly short of pianos, with an old Schanz square, a Longman & Broderip grand, and a "beautiful Fortepiano" (most likely a new Viennese grand) filling up his house already. And besides, he had started limiting his own pianistic activity to the clavichord.[26]

Beethoven's Revenge

So, who was to blame for these offenses? None other than that rapscallion Steibelt, of course. But now the old man has finished telling his stories, and it is Beethoven's turn. Hence the conversation shifts to *his* run-ins with the German expatriate. Steibelt came to Vienna in the spring of 1800, and Beethoven was initially curious to hear him play. As Owen Jander has suggested, it is entirely possible he attended Steibelt's public academy in the Vienna Augartensaal in March or April 1800. Steibelt's immensely popular piece, *L'Orage précédé d'un rondeau pastoral*, which as always was on the program, might even have been a source of inspiration for Beethoven's "Tempest" Sonata, Op. 33 No. 2.[27] Nevertheless, critical responses to Steibelt's musicianship tended to sour upon closer listening. The review of the Augarten concert by the Vienna correspondent of the *AmZ* is a case in point. At first he pronounces Steibelt "a very skilled player, full of fire, and not without expression," and calls his concerto (that is, both composition and performance) "very brilliant." But the critic's enthusiasm soon dwindles: "The rondo with the thunderstorm (which he had especially announced), however, is a very weak copy of the one that *Hr.* Vogler played on his concert trips on the organ some ten years ago." His concluding remarks border on derisory, branding Steibelt's fantasy and variations "somewhat shallow" and asserting that they "betrayed little knowledge of deep composition."[28] Similarly, any shred of admiration Beethoven had for Steibelt seems to have quickly developed into "utter contempt."[29] The catalyst was almost undoubtedly the galling competition hosted in Vienna by Count von Fries during Steibelt's visit.

The only known record of this protracted engagement was written many years after the fact, in 1838, by Beethoven's pupil Ferdinand Ries:

> When, preceded by his great name, Steibelt came from Paris to Vienna, several of Beethoven's friends were afraid lest he should harm Beethoven's reputation. Steibelt did not visit him; they met for the first time one evening at Count von Fries's, where Beethoven first performed his new trio in B-flat major for piano, clarinet, and cello (Op. 11). The pianist cannot show himself particularly well in this work. Steibelt listened with certain condescension, paid Beethoven a few compliments, and felt confident of his victory.—He played a quintet of his own composition, improvised [lit., fantasized], and produced great effect with his *tremulandos*, which were something quite new then. Beethoven could not be persuaded to play again. Eight days later there was another concert at Count Fries's. Steibelt again played a quintet with much success, but in addition he had *prepared and practiced* (one could sense this) a brilliant fantasy, choosing the *identical* theme on which the variations in Beethoven's trio were written: this angered Beethoven's admirers as well as Beethoven himself; it was now his turn to improvise; he walked in his usual, I would say unmannerly, fashion toward the instrument, almost as if he had been pushed, along the way grabbed the cello part of Steibelt's quintet, placed it (intentionally?) upside down on the music stand, and hammered out a theme from the first few bars with one finger.—Insulted and angered, he improvised in such a manner that Steibelt left the room before Beethoven had finished, never wanted to meet him again, yes, even made it a condition that Beethoven not be invited when his own company was desired.[30]

William Meredith has identified the random cello part in this narrative as the first page from Steibelt's Quintet, Op. 28 No. 2.[31] When turned "upside down," as in the Ries account, Meredith maintains that it reveals characteristics evocative of the disjointed Basso del Thema (*sic*) of Beethoven's "Eroica" Variations, Op. 35 (ex. 6.1, top): single notes, jerky rhythms

EXAMPLE 6.1 Beethoven, Fifteen Variations with a Fugue in E-flat Major, Op. 35, theme (*top*); Steibelt, Caprice in G Major, Op. 24 No. 3, mm. 55–59 (*bottom*).

resulting from backward reading, rudimentary intervals of fifths and octaves reminiscent of the bass progression of a perfect cadence. These shared qualities indeed lend some support to the notion first entertained by Herbert Westerby in 1931 that the famous Eroica theme, easily "hammered out with one finger" on the piano, found its origins in those moments of anger provoked by Steibelt. Still, while this resonance suggests that Ries's version of events has some truth to it, his story must be taken with a pinch of salt, containing as it does several factual errors: on his 1799–1800 continental tour Steibelt traveled to Vienna not from Paris but from Prague; and the premiere of Beethoven's Trio, Op. 11, had actually taken place two years earlier, in 1798. More important, Ries himself did not arrive in Vienna until early in 1803, almost two years after the contest he recounts.[32] Clearly, his telling is secondhand, at best.

How can we be sure, then, about the most dramatic part of the story, that Steibelt walked away, utterly defeated? Did it happen, or did fact and fiction fuse with the telling? and who did the telling? If the Westerby–Meredith hypothesis holds (that Op. 35 encapsulates trails of the Steibelt–Beethoven competition), I would be inclined to nominate Beethoven himself, in his role as the teacher of an impressionable eighteen-year-old Ferdinand Ries, who would have eagerly soaked up anything his new master told him. Imagine a new scene, student and teacher now seated around Beethoven's 1803 Erard. We know that Ries received intense coaching from Beethoven: during a lesson that took "almost two entire hours," Beethoven made him repeat the final variation of Op. 34 no fewer than seventeen times, never satisfied "with the expression in the little cadenza," even though Ries thought he "had played it just as well as [Beethoven] did."[33] It is no stretch to assume that Ries also played Op. 35 for Beethoven, the second of a pair of variation sets (along with Op. 34) that Beethoven had offered to Breitkopf & Härtel in the fall of 1802.[34] "Both," as Beethoven had stressed in his pitch to the publisher, "are written in a truly *new manner*, each in an *entirely different way*" (emphases Beethoven's). Ries came under Beethoven's tutelage shortly before the sets appeared, in April and August 1803, respectively.[35] The maestro would no doubt have been pleased and proud to hear Ries play two of his recent publications.

The grand finale of Op. 35 consists of two parts: the Alla Fuga, reconnecting with the *basso* version of the theme, and the ensuing Andante con moto, a final, elaborate rerun of the fully harmonized theme. The fugue is highly effective precisely because of the initial subject's skeletal nature, which lends itself superbly to contrapuntal elaboration. If Steibelt, in the words of our German reviewer, showed "little knowledge of deep composition," then the Albrechtsberger-trained Beethoven must have known there to be little risk in selecting a random theme, *especially* from a cello part, that would give him exactly the slow, naked fifths desirable for an improvised fugal demonstration certain to impress everybody in that room. In the presence of Steibelt, moreover, nobody would have failed to understand the intent behind the Andante con moto, wherein with mind-boggling skill and pianistic finesse, Beethoven combines all possible means of surface-level or (dare we say) "Steibeltian" filigree, such as trills, diminutions, and yes, even tremolo, albeit a highly rhythmic version of it and in the right hand only—Beethoven beating Steibelt at his own game. The Op. 35 variations have "competition" written all over them, and Beethoven rubs it in with an arrogance matching only that of his French opponent and worthy of the "dissing" that occurs among today's rappers. If Steibelt had not "left the room" yet, he might just as well have: this is the kind of rhetoric expected of such a musical competition, where any successfully executed idea in musical improvisation becomes a metaphor for real life. An admiring pupil, receiving a lesson from the uncontested number-one pianist-improviser (who at age thirty-two was still at the top of his game), may not have understood the difference. Steibelt, however, would have known that giving in to his emotions and leaving the room would generate the kind of news an *AmZ* journalist would devour.

Steibelt's Magic

Steibelt was the man Germans loved to hate. Yet, invariably, *AmZ* critics always had something positive to say as well. His compositions may not have had much science (*Wissenschaft*), as the Dresden correspondent reports, "but [they] were crafted with a good eye for effect [*Effekt*], with pleasantness [*Annehmlichkeit*], and with true taste [*mit wahrem Geschmack*]."[36] The first half of Ries's story suggests that Beethoven himself may have been so impressed that he knew better than to take the stage after Steibelt had made "much effect" with his tremolos. Unfortunately, we do not know which piano the two contenders used at the Count's. "To execute these kinds of things well, [Steibelt] only plays on English fortepianos," the Dresden reviewer wrote, and there, it was the English ambassador who had loaned out "his very valuable instrument." In the same review we read about Steibelt's "ever-continuous *tremulando*" and his efforts to "make it swell and more striking still through the various stops of his instrument." Did Steibelt in Vienna likewise insist that an English-style piano be provided, so as to show off his tremolo magic and dexterity with the pedals?[37] If so, did Beethoven feel intimidated by Steibelt's mastery of this still unfamiliar technology? Could he himself "not be persuaded to play again" because he felt insecure confronted by this alien instrument? If Steibelt had indeed just played on an English piano, Beethoven may not have known immediately how to retort. A delay of several days would have allowed him to plot his revenge. Thus, his anger at Steibelt for having "prepared and practiced" a fantasy may have been just a smokescreen for his own secretly hatched plan, which was to beat Steibeltian elegance with Beethovenian science by improvising a learned fugue, certain to impress on *any* instrument.

What was it that made Steibelt's tremolo at once so irresistible and so irritating? Our Dresden critic writes, "It is true that his *tremulando* is attractive to listen to—*once*, but then it becomes tiring" (emphasis his). I will devote a separate chapter to the science of the tremolo in the context of the French ideal of *son continu*. For now, example 6.1 may serve as an introduction to Steibelt's trademark effect and, more generally, to his status as the unbeaten champion of piano stops.

In this early Caprice, published in 1795, Steibelt's directive for an extended tremolo section reads, "*Il faut mettre les étouffoirs du Piano* [One has to employ the dampers of the piano]." Steibelt obviously means the opposite, that is, that one has to employ (the pedal by which one lifts) the dampers of the piano. The opening bars of this thirty-six-bar-long vibrating Adagio allow Steibelt to ease into the ideal speed for alternating his fingers. Through a prolonged, single C-major chord, his hands and ears adjust both haptically and sonically to a perfect four-part texture, from which a simple melody emerges, giving rise to an unavoidable *crescendo* in m. 2. The double appoggiatura in the next bar similarly creates a swell— their resolution on the dominant chord marking the end of this opening phrase. Fingers, hammers, and keys all move in perfect synchronicity, and the soundscape they elicit from the instrument's soundboard breaks any acoustical precedent to a Viennese audience: the damperless vibrations are nothing short of breathtaking. We're looking at an effect descriptively notated by a sensitive pianist, who has applied himself with the same earnestness to the execution of a tremolo as the generation of C. P. E. Bach, say, to the perfect execution of a trill—but to the extent that the tremolo is no longer an ornament but the generator of ever developing sound.

As I impersonate Steibelt (video clips may be found at the website for this book), I try to reconstruct his *tremulando* art one step at a time—but together, the complexity is not unlike what typically happens in a mixing studio when one layer of recorded sound is combined with another. First, at our Erard replica, I use only the damper pedal (no. 2), which I depress with my left foot. Then, I attempt to make the initial tremolo much softer, while still allowing my fingers to move more freely: in addition to the damper pedal, I also engage with my right foot the *una corda* (no. 4). At this point, my full body gets engaged—and at this level of self-consciousness, I'd invite my listener to do the same, by closing their eyes (just as Steibelt insisted the young Chaulieu do; see chapter 4). Does the *crescendo* followed by *diminuendo* in m. 3 sound better when I create this swell with finger pressure, or rather when I exploit the pedal technology to do the job, making the out-of-case spring ever so gently relax and tense up again, that is, moving from *una corda* to *due corde* and back? (Doing any more—*tre corde*—would be too much, and thanks to the spring, I know perfectly well where to stop.) I confess here to seeking confirmation for what I already know: the latter rendition is much more satisfying.

It is also exactly how I envision Steibelt pulling it off, his ears carefully monitoring the results of what must sound like a four-voice chorale, while the tips of his far-right fingers get busy sculpting the top notes of a spun-out melody. As he works his way around the pedals, he keenly focuses on keeping the alternation of his fingers *as even as possible within a single sustained dynamic level*. His physiological awareness is such that it resembles a state of self-hypnosis. From afar, the method behind these magical effects might come across as mechanical or artless (think of the sight of a bobbing lid on a square piano); it is not until one sits down to produce such tremolos oneself that one realizes the deft and intense coordination involved in playing them: the line between success and failure is very thin.

So far we have used only pedals nos. 2 and 4, or the two pedals that would have been available also on an English piano, if such an instrument had indeed been brought to Fries's salon. But at our Erard replica, I can continue to raise the bar of technical difficulty, as Steibelt would have been able to do back home in Paris, along with the potential payoff. With my right foot, I now depress not just one but *two pedals at once*. This is a trick stolen from Steibelt, who in his 1809 method promotes the use of the far-left harp pedal (no. 1) in conjunction with the following damper pedal (no. 2), both to be played with the same foot: "*Il faut prendre aussi, et avec le même pied, [la pédale] qui suit.*"[38] For the sake of experiment, I next combine the *una corda* (no. 4) with the celestial stop (no. 3). By turning in my right foot, I manage to continue producing the swell with the ball of my foot. Finally, we may pull out all stops at once: pedals nos. 1, 2, 3, and 4, played by left and right feet, with each foot anchored in the center by the heel and symmetrically turned out. This is no longer Piano Magic 101, but advanced

Hatha Yoga. In the land of knee-levers and hand-stops, foot contortions of this kind would in all likelihood have left unsuspecting audiences unsure whether to be amazed or amused.

Through these descriptions of my own limit-pushing adventures with the tremolo, I have started to fill out what Steibelt meant by his single, generic, and imprecise directive, *Il faut mettre les étouffoirs du Piano*—an instruction so vague that he might just as well have written, "Be sure to make good use of the pedals." With the release in 1809 of his *Méthode de piano / Pianoforte-Schule*, however, Steibelt stopped concealing the secrets of his artistry. On the contrary, he proudly articulated his approach and defended it against former critics:

> To mask [the piano's] monotony, I wished for the only means it has to serve to its glory. The manner of attacking the keys, that of folding one's fingers, the well-notated use of the pedals, which have remained unused for so long and of which I was the first to make known the advantages, give this instrument an entirely different expression. People at first decried this activity of the pedals as *charlatanism* [emphasis added]. They tried to put the pupils off them. But those who banned them, all retraced their steps: many, however, still use them badly. I will soon show how this important addition to the instrument serves to pronounce better the colors, mark the shades and their degradations, and that the ways of using them are subject to the rules that [good] taste has traced.[39]

One has taste, or one doesn't. In Steibelt's commentary, the French noun *goût* is unmodified, absolute, taste *tout court*, whereas the German version adds the adjective "good" (*guter Geschmack*). The two versions, French and German, appear side by side in Steibelt's book, which was published by none other than Breitkopf & Härtel, whose *AmZ* for so many years had been harshly critical of Steibelt's person and musicianship.[40] Despite the German imprint, however, the aesthetic message that permeates Steibelt's bilingual text is unmistakably French. When Steibelt professes, "It is with a method [*méthode / Spielart*] that combines the mechanism of the keys, the fingers, and the pedals, that I have succeeded in almost spinning the sounds [*filer les sons / die Töne auszuhalten*]," he ascribes to a French way of conceptualizing sound for which there existed no adequate translation:

Töne aushalten ("to sustain tones") hardly captures the delicate skillfulness involved in a process that relies on the four pedals not as accessories to the piano but rather as essential extensions of the keyboard, the four rods extending the musicality of the instrument all the way down, just as the pianist's performing body extends all the way to their feet.[41]

With this in mind, it becomes easier to comprehend the sequence of pedals on the Erard. Consider again the various foot choreographies I have outlined, from simple to complex. In each of the tremolo realizations, it is the left foot on the damper pedal that maintains an anchoring position, while the generally more versatile right foot helps "pronounce better the colors [and] mark the shades and their degradations." Playing a tremolo like the one in example 6.1 means to keep moving one's fingers in a very calculated and contained manner: it is significant that Steibelt writes out every single note. Exactly this upper-body restriction—we're locked into firm hand positions that change only at a slow and carefully controlled pace—allows the pianist to devote their equally divided attention to the lower body. Hands and feet start mirroring one another—the former gently swaying over the keyboard, the latter engaging in a slow and intimate dance with the pedals. Both as initiator and privileged listener, the pianist adjusts their decisions—a small swell here, a celestial touch there—as they coordinate the two halves of their body in the sculpting of that ever fluid soundscape. Beyond its status as ornament or effect, the tremolo becomes the ultimate manifestation of the French ideal of *filer les sons*, or spinning the sound.

To take Steibelt's tremolo seriously, then, demands that we appreciate a school of piano building and music making that lies outside today's prevailing Germanic norms, as well as those that pertained for Beethoven. Many of Steibelt's German contemporaries clearly had not yet learned to open their sensibilities in this regard. It is telling that, when listening to Steibelt's *L'Orage*, the Viennese *AmZ* correspondent quoted above was reminded of a similar musical feat by Georg Joseph ("Abbé") Vogler, who was known for his so-called eccentricities and who, like Steibelt, was considered a charlatan by many. Vogler was also the son of an instrument maker, and his name was attached to the model of a chamber organ called the Orchestrion, which in its earliest design had four manual keyboards with sixty-three keys each (from FF to g^3), thirty-nine pedal keys (FF to g^1), twenty-four stops, and no fewer than three kinds of swells—all contained in a 9 × 9 foot (or 275 × 275 cm) square box that was comparatively easy to transport.[42] An older, tradition-bound audience might therefore have associated Steibelt's gymnastic footwork on the piano pedals with other instruments, like this absurdly complicated organ; but for a new generation of *piano* players (i.e., those no longer trained on the organ as well), it would have been revelatory to witness someone use the pedal in a radical new way: the sight of it may have been funny, but the ever changing sounds and colors produced were irresistibly magical.

Conclusion

"*Ergo*: all Germans hate piano stops." Or do they? The austere logic no longer holds. Something happened in that Vienna room in the spring of 1800, and Beethoven took note:

> A pianist, fresh from Parees,
> Was invited to Count von Frees':
> *Sempre tremulando*,
> *E molto arrogando*,
> But his feet were an interesting tease![43]

Or do we believe Ferdinand "Rees"? And was it the local hero who brought the French charlatan to his knees? I suggest that even if Steibelt did retreat from that room, the memory of his bizarre yet delightful skills lingered. In this sense, what did *not* happen in that spring of 1800 may well be the most significant part of Ries's story. Upon his arrival in Vienna, "Steibelt did not visit Beethoven; they met for the first time one evening at Count von Fries's." Had the two musicians met privately first, what fruitful exchanges might have taken place? Would they have exchanged insight and knowledge, the one relating his experiences with French and English pianos and effects, the other talking about his love-hate relationship with the German-Viennese fortepiano? But pride took the upper hand, and two personalities ended up clashing in the public arena of a Viennese salon.

Haydn's Erard was a less than welcome gift that did not yield new piano works; Beethoven's Erard, however, would make up for that. His desire to possess a French piano and all the effects that came with it arose far less from envy of his former teacher and his lavish new instrument than it did from ambition. If anything, Beethoven sought vindication for them both: whatever Steibelt did, Haydn's star pupil Beethoven would do better. But for that to happen, Beethoven would first have to explore the technology of his new French piano—its pedals, especially, provoking new questions and, through those questions, new experiments.

CHAPTER SEVEN

Continuous Sound

Vive la république! And long live its bureaucracy. To them we owe an on-line database of all French patents that the Institut national de la propriété industrielle (INPI) has awarded since 1791.[1] If you type in "Erard," no fewer than twelve show up, each with its separate file. One application in particular draws our attention. It is signed "Erard Frères" by Jean-Baptiste, though someone else with a clear and beautiful hand wrote the actual text of the application. This is application no. 3. It is grouped with two others for a *brevet d'invention de 15 ans* (a fifteen-year patent). Application no. 1 began with a confident note: "After having obtained last year a patent for our new Forte Piano *en forme de clavecin* and having received the approval of the public for this perfection, we occupied ourselves with new research on this instrument that has been the object of our diligent work during more than thirty years."[2]

If Jean-Baptiste had the honor of signing the applications, the supplementary technical drawings betray the hand of an engineer like Sébastien. Figure 7.1 thus reproduces the drawing corresponding to the prose description, which table 7.1 offers in translation. Imagine a patent officer examining the two sheets of paper side by side, making clarifying pencil marks on the diagram in the process. Application no. 3 is dated "*à Paris, le 6. 9 [September] An 1811,*" nearly two months before the November 4 dates on the two preceding submissions. Had the third application been prepared first, and then shuffled to the back of the others? The filing date is the same

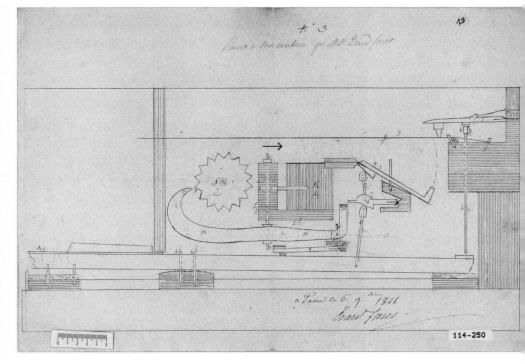

FIGURE 7.1 Technical drawing added to an application of Erard Frères for a *Brevet d'invention* of a *Forte-piano à son continu*. 1BA1484. Institut national de la propriété industrielle.

for all three: on November 6, 1811, they were classified under "industrial arts" (*arts industriels*) and within that category under "music" (*musique*). On February 4, 1812, file 1BA1484 was officially closed and a *brevet* granted. This is bureaucracy at its most efficient, even if three months into the process Jean-Baptiste wrote to inquire of His Excellency, Monseigneur le Ministre Intérieur Comte de l'Empire, why the process was taking that long. This letter, incidentally, is also included in the file—where it now serves as a nod to a future time when nobody would even think of filing a complaint just three months into any application.

Despite their inquiry, the Erard brothers could not have been that impatient to move ahead with production. At least for invention no. 3, there's no evidence to suggest that they ever did; no such instrument has been preserved.[3] Technically, as it turns out, the invention wasn't even theirs: Robert Adelson has discovered, in a letter dated June 16, 1811, as yet

TABLE 7.1 Translation of the application for a *Brevet d'invention* of a *Forte-piano à son continu* by Erard Frères (1811)

N° 3

N° 3 is a fortepiano with continuous sound; the drawing represents the cross section of the action in profile view.

A key, **B** balance point, **C** hopper [of the "real" hammer, attached to the key], **D** false hammer, **E** hopper of the false hammer, **F** hammer, **G** string, **H** hopper of the damper, **J** damper—all these parts belong to the existing action of pianos with two and with three strings;

Now we will describe the mechanism designed to create continuous sounds.

K is a strong bar with the length [equivalent to the] width of the keyboard

L is another bar in the shape of a right angle with the same length as the previous one.

M is a double lever. **N** is a strong hopper cut in the form of a screw with two ends, and at each end a nut is fitted. **O** is a small hopper screwed in bar **P**—at bar **P** there is a false hammer **Q**. Up to now this whole mechanism does not show the effect that one wants to produce; but as one pushes, by aid of a pedal, bar **L** against bar **K**, one end of the double lever **M** passes under the false hammer **D**; and the beak of the same lever **M** passes under tooth **R** of cylinder **S**; this cylinder **S** has a pivot **T** at each end; the one on the left fits in a wheel that one turns with the foot or by any other means. One observes in this description that when the end of the double lever **M** sits under the false hammer **D** and the beak of the same lever under the tooth **R** of cylinder **S**, it is obvious that the sound of each note becomes continuous, that is, of each note for which one presses key **A** when the cylinder is moving.

V indicates the springs. When one lets go of the pedal the continuous sound stops.

Paris, September 6th, 1811
Erard Frères

unpublished, from Jean-Baptiste to Sébastien, that they'd actually bought it from another, unnamed inventor.[4] Why, then, was it so important for the Erards that they claimed it as their own? Because the concept it embodies is one that occupied the minds of many French musicians, including the builder whose vision and work are the central focus of this book. The concept was in many ways already essential to their own flagship *piano en forme de clavecin*. As the *nouveau modèle* of this flagship piano started rolling off the factory floor, well into the second decade of its production, nobody else could be allowed to walk away with the credit.

The Erards called the new invention a *forte piano à son continu*, or a "piano with continuous sound." This is not some other "piano with a funny name," to quote Emily Dolan and Robin Blanton, such as the German builder Johann Andreas Stein's hybrid invention, the Poly-Tono-Clavichordium—its name a convoluted mix of Greek, Latin, and German.[5] Rather, *son continu* (savor the long vowels in these French words, and they take on the quality of onomatopoeia) conveys a deeply powerful idea—one to which every piano should ideally subscribe and to which a single *brevet d'invention* cannot do full justice. Proof of the strength of *son continu* as the term for an all-encompassing concept of sound is the fact that Maria Rose–van Epenhuysen, the author of the single authoritative doctoral dissertation on the French piano school before 1820, uses it repeatedly (starting in her preface, in which she professes a "fascination with *son continu*"), without ever acknowledging that her only source for this particular wording is the very instrument that we are also intrigued by—one that, intriguingly again, *existed on paper only.*[6]

To modern-day fortepianists, who have typically taken their first steps in historical performance on Viennese instruments, the desire for continuous sound seems naïvely prescient. Most of us have spent years *un*-training ourselves from relying on those long-developing vibrations of the modern piano, instead learning to embrace the much faster decays of historical piano strings and reviving a more declamatory and historically appropriate approach to "singing" at the piano. Nevertheless, through our fascination with Daniel Steibelt and his *tremulandi* we have also come to recognize *son continu* as a Holy Grail for French piano builders and players alike. By Steibelt's own c. 1809 account, his technique had brought him to the point where he "succeeded in almost spinning the sounds [*parvenu presque à filer les sons*]." This image of a "spun thread" of consecutive sounds taps into the ideal of a single *son continu*. But note Steibelt's qualifier, "almost." Is it to be read as a veiled criticism of the machine's imperfection—something along the lines of, "It cannot be done, but I came pretty damn close"? Indeed, earlier in the same account, Steibelt had declared the piano potentially "the first of instruments," throwing down a gauntlet for piano builders like Erard: "The piano would incontestably be the first of instruments if it could imitate the voice that spins sounds [*sic*], the wind instruments that can make them swell or diminish, and the bowed instruments, which in this respect are the rivals of both."[7]

A Fortepiano *à son continu*

In the proposed invention, there is no "almost." The machine is designed to realize the impossible, a "fortepiano *à son continu*"—all it takes is to press down a key. Anyone can do it, no Steibeltian skills required. So how does it work? The drawing depicts a cross-section of the action, which resembles that of a square piano *à double pilote*. This means that it has two hoppers (C and E) and two hammers (D and F). (To be sure, the corresponding text does not specify that this is a drawing of a square piano, but in a grand piano, there would be no room under the wrest plank for the additional components.) The hammer F that actually hits the string (G) is the real hammer, while hammer D is only intermediary and thus false (*faux*); the same holds for the hoppers: hopper C is attached to key A, and hence real, while hopper E, attached to false hammer D, is also "false." (The string is drawn as a line parallel to the key, although in reality it would run perpendicular to it.) Crucial to generating the continuous sound is a cylinder (S), which is made to turn "by foot or any other means." If by foot, the mechanism would be similar to those on a treadle sewing-machine or a spinning wheel. The other foot is needed to operate a pedal that moves the whole construct of bar L (incidentally also in the shape of an L) toward the fixed "strong bar" (K). I have added an arrow in the drawing to indicate this movement. The prose description mentions the existence of springs (V), but none is represented in the drawing. It seems safe to imagine one between movable L and stationary K, where it would bounce the system back to its default *off* position. The other likely location for a spring would be to the left of bar L, where it would move the bar to the *on* position; however, this is harder to conceive, for such a spring not only would need to be very robust but also would have to compete for space with cylinder S and a large double lever (M). Lever M is attached to bar L. As soon as L engages, the pointed left end of M (which Erard calls its "beak") catches under one of the cylinder's teeth, causing the lever to teeter. This seesaw motion causes the other end of M to repeatedly hit false hammer D.

"Repeatedly" is the operative word here: the continuous sound is ultimately realized by hammer F's repetitive contact with the string. "It is obvious," Erard explains, "that the sound of each note becomes continuous, that is, of each note for which one presses key A when the cylinder is moving." One can only speculate about how fast the repetitions occur, but what is certain is that the cylinder's revolutions would have to be carefully calibrated according to the time it takes for the hammers to rebound. Meanwhile, for as long as the finger continues depressing the key, damper J remains elevated so as not to interfere with the repeated strokes of the hammer. Let go of the pedal, and damper J and real hopper C resume their regular function. The piano goes back to normal.

The technical design seems sound enough—but what about its execution? Just as a French bureaucrat in the patent office might have solicited the opinion of an expert, I consulted piano maker Chris Maene for his take on this issue. According to Chris, the mechanism as portrayed looks "like it could work." Certain details have received close attention, including options for finely regulating the interlocking parts. Other specifications, however, have been omitted. These include where the springs would sit, whether hand or foot would propel the cylinder crank, and what the double lever would be made of. But even if the blueprint for the apparatus had been complete and could be built to run with the clockwork precision of an automaton, its mechanics in operation might well have been so loud that the machine would be better named a piano with continuous noise than one with continuous sound. In short, if Sébastien Erard had been summoned to the patent bureau for a follow-up interview, he would have had major omissions to rectify. It may thus have been wise of the brothers Erard to make this particular application the last in a portfolio of three, in which the first two represented more straightforward variants of the piano, with few if any profound changes to the instruments' internal workings: no. 1 was for a "*forte-piano ayant la forme d'un secrétaire* [piano in the form of a writing desk]," and no. 2 for a "*forte-piano d'une forme et d'un mécanisme particuliers* [piano in (some) particular form and with (some) particular mechanism]."

For all our focus on the inventive aspect of this patented *son continu* instrument, we should not forget that it, too, is fundamentally a regular piano. With the exception of the cylinder apparatus, "all these parts," the application explains, "belong to the existing action of pianos with two and three strings." The piano transforms into an instrument of continuous sound only once the pianist has undamped the strings and set the cylinder in motion. To do this would require deliberate preparation—exactly of the kind that occurs in works by Steibelt or Adam, where the pianist at some important juncture in the composition shifts from playing plainly, letting the tones decay, to producing a tremolo-like texture. This transition would typically occur where an Allegro begins to subside into an Adagio, giving the performer a chance to prepare their pedal(s) of choice. A listener familiar with this style of playing would have thought, "Ah, yes, here it comes."

Another striking analog for the pianistic reality of a tremolo can be found in the teetering motion of the moustache-shaped lever (M). One can see in it the equivalent of a hand playing a tremolo, say, a pure fifth using the thumb and pinkie wavering back and forth: the lever seesaws much the same way. While the human fingers have the mechanical *advantage* of individual independence and flexibility (we do not need to rely solely on the lateral movement of our wrist to press the keys, but can simultaneously move the individual fingers vertically, increasing both elegance and control), the human *disadvantage* is that there is a limit as to how many levers (or the human equivalent of them) we can create in a single hand. The machine, in contrast, provides a shaking lever for every note one plays, and one may combine as many notes as one has fingers. The resulting sounds are not tremolos but individual repeated notes. The invention may not be a piano *à tremendo*, but the inspiration is clear: the inventor (and by proxy Erard) must have wanted to build the perfect *tremulando* machine. Conversely, the tremolo is the closest a human hand can get on a regular Erard piano to *son continu*.

So, assuming that its construction equaled if not outdid the performance of a human hand, then who were the practitioners of *son continu* after whom the newly invented piano would have been patterned? The mention of Steibelt and Adam so far has not been arbitrary. Writing in 1834, Charles Chaulieu remembered both pianists' success in this domain: "These tremolos, in which one never heard the *battements*, and which produced veritable spun sounds [*sons filés*], I have never heard them played well after [Daniel Steibelt] than by Mr. L. Adam."[8] But what did Chaulieu mean by *battements* (beats)? That one is not supposed to hear the sounds of hammers hitting the strings, or that one is to become oblivious of alternating pitches altogether and instead hear a single, continuous sound? The former, of course, leads to the latter, and by removing ourselves with Chaulieu from the machine-mechanical side of things, we start tapping into the secrets of what it meant to play a truly fine tremolo. Still, to acknowledge such a "true art of playing the tremolo" begs the question of why the French piano was so well suited for it.

An Experiment

On the top floor of the Orpheus Institute we organized an experiment, initially to observe the mechanics of tremolo execution. We set up two keyboard models, one with a Walter action and the other with the action of an Erard. I was to play a tremolo, first on one model and then on the other. Bobby Giglio would record these using our slow-motion video camera. While we focused on observing the movement of action parts and fingers (as two sides of the same mechanical coin), we also recorded the sound of the tremolo runs, at least those on the Erard (for some reason, we neglected doing so for those on the Walter). It was only as we started analyzing the visual results that investigations branched out to deliberately address sound and questions of acoustics. At that second stage, our team expanded to include Prach Boondiskulchok and Song Hui Chon.

What was I to play? Studying the tremolo had been one of the priorities when planning the construction of the two models, so among the six chromatic tones from middle C to F available to me, the choice was easily made: I settled on the third c^1–e^1, also the plausible beginning of a tremolo section in French scores (see below) and with the added advantage of a near-perfect C-major third. (Chaulieu would have been pleased to hear that also from this tuning perspective, any distracting "beats" had been minimized: I used a Vallotti well-temperament.)

The intent was to study what it takes to produce a *good* tremolo. If Erard had been on our team, he might have offered to make us a cylinder-cranked lever to eliminate human subjectivity, but we would have politely declined. An experimental psychologist, for their part, might have insisted that several pianists participate in order to ensure greater objectivity. But we decided that it was more useful to have a fully human pianist try both actions, and to compare these distinct environments from the perspective of a single subject. The historicized version of that person could be Beethoven, wishing to imitate Steibelt, and doing so on two pianos: first on his familiar Walter, then on his new Erard. Familiarity with one or the other action, though a potentially obstructing factor from a scientific point of view, became an added element of strength because, like Ludwig, I had a much longer experience of playing Viennese fortepianos than French ones.

Establishing a premise of proficiency, however, brings us no closer to establishing what makes a tremolo "good." Cultural differences complicated the process. As in the experiment of a single strike (see chapter 2), rather than attempting to define the criteria among ourselves, we looked to a proven expert for guidance. The most detailed description of the tremolo is to be found in Louis Adam's *Méthode* (1804–5) in the section on "How to use the pedals":

> The two pedals combined [i.e., the second and the third pedal] express very well the sustaining of chords by way of the *Tremendo*; but *Tremendo* does not imply the [mere] beating [*battement*] of the fingers that one uses to strike alternately one note after the other: the *Tremendo* must be done with such a speed that the sounds present only a continuity of sound to the ear [*une continuité de son à l'oreille*].
>
> To succeed in executing this the fingers must barely leave the keys, and with a small shuddering they vibrate the strings without any interruption to the sound, especially in the *diminuendo* and the *pianissimo*, where the sounds must extinguish themselves in such a way that one no longer hears any movement of the keys.[9]

Let's try and break this down:

1. Tremolo (or what Adam calls *Tremendo*) is a damperless affair involving (on the French piano) the damper pedal and the *jeu céleste*.
2. As we suspected already from our reading of Chaulieu (himself a former student of Adam's), *battement* refers to the movement of the fingers. The goal of a tremolo is not some fast alternation of fingers but rather the combined perception of "sound continuity" *as a single entity*. Musically and semantically, Adam's *continuité de son* is but one small step removed from Erard's *son continu*. They may even mean the same thing.
3. Or, to put it another way, the plural *sons* of those alternations must become a singular *son*—one uninterrupted sound that largely subsumes yet resonates with the constituent pitches.
4. The ultimate judge of success is the human ear (*l'oreille*).

5. Any movement of fingers (and through them, action parts) is designed to make the strings vibrate and must be kept *to a bare minimum*. On the one hand, the hammers should be made to hit the strings and get out of the way as quickly as possible for freest possible ringing. On the other hand, one needs to aim for just enough impact of the hammers so as to ensure that their attacks do not interrupt those vibrations for any longer than necessary. In *diminuendo* and *pianissimo* this may mean occasionally not producing any sound at all, or creating the illusion of a continued sound by the visual signal of a silently moving key.

To Adam, finger strokes and sounds on the piano are utterly symbiotic, so intimately and reciprocally connected as to blur cause and effect. When he writes, "The sounds must extinguish themselves in such a way that one no longer hears any movement of the keys," he must mean that the keys do actually move, but that sounds no longer result from that movement. From a modern perspective, this reading may be surprising. Those of us familiar with mechanical noises in historical piano actions (especially in recording contexts, where these things matter even more) might rephrase Louis Adam's statement and say that "sounds must extinguish themselves in such a way that the only thing left to hear is any movement of the keys."

From the fine detail of these instructions, it is evident that the French took their tremolo very seriously. Adam's use of qualifiers like "barely," "only," "small," or "any" suggests extreme caution and care—unrelenting attention to the subtleties of execution. Like tasting wine, the degustation of a tremolo cannot be rushed, which may explain why it demands its own ritual and why it comes with its own conventions and rules, to the extent of becoming its own piece or section within a piece.

Learning from the Masters

Two Adam examples (see ex. 7.1) may shed some light. The first is from his method: a *Tremendo* version of the popular Swiss air "Le ran[z] des vaches imitant les échos," a traditional cow-calling tune (think Swiss Alps and alphorns).[10] The second is from the slow movement of Adam's Sonata, Op. 8 No. 2, written for the *premier prix* exam of his pupil Frédéric Kalkbrenner.

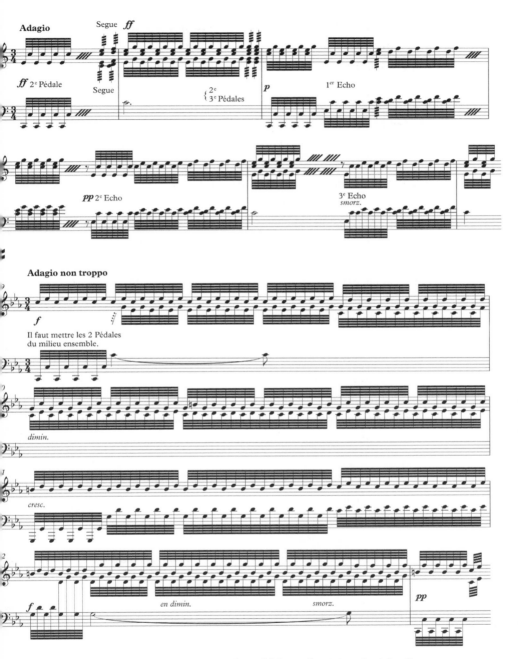

EXAMPLE 7.1 Adam, "Air Suisse nommé le ran[z] des vaches imitant les échos," mm. 1–6 (*top*); Sonata in C Major, Op. 8 No. 2, second movement, mm. 49–53 (*bottom*).

To these we may add the Steibelt tremolo from chapter 6. What are their shared characteristics?

It is always the lower note that comes on the good or metrically strong part of the beat *in both hands*: this means that the hands move asymmetrically with respect to one another. Notable, too, is how the left hand tends first to establish a low foundational bass, taking up its tremolo position next to the right hand with a slight delay. A default four-voice texture (two notes per hand) is augmentable to five or six, and the slow tempo (typically an Adagio) combines with mostly triadic harmonies to form a chorale-like structure: the simpler, almost, the better. In contrast to such perceived simplicity, however, the notation is impressively detailed and meticulous down to the smallest note values (64th notes), which implies an expectation of equal accuracy in performance. The advice, "Don't count: just play a tremolo," is clearly not applicable here. Adam also consistently specifies the use of the second pedal (to raise the dampers), thereby confirming the intrinsic importance of freely ringing strings. With *Tremendo* (a gerund with a capital, or somewhere between a proper noun and a verb), Adam thus has more in mind than a manner of playing: *Tremendo* stands for a style, type, or topos—a Trembling, to be executed while following strict rules and exercising utmost care.

Adam's recommendations and examples yielded the following three instructions for the experimental tremolo (ex. 7.2):

1. Alternating thumb and middle finger, play three quarter-notes with 64th-note tremolo subdivisions on C and E, with the thumb on C (as the "good" note) and the middle finger on E (as the "bad" note).
2. Take it easy at the outset, making sure your muscles are relaxed and that you consciously feel the weight of keys and hammers; then swell

EXAMPLE 7.2 Tremolo for experiment, as prescribed (*bottom*) and as played (*top*).

and reach your maximum speed by the second beat (without ever tensing up).

3. Play a *smorzando* by the end of the third beat; not producing actual sound at the very end is allowed and encouraged.

Walter vs. Erard

The first experiment consisted of playing tremolos on the Erard and Walter action models, in front of an all-observing, slow-motion video camera—a process that resulted in two situations of performance anxiety. After taking care of external circumstances (tuning the two notes, making sure all action parts were optimally functioning, sitting as Adam would have required "with elbows a bit higher than the level of the keyboard,"[11] and this after Bobby had spent many days optimizing filming conditions, adjusting lights, finding focus, adding markers to the mechanisms), there was pressure to perform ("Ready? Go!"), invariably followed by moments of self-evaluation. Three takes was all I got, on each of the actions. On the Erard mechanism, my fingers felt more readily "locked" in a certain speed of alternation, in response to the moving hammers and keys. The Walter mechanism, by contrast, seemed to shift the choice of speed to the fingers: at every run, a faster tremolo felt within reach, provoking uncertainty as to exactly what to aim for or listen to (and prompting me to ask for an unplanned fourth trial). "Should I have played the tremolo faster? Exactly what information did I just get from these Viennese keys or hammers?" This perceptual second-guessing applied to hearing as well: while the clearer and harsher hammer strokes of the Walter produced alternating sounds that can be compared to those produced by mallets on some imagined cimbalom, the Erard tremolo lacked exactly this kind of clarity and somehow allowed the two repeated notes to gel with one another much more.

Granted, these are subjective impressions, but they are confirmed by visual observations upon comparing the slow-motion videos. The Erard clips show cause and effect taking place right in front of our eyes, the movements of hammer-shanks and hammers mirroring exactly those of the fingers (as in, finger going down, shank going up); meanwhile, engaged in a balancing act on their own, keys bounce off the front and back paddings respectively (watch the extreme left and right ends of the key): *there is always something in motion*, with every component *smoothly following a predictable choreography*, going back and forth, or up and down, or down and up, or forth and back. This is keyboard-action ballet at its most elegant—an intriguing display of continuous movement, even when slowed down at 3/125 of the normal speed (which corresponds to the camera's recording at one thousand frames per second).

The Walter clips could not be more different: we see jerky movements— a hammer picking up speed toward the strings, but then just as quickly falling down before repositioning itself behind the back-check, waiting until it is pulled up again, with sudden force. *There is less sense of regularity*, and unexpected things happen: a hammer, for example, may fail to rest and erratically jump up. Under the front side of the keys (where the fingers are) there is no padding (since the movement of a Viennese-action key is blocked at the key's back or beak), resulting in not much of a bounce at all, felt or seen. The overall impression is one of speed and efficiency, but certainly not of elegance or continuity.

None of this was particularly surprising, given what we already knew about the pianos' tendencies. In general, the Viennese piano *speaks* more than its French counterpart, for it can project the kind of energy equivalent in speech to the unleashing of a previously blocked airflow after plosive consonants like *t* or *k*. The French piano, in contrast, *sings* better, because its English-style action allows for powerful but less explosive strikes and thereby greater continuity of sound. But seeing is believing, and the video clips did serve to strengthen the hypothesis that the Erard would demonstrate a more regular tremolo than the Walter. Still, in order to make sure that our observations were credible, we set out to time the intervals between consecutive hammer strokes. Our strategy was to watch for the highest point of contact between hammer and string, just before the hammer starts its descent, and then record the number of the video file frame where this peak occurs.[12]

So what do the data reveal? The protocol for each tremolo run was to play the equivalent of three quarter-note beats of 64th notes, so 48 notes in all. As it turns out, the note count in every run exceeded the intended number by at least four. (So much for following instructions.) The Erard runs consisted of 58, 64, and 56 notes, whereas those on the Walter consisted of 52, 52, and 57. The higher counts on the Erard may reflect the compelling impetus of the action, which had locked in, as it were, both my fingers and mind, so that they just wanted to keep going. The Walter's clearer sounds and more instantaneous responses, in contrast, may have allowed me to react faster to my brain's command to stop.

We categorized the hammer action for each note played, depending on the extent of its contact with the string. A "miss" designated any situation where the hammer did not meet the strings, either "not at all" or "not quite." "Not at all" meant that the hammer failed to engage altogether, typically because the hopper or escapement tried to set it in motion again too soon, invariably due to an over-eager finger. "Not quite" meant that the hammer rose as it should, but did not achieve contact. The Erard runs included a total of fifteen overall misses (5, 8, 2 misses in each run), compared to only five (2, 1, 2) on the Walter. Of these, eight were "not at all" instances on the Erard (3, 3, 2) versus only two on the Walter (1, 0, 1). The Erard also had seven "not quite" strikes (2, 5, 0) whereas the Walter had three (1, 1, 1). Six of the "not quite" instances on the Erard, finally, were intentional: they happened toward the end of longer runs 1 and 2 as a result of the required *smorzando*. No such near misses occurred on the Walter, almost certainly because moving the keys silently is next to impossible on a Viennese action. On the one hand, when playing such a *prell*-action, the finger carries the full weight of the hammer even with the slightest downward movement of the key, which means that there is a substantial difference between pressing the key ever so slightly or not at all. On the other hand, once the key has moved down, there is a good chance that the hammer (which should be sufficiently free to pivot within its *Kapsel*) will actually hit the strings: the let-off point, that is, the moment when the hammer is allowed to escape, is regulated as close to the strings as possible, which means that, in order to keep a hammer from hitting the strings, one would have to depress the key very, very slowly.

The graphs in figure 7.2 chart the intervals between hammer strokes for the Walter and Erard models, based on averages for the three runs. On the horizontal axis is the note index: odd numbers correspond to the transition from C to E in the tremolo, and even numbers correspond to the event from E back to C. Vertical bars indicate the amount of time between hammer strokes at a particular note index measured in milliseconds. The top of each bar shows the average of three runs, while the brackets that extend above

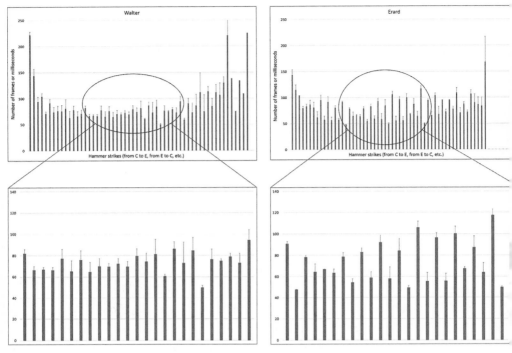

FIGURE 7.2 *(left)* Walter tremolos: time difference between strikes, based on the average of three runs; *(right)* Erard tremolos: time difference between strikes, based on the average of three runs.

represent the standard deviations. An oval marks the plateaus or the middle area of a tremolo, where momentum can be expected to be at its fullest and most regular; these are amplified as separate graphs. Comparing the data for the Walter and Erard, one can see that the very first average intervals on the Erard are shorter, confirming my impression that the Erard action invites the player to settle into the tremolo more quickly. On the other hand, none of us was prepared for the results in the plateau segments. Of the two actions, it is the Walter that displays less variability in the speed of alternations, the fastest clocking at 50 ms and the slowest at a little under 100 ms. On the Erard, meanwhile, both faster and slower alternations occur with greater frequency, and the difference between them is more pronounced: many more fast alternations approach the 50 ms mark, while no fewer than three clock in at the 100 ms mark or more. In other words, *the Walter intervals show greater regularity all the way across the stable region of the tremolo*. But a distinct sub-pattern emerges: *consistently, on the Erard, there is a longer interval between C and E strikes, followed by a shorter interval between E and C strikes*. That is to say, the durations of the two notes differ, albeit by milliseconds, so that longer Cs virtually always precede shorter Es. While the Walter action, then, is more regular on average, the Erard's pattern of long and short between C and E reveals a consistency of a different kind altogether—a regularity within irregularity, which establishes itself already from the seventh note onward. In contrast, both C and E on the Walter can be either long or short—in other words, there is irregularity within regularity.

Playing notes of unequal duration does not in itself warrant surprise: it is the basis, after all, of the French baroque practice of *notes inégales*. What is startling, however, is that they occur when skillfully deploying an effect whose essence is supposed to be the *equal* alternation of two *equally important* pitches. If C and E are supposed to contribute fifty-fifty to creating a single continuous sound, then why should one be longer than the other? Where should we look for answers? We decided to focus on what started it all: continuous sound, with an emphasis on singular sound.

The Ear Decides

I recorded another three runs of a tremolo, this time on the actual Walter and Erard replicas—soundboard, case, lid, and all—for a complete acoustical experience. The results came out exactly the same: a more or less regular Walter tremolo versus a regularly irregular one on the Erard. Instead of counting time frames on video, we easily reached this conclusion by playing the sound files at a speed four times slower than normal. But then, a new set of questions arose: was the particular inequality of the notes due to the heavier touch of the Erard and/or to a thumb moving more sluggishly than an agile third finger?

Back at the piano, I played several versions of the tremolo with different fingerings: 1–3 again (for reference), 1–2 (for more wrist rotation), and 2–4 (to replace 1 by a much stronger finger and 3 by a weaker one). The variations in fingering had no measurable effect. Note C consistently lasted longer. Along the way, though, something unforeseen happened. Hypothesizing that the insistent C had something to do with the perception of overtones, I started listening for the specific pitch of the major third E. The result was a tremolo where the weight shifted from a consistently long C to a consistently long E. Is there value, after all, to the proposition that the heavier touch of the Erard encourages a pairing of notes, weighted in whichever direction? But Prach noticed the subtle shift in my approach and reminded me to just concentrate on producing a *single, combined* continuous sound. Remarkably, after this reminder the long C reestablished itself—along with the initial question of why.

Only when sounds C and E mix is there a continuity of sound, to paraphrase Adam. But from an acoustical point of view, what exactly does it mean for those sounds to *mix*? Here we broke out a different toolbox. Spectral analysis would enable us to compare the frequency spectrum of a single tone on the Walter to one on the Erard.[13] For this experiment, Prach played a single c^1 (or middle C) on each of the pianos, striking it at medium loudness. Each pitch was recorded for its full duration. The respective power spectra appear in figure 7.3, top. (A power spectrum plots the average power level, usually in dB, of the complete frequency contents throughout the length of the played note.) The frequencies of the fundamental tone c^1, or 255.7 Hz in a tuning of $a^1 = 430$ Hz, as well as all its overtones, display as peaks. The first peaks show that the Walter has a much stronger fundamental frequency than the Erard. However, the first harmonic overtone on the Erard is almost as strong as the Walter fundamental, and considerably exceeds the power of subsequent overtones on both pianos. More important, it is higher than its own fundamental. The Walter shows a steadier decay in that its overtone peaks, each as distinct as the next, more or less descend in power as the frequency increases. One also observes that the Walter contains more power in the higher end of the spectrum, including more inharmonic frequencies, while the Erard piano's more focused emphasis on lower overtones contributes to a much stronger sense of purity and harmonicity among them, undiminished by the higher overtones, either harmonic or inharmonic.

Figure 7.3, bottom, zooms in on the decays over time of the fundamental frequency and the first harmonic overtone, respectively. We see clearly that the Walter's fundamental tone has a slower decay than the Erard's, but the general temporal pattern of the respective fundamentals (an impetus followed by a decay) is very similar. By contrast, the first harmonic overtones

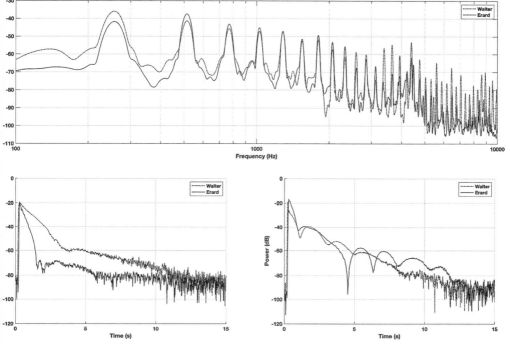

FIGURE 7.3 Power spectrum of c¹ (*top*); decay analysis of fundamental tone c¹ (*bottom*, *left*); decay analysis of first overtone c² (*bottom, right*).

for each piano behave quite differently. The Erard's first overtone (corresponding to c²) shows remarkable endurance, confirming its status as the dominant spectral component of the French sound. After an initial dip at the 4.5-second mark, it resurges spectacularly, and through a series of four rejuvenating waves ("wa-wa-wa-wa") ends up resounding for more than 12 seconds, all while maintaining a power level higher than the fundamental frequency's. "Continuity," then, seems embedded in the overtone of an Erard tone, and this shows most vividly in the seething waves of its decay: it is as if the instrument were spinning a fragile thread of sound, one wheel rotation after the other.

If a single Erard tone aspires to continuation, then an Erard tremolo goes a long way toward achieving it. This was definitely our expectation after evaluating our visual observations and aural impressions on the action model. Figure 7.4, top left, shows the power spectra of a tremolo on a Walter and on an Erard. An entire tremolo run is here represented as if it happened in a single moment. Larger levels of higher frequency energy present can be seen in the Walter tremolo. Harmonic overtones are partly responsible for this presence, but there appears also to be a great deal of inharmonic content—that is, frequency components that are not integer multiples of the fundamental frequencies of c^1 and e^1—including any friction noises of the piano action. Since every note in the Walter tremolo is accentuated by these percussive high frequencies, they emerge as an interrupted sequence of highly articulated sounds rather than as a single, blurred stream. The Erard has many fewer disruptive elements, and the lower presence of inharmonic content results in a more sustained listening experience. For an impression of continued sound to succeed, the fewer high-frequency inharmonic components there are, the better. Treble means trouble, and in this respect it is the Walter that loses out.

This brings us to a rather stunning observation. In the Walter tremolo (still fig. 7.4, top left), we see two strong fundamental frequencies positioning themselves closely side by side, which correspond to the pitches of c^1 (255.7 Hz) and e^1 (322.1 Hz): these are the "beats" that Adam does not want to hear. On the Erard, however, the most forceful sounds instead manifest themselves as a triad of peaks one octave higher. Together, these fundamental frequencies for c^2 (511.4 Hz), e^2 (644.2 Hz), and g^2 (767 Hz) dominate the overall spectrum. They represent the first harmonic overtone of c^1, the first harmonic overtone of e^1, and the second harmonic overtone of c^1, respectively. The strong presence of the same three frequencies can be clearly observed in the righthand image shown next to it (fig. 7.4, top right), which shows the spectrograms of the Walter and Erard tremolos, no longer as a single moment, but as they develop over time, the strength of their respective signals either augmenting, sustaining, or diminishing.[14] The horizontal axis shows time, and the vertical axis shows the frequency components in the signal. A lighter shade in our spectrogram signifies a higher level of energy, or a louder frequency component. On the left, the Walter sound exhibits the strong fundamental (around 250 Hz) that we have already indicated, as well as some almost-as-strong harmonics two octaves higher (around 1,000 Hz). Even though the harmonics at c^2, e^2, and g^2 are visible, they are less intense than their neighboring partials, both above and below. In the Erard spectrogram, however, the harmonics at c^2, e^2, and g^2 clearly stand out just above the 500 Hz mark. This pattern,

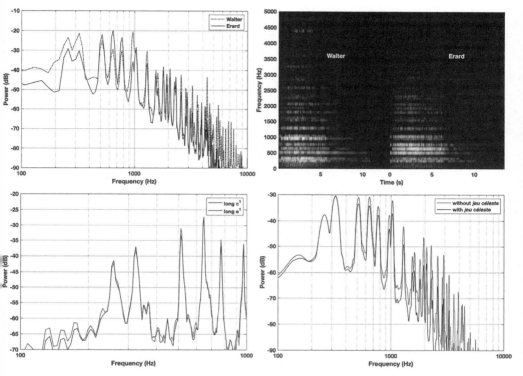

FIGURE 7.4 Spectral analysis of tremolo c^1/e^1 (*top, left*); time-dependent changes in frequency spectrum of tremolos (*top, right*); spectral analysis of a tremolo on Erard with longer c^1 versus longer e^1 (*down, left*); same with or without *jeu céleste* (*down, right*).

together with the weaker high frequencies in the Erard spectrum, allows the pure C-major triad to rise above everything else, creating a sonic halo that hovers one octave above the actual tremolo pitches. Our ears are thus directed away from the physicality of repeating notes to the higher spheres of the C-major triad.

If there is such a sonic halo to reach for, then can it also be made clearer? We are now able to solve the mystery of the longer c^1. Figure 7.4, bottom left, shows the power spectra of two versions of the tremolo as played on the Erard, the first with a longer c^1 and the second with a longer e^1. (These are the trials in which I was consciously focusing on the continuation of that higher pitch, to the expense of the combination of both.) The first and third peaks of the C-E-G triad are about three decibels stronger in the version with a longer c^1, which makes sense, since c^2 and g^2 are the first and second harmonic overtones of c^1. However, there is no significant increase for the middle peak E in the version with the longer e^1. When it comes to projecting the three-peaked overtone triad, therefore, the version with the longer c^1 wins out—even though *in both cases* the harmonic triad sticks out firmly above the weaker fundamentals. The tremolo, then, should be seen as a spun-out version of c^1 (with its C-major content) more than of e^1 (heaven forbid, with its own E-major content). The conclusion must be that from an acoustical point of view, sustaining C ever so slightly is a very good idea indeed, if one wishes to latch on to that higher sphered triad.

Finally, since the very nomenclature for Erard's third pedal makes the question relevant from an acoustic-cultural perspective, is there any further advantage in using *jeu céleste*? Adam holds that this particular stop is "only truly celestial when one adds the second to it,"[15] and by calling for the "two pedals in the middle together" in example 7.1, he explicitly links the association with the effect of a tremolo. Lured by that C-major triad, we have already redirected our senses to something higher than the actual tremolo notes. But, as we found out from our attempts with the Walter piano, we should not set our gaze too high into the stratosphere of dissonant harmonics. The power spectra in figure 7.4, bottom right, show how the *jeu céleste*, with its leather strips, further mellows the high-frequency inharmonic content in the Erard. Yet, even as it preserves the essential message of our C-major beacon triad, it somehow also imparts to it a purer—and, indeed, *truly* celestial—aura.

Like Adam, I also apparently find it hard not to invoke spiritual language in reference to the tremolo. But unlike Adam, who was writing the textbook for a national institution in a secularized, postrevolutionary France, I do not need to censor myself. A Christian version of the message would read: a divine Trinity of tones sits high—yet is firmly in reach—above a single foundational tone that seeks eternal life through *son continu*. Playing a tremolo becomes, if not a prayer, then a meditation of some sort—a practice requiring as much concentration as Tibetan throat-singing or playing the glass harmonica.

Spirituality aside, there was a true art to playing the tremolo. This art, furthermore, was distinctively French. To the German ear, *tremulando* may have been tiring, but the French could not get enough of it. But then Beethoven, always determinedly probing, developed an interest in the effect, despite his Germanic origins and training. This interest became so compelling that he sought to acquire a French piano, and, along with it, its *Tremendo* potential. His efforts to exploit this potential would show nowhere else as clearly as in the first movement of his Sonata, Op. 53 . . . in C Major. Several years later, Sébastien Erard would patent an instrument that was intended to achieve the impossible—a veritable automaton for *son continu*. One might be thankful, however, that this machine never came to be. It would have unmasked, if not made seem ridiculous, the magic of a human hand capable of drawing continuous sounds from a hammer-striking machine that essentially prescribes the contrary. In this artistic meeting of opposites, it is the ear that leads the pianist's fingers in unpredictable and *almost* inexplicable ways.

A Gift Not a Given

with Robin Blanton

To a business owner of today, bookkeeping may feel like a modern curse, but it is a far from recent invention. The ordinance *Pour le commerce* was enacted in France under Louis XIV in 1673: it required "tradesmen and merchants" to keep books that detailed their financial dealings on a daily basis. Two years later its main author, Jacques Savary, published *Le parfait négociant*, an impressive two-volume, one-thousand-page manual for merchants that was widely consulted and relied upon. Reissued in new editions in French throughout the eighteenth century, it was translated into multiple languages. Savary advocated keeping no fewer than *seven* separate books of account, some of which he said should use a double-entry system—a mathematical method of balancing debit and credit codified in 1494 by Fra Luca Pacioli, who is sometimes called "the father of accounting." But Savary himself allowed that his recommendations far exceeded the requirements of the law he had written, and he also described a simpler method using fewer books and adding such conveniences as a customer index at the rear of the sales register, for quick reference.[1] Later, one of Savary's sons, also named Jacques, in a kind of gloss on his father's ordinance, offered businessmen even more practical advice about how to comply with the legal requirements. In his 1723 *Dictionnaire universel de commerce*, we read, "Tradesmen and merchants both at wholesale and at retail shall have a *livre* which shall contain all their business." In such a *livre journal*, Savary's *Dictionnaire* continues,

One writes day by day all the transactions as rapidly as they occur. Each item that one enters should be composed of seven parts, which are the date, the debtor, the creditor, the sum, the quantity and kind [of goods], the *action* or how payable, and the price. Ordinarily this book is a register *in-folio* of five or six *mains* of paper [i.e., five or six times twenty-five pages = 125–50 pages], numbered, and ruled with one line on the side of the margin and with three on the other for extending the sums.[2]

The sales books (*livres de ventes*) of the Erard Frères firm were kept as required by law and are preserved for nearly every year of the firm's existence from 1790 on.[3] They consist of a series of bound volumes in journal form, listing sales of instruments in running chronological order, with some multiple sales to single customers gathered into single entries. While the sales books record credits and debits for each customer account, they are not a component of a larger double-entry system; there is, for example, no general ledger.

Turning to the alphabetical index at the back of the sales book for the years 1802–6, you will find a page with a tab stamped "B." On this page, the list of names spans two columns on the front and spills over onto the back. If you run your finger down the lefthand column on the front of the page, you will find, second from the bottom, the name "Beethowen [*sic*]" and the number 93.

Folio 93 of the sales book for 1802–6 is reproduced as plate 7, and transcribed and translated as table V3.1. (As in the original books, "folio" refers not to a single page but to a pair of facing pages.) Folio 93 has the same layout as every other numbered folio in the book, and indeed in nearly all of the sales books.[4] Highest up on each of the two facing pages is the stamped folio number, and the notation *F.° J.ᵃˡ* (for "journal folio") is written in the top left corner of each page. Each page is also headed with the year: "*An 11*" of the French republican calendar, corresponding to 1802–3. Finally, the lefthand side of this and every folio is headed "*Doit*," while the right-hand side is headed "*Avoir*"; these may be translated as "owed" and "received," or "debit" and "credit."

Below the header, the main part of every folio is ruled off into dated entries that span the entire width of the two pages. Folio 93 has four entries, each for a different customer, and each entry recording the sale of just one instrument. This was a typical scenario, but more complicated variations also appear: customers often bought multiple instruments. In such cases, the entries could be subdivided by date, creating a running account. Sometimes entire folios are dedicated to customers or dealers who purchased many instruments, tracking their accounts over a long period.

On every folio, the entries themselves follow a standard formula. They record the same elements of information for each sale, in the same order and using the same wording. Each entry has a *doit* side and an *avoir* side, with a wide column for text and several narrower columns for numbers on each side.

Doit

The *doit* side of the folio records the details of each sale and the total to be paid. Each entry begins with the date, set in the middle of the text column. After the date comes the customer's name. Customers are identified by honorific (Monsieur, Madame, or Mademoiselle; between 1797 and 1802 Citoyen and Citoyennne also appear), and a surname written in large, bold letters. The country and/or city of residence may follow; occasionally a street address is also given. Sometimes, too, an occupation is noted, especially for musicians. Thus, on folio 93, the first entry is for a "*Mme Roulet née Mezerac à Neuchatel en Suisse*"; the second identifies Beethoven as "*Mr Bethowen* [sic] *Claviciniste* [sic] *à Vienne.*"

Next comes a formal statement of exchange and price. The same stock phrase is used in every entry: "*D^t £ . . . p^r Vte de* [owes £ . . . for the sale of]." The goods being sold are then specified. Standardized model names are used. On folio 93, for instance, we see that Mme. Roulet and the third customer, M. Mayer Marx, each bought a "*piano à 3 Cordes à L'ut*" (a triple-strung square piano with a compass reaching to C, that is, 5 ½ octaves). The fourth customer on the folio, Mr. Solere [sic], bought a "*piano à 2 Cordes à L'ut*," or a bichord 5 ½-octave square. Beethoven's piano, as we know, was a "*piano en forme de clavecin,*" or grand piano. The serial numbers of the instruments sold are noted in every entry, on this folio and unfailingly throughout the sales books. Instruments with special decoration are described as "*orné,*" sometimes with additional detail. The piano purchased by Mr. Mayer Marx, for example, had "legs surmounted with Zephyr

TABLE V3.1 Folio 93 from the Erard Frères 1802–6 sales book, transcribed and translated

93

F.°J.ᵃˡ

An 11. _____ 16 Therm.ᵈᵒʳ 11. _____	Doit		
M.ᵐᵉ **Roulet née Mezerac** à Neuchatel en Suisse D.ᵗ £ 1200. pʳ V.ᵗᵉ du piano à 3 Cordes à L'ut N.° 5512.	1200.	,	,
_____ 18 Therm.ᵈᵒʳ 11 _____ M.ʳ **Bethowen** Claviciniste [*sic*] à Vienne D.ᵗ £ 1500 pʳ V.ᵗᵉ du piano en forme de Clavecin N.° 133..............	1500.	,	,
_____ 23 Therm.ᵈᵒʳ 11 _____ M.ʳ **Mayer Marx** D.ᵗ £ 2000. pʳ V.ᵗᵉ du piano à 3 Cordes à L'ut N.° 5524. orné, les pieds Surmontés en Têtes de Zephir.................................. par M.ʳ Lemoine	2000.	,	,
_____ 24 Therm.ᵈᵒʳ 11. _____ M.ʳ **Solere** D.ᵗ £ 912 pʳ V.ᵗᵉ du piano à 2 Cordes à L'ut N.° 5607. par Von Esch L'ainé..............	912	,	,

heads." Zephyr was the god of the west wind; one imagines ornamental heads on the front legs of the piano, facing candleholders incorporated into the decoration.

After the stock description of the sale, the name of the agent or intermediary of sale, where applicable, was recorded, prefaced by the word *par* (via). Thus we see that M. Mayer Marx purchased his piano "via M.ʳ Lemoine," and M. Solere his "via Von Esch the Elder." No intermediary agent is noted for Mme. Roulet, or for Beethoven.

The final element of each entry on the *doit* side is the total amount of the sale, usually given in livres. This figure is entered in the column immediately to the right of the text column. On folio 93, each of the four entries

93

F°J.ᵃˡ

An 11._____ 18 Therm.ᵈᵒʳ 11. _____	Avoir		
Avoir £ 1200. par les mains du M.ʳ			
Scherer ci	1200.	,	,
_____ _____			
	𝜂[ul]		
_____ 23 Therm.ᵈᵒʳ 11 _____			
Avoir £ 2000.			
Especes [*recte*: espèces]............1300.			
Piano de Retour N.° 4181 à 3 Cordes au fa ..700.	2000.	,	,
_____ 24 Therm.ᵈᵒʳ 11. _____			
Avoir £ 528. par Retour du piano			
à 2 pedales N.° 5611.........................528.			
_____17 floréal 13._____			
Avoir £ 384. Especes			
p[our] Solde Ci........ 384	912.	,	,

involves just one instrument, and so the total amount in each case simply
equals the price already given for that instrument. On other folios, when
an entry includes multiple instruments, their separate prices are totaled up
in this column.

Avoir

The *avoir* side of the folio holds information about payment. Perhaps the
simplest case on folio 93 is that of Mme. Roulet, who paid for her piano
in full almost immediately. The payment date is recorded as August 6,
1803, which is just two days after the sale date, and the text column notes

TABLE V3.1 *Continued*

93

Journal Folio

1802–3 _____ 4 August 1803 _____	Debit		
Mrs. **Roulet born Mezerac** in Neuchâtel, Switzerland, owes £1200 for sale of piano with 3 strings up to C no. 5512.	1200	,	,
_____ 6 August 1803 _____ Mr. **Bethowen** harpsichordist in Vienna owes £1500 for sale of *piano en forme de clavecin* no. 133	1500	,	,
_____ 11 August 1803 _____ Mr. **Mayer Marx** owes £2000 for sale of piano with 3 strings up to C no. 5524. ornamented, legs surmounted with Zephyr heads. . . . . via Mr. Lemoine	2000	,	,
_____ 12 August 1803 _____ Mr. **Solere** owes £912 for sale of piano with 2 strings up to C no. 5607. via Von Esch the Elder.	912	,	,

a payment of £1,200, which is the exact purchase price. The payment was received "via the hands" of a third party, Mr. Scherer. The figure of £1,200 is transferred over to the adjoining number column, where a quick comparison with the *doit* page confirms that the total paid matches the total owed.

Customers sometimes traded in an old piano for credit toward a new one. Typically, the trade-in piano was also by Erard Frères, in which case the entry notes the model and serial number of the trade-in, as well as its value. M. Mayer Marx, for instance, traded in a 5-octave trichord square ("*à 3 Cordes au fa*") by Erard Frères, serial no. 4181, in partial payment for his new 5 ½-octave instrument, and made up the difference in cash. Like Mme. Roulet, he discharged his full debt right away: both the credit and the cash payment are recorded on August 11 ("*23 Therm.*^dor"), which was also

93

Journal Folio

	Credit		
1802–3 _____ 6 August 1803 _____			
Received £1200 through the hands of			
Mr. Scherer..	1200	,	,
_____ _____			
	N[ul]		
_____ 11 August 1803 _____			
Received £2,000			
Cash..1300			
Returned piano no. 4181 with 3 strings up to F....700	2000	,	,
_____ 12 August 1803 _____			
Received £528 by return of piano			
with 2 pedals no. 5611.............................528			
_____ 7 May 1805 _____			
Received £384. Cash			
for outstanding balance......384	912	,	,

the sale date. The two values are summed (indicated by a bracket) in the number column, and again, a quick glance back at the *doit* side of the entry confirms the match: payment in full.

Some customers, however, took much longer to pay. Mr. Solere is an example. He was credited £528 for the return of his two-pedal square on August 12, 1803, the same day he bought his new piano, but he did not pay the remainder of the balance due until nearly two years later, on May 7, 1805, when the receipt of "£384. Cash for outstanding balance" was noted. In this case, each time a payment was received, the figure was carried over to the number column, and the two payments are totaled there.

A fourth scenario, unique on this folio, occurs in the case of Mr. Bethowen. For him, almost nothing is recorded on the *avoir* page. The text column is completely empty, and the number column holds no numbers: nothing but a swooping flourish of the pen. Is it an initial or an abbreviation? What does it signify?

The *Nul* Hypothesis

The swooping symbol in the Beethoven entry is an outlier on folio 93, but it is not unique and in fact not even that uncommon in the sales books as a whole. In fact, it appears some thirty times in the 1802–6 volume, and frequently in the volumes before and after it as well. Sometimes, as in Beethoven's entry, it appears when the *avoir* column is otherwise empty, seemingly in lieu of any payment at all. Sometimes, it is penned below one or more recorded partial payments. Undoubtedly it signals the clearing or cancellation of an outstanding balance.

Recall that although the sales books do employ debit and credit columns, they were not part of a double-entry system as such, as there is no indication that the debits and credits in the customer accounts were offset by entries in other accounts (cash, goods, and so forth). The books may not have been balanced annually, and they were probably never intended to convey a picture of overall profits and losses. More likely, their main purpose was simply to keep track of credit relationships with individual customers on an ongoing basis.[5] At a glance, the books made it possible to identify how much credit the business had extended to any given customer over time, how much of the money owed had been received, and the amount of the outstanding balance. Perhaps the books were also an aid in tracking the overall credit extended by the business at any one time, as credit, like cash, was a business asset that extended the firm's overall purchasing power.[6]

Whether the symbol is an initial that stands for a specific word, or some other form of abbreviation, is difficult to say. It may, perhaps, be an elaborate N, standing for *"nul"* (void) (our thanks to Pierre Gervais for advancing this suggestion).[7] Its function, however, appears unambiguous. By all appearances, it was used to discharge a debt and reconcile a credit relationship: to say that a customer no longer owed, or perhaps had never been considered to owe, any money.

A Gift? . . . Not a Given

The idea that Beethoven received his Erard piano as a gift has been the subject of much recent debate. As already discussed, the diplomat Griesinger, writing to publisher Härtel in Leipzig on December 14, 1803, specifically said the piano was a present: he wrote that the Erard brothers had "made a gift" of a piano to Beethoven, "as they did earlier to Haydn."[8] The Erard firm itself affirmed Griesinger's claim in 1875.[9] More recently, however, the gift claim has undergone a reevaluation. When Rose–van Epenhuysen in 2005 first drew attention to the Beethoven entry in the sales book (previously unknown), she suggested its existence implied that Beethoven must in fact have ordered the piano from Erard Frères, and simply never paid for it. By way of contrast, the piano given to Haydn, although listed in the Erard Frères register of manufacture, never passed through the sales books.

If we accept the "*Nul* hypothesis" for the meaning of the swooping sales book symbol, then it seems likely that neither Beethoven nor anyone else ever paid Erard Frères for his piano. But whether the Erards intended it that way from the beginning or not may never be entirely clear. Possibly they initially expected to be paid, and later cancelled the debt. What seems most likely, however is that they did indeed intend the piano as a gift, but the gift, in contrast to the picture handed down by traditional scholarship,[10] was a *solicited* one. Beethoven's letter to Zmeskall of November 1802 (see vignette 1) is too explicit to ignore. In other words, we should probably imagine that Beethoven did place an order for an Erard piano, either directly or through an intermediary, and the idea of a business gift materialized along the way, perhaps instigated or reinforced by someone like Louis Adam— who may furthermore have been kind enough to select a specific instrument from the Erard showroom to send to this eminent foreign *claveciniste*.

If something like this scenario occurred, it would have made Beethoven a member of a rather large company. The list of customers who received Erard instruments for which they paid only in part or not at all is quite long, and includes a number of high-profile keyboardists. Here are a few examples, selected for their relevance.

In the 1799–1802 sales book, an entry dated October 26, 1801, is for a square piano valued at 384 livres for one "M Herold." The *avoir* side is completely blank: no payment is recorded, but neither is there any swooping flourish like the one in the Beethoven entry. This must be the Alsatian-born François-Joseph Herold (1755–1802), a pianist-composer who had studied with C. P. E. Bach in Hamburg before coming to Paris, "sometime between 1780 and 1784." On arrival in Paris, Herold struck up an intense friendship with Louis Adam, who became the godfather of Herold's son Ferdinand. Ferdinand would grow up to win first prize in Adam's class at the Conservatoire, but at the time of the sales book entry, the eleven-year old had just entered the prestigious Hix boarding school at the Champs-Elysées, where Adam also used to teach and where Ferdinand would befriend Pierre Erard, son of Jean-Baptiste. The Herold, Erard, and Adam families were close, and their sons Ferdinand, Pierre, and Adolphe seemed destined to become significant musical figures themselves. Almost certainly, the gift of a piano was to mark an important moment in Ferdinand's education.[11]

In the same volume, an entry dated July 14, 1802, is for a six-octave *piano en forme de clavecin* valued at 1,200 livres that went to "Mme De Montgeroult." Once again, the *avoir* side of the entry is blank, with no N-shaped flourish like the one in the Beethoven entry. What is interesting here is that Hélène de Montgeroult (1764–1836) received a rare six-octave grand piano, her profile as a progressive musician making her deserving of the latest update. (De Montgeroult will make her appearance in chapter 9 as the younger, brilliant, and female colleague of Louis Adam.)

In the 1802–6 sales book is an entry on December 20, 1804, for a square piano that went to "Mr Kalckbrenner," valued at 1,200 livres but discounted to 1,008 livres. The *avoir* side contains an N-shaped flourish like the one in the Beethoven entry. This must be upon the young Frédéric Kalkbrenner's return to Paris after his concerts and studies in Vienna and Germany. He re-enrolled at the Conservatoire as a composition student in January 1805.[12]

In the 1806–9 sales book is an entry dated September 7, 1808, for a grand piano that went to "Mr Steibelt," along with another entry dated March 18, 1809, for a harp that went to his wife. On the *doit* side, a note next to the piano says "*Donné* [given]," and no price is listed. On the *avoir* side we find another N-shaped flourish.

Finally there is the case of Józef Elsner. In the 1806–9 sales book is an entry dated October 28, 1806, recording the transfer of a grand piano valued at 3,500 livres, to "Mr Elsner à Varsovie." On the *avoir* side of the entry, once again, we find no record of monetary payment but instead the now familiar N-shaped flourish. As we know from vignette 2, Erard Frères had offered a grand piano to Elsner, when he visited their establishment in Paris, "as a trial"—"so long as I would be kind enough to receive it on consignment," as Elsner later recorded in his memoirs. Interestingly enough, in Elsner's report it is not quite clear whether or not the Music Society actually sent money for the piano. It seems that it was their intent to do so as of 1806, but Elsner also says it was resolved that he would wait to "retrieve" the money owed until 1807, after which time we have no further report.

To sum up, we may never know the precise circumstances under which Beethoven acquired his Erard. On the one hand, it seems quite likely that he sought it out deliberately: as much is suggested by the letter to Zmeskall and by the fact that the order appears in the sales books at all, unlike in the case of Haydn, who we know placed no order. On the other, it appears quite probable that the Erards did indeed "make a gift" of the piano to Beethoven, although in a rather matter-of-fact way, as part of their normal business practice.

CHAPTER EIGHT

The Vertical/ Horizontal Paradox

"Beethoven wanted an Erard piano so he could write his 'Waldstein' Sonata." Since we tend to think through the prism of finished works, this way of reasoning has been more common than we realize. We're interested, after all, in Beethoven's Erard piano precisely because something like "Waldstein" exists. But surely, the wanting can apply to the piano only. Beethoven could not possibly have known he would write a "Waldstein" until he had his Erard piano. As I've argued so far in this book, especially when it comes to Beethoven's artistic responses to a piano as unique as his Erard, we must put materiality first. Might not Beethoven's thinking have run more along these lines: "I want a piano just like Haydn's; I don't quite yet know what I'll do with it, but I look forward to being inspired by it."

Over the past few years, as I rediscovered Beethoven's "Waldstein" Sonata through the materiality of our newly built Beethoven-Erard, I've been associating the repeated C-major chords of its opening (fig. 8.1) with Beethoven enjoying the feel of his new piano not once, but over and over again, through the sensation of playing a single chord. A four-voice chord is spread out over two hands and has its major third on top; not just any third, but the mother of thirds: C–E, as the purest in almost any historical well-tempered tuning. My hands, fingers, and joints bounce up and down as the key levers under them rock back and forth at the exact same pace and in what feels like perfect synchronicity. Among the team, we started referring to those repetitive chords as the pianistic equivalent of a "basketball dribble," and that's exactly how I started to feel: like a basketball player, whose body rehearses that off-and-on contact with the ball over and over, both on and off the court. The sheer physicality of playing these selected keys never fails to exhilarate me, and the feeling is reinforced when I push down the *una corda* pedal in response to Beethoven's *pianissimo*—making me revel, with Beethoven, in a one-string register of the sort I've never experienced before. Reduction in volume, coupled with an increased purity of sound (because playing on only one string decreases the likelihood of disturbing unisons), allows me to hear even more with my hands than with my ears, making the experience more visceral still. To summarize, I embrace those opening chords from "Waldstein" and never tire of playing them, celebrating a physical connection with the new keyboard in my life, just as Beethoven wrote them originally to celebrate his.

But how literal can this connection be? Does my subjective experience count as evidence for something that Beethoven might also have felt about those opening chords? What place does pianistic inspiration have in our assessment of a long since composed work? Finally, how much of this matters, in terms of increasing our understanding of what we now know as the "Waldstein" Sonata?

Let's start by examining Beethoven's sketches. The official sketches occupy twenty-five uninterrupted pages of the so-called "Eroica" Sketchbook, also known as Landsberg 6, and can be dated roughly between December 1803 and early January 1804. In addition to these, Barry Cooper has identified many loose ideas that are all relatable in one way or another to "Waldstein." These "preliminary sketches" are spread out over no fewer than ten additional pages that all precede the noninterrupted batch of official "Waldstein" sketches. Their existence allows Cooper to conclude that Beethoven's "delight in receiving a wonderful new piano may well have prompted him to make an almost immediate start, however tentative, on a grand new sonata in C major."[1] The "earliest definite sign of an embryonic piano sonata in C" he identifies is shown in example 8.1, top, and if true, this is evidence that Beethoven thought of "Waldstein" almost immediately after the piano arrived, that is, after completing his "Eroica" Symphony (the sketches on the pages before) and while awaiting the text of the

FIGURE 8.1 Beethoven, Sonata in C Major, Op. 53, first movement, mm. 1–42. First edition (Vienna: Bureau des arts et d'industrie, 1805), with annotations.

EXAMPLE 8.1 Beethoven, sketch, Landsberg 6, p. 97, st. 7–8.

projected opera *Vestas Feuer* (the sketches on the pages after).[2] Naturally I was thrilled to recognize the same C-major triad through which I took delight in experiencing my new piano. That Beethoven also made it the main event of the finished version (spreading the bouncing over both hands) strengthens our bond created by our identical instruments. Also Cooper seems excited: "The similarities to the start of the 'Waldstein' Sonata are conspicuous, and include the key and time, the low register, the repeated quavers, and the prompt return of the initial figure in a foreign key—here A major and in the sonata B♭ major."[3]

My alliance with Cooper, however, is temporary: he stops short of acknowledging any direct link between "Waldstein" and the Erard piano per se. Instead, Cooper emphasizes Beethoven's initial resistance to use any notes above the five-octave range of the standard Viennese piano, to suggest that Beethoven's pianistic ambitions were elsewhere—that is, *not* with his new French piano. Beethoven does end up going over f^3 as the highest note of a five-octave range, but "only," as Cooper points out, during "stage VII" of the sketching process—implying that the expanded range had remained off his radar during stages I through VI. And even then, from stage VII onward, he only goes up to a^3, which is not quite the highest key of his 5 ½-octave Erard. Taking into account that 5 ½- octave pianos were still a rare commodity in Vienna, however, this kind of argument leaves Beethoven no place to go: he's damned if he does exceed the normal range of a piano (if he was counting on having any customers), and he's damned if he doesn't (for the present-day scholar looking for evidence of an Erard). In fact, the argument might go the other way: yes, for marketing reasons, Beethoven initially tried to adhere to the conventional five-octave range, but the temptation to expand on it proved too great, leading to a compromise range of FF–a³, not quite up to the highest note c⁴. Op. 54 would again conform to the conventional five octaves, FF–f³, while in "Appassionata," Op. 57, Beethoven would go all the way, FF–c⁴.

More important, Cooper points out that Beethoven didn't "attempt to exploit the Erard's extra pedals or its distinctive sound through a dramatic change of style." But this begs the question of where to look: solely in the score, or the score in combination with the instrument whose relevance we are seeking to understand. That Cooper essentially takes the instrument out of the equation is confirmed by the following conclusion:

> One can surmise, then, that it was the quality of the piano, rather than its extended compass or other characteristics, that inspired him to compose a new sonata. To do so was actually in direct contradiction to his view expressed through his brother Carl only a year earlier [in a letter of November 23, 1802], that he no longer bothered much with such trifles as piano sonatas, as he preferred to write just operas and oratorios. Thus the new piano evidently had a major impact on him at that time, and without it the "Waldstein" might not have been written when it was.

"The new piano," in other words, affects the when, but not the how. The Erard was of such quality that it restored Beethoven's faith in "the piano" and rekindled his interest in the genre of the piano sonata. Beethoven may have "acquired" the piano (the term is Cooper's), but Cooper does not acknowledge or dwell on any desire on Beethoven's part to own a French piano, his focus remaining on a timeline of works rather than of instruments.[4]

With "Waldstein," Donald Tovey in 1931 also famously saw Beethoven "crossing the Rubicon." The point of no return that Tovey had in mind is the one leading to Beethoven's heroic or middle period, and "Waldstein" constitutes for Tovey "the first act after long hesitation in hopes of compromise with the old regime."[5] Stylistic overviews of Beethoven's piano sonatas since Tovey have tended to assume that for Beethoven there was just one such Rubicon moment. But what if there were other metaphorical rivers to be crossed? What if Beethoven had resisted the temptation to buy a French piano, or what if that Frenchman hadn't shown up at the luncheon in November 1802? What if Anton Walter and Beethoven had put their heads together, and this meeting had resulted in the design of a new kind of Viennese piano? What if Beethoven had ordered an English piano by Clementi & Co. or one by John Broadwood & Son instead? Would we still have had a "Waldstein"?

I here propose something drastically different. I have in mind a double perspective that, on the one hand, looks at Beethoven's Erard not as merely capable of having "an impact," but as the very space in which creation happens; and, on the other, acknowledges object-oriented experimentation as actual compositional content, which in its turn cannot be separated from performative realization. Through "Waldstein" we witness Beethoven familiarizing himself with his new instrument, and those very first printed notes of a new sonata—or the very last ones, for that matter—encapsulate a relationship just as strikingly fresh, unpredictable, and alive as any preliminary sketch.

As a first step, I suggest banning the name by which the world knows Op. 53. So far in this chapter I have used the name "Waldstein" sixteen times—seventeen if we include the reference to the person on the following title page: *Grande sonate pour le Pianoforte, composée et dédiée à Monsieur le Comte de Waldstein, Commandeur de l'ordre Teutonique à Virnsberg et Chambellan de Sa Majesté I. & I. R. A.* We're reading from the first edition by the Vienna Bureau des arts et d'industrie, which was announced on May 15, 1805. Typically, an author on Op. 53 at this point recalls Count von Waldstein's generosity to the young Beethoven, explaining the dedication as Beethoven's long overdue "proof of gratitude."[6] But this association with the man who sent Beethoven off from Bonn to Vienna with the prophetic words, "You will receive Mozart's spirit through Haydn's hands," should not obliterate the outspokenly French *raison d'être* of Op. 53.

Instead, I propose to think of Op. 53 as the *grande sonate* that Beethoven should have dedicated to Jean-Louis (Johann Ludwig) Adam. We know from Ferdinand Ries, writing on the topic of the "Kreutzer" Sonata, Op. 47, to the publisher Simrock in Bonn on October 22, 1803, that "it will probably be dedicated to Adam and Kreutzer as the premier violinist and pianist in Paris, because Beethoven owes Adam a courtesy on account of the Paris piano, about which you can learn more from my father, to whom I wrote about all this."[7] We can no longer ask Ferdinand's father Franz, but

I hope to make clear that Beethoven owed Adam on account of much more than just the brokering of a Paris piano. If not in dedication, then certainly by acknowledgment and indebtedness, Op. 53 ought to be known as the "Adam" Sonata—with the name Adam standing for much more than the personality of the man himself.

Addressing some of the strongest entanglements in Beethoven's life after receiving his Erard, I formulate the following hypotheses, each revealing a specific dependence, either on the new thing (the Erard) or on humans (Beethoven's peers). As Op. 53 celebrates a fresh relationship, there are dependences only (i.e., those that Ian Hodder defines as positive affordances), and not yet dependencies (i.e., limiting or constraining relationships):[8]

With his "Adam" Sonata, Beethoven wrote a piece that

with respect to his Erard:
- Both continues and reflects his studies of a new finger technique, turning the questions and solutions into the fabric of a multimovement piece
- Explores and shows off all the piano's pedals, both in and of themselves, and in all possible combinations
- Investigates with uncanny sensitivity to detail the acoustical characteristics of his Erard
- In short, reveals a proud new owner-composer who is demonstrating "what works" on his French piano

and with respect to his fellow humans:
- Beats his old rival Daniel Steibelt on his own turf, *tremulandi*, pedal effects, and all
- Ticks many boxes from Louis Adam's textbook on playing the piano, the soon-to-be standard of French pianism
- Is at least as *grand* as the grandest French *grande sonate*—a genre that both Steibelt and Adam actively pursued
- In the hands of a gifted pupil such as Kalkbrenner would be certain to win the yearly *concours* at such a prestigious institution as the Paris Conservatoire de musique
- In short, *is deserving of a place in the Paris Conservatoire library of musical scores*

A Pianistic Exercise

Plate 8 reproduces page 107 from Landsberg 6. On the top eight staves we see a series of scales—or at least the beginnings of them: Beethoven writes out in full only the first, but the others can easily be filled out. Written in dark ink, they stand out from the pale-inked sketches that surround them. Their entry may be dated with remarkable accuracy between October 22 and November 2, 1803 (the former date applying to the letter by Ries and the latter to a letter in which Beethoven announces having started work on *Vestas Feuer*).[9] Experts agree that Beethoven must have written the scales at the same time as the sketch shown in example 8.1, which appeared ten pages before, on page 97 of the sketchbook.

So, after jotting down an embryonic idea for a new piano sonata, what made Beethoven skip multiple pages to write down a bunch of scales—in the simplest of keys? The timing is too intriguing to leave unexplored: is there a connection?

Let's start by imagining the physical reality of a prebound sketchbook.[10] One sheet of paper is folded in half to make a bifolium of two leaves, or four pages. Four of them are stacked and sewn together to create a gathering. Twelve gatherings are bound together to make an oblong book. By these calculations, Landsberg 6 should have consisted of 192 pages: 12 × 4 × 4. Five leaves, all from the first gathering, however, are missing. Beethoven must have ripped them out for use elsewhere. This leaves a total of 182 numbered pages.

Our page 107 is the first *recto* side of a bifolium. This bifolium is the second of four (counting inside out). It belongs to the eighth gathering. This means that this page appears well past the center point of the volume.[11] I enter into this kind of detail because, as I placed the facsimile of the sketchbook on my Erard music stand, something hit me: the act of flipping the pages may have been casual, but settling on that particular page was not. Looking for an empty page, Beethoven settled on one that not only allowed him to write easily while seated at his Erard (holding his quill in his right hand), but that also stays relatively flat on a piano desk at a 70-degree angle. This suggests that Beethoven wrote these scales not just as a memento for composition, but *for repeated use at the piano*. Why?

Transcribed to modern-day notation (as in ex. 8.2), they look like your routine, Hanon-type exercise. Two hands, one tenth apart. Play the scales first in parallel motion, from bottom to top, and from top to bottom; then in contrary motion, outside in, and inside out. Simple. For Beethoven, however, still at the dawn of modern pianism, it must have been anything but. Just a few years earlier (in the winter of 1799–1800), he had still insisted that the ten-year-old Carl Czerny buy a copy of C. P. E. Bach's *Essay on the True Art of Playing the Keyboard*, the third, slightly enlarged edition of which had appeared the year before Bach's death in 1787. Only in 1826 do we find him providing another boy, Gerhard von Breuning, age thirteen, with a copy of *Clementi's vollständige Klavier-Schule*, a translation of Muzio Clementi's popular method, *Introduction to the Art of Playing on the Piano-forte*, published in Vienna by Mollo in 1807.[12]

Thus, even if it was old-fashioned by 1803, we may still look at Bach's illustration of a C-major scale by way of reference (ex. 8.2, bottom). At stake for Bach was the issue of fingering—and this must be true for Beethoven as well. Bach gives no fewer than three options: two of these feature what we now like to call the new fingering, with the thumb passing under the third finger, while the third option recalls the old fingering, with strong finger 3 on a good note crossing over weak finger 4 on a bad note, creating paired and *inégal* articulations and avoiding the thumb altogether. Bach then gives examples that combine the new principle of passing under the thumb with the old principle of shifting one's hand—the latter ideally happening on good parts of the beat. Still, for an entire generation of keyboardists, including Bach himself, the new thumb technique would have been hard to dissociate from the old one of shifting one's hand from one position to the next—so why not combine both? This is why we find examples like the first and fourth in Bach's figure II: the thumb is used, yes, but on a good part of the beat, where shifting the hand results in the kind of emphasis that can be positive and exhilarating. Conversely, for similar reasons of articulatory elegance, as in the third example of Bach's figure II, old fingering keeps its usefulness—especially on relatively light keyboards with relatively low key dips, like the Walter fortepiano that the auditioning Czerny had encountered at Beethoven's. This is the kind of teaching—among others, through Christian Gottlob Neefe in Bonn—that the young Beethoven would have been subjected to.

But in Beethoven's 1803 exercise, there's no escape: the thumb *must* be used also on the bad parts of the beat. New fingering supplants old. I found fingering advice in Louis Adam's exercise No. 48, from his 1804–5 *Méthode*, reproduced here as figure 8.2. Going up the scale in the first bar, my Viennese-trained right hand still finds comfort in two groups of four notes, each to be fingered 1, 2, 3, and 4. Also the descent in the same bar feels safe: I can gently turn my wrist as I play a full hand down (5, 4, 3, 2, 1). In this slanted position, three extra notes (4, 3, 2) may be tagged on, before decisively straightening my hand again, ready to take on the next scalar pattern, one piano key higher. I think of these three notes as an upbeat of some sort, helping me connect the one scale to the next. But when the pattern descends in m. 5, the problems start. The descending scale in m. 5, again, feels natural enough, but when going up in the same bar, I feel jerked out of my comfort zone, forced to give up my habit—or worse, my instinct—of using my thumb on a good note: Adam's priority is with the top note B, which he wants to see played with the fifth finger, forcing the thumb to move into action one note earlier than expected. Four-note articulations (like those in the fourth example of Bach's figure II) or pleasant slanted-wrist positions yield to more erratic combinations of fingers, where I must count on an agile thumb and an alert mind to carry me through. Anything just said about the right hand holds for the left, but in the opposite direction—and it is in this methodical order, swapping right for left, that Adam makes the pupil master the difficulties.

But Beethoven ups the ante. He *combines* the hands no fewer than four times, in each possible direction. His scales become a pianist's version of a Rubik's Cube, where for each hand, the one and only possible fingering must be found, while one's brain is forced to think right and left at the same time. It is meaningful that, in contrast to Adam's, Beethoven's exercise is *not* fingered, nor is every run written out in full. The solutions are not to be read off a fingered textbook exercise: instead, the puzzle is Beethoven's to solve, live *at his new Erard*, looking down at his hands. Contrary to what he would have been accustomed to on a Walter fortepiano, there's no comfort in recognizing groups of 2, 3, 4, or 5 notes and shaping them accordingly. The larger key dip and altogether heavier keyboard necessitate a new technique—one where individual finger strikes need sufficient strength to make each key speak. Instead of 14 groups of notes (counting

EXAMPLE 8.2 Beethoven, scale exercise, Landsberg 6, p. 107, st. 1–10, completed and with added fingering (*top*); C. P. E. Bach, C-major examples (1787, Tabula I) (*bottom*).

the hand positions necessary for the right hand to get through the first line), two hands together produce 114 individual key strikes. And that's the first run only. When played as a single exercise, the four runs together produce 456 key strikes.

When I focus on making each of my fingers behave independently, another type of grouping starts to foreground itself. Every ninth note in each hand coincides with a new tenth (or third), to be played by either one's thumb or little finger, not to emphasize any "good" note but simply to mark a turn in direction. These tenths (circled in ex. 8.2) reveal an *Ur*-version of the scale. Appearing at regular intervals and undisturbed by any internal shaping along the way, they're easy to follow. Step by step, they create a

Exercices et Exemples de Gammes ou il est nécessaire de s'écarter des principes établis pour le doigter des Gammes.

FIGURE 8.2 Exercise No. 48, from Adam (1804–5), 29.

hypermeter of some sort. (At the end of the first run, Beethoven replaces the tenth C/E by a more conclusive octave C/C: the significance of this contrapuntal reflex will be discussed below.)

I dare say that taking time out on an empty sketchbook page was about more than sharpening his technique. Beethoven appears to be studying a new aesthetics altogether—one in which equality of sound (those equal finger strikes) creates hierarchies of a different order than anything that typically happens on a Viennese piano. While his Walter would have allowed him to spontaneously shape passagework, his Erard has the potential of imbuing passagework with the simplest of melodies that are also deeper and on a larger scale. Beethoven's exercise, while almost identical to Adam's, outdoes his colleague's on two levels: first, he increases difficulty by fusing right and left hand, and then, by having them move in parallel tenths, he creates melodic-harmonic opportunity. This insight revealed itself only after focused practicing, during which I had to give up some deeply ingrained Viennese expectations. Along with Beethoven, I discovered a new kind of virtuosity—more mechanical, yes, but ultimately more serene than anything I had heard or felt on a Viennese piano.

Vertical vs. Horizontal

Let's now go back to figure 8.1 and resume our basketball pattern, which (the pianistic exercise firmly in our ears) features the third E on top. In m. 4 the right hand breaks out from this rhythmic activity to play the simplest of five-note figures: 5, 4, 3, 2, 1, slurred together. These numbers refer to fingers, but they may just as well apply to scale degrees, in the dominant harmony of G. Viennese instinct makes me focus on gesture rather than on individual notes. Turning my wrist sideways in the direction of the lowest key, I aim to just caress the keys along the way. This is the language of the slur that German-Austrian musicians knew and applied so well, and that both Beethoven and I have also taken for granted. Playing the five-note figure on a Walter instrument, I never fail to make that last note G sound exquisitely soft, yet audibly present and crisp. Imagine a lively glissando off D, softly landing on G. In this Viennese context, Beethoven's addition of an invariably short appoggiatura on the high note seems bizarrely superfluous. "Make me count," the high note cries out—as if I wouldn't have done exactly that.

Beethoven and I share this kind of self-consciousness on a foreign instrument. A simple five-note caressing gesture, which has served us well through many years of playing Viennese instruments, simply *does not work* on the French keyboard. It may result in beautiful optics: in figure 8.3 (left), the photo, extracted from a slow-motion video, shows adjacent fingers pressing multiple keys of the action model at different moments of descent or ascent. But by the fourth key (the lowest on the model action), I realize that there's little power left for my thumb, which is why that lowest key almost always fails to send the hammer all the way up the strings. (By comparison, the risk of not playing the last note is practically nonexistent on a Walter fortepiano.)

It may be useful to recall Adam's words on finger strikes (table 3.1):

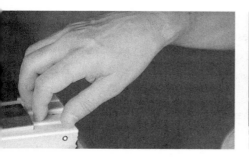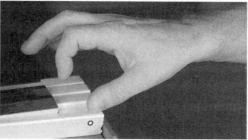

FIGURE 8.3 Playing the slur (*left*) vs. playing the *staccato* (*right*).

When placing the right hand [...] in order to strike the five notes: *ut,*
re, mi, fa, and *sol* successively [...] it is necessary that all the fingers are
placed at the same time on the surface of the keys that one will have to
make sound, so that they are ready *to strike* [*toucher*]; then one will lift
the fingers a little above the keyboard [...] and one will make them fall
perpendicularly and successively [*perpendiculairement et successivement*]
on the indicated keys. (Original emphasis)

We've explained *perpendicular* before: the Erard hoppers need that downward determination from the fingers to send the hammers in free flight.
But what about *successive*—a term Adam uses not just once, but twice in
this passage? Comparing the execution of our five-note run on Walter vs.
Erard, one realizes that Adam is *not* stating the obvious: each finger must
contribute its part. No reliance on a light and crisp action to amplify the
slightest movement in my finger, as I casually turn my hand. To make this
point, a resourceful teacher like Adam might slide a ruler under my forearm: "You must keep a straight wrist and play each finger or key *successively*." Figure 8.3 (right) conveys this newly found efficiency and determination for the last of the five digits, the thumb. (The sketched classroom
memory may have inspired Kalkbrenner to later invent and take credit for
his own *guide-mains*, a rail to be screwed from the left to the right of the
keyboard for the pianist's wrists to rest on and with which to remain in
constant contact. This was to be the central didactic tool of his 1831 *Méthode*
pour apprendre le piano-forte à l'aide du guide-mains.)

I believe that the described juxtaposition of Walter and Erard is fundamental to understanding the object-inspired rhetoric in Beethoven's

"Adam" Sonata. Within this dichotomy of technology and expectation, the pianist (Beethoven, me, our Viennese peers) deliberately flirts with failure. They literally test boundaries and experiment with new techniques. In m. 4, for example, Beethoven writes a *staccato* on the last G, but I understand his reasons only in m. 8, when I get a second chance, on the next five-note figure, one step lower. In my performance of "Adam," I consciously play the figure of m. 4 in the old, Viennese way, feeling successful, ironically, when that last note *fails* to come out. I take the step of French-izing my technique only by m. 8 and then *never* fail to bring out that low note F, now taking my cue from the *staccato* stroke. What to my Viennese fingers feels like overcompensating ends up sounding on those Erard keys *just right*. In fact, right at the moment when the neurological sensation of physical movement (way too much for what's needed) clashes with sonic result (surprisingly, not very crisp at all), a new question pops up. Which of the two is more important—the high note of a five-note slurred group like the ones I just played, or the low one? the beginning of a gesture, or its end? the note marked by an entirely superfluous appoggiatura, or the one with the all too keen *staccato? Of course*, it must be the higher one. Just raising the question in pre-Erard Vienna would have been absurd. But through the following bars, Beethoven proceeds by exploring what any Viennese-trained musical mind would find unthinkable.

There are two ways of fingering the right hand's figuration in mm. 9–10, circling back and forth between keys F and B. First, the elegant one: 5, 4, 3, 2, and 1—as we did for the two five-note figures before, keeping the extremes 5 and 1 for beginning and end. "This way of fingering gives much grace to the hand, and allows it to avoid too much movement," Adam writes—and this endorsement makes all the more sense in reference to the key f^3 in particular, as the highest of a conventional five-octave keyboard.[13] (Even when sitting at his 5 ½-octave Erard, the memory of f^3 as an absolute outer limit must still have been firm in Beethoven's mind.) But here's the dilemma: do we see F and B as the beginning and end of a circular five-note group, or as each starting a *new* group on its own, one down and one up, twice four notes instead of a single five? When I use my fourth finger on that once highest F, I feel the shape of what could be the lower part of a C-minor scale—and the feeling is both comforting and powerful. Then, turning my index finger over my thumb to grab leading tone B one key below, I give that tone the stand-alone harmonic attention it deserves. In other words, I cling to Viennese habit—favoring shape and clarity over elegance and grace. Remarkably (though not surprisingly, given my shared background with Beethoven), I get away with it on the Erard. Extending the rhythmic groove that I've established from the outset, I bring my two hands in sync once again—both hands accumulating energy through beat-by-beat impulses that may be transferred into the keyboard.

In my description of a motoric-neurological chain of events, I've deliberately shunned emotional-rhetorical language. There *is* musical drama, of course. There are, for example, the hints to C minor in mm. 9–10 and again in m. 12. Where do these shadings come from, so early in the game of a grand C-major sonata? Do they evoke wonder or mystery? Just as Beethoven retold the Orpheus and Eurydice myth so vividly by submitting himself to the mechanics of a single *una corda* outer spring (see chapter 4), the core of the drama here lies in the actions of a man exploring all the bells and whistles offered by his new machine, deliberately testing deeply ingrained bodily instincts. What from the *crescendo* in m. 9 onward appears like an emotional outburst of some sort may in fact be most effectively realized not by increased tension in fingers or hand (since just making them "strike" the heavy keys is already quite a workout in itself) but by the simple operation of one's foot: the gradual release of *una corda*—the equivalent of the old *jalousie* or swell. Directing my right foot in m. 9 to start ascending, while allowing my fingers to just keep rolling through those repeated four-note patterns, I've been consistently amazed by the force amassed by sheer multiplication of strings: you'd almost swear that I did play louder and louder. But here we're entering a new definition of "playing." Just as Beethoven may have felt when playing his "Eroica" Symphony to Ferdinand Ries on his newly received Erard, I feel like I'm conducting a whole orchestra of keys, hammers, and strings—making *them* do the work, realizing *my* ideas. I'm becoming a robotic version of myself—my body operating as an interface with the complex machine before me.

Hand Keys and Foot Keys

Here's the interesting part—also what sets Beethoven's "Adam" apart from Adam's own Grand Sonata in C Major, Op. 8 No. 2, which (as we know) won Kalkbrenner the first prize at the *concours* of the Paris Conservatoire in 1801. The score has "competition" written all over it, not only for the kind of pianistic skills it espouses, but also for how and in what order it does so. For example, while the second and third movements contain quite precise pedal indications (and we've encountered one of them in the Adagio tremolo already), there are none in the first movement. "Some people," Adam writes in his 1804–5 method, "consider the use of pedals as *charlatanisme*."[14] It is tempting to interpret "some people" as colleagues Adam would have known. "Start by impressing the judges by your finger work alone," we imagine overhearing Adam tell his protégé. And then, a warning: "At all cost, leave your feet visibly on the floor, lest some jury members would suspect you of charlatanry." Once cleared of that suspicion, having earned the respect of the most conservative harpsichordist, the second and third movements would give his star pupil ample opportunity to draw exquisite and tasteful sounds from the piano through a deft use of all available pedals, winning over the entire jury.

By contrast, in the first movement of Beethoven's "Adam" Sonata, there's no holding back: fingers, feet, and ears are all engaged at once. Right away, Beethoven makes me conscious of a uniquely balanced C-major chord. Through the single *staccato* at the end of a first five-finger group, he forces my thumb to behave in a particular way and triggers my brain to keep alert for what's next. And even before I start playing, his careful dynamic markings direct me toward a well-calculated use of the pedals. The "I/me" in these statements, however, implies that, like Beethoven, I own a *piano en forme de clavecin*—just as Adam's pupil could expect to have one during their exam, with the exact same four pedals, in the exact same order. It is in within the context of this single, ideal instrument that I added the pedal markings in figure 8.1, copying the language from the score of Adam's *concours* sonata: "*Mettez la 4ᵉ Pédale entièrement* [Push the fourth pedal entirely]" in response to the *pp* in both hands, then, "*Ôtez la 4ᵉ Pédale peu à peu* [Gradually release the fourth pedal]," to realize the *cres:* mark, and so on.

Throughout the first movement, I explore all kinds of pedal combinations. These explorations take place between the following two extremes: the pushing down by one's foot of a single pedal (*perpendicular*, just like the movement of a single finger); and the turning of one's foot sideways to press two pedals at once (*lateral*, the equivalent of a hand rather than individual fingers playing a five- or four-note group). So far, we've discussed single-foot perpendicular operation. Double pedal use, by two feet, occurs in mm. 14 and following, open dampers ("*2ᵉ Pédale*") combining with *una corda* ("*4ᵉ Pédale*"). But the first execution of the most lateral kind of pedaling (like the one I found myself experimenting with in the "Moonlight" Sonata in C-sharp Minor, Op. 27 No. 2, and in Steibelt's *Caprice*, Op. 24 No. 3) presents itself in m. 35, for the theme in the mediant key of E major. Four bars of transitional material (mm. 31–34) give me plenty of time to prepare what I consider a genuinely Steibeltian move, putting my heels together, toes facing either side, my feet pressing down all four pedals. I've come prepared with a pair of dancing shoes: their thin leather and soft soles lend me the necessary freedom to turn and glide my feet over the wooden and sharp-edged pedals. Ready to please a salon full of Parisians guests, I feel in character as a dandy, straight of an 1804–5 issue of the *Journal des dames et modes* (fig. 8.4).

The acoustic purpose of this fancy, however, is as serious as it is refined. It has been endorsed, furthermore, by two of Beethoven's peers (see ex. 8.3). "In a sequence of chords where the high notes form a melody [*un chant*], one must almost always arpeggiate the chords," Adam writes in his method, giving an example that seems relevant for Beethoven's theme:

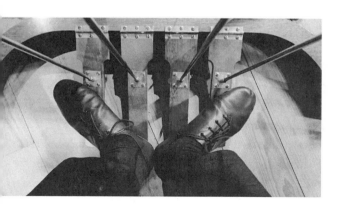

FIGURE 8.4 Steibeltian footwork for Op. 53, first movement, 2nd theme (*left*); male fashion, illustration in *Journal des dames et des modes* 9, no. 53 (Paris, June 14, 1805) (*right*).

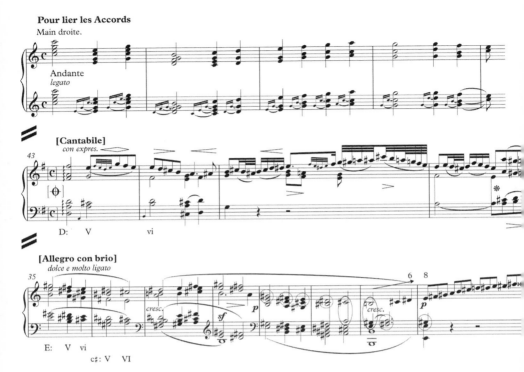

EXAMPLE 8.3 Adam, "To connect chords" (1804–5, 61) (*top*); Steibelt, Sonata in G Major, Op. 64, first movement, mm. 43–46 (*middle*); Beethoven, Sonata in C Major, Op. 53, first movement, mm. 35–42 (*bottom*).

Beethoven also spins a melody out of single-hand chords.[15] Arpeggiation evokes the "sound of a lute or a harp," and for Steibelt this automatically means combining the first and second pedals: "Whenever one selects the first pedal, one must also, *with the same foot*, select the one that follows," he writes.[16] In the first movement of his *Grande sonate* in G Major, Op. 64, Steibelt could have gone, but did not go, as far as to prescribe harp-like registration for his D-major theme (the third in a protracted sonata form), but the damperless indication is his, and cannot be ignored. (Steibelt even invented his own symbols for "on" and "off.") To make sure, we're not talking here about the modern-day habit of leaving one's foot to float on the damper pedal, constantly cleaning the reverberations, but about leaving one's foot completely down and resisting any temptation to change. In this long first movement, marked "Cantabile" from the start, damperless playing is the norm, with few rejuvenating bars of brilliant passagework in between.

The similarities between Steibelt's and Beethoven's themes are striking. In both themes, root-position chords safeguard a degree of clarity to the bass. In the context of damperless playing, this crucially allows the pianist to push into the past any previous harmony. Consciousness of space is crucial for this now lost art, and just dropping that additional fraction of time, allowing that particular bass to assert itself, can make the difference between gorgeous blending or a disturbing mix. Another trick is to have a strongly present V-harmony followed by a less assertive ("deceptive") vi—the latter as a tail to the former (and in Beethoven's case, also with fewer notes). Both composers do this, Beethoven twice in a row, first in E major (vi), then in C-sharp minor (VI). Steibelt, for his part, has a final trick up his sleeve. In mm. 43 and 44 he subtly doubles the bass notes, giving each harmony support from the ground up.

If this were a competition in damperless playing, Steibelt would be the winner, hands (or, in this case, feet) down. I convinced myself of this when adding double-bass notes *à la* Steibelt for Beethoven's mm. 36 (G♯ and A) and 38 (B). But before we try to improve Beethoven, we should look at the bigger picture. Beethoven's harp-like chords (visualize both hands strumming a single area on the harp just next to one another) do not accompany some *bel canto* melody (what Adam called *chant*)—rather, they *are* the melody. They're a magnified version of the five-tone descending gesture that we attempted in m. 4—both hands and feet now achieving what a single hand could not, while celebrating a newfound aesthetics. No more worrying about not-quite-connectable single strikes: the strumming creates a halo around each chord anyway. No worrying, either, about *legato* fingerings: with raised dampers, the overall effect is *legato* already. We play a simple five-note scale under a single slur—now really *dolce e molto ligato*. There's room even for an exquisite and time-defying *diminuendo*. Most pianists are unaware of the two-bar slur over mm. 35–36, but even thinking of this moment as taking up two bars is to miss the point: we're in a zone where there's no gravity; we're in free-fantasy land, where no counting is allowed.

From a material point of view, however, there's nothing simple about those top keys of G♯, F♯, E, D♯, and C♯. Sitting high and narrow on the keyboard, four of them cast a black shadow over C-major whiteness. We start in E major, yet by the end of the two-bar slur we end up in C-sharp minor—as if being drawn into the same irrational and self-hypnotic key of an earlier Beethoven sonata, like the first movement of his "Moonlight."[17] But as the descent reverses into an ascent, something happens. The *sforzando* in m. 38, positioned by Beethoven in application to middle voice b[1] alone,[18] always makes that particular pitch pop out from my Erard much more than anticipated. (I trust the same must have been true on Beethoven's instrument, for the same acoustic-technical reason.) This sudden surplus of energy (middle voice taking the lead to create a connection with next bar and phrase) explains the now much longer slur in mm. 37–41—stretched over five bars, as a new scale unfolds one octave lower. We're now more exclusively in E major, and the scale is one of thirds: see the circles in example 8.3 (bottom). While these thirds complete their downward roll, a four-note motive emerges: b, c♯[1], d♯[1], and e[1]. Exactly as in the first of the preliminary scale exercises, Beethoven's instinct is to lend closure, by cadencing on the first scale degree of E. But our ear does not have to choose: it may continue in either direction along a contrapuntal fork, either toward the tonic (E), or toward the third (G♯): see the arrow vs. the circles in the example.

Since the beginning of the E-major/C-sharp-minor theme, I've felt like I'm undergoing events rather than creating them. But the *sforzando* on a single B never fails to startle me, in spite of the preceding *crescendo*. It snaps me out of blissfulness back to a world where dampers will again be the norm ("*Ôtez la 2.ᵉ Pédale*") and where my mind had better be alert again. Where does bliss end and self-consciousness begin? We have flirted with notions of sound and spirituality on the topic of *son continu*, arguing that, for the French musician, the default intent would be to blur boundaries between these two states of mind. Our study of C/E as the interval of a pure and blissful third was not coincidental; its choice as *Ur*-sound for Beethoven's "Adam" Sonata seems just as deliberate. Paradoxically, it takes the most non-C major moment in Beethoven's sonata to make the link.

C-Major Mystery

The single C at the outset of the piece (capital C here referring to the specific pitch; see the first single bass note of figure 8.1) has baffled many an analyst.[19] "It seems significant," Carl Schachter thinks aloud, "that the piece begins with the tonic note alone, set apart from the chords that follow."[20] But how separate are they? To what extent can one insist on making a distinction between a solitary note and a four-voice chord? Kenneth Drake suggests that a "seemingly never-ending rhythm" has somehow been ongoing already: "Beginning with a single note on the downbeat, one may feel like a runner in a relay race grasping the wand from Beethoven."[21] His metaphor resonates with mine of a basketball player, but then, why not run with the full chord *immediately*—just as Beethoven did, in fact, in his earliest sketch?

Here's what my experience on Erard tells me. Rather than separating itself from anything that follows, a single-sounded C not only defines the soundscape within which *son continu* on the Erard is about to happen but also blends with it instantaneously. C-major soundscape will expand gradually and steadily, with ever more foreground detail. The ways in which Beethoven will prolong singular *son* are manifold, but in Vienna as well as Paris the mother of all sound-sustaining techniques remains *tremendo*.

Let's play the single C on our Erard and compare it to the Walter fortepiano. Figure 8.5 displays its respective power spectrum. As we might expect from similar measurements in chapter 7, while the Walter is altogether more overtone-rich, the Erard highlights overtones nos. 1, 2, 3, and 4 (or c, g, c^1, and e^1) before its curve plunges below the Walter, with the exception again of c^2 and g^2. A single Erard-C, thus, comes with a much more filtered version of triadic "C-major-ness" than the Walter-C.

Carl Czerny gives a fascinating perspective on the first movement, significantly not in his "On the Proper Performance of all Beethoven's Works for the Piano Solo," but in an appendix to his 1832 translation of Anton Reicha's *Cours de composition musicale*, aimed at students of composition rather than at Beethoven-interpreting pianists. Czerny cites two "exceptions to the rule" that any sonata-form movement in a major home key must have a middle part in the dominant key. The major tonic may also modulate to the "upper mediant, that is, to the major third, e.g., from C major to E major, or from G major to B major." The latter must be in reference to Beethoven's Sonata in G Major, Op. 31 No. 1, while the former, an explicit reference to Op. 53, prompts Czerny to elaborate on the "harmonic

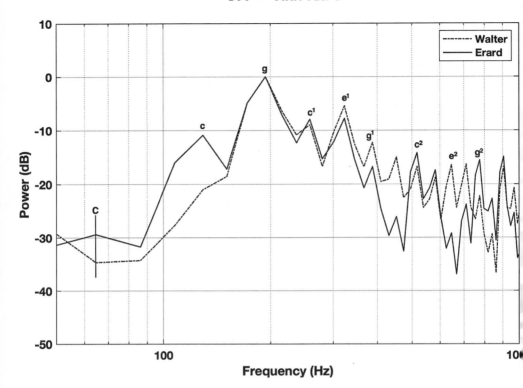

FIGURE 8.5 Power spectrum of a single C on Erard vs. Walter.

outline" of this first movement of what he calls "one of the shiniest, most brilliant, and most difficult Beethoven sonatas." His reduction, of which example 8.4 reproduces the first twenty-three bars, is designed to impress the reader: "If one plays the outline from beginning to end in the exact same tempo [as the original], how pure and noble emerges the whole sequence of harmonies! When set for choir, it would be entirely appropriate for the most serene and serious chorale."[22]

In chapter 7, we also evoked the four-voice chorale in association with the French art of tremolo. It is only a small step to imagine, in exact imitation of the human voice, a tremolo performance of Czerny's reduction. All the hallmarks of a French tremolo slow movement are present: a low fundamental bass that sets in motion a sonic-vibrational feast for the ears; fluttering hands seeking the shortest path on the keyboard; first-inversion chords typically following root-position ones; various shades of *pianissimo* and swelling requiring a deft use of the pedals.

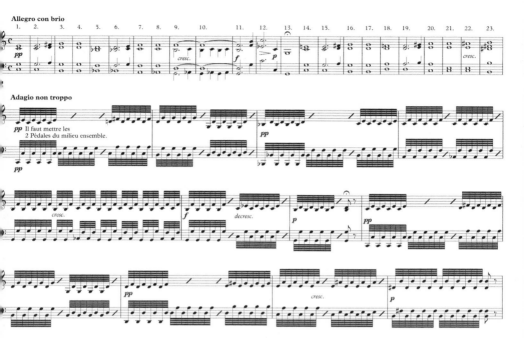

EXAMPLE 8.4 Beethoven, Sonata in C Major, Op. 53, first movement, mm. 1–12: harmonic outline ("*harmonischer Grundgeriss*") by Czerny (1832, 324) (*top*); rewritten as an Adagio tremolo (*bottom*).

But we need not resort to Czerny's reductive method—and even less to any suggestion of the church—to recognize a context of tremolo. In the "original," to use Czerny's term for the finished score, tremolo is what occurs in mm. 14–15 and again in 18–19, and it is in this foreground appearance that the true C-major tremolo-chord materializes: C, c, g, c^1, e^1, or the fundamental bass, followed by its first four harmonic overtones. The gambit of the opening single bass here reveals itself, too. Beethoven makes explicit what had been implicit already, or helps the ear to hear what had been there all along. This emphatically applies to the major third e^1: it would be a mistake to say that Beethoven *puts* it on top, because it *has been* on top *already*, ever since the first note of the piece—and quite audibly so.

Czerny may have linked his notion of original with the published score (as the first and also final word of his old teacher), but we must dig deeper: what did Beethoven have in mind when first jotting down his ideas? Cooper has pointed out that in the sketches, "the theme [first] appears in its tremolando [*sic*] form, as in bar 14 of the final version, rather than as repeated quavers."[23] To his example from Landsberg 6, page 120, I add another, from the opposite recto page, with an idea for a slow movement, later to become the Andante favori, WoO 57 (see ex. 8.5). This idea is still in E major, or the same key as the prospective second group in the first movement, but by the next system already, Beethoven changes his mind and switches to F major.

It is rare to see *any* articulation mark in Beethoven's sketches, so the two slurs in the Andante fragment must grab our attention. When interpreted next to the printed version, they tell a sophisticated story. First, it seems significant that Beethoven initially focuses on alternation *involving both hands* as the main principle, not only for the upbeat, but also for what happens in the next bar. Tremolo defines the texture, and a paired approach ("ti-a, ti-a"), exactly as the slurs imply, is essential. Slurring the four notes in the Viennese manner (with a *diminuendo*) would be all but impossible: the heavier and less responsive French keyboard simply demands a new impulse on each pair—and Beethoven acknowledges, even embraces this new reality.

EXAMPLE 8.5 Beethoven, sketches, Landsberg 6, p. 120, st. 10–12, and p. 121, st. 11–12; and published Andante WoO 57, mm. 11–12.

Just as with the opening theme of the first movement, for this little phrase of the second movement it is the tremolo version that existed first. Beethoven proceeds not only by creating a reduced version (only one instead of two hands engaging in tremolo), but also by adding longer slurs, some even crossing the bar line, and in any case obliterating the two short slurs that had been essential to the sketch. What do the longer slurs convey? I would argue that we're witnessing a redefinition from an articulatory to a more loosely connective slur, where it's no longer clear what remains articulation and what becomes what the nineteenth century started calling "phrasing." But this shift does not make those short, paired slurs any less essential at the more phonological level. Both Beethoven and our Erard insist on such a consistently paired performance, from a higher note to a lower one, honoring the tremolo origin not only of this particular idea, but also of many more in the Erard-inspired Andante.

Throughout the sonata, tremolo is at its most obvious in mm. 14–15 and mm. 18–19 of the first movement, reminding us of the French examples presented in chapter 7. There's one important difference, however: whereas in their Adagios his French colleagues always favor parallel motion of the hands, placing the highest note on the weak part of the beat (which, as we argued, created a more celestial experience), Beethoven sticks to a much less challenging, symmetric alternation of the hands, placing the top note on the good part of the beat. Is Beethoven *viennicizing* a French technique, not capable of letting go of rhythmic clarity in favor of nuance and suggestiveness? One may object, of course, that Beethoven is writing a *con brio* movement rather than an Adagio, but example 8.4 suggests precisely that such an Adagio tremolo was in the back of his mind. It is true, furthermore, that in 1808, when he wrote the Largo movement of his "Ghost" Trio, Op. 70 No. 1 (which is the closest he ever got to a true French tremolo Adagio), he would continue clinging to the security of the good parts of the beat for the melodically relevant tones of the tremolo. In fact, during those post-Erard years he seems to have developed a fascination with alternating hand symmetry altogether in combination with the effect of *son continu*: a good example is the long middle-voice trill in the second movement of his Sonata in E Minor, Op. 90 (1814), which is technically also a tremolo, albeit of dissonant intervals.

From Scale to Sonata

Beethoven's end game, however, is *sonority*. Let's recapitulate. First, C (as a single pitch) also means C-major-ness, best represented by a four-voice chord with the third on top. Second, once this open-third sonority has established itself, it's there to stay—until the next one comes around. Third, something as mechanical (from both piano-technical and pianist perspectives) as playing a scale reveals a paradox of verticality (the downward strikes) and horizontality (a pattern that forms an interesting whole). At some point Beethoven must have wondered whether these elements (C/third, scale/thirds—C-major-ness) could combine in the composition of a sonata.

Example 8.6 traces eight such open-third sonorities in the first movement of Op. 53, along with three moments where the third has moved to the lower voice. They are numbered by scale degree, with low C standing for no. 1 and high C for no. 8. Together, they complete an ascending scale of thirds, from C–E to C–E, identical to what had transpired from our C-major piano exercise—with one exception. No. 3 changes G to G♯, turning E minor into E major. There are two outliers: while no. −7 positions itself one step below the scale, the decimal number of no. 1 ½ for D-flat suggests nonbelonging altogether.

Finding nos. 1–8 represented in this precise order through a major-key, sonata-form movement is remarkable in itself. But do these sonorities also have structural meaning? And how is such an ascending scale compatible with sonata form? Here's the challenge: how to celebrate the harmonious world of a tremolo in the context of a *con brio* first movement? Steibelt knew how to dazzle listeners through his Adagio improvisations, but Beethoven sets the bar much higher, as he seeks to combine French filigree with Viennese form—not as some *divertissement* in the middle (like Adam's Op. 8 No. 2, also Steibelt's Op. 64), but head-on, at the outset of a multimovement sonata. Example 8.7 reconstructs the process. We pick up at the moment when those C-major thirds (those salient turning points in our key-by-key explorations of the French piano) have started clinging to us like earworms.

First phase. Let's play the C-major thirds slowly by themselves— without the previous distractions of mechanical practicing. Each third is unique, and not just because they are either major or minor: in a well-

EXAMPLE 8.6 Beethoven, Sonata in C Major, Op. 53, first movement: third/tenth sonorities.

tempered tuning, every one has a different character. Mostly, even after playing just the first two, we give in to an expectation of completeness: we want the scale to finish, and anything less would be a disappointment.

But how can something so linear become an outline for a musical narrative that thrives on rhetorical contrast and tonal resolution? Let's remind ourselves of the structural principles of a sonata. A sonata form is both bi- and tripartite. The first part of two, coinciding with the *exposition*, feeds off the harmonic tension between *first-group* and *second-group* material, respectively in the home and (usually) dominant key; the second part contains both a *development*, where more or less anything goes, and a *recapitulation*, where first- and second-group material is revisited in the home key, and any harmonic tension removed. Normally, each part is repeated.

Second phase. We contemplate the challenges. For the exposition, we must create a second key area. A simple change from G♮ to G♯ establishes a sufficiently strong contrast between C major (no. 1) and E major (no. 3). The same accidental of G♯ has the potential, furthermore, of functioning as a pivot toward A minor (no. 6), which will later on facilitate a smooth reintegration in the home key, for the second part of the recapitulation. The beginning of the recapitulation poses a more serious challenge. After dominant no. 5 we must return to tonic no. 1, but how can we simultaneously keep alive the expectation of a step-wise ascent to sub-mediant no. 6? One option is to emphasize the close connection of C major with its relative minor, A minor, so as to create the illusion that once you've heard one, you're also hearing the other. (This means that in the A-minor triad, C and A become interchangeable.) It remains to examine no. 7, or the penultimate step before closing back to tonic no. 8. It makes little sense to lend B–D any third-status on its own (as in treating it as B minor), so the obvious decision is to downplay its potential as a separate sonority, instead making B and D part of a first-inversion dominant harmony. This creates a new principle: like no. 5, third no. 7 joins the bass, in a facilitating rather than a "look at me" kind of role: they both have a dominant/tonic harmonic-functional job to do. (This provides the key to integrating scale within sonata: where it matters, dominant and interval of a fifth still rule.)

Third phase. Having worked out these principles, we can start forging connections between our eight (or six) sonorities. We rely on chromatic tones to be the leading forces of pre- or secondary dominant harmonies.

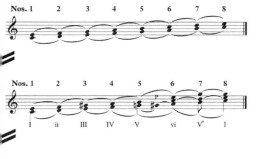

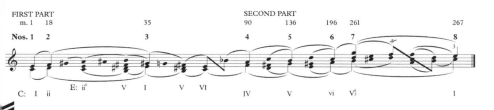

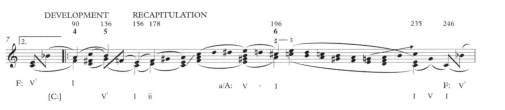

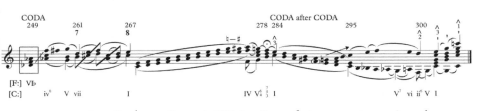

EXAMPLE 8.7 Beethoven, Sonata in C Major, Op. 53, first movement: sonority and structure.

The same pivotal G♯ from the previous phase takes the initiative: G♯–A–A♯–B between nos. 2 and 3 (see the high voice) and leading us from no. 3 all the way to no. 6, E–F–F♯–G–G♯–A (in the middle voice). Nos. 6, 7, and 8, from their side, join their usual forces to generate a structural cadence in C major. Nos. 1 and 2 convey the idea of parallelism most courageously. They're juxtaposed—plain and clear.

Each of the two major parts is to be repeated. This means that between no. 3 (E major) and no. 4 (F major) we need a hinge between the two major parts. We must be able to repeat the exposition as well as proceed to the development. A deceptive cadence on C major provides the solution, as it is capable both of reconnecting with no. 1 (as its tonic) and with no. 4 (as its dominant). As to the second part, we can reconnect with no. 4 (F major) through the exact same harmonic progression (since that deceptive C-major cadence is also the tonic).

We conclude with a graph that represents the harmonic events as they appear in the score, but still with two repeats—that is, one for each part (as Beethoven originally intended, before he would do away with the second repeat: see chapter 9). In phase 2 we anticipated that, for any continuity to be felt from no. 5 through the recapitulation of no. 1, no. 1 (or the home key of C major) would need to fuse with no. 6 (the key of its relative minor A). Initially, Beethoven presents no. 6 in its own right—as an A-major theme that mirrors its E-major counterpart of the exposition and whose fuller chords invite even broader, harp-like arpeggiations. Lusciousness yields to austerity as major changes to minor, one octave down, in mm. 200–202. But while beginning in A minor, the phrase closes in C major—with G-A-B-C as its closing formula, rather than E-F♯-G♯-A. When I play the varied version of the theme again in m. 204 (the whole phrase now starting one third higher, no. 6 A–C imperceptibly swapped with no. 1 C–E), I'm no longer sure: there's G♯—but there's also G♮. Are we in C major or in A minor? I ask the question as I play the same descending foreground version of the scale in thirds as during the exposition in E major before. If the E-major scale evoked some dream-like fantasy before, then the one mixing A minor with C major represents grounding wisdom. Within the scale of sonorities, one might interpret A minor's role as uniting—its raised seventh scale degree seamlessly yielding a natural one.

I announced them up front, but included their presence only in the concluding graph. The "one step down" B-flat-major chords, a mere four bars into the piece (mm. 5–6), are the first striking harmonic event of the whole Grand Sonata. We have labeled them as no. −7, and their identification as a third-sonority in their own right seems more than warranted when compared to nos. 1, 2, and 4. Yet, to insist on their prominence is also to overlook their role in brokering a thirteen-bar opening phrase. Just as G♯ (in the treble) brokered a four-chord chromatic transition from the one main sonority to the next (see the discussion of phase 2, above), at this earliest possible moment in the piece, B♭ (in the bass) facilitates a downward chromatic progression from C down to G, or from tonic to dominant. Paradoxically, our recognition of B-flat as no. −7 serves another purpose: it sends us in the "wrong" direction—something we realize only when we start over with no. 1 proceeding to no. 2, no longer simply bouncing, but in true tremolo. Initially taking a step back—quite literally, as a negative number outside of the scale—the B-flat chords attune our ears to the fantastic, step-by-step sonority drive that's ahead of us. But its outlier status as −7 (harmonically a ♭VII) may be interpreted as compensating for the lack of individual harmonic attention given to +7, which fulfills its structurally much more important role as diminished vii within both scale and sonata.

Coda after Coda

Arguably the most conspicuous structural consequence of our *Ur*-scale is the Coda followed by yet another Coda-after-Coda.[24] From a sonata-design perspective, the cadence of C major in m. 235, cadenza-like trill and all, could have amounted to structural closure. But there's unfinished business: after no. 6, sonorities nos. 7 and 8 still need to play out their course. The deceptive cadence to VI of F minor in m. 249 (our sonority no. 1 ½) plays a special role here. Why is it even there? To argue that it's there to introduce a Coda is to miss Beethoven's intent also to repeat the second part. Example 8.8 reconstructs this repeat sign, while showing Beethoven's change of mind ("vi–de," or "from here to there," as he himself wrote in his manuscript). What's important to understand is that the shift from F major to F minor, or from *primo* (the first run-through) to *secundo* (the second time around) is necessary only when anticipating a repeat. One may well imagine a more drastic shortcut, indicated in the example by an arrow,

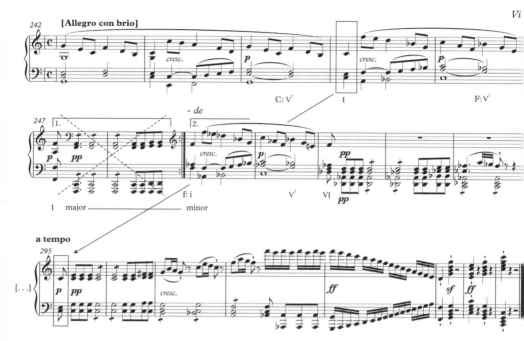

EXAMPLE 8.8 Beethoven, Sonata in C Major, Op. 53, first movement, mm. 242–51 and mm. 295–end.

from m. 245 to m. 295, reconnecting with concluding C-major bouncy chords rather than the D-flat major ones that send us on a long detour.

But we're still following Beethoven's train of thought in a scenario that does involve a repeat. After closing in C major in m. 245, he retraces his steps and modulates to reconnect with the same tonality as no. 4, allowing him to repeat the development. With an eye on our third sonorities, there's virtue in repeating nos. 4–6 as the second part, just as sonorities nos. 1–3 had been repeated as the first part of a sonata. It helps, for recognition, that no. 1 and no. 4, as the first of three, each feature the catchy basketball dribble, as does the version in D-flat, which marks the beginning of yet another part, starting in m. 249. From a sonata-structural point of view, this may be called a coda, but for the rollout of the eight sonorities (with two more to go), it is just as essential as the two previous parts. It is here that the desire to allow the ascending scale to take its full course takes over.

Highlighting D-flat as one of the other sonorities reminds us of the trajectory so far (nos. 1–6) and sets us up for the final two (nos. 7–8), while raising the bar of excitement, as we get ready for the final act. When in m. 259 we land on what, this late in the game, must be the structural dominant (replacing any such expectation held before), it seems appropriate to ever-so-briefly clear the air. My right hand in mm. 259–60 keeps the momentum going, but it's my left hand that's about to take the lead—and change the rules. Figure 8.6 reproduces the score from this point onward.

Thematically and texturally no. 7 still bounces around, but any physiological and harmonic pleasure has disappeared. Grounded perfect fifths, in harmony with complementary major thirds above, are replaced by lonely minor thirds—tight and narrow, without much context or support. Worse, octave syncopations in the right hand throw me off balance: forcing what is supposed to be rhythmically weak into rhythmically strong, they make me rush ahead even more. All the while I'm pressing down the *una corda*—in an attempt to retain physical contact with my French keyboard, staying within a *pianissimo* range without having to underplay. I seriously struggle to maintain my aplomb. This overall sense of instability, however, befits the harmonic position of no. 7 as the penultimate step in an ascending scale.

If by way of compensation one expects a strong arrival point with no. 8, then one is disappointed, too. Where no. 1 had started with a clear downbeat, no. 8 just rolls in, tagged on at the end of yet more bouncing around in m. 267, not at all bringing the stability of a structural cadence. Instead, one feels caught up in the whirlwind start of a potpourri. No. 8 also being no. 1, we *start over* with the left hand alone, while our right hand traverses scale after scale, agilely turning under the thumb, albeit always on a good part of the beat in the Viennese manner. *The left hand plays tenth after tenth*, relentlessly working its way up the keyboard, *going through the exact C-major scale all over again*, while also integrating the five-note, scalar motive. (See especially the circles in figure 8.6.) In these wild celebrations, there's no savoring of sonority. Overshooting our scale in m. 274, we rush up to G by m. 275, emphatically shifting to G♯ by the middle of the bar, before what by all expectation should now really become the final cadence—the sonata-structural equivalent of the sonority-textural closure we already had.

But there's a twist. In m. 284, after a double pause on the dominant seventh, Beethoven again introduces the downward A-minor/C-major scale from the recapitulation, with pitches G♯ and G♮ equally at home.

[Allegro con brio]

FIGURE 8.6 Op. 53, first movement, mm. 267–end. First edition (Vienna: Bureau des arts et d'industrie, 1805), with annotations.

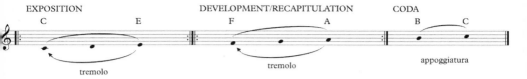

EXAMPLE 8.9 Tremolo as a structural principle in Op. 53, first movement.

Each of our thirds makes a final appearance, now reversed, from back to front. I play these bars as a serious chorale, my hands shifting *en bloc* from one chordal position to the next: cruising their way across the French keyboard, these hand positions inhabit a spirit of *legato* as I refuse to give in to any distraction from the damper pedal. During these solemn moments, I leave behind all tricks that previously helped me come to better terms with the *verticality* of the deep French keys. Tremolo and harp-like strumming yield to naturally sustained sounds, played in the plainest way possible, but with a human intent that honors the songful or *horizontal* capacity of the French piano. These are the blocks of sounds that Czerny recognized in Beethoven's score. But instead of being spread over many bar-lines, we now manage to hear and play them under a single slur that is much longer than any singer could hold their breath. The singing voice of the Erard reveals itself, even if, to paraphrase a poet among the early nineteenth-century French pianists, "illusion must come to the aid of reality."[25]

Beethoven would not be Beethoven if it stopped here. Our reconstructive exercise started with playing the simplest of scales and the question of how such a scale of thirds might be integrated in a sonata structure. By way of conclusion, let's play the scale again, stripped of its upper thirds, but ordered to reflect the structure we've just explored (see ex. 8.9). The first part moves from C to E, while the second inhabits a tonal space between F and A. (F major will indeed become the key of the Andante later on, and seen from this sonata-wide perspective, there's logic in Beethoven giving up the key of E major early on.) These two major thirds are separated from one another by repeat signs. Repeating each of them implies alternation and continuity. *We're looking at two major-third tremolos within the C-major scale.* In the Coda, finally, B and C (nos. 7 and 8) stand in relation to one another as a different kind of pair: an appoggiatura complete with its resolution. Not to be repeated, they stand outside of the double-tremolo structure, and like that final octave in the first of Beethoven's scale exercises, they bring structural closure to a movement that combined French sonority with Viennese structure. They also reveal how an unfamiliar keyboard and a set of scale exercises led Beethoven on a path of discovery and transformation. And this is only the first movement of Beethoven's "Adam."

CHAPTER NINE

A Grand Sonata

The following anecdote has come to us through Ferdinand Ries:

> In the sonata (in C major, Op. 53), dedicated to his first patron, Count von
> Waldstein, there originally was a grand Andante. A friend of Beethoven's
> suggested to him that the sonata was too long, whereupon [this friend]
> was taken to task most severely. Only quieter reflection soon convinced
> my teacher of the accuracy of the observation. He then published *das
> große Andante* in F Major in 3/8 time on its own and later composed the
> interesting Introduction to the rondo, which is now part of the sonata.[1]

The sequence in Ries's telling, of course, is wrong: Beethoven composed
that "interesting introduction" *first*, so that Op. 53 could be published, and
then published the original Andante separately. Important, however, is
what Ries got right: not only do we have extensive sketches of the original
Andante in connection with the other Op. 53 movements, but there are clear
signs in Beethoven's autograph that its pages were removed and replaced
by two newly stitched leaves with an alternative Adagio Introduzione—
keeping the key of F major of the previous Andante, but also acting as a
transition between the two outer C-major movements.

But why? Because the sonata was "too long"?

In hindsight, it's tempting to admire Beethoven for having the guts,
by making a major cut, to create that perfectly proportioned piece we've

come to love, but if we look at all this from the perspective of Beethoven's Erard, a different story emerges—one in which length may not have been a decisive factor at all.

* * *

That such an Andante was meant to live between the first and final movements is corroborated by the position of the continued sketches for this slow movement, both occurring in between and overlapping with the first and final movements.[2] It made it all the way to the finished manuscript, from which Beethoven would have played the sonata for his friends. The manuscript has been preserved and presently lives at the Beethoven-Haus in Bonn. Anyone studying its superb facsimile can follow the various steps of a cut-and-paste revision.[3] First, Beethoven must have cut out the Andante pages. Then, he used two new sheets of paper to write an alternative Adagio Introduzione. (The term "introduction" is his—and why this is important will become clear later on.) Judging by the number of corrections, Beethoven did not take the time to try new sketches or even to write a proper draft, in contrast with the outer movements, which had been copied in a more decisive and clean hand. For the revision and for some additional adjustments on the existing pages, he used a different, brownish kind of ink: he lengthened the available system on the previous page, to recopy the final bars of the first movement, and similarly, on the last page of the new Adagio, he had to write the two first systems of the final Rondo again. The new folios were then glued and sewn into the existing overall manuscript.

While the manuscript of the revised sonata may be studied today, the whereabouts of those ripped-out Andante pages are unknown. Possibly, Beethoven sent them to Countess Josephine Deym in April or May 1805, calling them "*your—your* Andante" (underlining "your").[4] These pages would certainly have been resewn.[5] Imagine, then, one musical work being split into two newly bound manuscripts. On the one hand, we witness the glorious birth of "Waldstein," while on the other we are somewhat saddened to see the Andante relegated to a solitary existence. It will have to wait for Georg Kinsky and Hans Halm in 1955 to receive a proper "WoO" number ("WoO" standing for *Werk ohne Opus*, or "work without opus [number]"). That's a consolation prize at best, like the epithet "Andante *favori*" that was featured on the title page of its second edition in 1806.[6]

These minor acknowledgments do not lessen the irony that "Waldstein" became known as a monumental piece in its own right, celebrated for the expansiveness of style and form of its first and second movements, together considered so long already that a proper slow movement couldn't possibly be missed. In fact, if it weren't for the Ries anecdote, one might be fooled into accepting the Introduzione as the only slow movement there ever was, rather than the introduction to the final movement that Beethoven actually said it is.

This is not a typical case of a friend or an editor telling a creative writer or composer to "kill your darlings." Indeed, how can an *entire* Andante, as a perfectly conventional slow movement for a *Grande sonate*, be dismissed as self-indulgent or unnecessary? I would suggest, on the contrary, that at a certain point the story of Beethoven's Sonata, Op. 53, changed fundamentally, which is why I've slipped back into using the name "Waldstein," in reference to a time after this change. The argument of the previous chapter still holds: I still wish to temporarily lay aside the sonata's Vienna-oriented associations, including its status in later processes of classicization and canonization, and explore instead the various inscriptions that arrived along with the physical object of a French piano, inextricably linked to the sonata's genesis. This chapter continues these explorations by looking beyond the first movement to the sonata as a whole—whatever that whole turns out to be. Rather than explaining, let alone legitimizing, the reasons behind Beethoven's drastic edit of Op. 53, as distinguished scholars have done, I set forth to ask the exact opposite question.[7] What exactly happened when "Adam" became "Waldstein"? Did the trimming of the sonata also affect its *raison-d'être*, which I suggested was to celebrate the affordances of a new piano? In the context of such celebrations, had not self-indulgence been the very point of artistic production, allowing for lavishness and grand proportions? Thinking beyond Beethoven in the confines of Vienna, why wouldn't Beethoven have wanted to offer the world a full-blown "director's cut" of his French-inspired sonata, tapping into the experience of his peers while showing off his own confidence and genius? Given that the Paris Conservatoire had become the talk among professional musicians throughout Europe and that enthusiasm for piano was reaching new heights, might Beethoven not have fantasized about his new sonata being played at a *concours*, possibly joining a gallery of C-major, prize-winning sonatas: Clementi's Op. 33 No. 3,[8] Adam's Op. 8 No. 2—and finally Beethoven's Op. 53?

We should not forget that at the heart of such grand plans and expectations lay a simple human emotion. Without the genuine excitement Beethoven felt over the acquisition of a new piano, none of those larger questions is relevant. But that state of mind ebbed very quickly. We can assume that unreserved happiness only reigned for the period of November and December 1803, right after he received the instrument. By January 2, 1805, when Andreas Streicher wrote that Beethoven "has already had [his Erard] changed twice without the least improvement," it is obvious that Beethoven had become distinctly *unhappy* with the piano, first having agreed to revisions and then having lived with the consequences. In any reconstruction of a pre-"Waldstein" scenario, then, it is crucial to keep an eye on the exact timeline of Beethoven's Erard (see appendix A) and of Op. 53, the planning, writing, and publishing of which happened in conjunction with Op. 54 and 57 (see appendix B, which also serves as reference for any quote from Beethoven's correspondence in this chapter).

Three New Solo Sonatas

In August 1804, Beethoven offers the publisher Breitkopf & Härtel in Leipzig "three new solo sonatas" along with his oratory *Christ on the Mount of Olives*, Op. 85, his Triple Concerto, Op. 56 (for piano, violin, and cello), and a "new grand symphony" (his "Eroica," Op. 55, still referred to in his letter as "entitled Ponaparte" [*sic*]). Mr. Härtel expresses interest in all of the five works except the oratory. His argument for rejecting the oratory sounds perfectly reasonable: the score is too complex for a publication to be economically sustainable, and as proof he relates previous experiences with Mozart's *Requiem* and *Don Giovanni*, Händel's *Messiah*, and Haydn's Masses. It is clear from the correspondence that both parties initially think of "three sonatas" as a single opus. For repertoires intended for domestic consumption, such as string quartets, sonatas, or songs, compiling three, six, or twelve works as one opus was still the conventional publishing practice. It's clear, however, that Beethoven would break with this custom when in his first letter he points out (undoubtedly to impress his addressee in Leipzig) that "one pays me nearly 60 # [ducats] for a single *Solo sonate* [*sic*]."[9] This ambiguity between a single sonata and an opus of sonatas in the correspondence between a proud artist and a remarkably patient businessman will play a role later on.

In any case, Op. 53 and presumably also Op. 54 had been ready since August 26, 1804, the date of Beethoven's initial offer, and Beethoven sent fair copies of them in December 1804, which would have been a full year after initially composing Op. 53. *By this time, the Erard piano had either been revised already or was in the process of being revised.* Can it come as a surprise, then, that Beethoven started dragging his feet over finishing the third sonata, his Op. 57? On January 16, 1805, he blamed "a lack of good copyists" and "poorer health during winter," but the true reason may well have been the failing project to improve his piano and his emotional inability to reengage with the instrument. Härtel inquired again explicitly in February 1805, but two months later, in April 1805, there was still no Op. 57. Clearly, the arrangement of "biweekly" submissions offered by Beethoven and accepted by Härtel on December 4, 1804, hadn't worked: in normal circumstances Beethoven would very probably have liked and perhaps even needed clear deadlines for his artistic output. From Härtel's business point of view, conditions hadn't been met: he had every right to break the contract—but he didn't.

It was Beethoven, and not Härtel, who withdrew from a perfectly reasonable arrangement. Beethoven's brother Kaspar Karl had run a tough negotiation, which Härtel tried to tone down in the letter of January 30, 1805. Unfortunately, this important letter arrived in Vienna only in April, upsetting the Beethovens at a time when tensions must have already been high. To the brothers it looked as though Breitkopf & Härtel was dragging its feet: publication of the submitted works didn't proceed as quickly as they'd wished, in spite of Karl's insistence (underlined) on October 10, 1804, that the five pieces [5 *Stücke*] "*be published separately by virtue of their design.*" Lumping together the two finished sonatas (Op. 53 and Op. 54) with the three other works (a finished Op. 55, an unfinished Op. 56, and most significantly, an unfinished Op. 57) may have been part of a strategy by Beethoven to prompt Härtel to start publishing the sonatas individually, but in Härtel's mind it would have been three or nothing.

In any case, Ludwig's inability to send the third sonata and his repeated promise to do so "soon"—"within 4 to 6 weeks," he writes in his letter of

April 18, 1805, nearly eight months after his initial offer—are too significant to ignore. I suggest that a bout of writer's block got mixed with feelings of frustration related to his Erard piano no longer being the same. Beethoven had been on a roll—not just with Op. 53 but also with Op. 54—but then something caused him to just not feel it anymore. As a result, the remaining effort of a third sonata took on insurmountable proportions. In this charged context, Beethoven made alternative plans to publish his "Waldstein"— not even waiting for the fair copy to be returned from Leipzig, but sending the manuscript itself to a young publishing house in town, named the Bureau des arts et d'industrie.[10] Penciled marks in the autograph, with directives for engraving, indeed suggest that no new fair copy was made.[11]

Two Questions

Two pertinent questions emerge from this reading of the timelines. First, what would the Leipzig fair copy have looked like? Would it, or would it *not* have included the Andante? Second, along the same lines (since Ries gives no indication of time), when exactly did Beethoven play the sonata for his friends? Was it when he finished composing it (in January 1804)? or as he was about to send a fair copy to Leipzig (by December 1804)? or when he changed his plans regarding publication (late April or early May 1805)? In other words, would he have done so *before* or *after* revisions made to the Erard piano? The probability of "after" appears much greater than "before."

For his friends to share Beethoven's enthusiasm over an Erard-inspired piece, it would have mattered that they actually heard him play it on his Erard.[12] By the same token, Beethoven would have been more likely to accept their criticism after he'd already felt mismatched with a different, Viennese fortepiano (say, at one of his aristocratic friends' houses)—or, worse, with his revised Erard (at his own house). "You should have heard me when the Erard was still new" would have been an excuse unbefitting a composer selling his music to be played by others. But Beethoven might have been caught by surprise himself. Only when forced by circumstances to play on a different instrument than the one he'd grown accustomed to might he have realized just how Erard-specific his latest production had been. After all, this had been his first foray into writing for a foreign piano.

Absorbed in his cocoon, alternating between sketchbook and piano, he might not have realized how difficult it would be to translate his newly found language to a Walter, Streicher, Jackesch, or (worst of all) a viennicized Erard. But when confronted with criticism (undoubtedly mixed with *self*-criticism), he acted like a professional. He made the necessary cuts and saved his "work," even if this meant downplaying its French roots.

Three plus Two

The focal point of our analysis so far has been a long, single string of C. Think of it as a gigantic monochord that is made to ring freely within the enclosing structure of a piano. Its *corps sonore* (to use a term of Jean-Philippe Rameau) produces an array of overtones—their vibrations creating a tremolo-infused soundscape. Tremolo equals continuous sound. And *son continu*, ideally, is forever. So, by replacing the Andante, itself a beautiful testimony of the Erard's capacity to sing, with an Introduction, almost by definition fragmented, improvisatory, and recitativo-like, what exactly is Beethoven hoping to gain?

The answer is—yet again—*son continu*, but with a structural twist and now in application to the sonata as a whole. With the new introduction, Beethoven brings into focus a fundamental link between the two C-major outer movements, or between a sonata-form movement that engages with sonority in rondo-like fashion (exploring the individual components of a C-major scale within the structure of a sonata) and a rondo-form that features sonority as a single theme (making for unapologetic C-major-ness throughout, with nonthreatening *Sturm und Drang* episodes in the two related minor keys of A minor and C minor).

Let's imagine a performance on the Erard *with* the original Andante in F major (since E major was rejected early on). After eight minutes of sheer beauty (in line with what F major stands for in a well-tempered tuning), I play the Andante's final chords, themselves an echo of what came before. I take a break and think about my next move. There we go: a single C, just like the one I had started the sonata with. The implication is crystal-clear: we reconnect with the beginning of the piece, not so much stylistically (since we're now embarking on a pastoral movement rather than one with an intense rhythmic drive), but all the more acoustically.

If single C initially was the trigger for a *son continu* texture, we found the specific idiom of tremolo manifested in mm. 14–15 of the first movement, which was also our no. 1 sonority. For spectral analysis I recorded this particular manifestation of C-major tremolo with raised dampers, exactly as I perform it in the context of the sonata: see the bottom system of example 9.1. I did so on both Erard and Walter, the two instruments standing side by side. The results are shown in figure 9.1. The Erard version clearly projects the "ethereal" triad consisting of c^2, e^2, and g^2, each of which is highly prominent, their consecutive peaks following an ever so gentle downward slope; the Walter, from its side (dotted line), shows a clear peak on e^2, while g^2 is much softer and easily superseded by higher overtones that are significantly louder.

There's nothing unfamiliar about these results: they're consistent with what we found in chapters 7 and 8. But look now at the opening bar of the finale rondo movement in example 9.1. This is a famous passage in piano literature, known for mixing tonic and dominant tones in a single pedal. We have our low C as downbeat. The right hand colors in the same chord as the tremolo before, in the same middle register, with the same e^1 on top. It's the crossing left hand, however, that deserves our attention. As if plucking sounds from the ether, it plays the following pitches, in this order: g^2, e^2, d^2, g^1, c^2, and back to e^2. The left hand is made to cross over a boundary drawn by the fifth finger of the right hand (on e^1), entering a new dimension. Now study again the spectral diagram in figure 9.1: these five pitches (the divine triad *plus* g^1 and d^2) are all represented as overtone peaks, but again more clearly and in a more balanced way on the Erard than on the Viennese fortepiano. The one dissonant d^2 is introduced as the third note under a slur that both sustains and mirrors the decaying bass pedal C. In performance, I consciously place d^2 *below* (i.e., more softly than) the preceding e^2, exactly as its spectral analysis specifies. Consistent with what was argued before, it is the single C-sonority that counts: rather than combining two different harmonies (tonic and dominant), Beethoven reveals its full content through one.

Beethoven's very first sketch, also shown in example 9.1, indeed had the exact same pitches already, but in a different order. The triad appears first, from high to low (g^2–e^2–c^2), then dominant sounds d^2 and g^1, followed by resolution c^2. Beethoven writes down the overtones he has been hearing

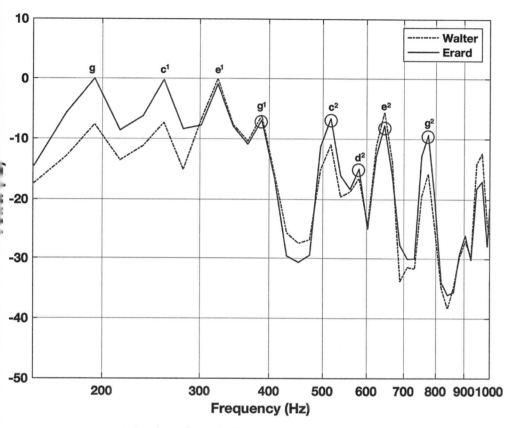

FIGURE 9.1 Spectral analysis of tremolo (first movement, mm. 14–15) as performed on Erard and Walter.

all along. As we compare the sketch with the finished version, we also understand the rationale behind lengthening the fifth (g^2) while minimizing the third (e^2). The latter being acoustically prominent by itself, Beethoven constructs a slim, long, and elegant column of sound that is made to stretch all the way up to g^2 or scale degree 5. This is soundscaping at its purest and most artful.

Louis Adam would approve: I have started playing *with my ears* rather than with my fingers. For these opening bars of the final movement, I've also adopted Adam's favorite combination of "the two pedals in the center together," which he prescribes at the equivalent spot in his Sonata, Op. 8 No. 2, for the final pastoral movement that similarly mixes tonic and dominant harmonies. Feet anchored by pedals, my body receives the message

EXAMPLE 9.1 Beethoven, Sonata in C Major, Op. 53, first-to-final movement continuity.

to sit straight. But as the angle of my legs becomes obtuse (by shifting my feet to the front of my body), I must also bend my torso slightly forward, to compensate for a shifted center of gravity. Meanwhile, my right hand, pointed to the center of the keyboard, locks in this firm position of my body. From this grounded posture my left hand reaches over to the upper echelons of the keyboard. It's not so much that my arms feel crossed or reversed: it's as if my left arm leaves my body altogether, becoming a virtual version of itself. In this unusual position, the only way to move the fingers of the left hand is by conscious brain command rather than visceral response. At this point, the only other loose part of my body is my neck, which I turn gently to the right, allowing my ears to follow the direction of the vibrations on the soundboard.

The photograph in figure 9.2 is taken at the precise moment of my reaching out to the high g^2. Remarkable in this image is the blending of human physicality and instrumental materiality. From bottom to top we see a straight column of feet, pedal rods, keyboard, arms, shoulders, and head—piano and pianist merging to form one *corps sonore*. Inciting, vibrating, listening, playing—it's no longer clear which or who is doing what, and this ambiguity, I suggest, reflects the trans-bodily experience just described.

The five special tones have existed not just as overtones, but also as sympathetic vibrations, as one string responds to another. Together they create a halo of sound, each component lighting up whenever its turn comes. If the subdued tremolo in the first movement held promise of something higher in some universal sphere of sounds, then the final movement delivers, by striking strings that have been vibrating all along. We enjoy a state of diffuseness, as enforced by the leather-moderating third pedal, never going beyond the dynamic level of *piano* for as many as fifty-four bars. In m. 55 we finally yield to the full materiality of hammers and strings that now strike one another as exuberantly as possible, as well as to the full physicality of fingers and arms, which now are made to move freely in their usual noncrossed position. One feels like congratulating whoever in France came up with the nickname "L'Aurore" for Op. 53. (This happened some time during the second half of the nineteenth century.)[13] It's entirely appropriate, indeed, in example 9.1 to see the five dotted lines as five single rays that are about to open up to a full explosion of sunlight: the wide arrow opening up to the sky above. In m. 55, a flurry of scales stretches our initial

FIGURE 9.2 My listening position at Op. 53, final movement, beginning.

single C to an immensely wide, three-octave version of itself, filling every diatonic step along the way: C, D, E, F, G, A, B, and C. Having received individual attention as sonorities in the first movement, these C-major-scale tones now collaborate in an unabashed and unfiltered celebration of all-encompassing C-major-ness, which will be revisited again and again until the final chords of the sonata.

Leading up to this breakthrough in m. 55 is a remarkable swell in mm. 51–54. Beethoven writes *crescendo*, and if I was right in having followed Adam's direction to use the third pedal up to this point, then now would be the time to release it. An association with the swell in mm. 9–10 of the first movement feels warranted. The memory of releasing my foot from the *una corda* pedal for the first ever time is still fresh and strong. However, while the physicality of operation is the same, the third and fourth pedals have quite different technological parameters. While the first movement's fourth-pedal swell could be realized by gradually shifting from one to three strings, the third pedal does not allow for such gradation. Soft leather strips either have an impact on the hammers or they do not: they necessitate an on-or-off kind of operation, and, when materialized by the release of one's foot, this exact moment of transition cannot be anticipated. But the *not knowing* becomes the point, as nobody, not even the player, can tell exactly when the inevitable crossover will occur. So, what's the connection with the first movement? While the fourth-pedal effect *there* was calculated and deliberately mechanical, the effect with the third pedal *here* is chaotic, unpredictable, and sublime. This fantastically uncontrollable, yet unstoppable shift from *pianissimo* to *fortissimo* brings to mind Haydn's Creation of Light (the unabashed release of C major) as arguably the epitome of sublimity in classical music.[14] Like Haydn himself, who never showed this particular page of the oratorio score to anyone (not even to his librettist Baron van Swieten), and who, during the first performance, had "the expression of someone who is thinking of biting his tongue, either to hide his embarrassment or to conceal a secret,"[15] the third Erard pedal holds a similar kind of oratorical power that only I as a player know to exist, and that only I can unleash, in full realization that once I do so, there won't be any return. I believe the outbreak of full C-major-ness in m. 55 to be the most dramatic moment of Op. 53, not only from an interactive instrument-and-player point of view, but also as an experience to be projected onto an audience. Like an orchestra, the piano follows my direction, but it has its own, delayed sense of timing. Nothing with similar force had been written for solo piano before.

A Viennese Reality Check

All of this is true on the Erard. And none of it—or very little of it—is true when played on the Walter. What to do? I can well imagine the panic Beethoven felt as he tested the results of experiments brought to fruition more than a year before. He was in for a sobering reality check. The first movement is still okay: on a Viennese instrument, the open-third sonorities sound sharper than on Erard, but at least there's a rhythmic drive that's interesting—of the kind, perhaps, that later inspired Schubert to write his "Wanderer" Fantasy in C Major, D. 760. Luckily, too, and along the same line, Beethoven had already viennicized the tremolo by rhythmically prioritizing the high notes: if no longer serving some higher sonic purpose, they nonetheless sound enticing and energetic.

The Andante is less salvageable, and I'd like to explain why by zooming in on its opening bars: see example 9.2, bottom. Already in the previous chapter, we've become aware of a tension between small-scale articulations—say, the equivalent of a word, or two, three, or four notes under a slur—and larger ones, either the equivalent of a ridiculously long word (of the kind that would be quite hard to find in a score by Mozart or Haydn) or of a phrasing slur. By using the latter term, I reluctantly tap into a well-known confusion between what's commonly called "articulation" vs. "phrasing" slurs, which caused Heinrich Schenker in 1925 to publish an infamous diatribe entitled "Away with the Phrasing Slur." Articulation slurs require instruments that articulate well (read: Viennese), while phrasing slurs are suited to instruments that favor sustain of sound over attack (read: French or English). Such "phrasing" is exactly what came into focus in chapter 8, when in the Andante we identified longer slurs with tremolo-like articulations underneath.

To understand the potential impact of his Erard on the concept of phrasing, it may be enlightening to compare our Op. 53 Andante with something Beethoven wrote at a time when he would have been unaffected by foreign technology. I propose the Adagio from his Sonata, Op. 2 No. 1, published in 1796, also in F major (see ex. 9.2, top). In each of the two melodies, I've boxed the dissonances, which on Viennese instruments are to be played noticeably louder and longer than consonances. A slur, like the one over the five notes in m. 1 of the Adagio, has the power to supersede this rule: from the dissonance the slur adopts the principle of release, which is why its beginning should always be played sufficiently strongly (so as to create room for a *diminuendo*).

While in the earlier Adagio example the dissonances consistently occur on the good part of the beat (where they belong, to create a "té-ah té-ah" kind of inflection), the Andante reverses this rule. There, dissonances occur on the bad (or weak) beats or parts of the beat and become part of a "long line," lasting all the way to a caesura at the end of the phrase, where a clear articulation (after the tension-increasing *crescendo* before, a typically Beethovenian ploy) dissipates the energy of the entire phrase. There's room for subtlety, of course, like the B-flat in m. 3 of the Adagio, which first appears as an offbeat dissonance that claims attention to itself in terms of length or strength. But the next pair of notes (on the third beat) immediately clarifies that B♭ was in fact a dissonance, and this kind of clarification is absent in m. 1 of the Andante. There, the same B♭ (seventh of the dominant chord) merges in a gentle overall flow of descending harmonies (I've marked their parallel tenth or third origins) that largely supersedes special attention to

EXAMPLE 9.2 Beethoven, Sonata in F Minor, Op. 1 No. 1, second movement, mm. 1–4; Andante, WoO 57, mm. 1–4 (dissonances are boxed).

dissonances. Beethoven, one could argue, finds a solution for the horizontal/vertical paradox we previously discussed by fundamentally changing his harmonic-compositional language.

What happens when we play the same beautiful phrase on a Viennese instrument? Making it *sing* suddenly becomes harder, since we can no longer rely on lusciousness of sound and sponginess of touch. Loosing this vertical side of the paradox, we can try and compensate, and imagine sustain where acoustically there's much less or almost none. This makes for a rather stiff performance, however. Or we can give in to Viennese horizontality, but then we risk that certain ideas start running off on their own. Take, for example, the octaves in the right hand during the last occurrence of the theme. Pleasant on the Erard, where a loose wrist can adjust its speed and level of bounciness to those of the French keys, these octaves easily feel too thin on a Walter, where the keys' lightness tempts one to compensate for a lack of tactility through excessive speed.

But the true make-or-break moment for the sonata as a whole—especially after a long Andante—remains the single C at the beginning of the final Rondo: is the link with the first-movement C-major soundscape still clear? The answer is a painful no. On a Viennese fortepiano, the C no longer has the acoustical breadth or physical depth that Beethoven remembers from those early days of his Erard. The solution? To give player and listener a helping hand: see the arrow in example 9.1. Beethoven introduces the high g^2 at the end of a new slow movement. Why? Of the divine overtone-triad, it is the g^2 that on Walter was the weakest (see fig. 9.1). Beethoven tweaks the way we perceive it—not by playing it more loudly (which would be grossly against the compositional idea of a self-inciting string), but by forcibly planting it in our brain just before we need to hear it. On a Viennese fortepiano, the *sforzando* is wonderfully effective: our brain cannot help but register an enthusiastically assertive but also quickly decaying impulse, and as the low C then makes its entry, we'd swear that g^2 is still there. Has it been there all along? This is make-believe at its most impressive.

But Beethoven did more. Doing away with the problematic Andante altogether, he expanded what could have remained a single-phrase transition (A, twelve bars) to a twenty-eight-bar ABA´-form. This act of substitution explains why the new Adagio molto starts in F major, just like the Andante before. But it also raises a question that has persisted up to this day: does the published "Waldstein" consist of two or of three movements? What seems certain from Beethoven calling his revision an "Introduzione" is that his mind had first and foremost been set on solving the problem of a link between the two C-major movements.[16]

Three Versions: "Adam," "Waldstein," and "Piano e.f.d. clavecin"

Once a revision is made, it is hard to unthink it. Who are we to question a *Fassung letzter Hand*, especially when this hand is so clearly Beethoven's? His perfect solution, furthermore, makes you forget there was ever any problem at all. But where does that leave me, from the perspective of my unrevised Erard?

I've already rejected "Waldstein" as a postpartum construct that breaks with the work's sociomaterial roots. Playing the sonata on my Erard, I want to reconnect it with those roots, to reflect what I consider also its rhetorical identity: a celebration of one's enthusiasm for a new piano. I haven't had mine revised—nor have I felt any reason to. As a result, unlike Beethoven, I've developed no desire to disentangle myself from its French inscriptions. As the date of my recording of Beethoven's "Adam" Sonata grew closer (a deadline not unlike that faced by Beethoven when publishing his "Waldstein"), the decision seemed clear: I would perform a version of the sonata that included not only the Andante favori but also an abridged version of the Introduction (namely, that single transitional phrase it could have been). It was a win-win. The Andante, with its abundant tremolo-like alternations, its pleasantly ruminative melodies, and, last but not least, its parallel-tenth harmonic textures, features the Erard in ways that would complement what I was eager to show in the first movement—and in a different key, F major. The transitional part of the new Adagio provided the perfect modulation from second to third movement, from F major to C major—a more spontaneous introduction than a movement-long Intro-duzione. Saving what I consider the best part of the Introduzione, I embrace Beethoven's revision as an improvement for a performance on my unchanged Erard: make-believe may no longer be necessary, but clarity doesn't hurt either. Example 9.3 shows what I played.

Introduzione: Adagio molto

EXAMPLE 9.3 Beethoven, Sonata in C Major, Op. 53: alternative transition between Andante and final movement, for use in "Piano e.f.d. clavecin."

We've focused on the status of the Andante, but there's another piece that Barry Cooper identifies as "clearly [. . .] intended as a possible minuet and trio for the sonata."[17] Beethoven's sketching of this little C-major piece (later published as Bagatelle, WoO 56) starts on page 138 of Landsberg 6 (near the end of the final movement) and continues on pages 145–46 (after finishing the final movement). So, after completing three long movements, did Beethoven still experience a sense of incompleteness? Or did he simply want to leave his options open, while executing an idea for a Minuet and Trio, not quite sure yet whether to actually use it?

An unforeseen four-movement "Adam" Sonata is coming into focus. Existing in the sketches, this sonata includes not only the Andante, but also a Minuet and Trio, which Cooper places between the Andante and the final Rondo. The addition of a short C-major piece at this juncture would relieve the single C at the outset of the fourth movement from having to fulfill a modulating function as well, by allowing it to vibrate in its own C-major habitat, as reestablished by the Minuet. For the original Erard, then, this would have been an improvement just as much as the prepublication revision would turn out to be for a different instrument.

For my commercially released performance of Op. 53, I've combined the best of both worlds: a four-movement sonata that includes the most useful part of the Introduzione from "Waldstein" and the Minuet/Trio from "Adam." Table 9.1 offers an overview of what are now not just two but three versions: "Adam," "Waldstein," and "mine." In my design, there's no longer room for a Scherzo or Minuet between the third and fourth movements, which are now firmly linked by tonal modulation. But the Minuet makes for an altogether better fit between the first and third movements—so, arguably, there's improvement again. As may be seen in the incipit scores of example 9.4, the Minuet continues a stream of creativity that had started in the first movement: we find the same interplay between G♯ and G♮. If the design of the four-movement "Adam" as constructed by Cooper corresponds to that of Beethoven's earlier Sonata in B-flat Major, Op. 22 (from 1799–1800), then mine is a forerunner to the "Hammerklavier." Written in 1817–18, the "Hammerklavier" Sonata in B-flat Major, Op. 106, also has four movements, with a Scherzo in second place, and a modulating Introduction between the third, slow movement and the fourth-movement Finale. Instead of the dedication to the Archduke Rudolph (there's already an "Archduke Trio," Op. 97), the nickname of "Hammerklavier" has stuck. Shining the sole spotlight on the object where Op. 53 all started, I similarly propose to call my version "Piano en forme de clavecin" or, abbreviated, "Piano e.f.d. clavecin."[18]

Cooper assumes that "Beethoven must have sensed that such an extended construction would be difficult for audiences to accept,"[19] but table 9.1 urges us to wonder: which audiences? Adam's Op. 8 No. 2 (in my performance clocking in at 31:53) is longer than Beethoven's "Waldstein" (26:12), while Beethoven's "Piano e.f.d. clavecin" (39:58) is significantly shorter than Steibelt's Op. 64 (44:38). Even if one decides to undo Beethoven's last-minute decision to omit the second repeat of the first movement, "Waldstein" would clock in at 31:03, some fourteen minutes short still of Steibelt's *Grande sonate*. For my recorded performance, I decided to embody Steibelt's legendary self-confidence, and I enjoyed every second of it. The man sure knew how to treat a French piano!

Length aside, we start seeing connections between Beethoven and his peers that cannot be coincidental, such as *attaca* transitions from the slow movement to the final movement. The Finales, furthermore, are always

TABLE 9.1 Five *Grandes sonates*

Adam, Op. 8 No. 2 (Paris: Pleyel, 1802)	Beethoven, Op. 53, "Adam" Fair copy [possibly] sent to Breitkopf & Härtel, 1804	Beethoven, Op. 53, "Waldstein" (Vienna : Bureau des arts et d'industrie, 1805)	Beethoven, Op. 53, "Piano en forme de clavecin" (CD EPRC 0036, 2020)	Steibelt, Op. 64 (Paris: Mlles Erard, 1805)
SONATE / *Pour le Forté Piano* / COMPOSÉE / *Pour le Concours des Elèves du / Conservatoire de Musique.* / PAR / L. ADAM / *Un de ses Membres* / NOTA[:] *Cette Sonate a été ex[éc]utée au Concert du Thé[â]tre / des Arts, par son Elève C. KALK-BRENNER, / Qui a remporté le Premier Prix.*	[Hypothetically:] GRANDE SONATE / pour le Pianoforte, / composée et dédiée / à son ami / *Monsieur Louis Adam / Professeur au Conservatoire de musique à Paris* / par / LOUIS VAN BEETHOVEN.	GRANDE SONATE / pour le Pianoforte, / composée et dédiée / à / *Monsieur le Comte de Waldstein / Commandeur de l'ordre Teutonique à Virnsberg et Chambellan de Sa Majesté I. & I. R. A.* / par / LOUIS VAN BEETHOVEN.	GRANDE SONATE / pour le Piano en forme de clavecin / par / LOUIS VAN BEETHOVEN.	*Grande* / SONATE / *Pour* / le Piano Forte / Composée et Dédiée / à Mademoiselle Cl[é]-mentine d'Epr[é]mesnil / Par / D. STEIBELT
Allegro di molto	Allegro con brio	Allegro con brio	Allegro con brio	Cantabile con espressione
C major	*C major*	*C major*	*C major*	*G major*
15:12	16:48	12:05	16:48	22:19

Romance: Andante grazioso un peu animé / Adagio non troppo / Allegretto *C minor / C major, V of C major / attaca:* 10:46	Andante grazioso con moto *F major* 8:41	Introduzione: Adagio molto *F major—V of C major / attaca:* 2:51	[Minuet/Trio:] Allegretto *C major* 1:55	Tempo di Minuetto: Scherzando *G major* 2:55
Finale Scherzando: Allegro vivace *C major* 5:54	[Minuet/Trio:] Allegretto *C major* 1:55	Rondo: Allegretto moderato *C major* 11:18	Andante grazioso con moto *F major* 8:41	Adagio: Fantaisie *E-flat major—V of G major / attaca:* 11:45
	Rondo: Allegretto moderato *C major* 11:18		Introduzione: Adagio molto—Rondo: Allegretto moderato *F major—C major* 1:16 + 11:18	Pastorale: Allegretto *G major* 7:39
TOTAL TIME 31:53	38:42	26:12	39:58	44:38

EXAMPLE 9.4 Incipits of Beethoven's Sonata in C Major, Op. 53, "Piano e.f.d. clavecin."

a Rondo in a pastoral style, with a theme that invariably mixes tonic and dominant harmonies over a single pedal. But while Adam's Op. 8 No. 2 and Beethoven's "Adam" share the largest percentage of C-major-ness, from a larger design point of view, it is Beethoven's "Piano e.f.d. clavecin" that most closely resembles Steibelt's Op. 64. I dare say, too, that the pedal effects in Beethoven (both the ones specified in the score and the ones inscribed in the piano) are audaciously Steibeltian rather than exquisitely Adamesque.

The Dedication

We are already familiar with the circumstance of Adam's Sonata: it "was executed [. . .] by his pupil C. [*recte* F.] Kalkbrenner, who obtained the *premier prix.*"[20] There's no dedication, but the institutional connection spelled out over a full title page espouses all the more prestige. For its part, Steibelt's *Grande sonate* is "composed and dedicated to Mademoiselle Clémentine d'Eprémesnil." Clémentine was the daughter of Françoise Augustine Duval d'Eprémesnil, who in the 1780s had hosted an artistic salon that Daniel Steibelt had frequented. Her salon, however, became so politicized that Mme. d'Eprémesnil ended up beneath the guillotine in 1794, along with her husband, Jean-Jacques Duval d'Eprémesnil, a known antirevolutionary. The young Clémentine must have grown up an excellent pianist—worthy of a new grand piano by Erard, not just once, but twice. Her name shows up in the Erard Frères *livres de ventes*, differently spelled as "Despreminil" and "d'Epreminil," on two different occasions. As a fourteen-year-old, on January 22, 1802, she receives her first *piano en forme de clavecin*, No. 69, for which Monsieur Thilorien (presumably a relative of Mme. d'Eprémesnil's first husband, who had died in 1784) pays 2,000 livres. Four years later, on November 6, 1805, she exchanges this piano for a more recent model, No. 191, adding 500 livres in cash (*espèces*) to cover a new balance of 2,000 livres. (Erard Frères thus considered a four-year-old piano as devalued by one-quarter of its original value.) Twice the sale is registered as "par Steibelt," no doubt her long-term teacher. That the purchase of a new piano coincides with the publication of Steibelt's sonata (announced by the *Journal de Paris* on November 14, 1805, or barely one week after the visit by teacher and pupil to the Erard Frères showroom),[21] adds to a hypothesis of a coming-of-age gift in the double form of a new grand piano and the dedication of a *Grande sonate*: the young woman had turned eighteen earlier that year. Clémentine's name does not show up in the register of *élèves* at the Conservatoire, and this need not surprise us.[22] Steibelt, the eternal entrepreneur, made his living (among many other things) by private teaching—and by brokering sales of pianos—and in any case, as also noted by the author of an 1801 report on the Paris Conservatoire in the Leipzig *AmZ*, he was not teaching at the institute.[23]

The social backgrounds of Frédéric Kalkbrenner and Clémentine d'Eprémesnil couldn't be more different: the one a product, the other a survivor, of the Revolution. What connected them most strongly was their youth and excellence. Worthy of a first prize and a new grand piano, they represented the best of a new generation of pianists. By contrast, on Beethoven's title page we find the name of a forty-three-year-old nobleman. Yes, he may have been "not only a connoisseur but also a practitioner of music" (and by all accounts, he was a decent musician, who "improvised at the piano in a truly delightful manner"),[24] but the dedication does not help clarify or promote the sonata's stellar potential. As we know, Beethoven had intended to include Louis Adam as co-dedicatee of Op. 47. So when in May 1805 he finally had the opportunity of going further and dedicating an actual piano sonata to his French colleague, what prompted him to settle instead on an old acquaintance, Ferdinand Ernst Joseph Gabriel, Count von Waldstein and Wartenberg at Dux?

The simple answer would be that circumstances changed. By 1805, any debt Beethoven had felt to Adam in the first flush of excitement over the new piano would have ebbed away, not least because the piano had become a headache; in any case, the matter of a dedication was never raised during Beethoven's correspondence with Härtel. But perhaps there's another perspective on the matter. Precisely because of its French roots, as well as its unmistakable similarity to a sonata like Adam's own Op. 8 No. 2, dedicating the sonata to Adam may never have been an option, in case contemporaries (particularly the French, who were bound to take notice) might mistake Beethoven's sonata as parody—or worse, plagiarism. (This assumes, of course, that Beethoven would have known Adam's Op. 8 No. 2, something for which we unfortunately have no evidence.) The dedication to Waldstein, who would not himself have picked up on any French connotations, may now seem like a lost opportunity, but back then would have been seen as business as usual: Beethoven dedicating a work to an aristocratic patron. The gesture was made, Franz Gerhard Wegeler wrote in 1838, "out of unwavering gratitude," and his Bonn connection with both Beethoven and Count Waldstein has helped make him a credible source in the matter.[25] Scholarship has since largely followed this line of thought, endorsing "the great and important Sonata in C Major" (as Wegeler calls it) as a self-professed fulfillment of Waldstein's famous prophecy that in Vienna Beethoven was "to receive *Mozart's spirit from Haydn's hands.*"[26] "Waldstein" (the piece now forever intertwined with the person) became the very symbol of a classicizing narrative, which back in 1792, on the eve of Beethoven's departure from Bonn to Vienna, had unwittingly been initiated by a handwritten note in a private album, intended more as the shared expression of a sentiment of loss (their mutual hero Mozart had just died, on December 5, 1791) than to predict any future creation of a Viennese classical triumvirate.

It is tempting, indeed, to see "Waldstein" as a default dedication—one that was bound to happen sooner or later, and applicable not to Op. 53 in particular, but to any Viennese-born piano sonata deemed worthy by the "mature" Beethoven of Count Waldstein's erstwhile trust.[27] But what if the dedication to Waldstein was rhetorically just as specific as my hypothetical one to Louis Adam? What if it was actually part of the complete overhaul of a sonata that had started with revisions of the score? Decisions on revision and dedication might have been made in tandem, and both perhaps in response to the reaction of his Viennese friends. In this new network of people and things, then, I'd suggest we focus on Count Waldstein, the friend—or "my friend Gr[af] waldstein," as Beethoven called him in a letter to Simrock in 1794.[28] The composer and the Count had reconnected in Vienna earlier that year, which was to be the only time they did so until as late as 1809.[29] Contrary to the speculations of many scholars, one might argue that it was the *absence* of the Count during the whole production of Op. 53 that may have been exactly what made him the appropriate dedicatee. As the meaning of Op. 53 shifted from actually French to sort-of-Viennese, Beethoven may have felt that a dedication to someone who was both an outsider and a long-time supporter would be the best course of action.

Let's read this dedication afresh (fig. 9.3): "Grande sonate pour le Pianoforte, composée et dédiée à Monsieur le Comte de Waldstein[,] Commandeur de l'ordre Teutonique à Virnsberg et Chambellan de Sa Majesté I. & I.R.A."[30] Waldstein became a knight of the Teutonic Order on June 17, 1788.[31] It was his employer who knighted him: the Archduke Maximilian Francis, Elector of Cologne and Grand Master of the Teutonic Knights. In *cf Appny.*

GRANDE SONATE
pour le Pianoforte,
composée et dédiée

à

Monsieur le Comte de Waldstein
Commandeur de l'ordre Teutonique à Virnsberg et Chambellan
de Sa Majesté J. & J. R. A.

par

LOUIS VAN BEETHOVEN.
Op. 53.

449.

f 2. 15 x.

A Vienne au Bureau des arts et d'industrie.

FIGURE 9.3 Title page of Beethoven's "Waldstein" Sonata, Op. 53 (Vienna: Bureau des arts et d'industrie, 1805).

1793 the Order assigned him the command over Virnsberg, a little village in Bavaria, but events in his life were to take him elsewhere. It is the last part of the title, however, that needs most scrutiny. "Imperial chamberlain" is a hereditary title that ran through the Waldstein family, thus applying to a generic *Sa Majesté impériale*, with "I." referring to the Emperor of Austria, whether Joseph II, Leopold II, or Francis II.[32] The second "I.R.A." (*[Sa Majesté] impériale et royale l'archiduc*), however, is a title reserved for possible pretenders to the imperial throne and must refer specifically to his service to Maximilian Francis of Austria, Archduke and Elector of Cologne, youngest child of Empress Maria Theresa and her husband, Francis I. Waldstein, in other words, was chamberlain twice: to the Elector *and* to the Emperor. (The phrasing on the title page assumes either a second "Sa Majesté," as clarified above, or mistakenly uses the singular for a plural "Ses Majestés.")

This full and formal title could not have felt more distant to what was actually happening in Waldstein's life. Since 1791 he had no longer seen eye to eye with the Archduke, whose prorevolutionary, anti-imperial political views turned Waldstein into even more of an Austrian patriot *pur sang*.[33] With the support of Prince Ludwig von Starhemberg, the Austrian envoy in London, Waldstein obtained permission to lead a German army regiment under English rule with the purpose of fighting against Napoleon—a training program he would transfer from Northern Germany to England, where he was based from 1796 to 1807.[34] It is hard to believe that Beethoven, who must have heard about Waldstein's projects through the brothers von Breuning, wasn't affected by the political idealism of his old friend, eight years his senior.[35] It may have made him more determined to get that noble title of Waldstein absolutely right, as proof of the latter's loyalty to Austria expressed in a manner the whole Viennese audience could see and take note of. In the dedication, then, it is the single, abbreviated "I." that counts most, in reference to the one and only Majesty—the singular perhaps carrying an implicitly patriotic message that "I.R.A." should have maintained his loyalty to the Austrian Emperor, too. (Maximilian Francis had passed away in 1801.)

"With the grace of God and that of Count Starhemberg, Colonel-proprietor in the service of His Majesty of England [*Par la Grâce de Dieu et du Comte Starhemberg Colonel propriétaire au Service de S. M. britan.*]" is how Waldstein described his real-life title at this period of exile, with a heavy dose of self-sarcasm.[36] Beethoven may have realized that Waldstein was walking a thin line between the official Austrian position with regard to France and his own military engagement under foreign royal rule in England. His dedication of Op. 53 to Count von Waldstein may well have had a political undertone: nothing as strongly emotional as the angry ripping out of the title page of his "Bonaparte" Symphony, but an act at the same time more lasting and more public.[37] As we saw above, at the time of his correspondence with Breitkopf & Härtel, the "Eroica" Symphony still carried its original association with the First Consul of France. If the subject of Op. 55 changed from hero to heroism by a mere change of title, then the shift in Op. 53 is more radical. Before it became "Waldstein," the true hero in the first of three solo sonatas had been not a person, but an unrevised object—this *piano en forme de clavecin*, arguably to be associated with the persons of Adam and Steibelt, as friendly facilitator and nemesis, respectively. But along with revisions made by the composer, to both piano and score, another person came into focus. Count von Waldstein was almost the opposite of a hero. Faithfully chasing his long-held dreams (ever since his youth, he had wanted to embark on a military career) and more of a patriot than his late Habsburg imperial employer had ever been, he represented loyalty, consistency, and decency—the perfect dedicatee of a piano sonata that was to become a classic.

What We Missed

So far, we've analyzed parts of a "Waldstein" we've known. If our Erard replica, however, also legitimizes the restoration of a four-movement sonata like the "Piano e.f.d clavecin" version that I propose, then how do the parts we have not known yet fit? Example 9.5 presents a collage of selected ideas from the early sketches and the finished score. I invite readers to play them at the piano. Start with the sketch excerpt at the center of the circle. Lyrical, songful, and in E major, it is a fitting contrast to the C-major tremolo that Beethoven initially jotted down as the opening theme for the first movement, just above. In many ways, it's a lyrical counterpart of the preliminary scale exercises, with which it all started. We recognize the parallel intervals (thirds, sixths) and the descending scale. But while the exercises served as a blanket experiment outside of the actual composition project (teaching us some core aesthetic principles of the French piano), this condensed E-major scale anchors itself within the actual composition. What is the driving force behind it? After settling on an opening theme, is Beethoven looking for a potential second theme of a sonata-form? Or is he fine-tuning the scale-experiment, zooming in on the descending part of the scale and exploring the lyrical qualities of his Erard? We see a long slur all the way from the beginning to the end: Beethoven listens to the long sustain that the piano is capable of producing. But now anticipating actual composition, he relaxes the principle of parallelism and introduces midway an 8 (B) instead of a 6 (G♯), creating a natural dividing point on dominant V, between the two tonics at beginning and end. Finally, note the bar-lines: he's thinking 4/4, with downbeat functions for dominant (m. 2) and tonic, respectively (m. 3). In other words, there's musical context; Beethoven is no longer just doing research.

We're ready to assess excerpts nos. 1–7, ordered clockwise in a circle around this mother sketch. The order corresponds to their appearance in

EXAMPLE 9.5 "//10" moments in Beethoven's Sonata in C Major, Op. 53, "Piano e.f.d. clavecin":

Center: sketch, Landsberg 6, p. 120, st. 13–14

1. Sketch, Landsberg 6, p. 121, st. 8–9

2. Sketch, Landsberg 6, p. 121, st. 8–12

3. Finished version, second movement, mm. 1–8, reduction

4. Finished version, first movement, mm. 35–42, reduction

5. Finished version, first movement, mm. 196–203, reduction

6. Finished version, first movement, mm. 204–11, reduction

7. Sketch, Landsberg 6, third movement, p. 146, st. 1–2

Landsberg 6, hence most probably also to the order of their creation. For excerpts nos. 3 and 7, I have adopted the final notation in the score, while for excerpts nos. 4–6, I made a harmonic reduction from the finished score. Excerpts nos. 1 and 2, finally, are copied exactly from the sketchbook. Some thoughts as we play:

Nos. 1 and 2. From the mother sketch, Beethoven looks for a complete period with antecedent and consequent for a possible Andante. He keeps parallel thirds going from E down to A. Appreciate the harmonies that these five consecutive thirds produce.

No. 3. At this early point, he abandons E major in favor of F major. This happens long before he resumes work on the Andante, which will be after the first movement is finished. Though more subtle and hidden, tenth/third parallelism remains inherent in this theme of the finished Andante.

No. 4. The E-major Andante theme (no. 2) has laid the groundwork for this second key area theme of the first movement. No. 4 keeps the antecedent-consequent design of no. 2, while maintaining more consistency with third parallelism. Play the two first measures and appreciate how G-sharp minor from before has transformed into a major secondary dominant (with B♯), now evoking C-sharp minor.

Nos. 5–6. Picking up with no. 4 (one fifth lower, to A major, to match the recapitulation), no. 5 also develops a new goal: to fuse main key C major with A minor—a fusion that no. 6 adopts and confirms.

No. 7. G♯ (A minor) vs. G♮ (C major) sticks, and now Beethoven has some fun with the idea. Of all excerpts, no. 7 is the one that has *everything*: A minor embedded in C major, antecedent/consequent (I–V followed by V–I), a descending scale (split between C to G in the key-by-key proceeding fifth finger of the left hand, and F to C in the key-by-key proceeding thumb of the right hand), and sixth-parallel voice leading. A nice detail: although from a voice-leading point of view the C-major scale descends, pitch-wise the beginning and ending points actually point upward: from low c to high c^2.

Excerpt no. 7 is the last. Effortlessly, it connects with the full cycle of sonorities that caught our attention in movement one. Beginning and end points are the same, and the fact that excerpt no. 7's descending scale actually ends up two octaves higher (from c to c^2) may well bring to memory the sonority-driven mission that the first movement's step-wise explorations of C-major components had taken on. More than voice leading, it's about color, to be savored almost in spite of register (which on a French piano is much less individually characterized than on a Viennese piano). Ultimately, however, it's about single C-major-ness. Itself the culmination of a series of variations on a sketched idea, excerpt no. 7 has the secondary function of drawing a connection between two Cs (which I've added in the example as a linear and ascending alternative to the descending slur of the mother sketch). Cutting through two octaves, this dotted line reminds us that there's only one C, at the center of a long piece of spectral composition.

Beethoven killed many darlings during various stages of revision, but in this case, he killed a complete sub-story—not as clear and compact as the one featuring eight sonorities in the first movement, but more cross-referential, more fragmented, and leading to a remarkable Minuet and Trio. Did Beethoven write them down as a bonus, to be placed second or third in a four-movement sonata—or were they just a little something, written on the spur of the moment and to be kept in a portfolio along with other stray bagatelles? Either way, this Minuet could not have been written without the previous hard work.

Much later, in 1818, Beethoven would tell Carl Czerny during a walk to Mödling, "Now I'm writing a sonata that is going to be my grandest."[38] The work in question was to be his "Hammerklavier," Op. 106. Back in 1805, however, I suggest his primary concern was not with length but with the higher principle of *son continu*. In this sense, Frenchness was to be saved after all. The acoustic and physical reality of a *piano en forme de clavecin* no longer being the same (because it had been either revised or pushed aside in favor of a more familiar Viennese instrument), Beethoven had to upgrade *son continu* from an aesthetic principle to a structural one. On the French piano sound itself breathes the air of *son continu* (and this would appear even more true from the perspective of a Viennese pianist), while on a Viennese piano one has to work for it, with logic, grand gesture, and sheer power of will. French materiality meets Viennese classicism.

Yet, when still faced with criticism, the best course of action for Beethoven the composer was to focus on the sustained experience of C-major-ness from the first to the last movement, at the expense of a playful Minuet and a favorite Andante. Thus, the outer movements became two grand pillars of one monumental sonata, with an Introduzione standing as an arch in between. This new structure—independent of any instrument, whether French or Viennese—espouses the kind of compositional force that may be readily recognized as Beethovenian.

The Adam Connection

Where does Louis Adam stand in all of this? He had possibly been the one who tested and selected Beethoven's French piano in the Erard Frères workshop, and, judging by his use of Beethoven's Op. 2 Sonatas as didactic material in his *Méthode*, he must have held Beethoven in high esteem. But was there more to it? Did Sébastien Erard include an advance copy of Adam's method in that crate destined to Vienna?[39] Did Adam write a letter to Beethoven, feeding off his contribution to the shipment of a piano to establish contact with a brilliant young colleague? No proof exists—apart from Beethoven's recorded words to Ries that "he owes Adam a courtesy on account of the Paris piano."

In a next chapter we will make an effort to get to know more about Louis Adam, the man, the teacher, and the pianist. For now, if we look for a flesh-and-blood link with Beethoven, we find it in Adam's prize-winning pupil Frédéric Kalkbrenner, who came to study in Vienna just around the time of the arrival of Beethoven's Erard piano. He would stay for about a year, from fall 1803 to fall 1804. Haydn sent the eighteen-year-old to Johann Georg Albrechtsberger for counterpoint lessons, just as he had sent Beethoven one decade earlier. But "every Sunday," as Charles Dumes wrote in 1842,

> Frédéric Kalkbrenner went to see Haydn to report on the work he had accomplished during the week; on his way over, he always made a stop with Beethoven, whose place was on the way and who took great pleasure in making him play preludes and fugues of Sébastien Bach, which he knew by heart.[40]

The intent of the French biographer is clearly to connect the young Kalkbrenner with the two musical giants in Vienna, confirming his future place in the pantheon. But what Dumes would not have known is that in both Haydn's and Beethoven's houses there was a French piano. For Beethoven this would have been the perfect opportunity to hear his instrument played by someone intimately familiar with its possibilities. Let's travel back through the power of the imagination and listen in on the conversation in Beethoven's apartment the first Sunday the young French virtuoso came to visit:

- [Beethoven:] So, how 's my old teacher doing?
- [Kalkbrenner:] Quite cheerful. Couldn't stop talking and asking questions, about my father, about the Conservatoire, about my teacher. He also talked about you—
- [B *(changing the subject):*] Speaking of Paris: you studied with Louis Adam, did you not? I read somewhere that you won the *premier prix.* Congratulations!
- [K:] *Vielen Dank.*
- [B:] What a strange concept, though, holding a competition in music: as if *Vortrag* is all that counts—or what is it that they call it in Paris, *exécution?*
- [K:] Yes, indeed: *la perfection d'exécution* is what our director Sarrette always urges us to aspire to.[41]
- [B *(pretending not to hear):*] I've been in a few duels myself. The clownery of it all, the sheer entertainment. If there's one good thing that comes out of them, it's that they help me keep up my improvising chops.
- [K:] Maestro Haydn told me—rather gleefully—that you gave Monsieur Steibelt quite a run for his money a couple of years ago.
- [B:] O yes: Da-nièl Stei-bèlt. Let's not talk about him. Let's talk instead about this beauty of an instrument. *(Beethoven leads Kalkbrenner into the adjacent room.)* You know, I really should send a token of gratitude to Monsieur Adam. *(Beethoven makes an effort to pronounce the name correctly: Adã, like* vent *or* champ.) I understand he was the one who selected it.
- [K:] He told me all about it. He also said it was an honor for Erard Frères to send one of their grand pianos to Vienna's greatest *claveciniste. Beethoven couldn't help but be annoyed by the label "harpsichordist": as if*

that was all he was known for in Paris, a player of keyboards, a Cembalist, *not even a pianist. Kalkbrenner did not say that Sébastien Erard had needed some serious prodding to consider the shipment a business gift. His nieces had published the "Pathétique" Sonata in 1801—what craziness and how detrimental for the piano!*[42] *"The man doesn't respect a fine piece of artisanship," Monsieur Erard had fumed, and Adam had admitted as much. "But what genius," he'd countered. "Clearly, he has the wrong instrument," he'd argued. "Send him one of yours, and it will teach him our* art de bien chanter. *Imagine the publicity for your company! Imagine the glory for our nation!" Jean-Baptiste Erard had nodded thoughtfully. "Leave it to me," he had whispered in Adam's ear as they walked him out.*

- [B *(back to reality, now standing in front of the piano):*] Play me something, young man! The old Albrechtsberger told me you know all of Bach senior's *Das wohltemperierte Clavier* by heart.
- [K:] One of the perks of studying at the Conservatoire. I had easy access to a manuscript copy of them in the library. Every week, I would diligently copy [*by hand*] another prelude & fugue—a project that took me a good year.
- [B:] Oh yes, I also read about that impressive library: what a terrific way to preserve the Classics, while also making them available to the young.[43]
- [K:] Monsieur Adam and also my harmony teacher Charles-Simon Catel shared my excitement about Bach's *WTC*. Monsieur Catel even predicted that one day all piano pupils would have to learn them.
- [B:] Show me! Why not start with the first?

  Kalkbrenner starts playing. His trained fingers hit the deep Erard keys with perpendicular precision, and holding down the keys of each chord for as long as possible, he produces some immensely beautiful harmonies. That's when it hits Beethoven. For the French it's not about shape or gesture: it's about sound, reverberation, harmonie—*all three in perfect balance and unity. His next piano sonata, he decides, is going to be in C major.*

Epilogue

As far as we know, Adam would have to wait until 1807 before he found a copy of Beethoven's "Waldstein" Sonata *chez* Pleyel at rue Neuve des

Petits Champs No. 1286, "opposite the National Treasury."[44] But then, he was all attention. Together with four extracts from Op. 27 No. 2 (all from the third movement), he incorporated no fewer than six excerpts from Op. 53 (from the first and third movements) in the second part ("lettre B") of the "Method or General Principle of Fingering for the Fortepiano, as adopted by the Conservatoire de musique de Paris, to serve the instruction of pupils in this institution." This was a new edition of the method that he had co-edited with Lachnith back in 1798, itself to be dated between 1813 and 1822.[45]

By way of conclusion, then, let's take a closer look at one of these excerpts and put it in context with Bach's C-major prelude and Adam's own advice on playing arpeggios: see example 9.6. "When the highest notes [of an arpeggio] may form a singing line [un chant] in places where there is a slur [une liaison] and the notes that accompany this melody may form a chord, one may hold all the notes under the fingers for as long as the chord may last."[46] Adam is referring to a single hand only, and the singing line is clear in Adam's example (top)—it starts with the high e^2 as the first note. The quintessential context of sound as multiple-voice harmony is clear, yet again. Beethoven (middle) goes a few steps further. He not only doubles the hands, but also constructs the overall harmonic effect from the bass up, saving singing tone e^2 in the right hand for last (second beat of m. 113). Clearly understanding the instrument, he exploits the Erard's capacity of producing rich, triadic clouds of overtones—an effect he expands beyond the C-major triad by introducing dissonances. While the seventh (B♭) in m. 114 is still very much part of an audible overtone spectrum (and thus part of the initial C-major sound), the ninth (D♭) has the power of catapulting the one chord to the next, turning C into a dominant of F; the same cycle unfolds then between F and B-flat. It's the stasis of each of these chords, held until a tipping point is reached and one cannot hold on any longer, that makes this sequence of harmonies (or, indeed, sounds) grand and monumental. In my performance (the added fingering in the example is mine), I deliberately try to feel each of the triads before moving my right hand from one position to the next. Keeping down the damper pedal as I shape these triads, it's as if I'm capable of combining a French acoustic experience with Viennese transparency: Beethoven writes long slurs, but it doesn't hurt to imagine a multitude of little slurs beneath them.

EXAMPLE 9.6 C-major arpeggios: Adam, "singing chords" (1804–5, 152) (*top*); Beethoven, Sonata in C Major, Op. 53, first movement, mm. 112–16, with author's fingerings (*middle*); Adam, exercise No. 282 (1813–22, part B, 104) (*bottom*).

Let's compare my proposed fingering with that of Adam (bottom). Instead of keeping the thumb in the right hand where it belongs (on the lowest note of each triadic constellation, whether consonant or dissonant), he forces the pupil into a complex fingering that loses touch with the passage's harmonic basis, dissociating it further from its C-major origin by calling it a "chromatic exercise." Beethoven, it could be argued, has here understood the French piano's acoustical and compositional possibilities better than Adam. So, what if Beethoven had made it to Paris after all, and the two men had befriended one another (granted, a big if)—interesting discussions might have unfolded in a Paris Conservatoire classroom, where the most advanced piano students might have gathered along with their teacher and his guest around the best French grand piano in the institute. A new educational format might have been born: that of a master class by a distinguished *claveciniste de Vienne*.

CHAPTER TEN

A Prize-Winning Teacher

BEETHOVEN, Germany's foremost *claveciniste* today, sees the palm of victory shine on STEIBELT & strives to challenge him for it.

—Advertisement for various scores of Beethoven works to be
had at H. Simrock, *Journal de Paris*, December 1, 1804, app., 6

Today, when someone is said to hold a *premier prix* in piano from a conservatory, does that mean they received first prize? I remember struggling with this conundrum when preparing English versions of my CV for applications to American graduate schools. Eventually, I decided to leave the French untouched. If the admissions committee had asked me to clarify, I would have replied, "No, a *premier prix* is a conservatory diploma, not unlike the Anglo-Saxon bachelor's degree, but it is awarded on the basis of a single exam. This consists of a closed-door technical challenge, followed by a publicly accessible performance. A final mark of at least 80 percent ensures a *premier prix*. If you obtain less than 80 percent but more than 70 percent, you are sent away with a *deuxième prix* and given a chance to present yourself to the judges again the next year." What I could have added is that I'd never felt at home in the very traditional confines of the conservatory, which in Belgium prior to 1999 had been the only path to a professional career in music.

Imagine my surprise, then, when beginning to piece together the details of the early years of the Paris Conservatoire, that godmother of all modern-day conservatories, to learn that my diploma experience did not match my predecessors'. A *premier prix* had originally been exactly that: a first prize to be won following a *concours*, or competition. Perusal of primary sources in Constant Pierre's two-volume study, *Le Conservatoire national de musique et de déclamation: documents historiques et administratifs*, published in 1900, reveals the extent to which competition became institutionalized. It permeates the language not only of evaluation but also of education in general. In the wake of the French Revolution, validation was bestowed on young talent through a new process that was democratic in ideology but proto-Darwinian in practice. The privileges of birth no longer guaranteed success in life; instead, it was through ability—and tenacity—that one earned a *premier prix*. Aristocracy was superseded by meritocracy.

While it was prestigious enough to call yourself an *ancien élève du Conservatoire national*, it was a mark of highest distinction to be recognized as the *premier élève de L. Adam*, as Frédéric Kalkbrenner was called in the Paris press.[1] Building one's career on the virtue of being a pupil of someone famous was nothing new. Beethoven was a pupil of Haydn, and everybody knew it, even if Beethoven himself downplayed the relationship;[2] Ferdinand Ries, in contrast, happily bore the epithet "Beethoven's sole pupil."[3] New, however, was the institutional context for such relationships, which could be mutually beneficial. Indeed, in January 1801 the public identification of Kalkbrenner as "first pupil of L. Adam" probably benefited the teacher as much as the student, since Adam was at that time actively positioning himself to become the *premier* piano professor at the Conservatoire.

The Paris conservatory became a major nexus of musical contacts, with Adam often at the center. In 1803, Ries informed the publisher Simrock in Bonn that Beethoven intended to dedicate his Violin Sonata in A Major, Op. 47, "to Adam and Kreutzer as *first* violinist and piano player in Paris" (emphasis added). By tapping Kreutzer and Adam jointly, both of whom were prominent members of the conservatory faculty, Beethoven could double down on a potentially fruitful institutional affiliation, one that might promote not only his violin sonata, but future compositions as well.[4] At the same time, he could settle a social debt with his French colleague-*claveciniste*, who had assisted him in obtaining an Erard piano. When Simrock eventually published the sonata in 1805, however, Kreutzer's name appeared alone on the title page (fig. 10.1). In the intervening

FIGURE 10.1 Title page of Beethoven's "Kreutzer" Sonata in A Major (Bonn: Simrock, 1805), Op. 47. Reproduced with permission of Beethoven-Haus, Bonn.

years, Beethoven's enthusiasm for his French piano had ebbed, taking his gratitude for Adam's help along with it. But the Conservatoire connection stuck, and the wording of the dedication reinforced it. Beethoven refers to Kreutzer as *Membro del Conservatorio di Musica in Parigi.* One can easily suppose that, by extension, Beethoven was addressing all the talented Paris piano and violin students who might one day play his *Sonata per il Piano-forte ed un Violino obligato scritta in una stile molto concertante, quasi come d'un concerto.* Noteworthy, too, is that at the bottom Nikolaus Simrock advertises where the score may be had in Paris: *chez* Heinrich, his brother, who was a teacher of horn and singing at the Conservatoire.[5]

It is well known that Beethoven had in fact crossed paths with Kreutzer, whom he would much later in life still turn to, describing himself as *votre ancien ami* ("your old friend").[6] In his diary, Count Karl von Zinzendorf recounted a musical soirée at Lobkowitz's on April 5, 1798: "Citoyen Creutzer [*sic*] played the violin and Bedhofen [*sic*] the *clavessin.*"[7] Kreutzer had stayed in the Austrian capital as part of the entourage of the French ambassador, Jean-Baptiste Bernadotte. This double encounter with a French colleague and a major political figure might well have kindled Beethoven's passion for Napoleon and postrevolutionary Paris.[8]

Adam, however, was someone Beethoven had never met—let alone heard. So, who was he? Given the number of times we've solicited his advice in our explorations of the French piano, we owe it to him to find out.

* * *

In 1878, Antoine Marmontel (1816–98) published *Les pianistes célèbres*, an omnibus containing thirty biographical sketches of pianist-luminaries. Eldest among them was Muzio Clementi, *le père du piano*—in adoption of the popular English epithet. If Clementi was the "father," then Adam, six years Clementi's junior, was *le doyen*.[9] The academic title is appropriate: Adam (1758–1848) had been teaching at the Paris Conservatoire for an impressive forty-five years, from 1797 to 1842. "The name of Louis Adam," Marmontel writes,

> merits to be added to those of the famous pianists, if not at premier rank—that of founders [*créateurs*] and great leaders [*chefs*] of a school—then certainly in the honorable role and especially interesting category of masters [*maîtres*], whose rational and methodical teaching has exerted a salutary influence on the progress of French art.[10]

By deliberately including Louis Adam in his pianists' hall of fame, Marmontel honored a new reality of institutionalized pedagogy that through the century had come to define both French and international pianism. But reputations do not arise *ex nihilo*, and Marmontel offers no glimpse into the circumstances that enabled Adam to arrive at the helm of a pioneering institution. During those first years of the Conservatoire, when faculty rosters were still being filled, classes formed, and that one crucial textbook was yet to be written, what made Adam the proverbial right man at the right time? In his biographical narrative, Marmontel has Adam leave his home region of Alsace in 1796 at age thirty-eight "to make it in Paris as composer and virtuoso."[11] If this is true, Adam's hiring by the Conservatoire by the next academic year (1797) comes across as a convenient alignment of fate between individual and institution: of course, the young Conservatoire snaps up a seasoned musician arriving from out of town. Two other reports, however, place Louis Adam in Paris much earlier. Choron and Fayolle (1810) have the budding musician arrive "in Paris at the age of seventeen," while Adam's own son Adolphe, interviewed in a work by Arthur Pougin (1877), claims his father was in the French capital already "at the age of fifteen."[12] Thirty-eight, seventeen, or fifteen: which is it? The fact remains that we know very little about Louis Adam's pre-Conservatoire activities in Paris. Adolphe Adam ties him with Gluck, as the latter's friend and protégé, and keyboard arranger for his operas, and explains further that "performers [*exécutants*] were rare at this time," which made "my father part of a trend that would benefit him during his whole long career."

A Female Colleague

Whether or not Adam responded to the Conservatoire's first *concours* for piano faculty on October 24, 1795, we do not know, but his name did not appear on the list of newly hired *professeurs*, announced on November 22, 1795.[13] On this list, one pianist stands out for her gender: Hélène de Montgeroult (or "Comtesse de Charnay") was given the rank of *professeur de 1re classe* as the first and only newly hired woman: she would teach the first class of men (*classe des hommes*) and earn 2,500 livres. The other new piano hire was a man, Hyacinthe Jadin, who like Montgeroult had been a pupil of Nicolas-Joseph Hüllmandel and who received the rank of *professeur de 2me classe*, earning 300 livres less than Montgeroult and teaching a class of women (*classe des femmes*). The third opening on the piano faculty was not filled. Even if Adam had thrown his hat into the ring, there would have been little chance against de Montgeroult. Jérôme Dorival, in a 2006 biography of de Montgeroult, cites a gut-churning episode that brought together Bernard Sarrette, soon-to-be Conservatoire director, and the indicted de Montgeroult before a revolutionary tribunal in 1794. The story originally appeared in 1873 in a highly romanticized chapter on Viotti and de Montgeroult ("Deux virtuoses au XVIIIe siècle") by Eugène Gautier, a Conservatoire alumnus and professor of music history at the same institute.

In 1794, we find Madame de Montgeroult confined in the prisons of the Conciergerie, and the Committee of Public Safety is about to determine her fate. "Fortuitously for the famous artist, her friend Sarrette, director of the Conservatoire, then called the National Institute of Music, ventured, like Orpheus, to penetrate Tenaron [. . .], and appealed for Madame de Montgeroult, arguing that the establishment that he leads could not proceed without the greatest piano professor then in France." A piano with "two unhinged pedals swinging wildly under the belly of the box" (i.e., a square piano, which for a moment was mistaken for a coffin by her "disturbed friends") was brought into the tribunal, and de Montgeroult, "pale after many days of captivity and anguish," was asked to "sit down and play for us La Marseillaise!" De Montgeroult complied, and as she continued to improvise variations, "the president could no longer contain himself." "He rose," Gautier concludes the stirring story, "and gesturing to his colleagues, launched into the national anthem in a thundering voice." Cityonne de Montgeroult, now a proven patriot, was acquitted, and asked to "come and receive the fraternal accolade!"[14]

Madame de Montgeroult was neither the only aristocrat nor the only musician to be shown clemency. During the Reign of Terror, *réquisitions* were granted to select nobles and foreigners, sparing their lives so they could continue to exercise a potentially useful talent or profession. Between April 16 and 24, 1794, a "Decree concerning the restraint of conspirators, the removal of nobles, and the general police" was proclaimed in Paris and distributed via public bulletin. Article 6 of the new policy stated in no uncertain terms, "No ex-noble, no foreigner of the countries with which the Republic is at war, shall inhabit Paris, nor the garrisons, nor the maritime towns, during the war." The vital exception, however, was stipulated in Article 10:

> The Committee of Public Safety is authorized to retain, by special requisition, the aforementioned nobles and foreigners, whose capacities [*moyens*] are deemed useful to the Republic.[15]

A 1794 list of requisitions begins with (as no. 51) none other than Daniel Steibelt, "Foreigner & composer of music, to be employed for the composition of patriotic works for national holidays, of which he will present proof to the committee." Among the 1,300 entries one finds other notable musicians and future Conservatoire faculty, such as Monsigny, Rode,

Ladurner, and Nicodamy. Next to the entry "No. 453 C[itoy]enne Gaultier-montgeroult [*sic*]," we read: "Artist, whose husband was cowardly assassinated by the Austrians, is to employ her talent toward patriotic holidays."[16]

Patriotic duty is also what Sarrette would appeal to—tables turned—when justifying his young institute to the republican authorities. "Is the *Conservatoire de musique* necessary?" This blunt opening question at a 1796 hearing by the budget committee of the Council of Five Hundred is answered by the thirty-one-year-old director succinctly and pointedly: "It is the only music school in France and the only means of performance [*moyen d'exécution*] that the government has at its disposal for the celebration of national ceremonies [*solennités nationales*]." To the objection that the Conservatoire has already cost too much, he rejoins that "to unite musicians for the service of each of the national holidays" would have cost much more.[17]

So, when in October 1795 it was Sarrette who presided over the committee in charge of hiring new faculty, there could be little doubt: following his own logic, de Montgeroult virtually had to be hired. All the more intriguing, then, is that *professeur* de Montgeroult ended up leaving the Conservatoire barely fifteen months into her new job. On January 16, 1798, she submitted her letter of resignation. Speculation abounds as to her reasons. Was it poor health? or, with the memories of terrible times gradually fading, did de Montgeroult wish to resume her old lifestyle? or might there have been a rivalry with a new colleague—Louis Adam? Of the three hypotheses floating through the literature, the last is the most easily verified by known institutional records. Hélène de Montgeroult, so the proposition runs, felt slighted when Adam was selected to write the official piano textbook. It took her another twenty years to publish her own textbook—celebrated in its own right but sadly irrelevant for those all-important early years of an emerging institution. (Her approach to the piano was diametrically opposed to Adam's: while, as we know, Adam praises "the French" for "having brought the forte piano to its highest degree of perfection," the only reference to the piano as an object in de Montgeroult's method is to its shortcomings [*défauts*], which one has to transcend through some *art de bien chanter*, which in her belief "is the same for whichever instrument one applies it to.")[18]

Meanwhile, on March 28, 1798, *inspecteurs* Méhul and Cherubini signed a motion to adopt the *Méthode ou principe général du doigté pour le forte-*

piano, co-authored by Louis Adam and Ludwig Wenzel Lachnith (also Lachnitz), a horn-player from Prague, composer of pasticcios (with Christian Kalkbrenner, father of Frédéric), and *instructeur* at the Opéra. The existence of this earlier textbook, later to be superseded by Adam's much more famous 1804–5 method, is crucial for our reading of the facts. March 1800 saw major personnel changes at the institution and commensurate discontent among outgoing faculty: no fewer than thirty-four faculty were let go.[19] Louis Adam not only remained on board, but also was promoted from the *2ᵐᵉ* to the *1ʳᵉ classe des femmes*. Later that year, on September 23, Adam was promoted yet again, now to the *1ʳᵉ classe des hommes*.

Adam's Early Classes

La Grandville's studies devoted to the two first decades of the Conservatoire (1795–1815) allow us to take a look at the class records of Louis Adam.[20] Unfortunately, there is a gap in the archival documents for the period of our interest (1799–1807), but a discernible trend nonetheless emerges when browsing Adam's class lists between 1808 and 1815. These include those of his teaching assistants—or *répétiteurs*, the single administrative term for males and females, though in this period Adam had far more female *répétitrices* than male assistants. Typically, these were older and more advanced students of Adam's.

In principle, Louis Adam taught all the male students. The only exceptions are three men in the class of *répétiteur* Edelmann in 1813 and one in the class of *répétitrice* Dutey in 1814. Thanks to the system of teaching assistance (which had been implemented in 1802), the average age of the women in Adam's class rose above the current college-level age of eighteen from 1811 onward. This is in stark contrast with his first-ever class of 1797–98, which had an average age of ten. Counting a single *"classe Louis Adam"* results in a peak in 1813 with a grand total of forty-three students (fourteen taught by Adam plus twenty-nine taught by his three assistants), but an overall class number of twenty-nine emerges as the norm in the period of 1809–14, with two or three teaching assistants. The year 1813 shows an exceptionally high enrollment, with 75 piano students out of 473 across the school: in this particular year, with those 43 students, Adam's class would have represented more than half of the piano department.[21]

Preserved class lists with actual student names allow us to oberve some broader tendencies from year to year. It is clear, first, that consistency (as in staying with the same teacher) was very much promoted by the institution (an ideal that has persisted until today). But one also notices names shifting within the global class, either from professor to assistant (amounting to a demotion) or from assistant to professor (a promotion). Since Adam remains the default teacher for male pupils, this happened more typically among the female students.

We may follow, for example, the trajectory of three boys aged ten, fourteen, and thirteen in the class of teaching assistant Jean Frédéric Edelmann—himself the son of Edelmann senior, the well-known Alsatian composer who in 1794 had been less fortunate than Citoyenne de Montgeroult and had been guillotined. (Louis Adam had himself been a pupil of the late Edelmann, so it is a compelling twist of fate that the latter's son, who had never known his father, grew up to enter Adam's class.)[22] After a year (when Edelmann appears to have left: "Doesn't come anymore," Cherubini wrote on December 30, 1813), Adam may have had second thoughts about the experiment of having someone else teach his young male pupils, since he took all three of them back under his wing. One of them was Nicholas Bach (b. May 5, 1803). In the inspectors' reports—which are comments made on individual students during regular class exams, diligently filed away and preserved to this day—we find that the boy, then eleven, is given the benefit of the doubt: "He'd do better if he had a piano at home," Cherubini wrote. But the young Nicholas continues to attract lackluster comments, and after an exasperated "Does not make progress and I doubt he'll ever make any," from the pen of Inspector Méhul, he leaves the Conservatoire altogether. Remarkably, the Moscow-born teenager returned to the institution after a few years, making it into the class of Zimmermann and at age seventeen winning a *1er prix du piano* with a piece by Cramer.[23]

Among the female students, Angélique Honorine Dutey (b. 1797) is an example of someone who worked her way up. On first entering Adam's class in 1808, Mlle. Dutey did not make a very strong impression. Méhul noted that she was "not as advanced as she could be, considering that studying the piano is her only occupation."[24] By April 1809, she was transferred to *répétitrice* Chanuel's class where she began making noticeable progress: over a three-year period, the term *progrès* showed up in her records no fewer than seven times. Eventually, with Méhul and Cherubini agreeing that "she will do honor to her masters," we find her back on *maître* Adam's list in 1813. Within a year, at age seventeen, she would have a class of her own as one of Adam's *répétitrices*, and she crowned her successful trajectory by winning a *premier prix* in 1818, playing a composition by her own teacher: Louis Adam's Variations, presumably those on "Air du bon Roi Dagobert."

The "Adam Project"

And so we're back to where statistics would have mattered most: with those pupils who made it all the way to the top. If Dutey's win marked yet another high point in Adam's twenty-odd-year Conservatoire career, then Kalkbrenner's win had firmly set it in motion. Of course, at the age of thirty-nine, Adam came to the Conservatoire with considerable experience already (he's said to have taught piano at an upper-class Parisian boarding school),[25] but his personality and dedication were demonstrated by the fact that, during those crucial early years at a new institution, he managed to consolidate his activities as both a teacher and a composer in a pedagogical project that was to bear his name. No longer co-authored, the 1804–5 piano method was to be by Adam alone—and advertised as such, in contrast, for example, with the 1802–3 violin method, which the bottom half of the title page clarifies was written by Pierre Baillot ("*rédigée / par Baillot*"), but only after sharing the overall credit with Pierre Rode and Rodolphe Kreutzer ("*Méthode de Violon / par / MM. Baillot, Rode / et Kreutzer*"), collectively representing the violin class as "*Membres du Conservatoire de Musique.*" Adam's old partner Lachnith was not a faculty member (so he'd have no choice but to understand why he'd been left out), but a linguistic comparison of the old method on fingering with corresponding sections in the new method reveals surprisingly little overlap: yes, some concepts, terms, fragments of phrases, and one exceptional paragraph are repeated, but the intent on Adam's part seems to have been *not* to repeat himself, and where this is unavoidable, at least not to do so verbatim. (This is almost to Adam's detriment, because the earlier prose was both more transparent and more polished, which may indicate that Lachnith was the better writer of the two.) Perhaps more strikingly still, all musical scores are new in the

1804–5 *Méthode*: not a single example or exercise has been repeated. Adam, in other words, is going solo, and only when reviewing the full contents (prose and musical scores) can we develop a sense of what the "Adam project" truly entailed.

With legalistic deliberation (not unlike the 1804 Code Napoléon), twelve "articles" unfold from preliminary topics such as the topography of the keyboard (Article 1), the position of body and hands (Articles 2 and 3), and proper fingering and scales (Articles 4 and 5), to the production and articulation of sound ("How to touch the piano and draw sound of it" and "On connecting sounds and three manners of detaching them," Articles 6 and 7), then on to ornaments, time, and expression (Articles 8–10), and culminating with "the use of the pedals" (Article 10), "the art of accompanying the score" (Article 11) and "style" (Article 12). The final chapter, on the need for a performer of a piece, just like its composer, to "have a particular style," makes sense, since it allows Adam to encourage those pupils "whose efforts have already been crowned" (read: who've earned a *premier prix*) to "not stop at this first success," but "to enter the temple of harmony and to become initiated into its secrets"—in other words, *to become composers themselves*, completing the circle. Anyone Adam's age or older would have been surprised to find no treatment or even allusion throughout the method to skills in composition, or at least figured bass and improvisation, especially as mastering these skills had traditionally been believed to go hand in hand with the mastery of a keyboard instrument. At this almost overdue point in a method geared toward aspiring professionals, Adam seems to argue that, if it's in you, it will happen—no longer simultaneously, but at least consecutively. By opening up the temple of composition to those happy few who have demonstrated "genius" on the piano, Adam appears to be providing the justification he may have felt he needed as the author of a method that singularly focused on the *métier* of pianist, leaving the subject of harmony to his colleague Charles-Simon Catel's 1801–2 Conservatoire-endorsed textbook.

For the same reason, Adam's penultimate chapter on the skill of arranging orchestral scores for the piano at sight seems oddly out of place. His brief remarks on a practice that requires a skillset far beyond the practicing of one's scales again reveals his age. Just two years Mozart's junior and twelve years Beethoven's senior, Adam and his generation would have found it unthinkable to promote a professional curriculum that revolved around playing the piano exclusively. We may recall his son Adolphe's words that, "performers being rare at the time, my father benefitted from a trend that he would adhere to during his whole long career." But at the same time, he "arranged for the harpsichord and piano all the operas of [Gluck] as they appeared in print." Article 11 may offer a glimpse into Adam's own broader skillset, one that ideally he'd share with his pupils, but the preceding ten certainly do not prepare them to follow in his footsteps: for this, a separate method—or training—would be required, and the shortage of accompanists would in fact become a thorny issue for the young institution.

Interspersed between the twelve articles are musical scores—"exercises," at first (again, with surprisingly little if any overlap with those from the 1798 method), but between Articles 5 and 6 yielding to what amounts to a method on its own, consisting of "fifty progressive lessons fingered for small hands," written mostly by Adam himself, expanded with airs, minuets, romances, and polonaises by Gluck, Haydn, Mozart, Dussek, and Cramer. For the more experienced player (those with bigger hands), an anthology of "fingered passages" follows (eighty of them) from a repertoire by Dussek, Cramer, Mozart, Haydn, Steibelt, and, last but not least, all three of Beethoven's Piano Sonatas Op. 2, which had first appeared in a French edition by Pleyel in 1798.[26] (This connection sheds significant light on the subject of this book: Adam must have practiced all three Beethoven Sonatas and found sufficient value in them to also assign them to his students.) Preceding Beethoven's excerpts are those by Adam himself, of his Sonata, Op. 8 No. 2, spread out as nos. 53–62. "Practice us," these fingered exercises call out (no fewer than ten from a single sonata), "and one day you'll be successful!"

Adam had Kalkbrenner to prove it. At age sixteen still finishing his first stint at the Conservatoire as a pianist (he would come back as a nineteen-year-old for separate studies in composition), he would have practiced Adam's sonata as if his life depended on it—scales, arpeggios, double-note trills, octaves, leaps, tremolos, and all.[27] It is significant that Adam introduces Op. 8 No. 2 roughly two-thirds of the way through the 234-page method—and not, for example, between Articles 9 and 10, where yet another "Method with a choice of pieces in different characters and tempos" is inserted, including movements from Mozart's Sonatas, K. 310 and K. 331,

Clementi's Toccata, Op. 11, and C. P. E. Bach's Probestück No. 6 in F Minor, as well as various fugues by Handel and J. S. Bach. Adam's Sonata is a demonstration not just of tempo or character (the topics of Article 9), but of *everything*. Designed in tandem with the method, it is the piece that the pupil must studiously keep on the side, to be broken down and practiced at first as single exercises, but eventually brought to one's lessons as a concatenated, three-movement sonata that proves first to the master that one has indeed mastered his method, and then during a classroom examination to the two inspectors that one is indeed ready for the ultimate step in one's training—"to compete."

EXAMPLE 10.1 Adam, Sonata in C Major, Op. 8 No. 2, excerpts.

If performed with perfection—an overall quality that Méhul was quick to connect with style and taste—Adam's Op. 8 No. 2 can be deadly effective as a *concours* piece. The first movement has an attention-grabbing exclamation at the outset, which is followed almost immediately by a most risky octave run: see example 10.1. Fail it, and you've created a serious disadvantage; nail it, and you're all but guaranteed instantaneous goodwill. (There's an added dimension of nerves: until you're on that stage, you just don't know what exactly will happen.) Playing the whole opening Allegro without using any of the pedals (as we discussed before) is not easy—especially during a prolonged *dolce* in the development part where the only way to create some semblance of *legato* is to be creative with one's fingering for the octaves (like the ones I added in the example, as learned from Adam's method).[28] But if you keep trying and eventually succeed, you have a chance of demonstrating mechanical mastery—in the widest sense, that is, not just of fingers, but of whole mind and body in conjunction with the mechanics of an Erard grand, the ne plus ultra of pianos. The second movement is like a grown-up version of those "lessons for small hands," combining the various genres of romance, polonaise, and (at the heart of it all) a true Adagio Tremendo in an A-B-A´-B-A rondo (with the Adagio as a variation of the romance). The third movement, finally, represents yet a different kind of rondo—one that made the careers of the like of Steibelt and that allows you to prove your intimate knowledge of all four pedals, combining sonic control with exquisite taste.

An Exercise in Historical Enactment

Who of us does not recall that the third sonata (in C) from Clementi's Opus 33 had such prestige that it was solemnly banned from the *concours* at the Conservatoire because it always made the person who played it win the prize?

—*Le pianiste* 1, no. 1 (November 20, 1833): 3

A piano sonata so irresistible that whichever jury member listens to it must award its player first prize: did it exist? At first sight we're looking at a rumor typical of the ones that circulate among those not privy to the goings-on in a jury deliberation room. A similar notion floats around today:

how many Rachmaninov Thirds or Tchaikovsky Firsts have been played in the final round of an international piano competition? But there's more than meets the eye. The quote is from the first issue of a new journal that was to have a brief run in 1833–35. Its founders, Henry Lemoine (1786–1854) and Charles Chaulieu (1788–1849), had been classmates at the Paris Conservatoire, both studying with Louis Adam. In this case, they could be considered experts on the matter, having won first prizes themselves in 1809 and 1806, respectively.[29] We don't know what pieces they played, but table 10.1 shows the ones we do know to have been performed, along with who played them, and whose class they belonged to.[30]

It turns out to be true: Clementi's Op. 33 No. 3 was played twice—but more to the point, it was played *twice in a row*. It won back-to-back first prizes for "Ozi *fils*" (the son of the Conservatoire's bassoon teacher) in the class of Ignace Ladurner and for Pierre-Joseph Zimmermann in the class of Adrien Boieldieu. Chance or logic? Either way, the next year Louis Adam may have decided that the only way to guarantee success was to write his own competitive sonata. The clarification on the eventually published title page of Op. 8 No. 2 may be factual and dry ("This sonata was played by his pupil [F.] Kalkbrenner who obtained the *premier prix*"), but the victory must have been sweet. It would have sent the message to the other boys that "if you practice, then maybe one day you can win too."[31] And practice they did. Win they did as well, one after another. Adam's class managed to win almost every *premier prix* during the years to come: Chaulieu (1806); Paul-Cécile Merland (1807); Charles-Pierre Lambert, Arnold Meysenberg and Henry Lemoine (the three of them exceptionally sharing the prize in 1809); and, finally, Ferdinand Herold (1810), who marks a new milestone altogether, playing a sonata composed by himself, "dedicated to his teacher *par son élève*," just as back in 1797 Cramer's sonata had been dedicated to Clementi.[32] And so a second Conservatoire legend was born—just as recognizable today, but one that Lemoine and Chaulieu would have been much less inclined to admit: if you want to win the *concours*, you need to be a pupil of Louis Adam.

Still, the question is worth asking: was there such a thing as a prize-winning sonata? During the first decade of the Conservatoire's existence, the confusion might have been both novel and unavoidable: which dazzles more—polished playing or a difficult composition? Through a two-week

TABLE 10.1 Pieces for solo piano known to have been played at the *concours* of the Paris Conservatoire, 1797–1819 (square brackets indicate suggested identification)

Piece	Pupil	Teacher	Result
John Baptist Cramer, Sonata [in F Major, Op. 7 No. 3] [Dedicated to Muzio Clementi, "par son élève"]	Louis Pradher (b. 1781)	Louis Gobert	*2ᵐᵉ prix* (1797)
Muzio Clementi Sonata [in C Major, Op. 33 No. 3]	Marie-Joseph Ozi ("Ozi fils") (b. 1787)	Ignace Ladurner	*1ᵉʳ prix* (1799)
	Pierre-Joseph Zimmerman (b. 1785)	Adrien Boieldieu	*1ᵉʳ prix* (1800)
Louis Adam Sonata in C Major, Op. 8 No. 2	Frédéric Kalkbrenner (b. 1785)	Louis Adam	*1ᵉʳ prix* (1801)
Johann Nepomuk Hunmel Fantasy Op. 18	[not known]	[not known]	[not known] (1806)
Ferdinand Hérold Sonata in C Minor/ Major, Op. 1 Dedicated to Louis Adam, "par son élève"	Ferdinand Herold (b. 1791)	Louis Adam	*1ᵉʳ prix* (1810)
Louis Adam Variations [*Air du bon Roi Dagobert avec douze Variations précédé d'un Prélude ou Introduction*]	Angélique Dutey (b. 1797)	Louis Adam	*1ᵉʳ prix* (1818)

Sources: Pierre (1900), vol. 1, 485, and vol. 2, 967–69; La Grandville (2017b), 251–52, 542–43, 715–16; La Grandville (2014), 226; Fétis (1839), 216.

Summer Academy at the Orpheus Institute in 2018 I decided to put this question to the test, partly tongue-in-cheek but mostly as a historically inspired experiment. First, I invited my former student Erin Helyard to be a colleague-teacher. With his intimate knowledge of Muzio Clementi, that "father of the piano," Erin would represent the foundation of the French curriculum.[33] Two experts, Jeanne Roudet and Frédéric de La Grandville, would join us for seminars, and would also be part of the jury, along with co-organizer Ellie Nimeroski (who would function as the jury's secretary) and our director of research, Jonathan Impett (representing the Institute, which like the Conservatoire back then is still relatively young and dynamic). My role was to represent Louis Adam, and to share my new expertise relating to our Erard piano with a younger generation. We invited eight participants from six different countries (Belgium, Brazil, France, Italy, United States, and Thailand) to come and experiment, with the intent of being judged during a *grand concours* by the end of the workshop. By accepting our invitation, everyone agreed to compete, even if we reasssured them that, in the spirit of research, there was no prize to win, or to put it differently: everyone wins.

We offered eight pieces from which each participant would select one to perform. These included the five competition pieces from table 10.1, plus what we liked to think of as three "control pieces"—pieces that, as far as we know, did not win a prize at a competition, but still had some link with the Conservatoire:

1. John Baptist Cramer, Sonata in F Major, Op. 7 No. 3
2. Muzio Clementi, Sonata in C Major, Op. 33 No. 3
3. Louis Adam, Sonata in C Major, Op. 8 No. 2
4. Ferdinand Herold, Sonata in C Minor/Major, Op. 1
5. Louis Adam, *Air du bon Roi Dagobert avec douze Variations précéde d'un prélude ou introduction*, in F Major
6. Johann Nepomuk Hummel, Fantasy in E-flat Major, Op. 18
7. Pierre-Joseph-Guillaume Zimmermann, Sonata in G Major, Op. 5
8. Hélène de Montgeroult, Sonata in G Minor, Op. 2 No. 1

Compiling the list required some interpretive decisions. For example, we know that in 1797 Louis Pradher played "a sonata by Cramer." With Op. 7

No. 3 in F Major (first published in 1792), I selected Cramer's then most recent solo work with most *concours* potential. The Adam Variations that Angélique Dutey played in 1819 I assumed to have been on "Roi Dagobert" in F Major from 1808. This piece was prize-winning, but only by default: in 1814, the rule had changed from the option for pupil and teacher to choose their own competition piece to the concept of an obligatory work (*morceau imposé*) to be assigned to every contestant.[34] The sixth variation, in particular, with relentless thirds that run from the middle of the keyboard all the way to the top key of a five-and-half-octave piano, would have allowed for ruthless comparison.

Our first "control piece" was played at a *concours*, but most probably did not win. "Cherubini had brought from Vienna Hummel's grand Fantasy in E-flat, Op. 18, which was executed at the *concours* that same year," Fétis wrote in 1866. His next statement, "It was understood only by true artists," clarifies that it was not a good fit.[35] As to Zimmermann, while he had already won first prize in piano performance back in 1800, there's a record of him as a composition student performing a sonata of his own, presumably his Op. 5 in G Major, at an 1807 school concert.[36] Grand in proportion (it has no fewer than four movements), the sonata nonetheless breathes understatement: soft shades, "not too much" (*non tanto*, in reference to tempo), melodies that are both harmonious and pleasant but never catchy. Finally, we felt that Hélène de Montgeroult, as the distinguished colleague who briefly overlapped with Adam, could not be absent. I selected her two-movement Sonata in G Minor, Op. 2 No. 1 (published in 1800), as the only piece among the eight in a minor key throughout.

This repertoire, of course, came with an expectation of how each piece would fare during the competition, so the next step of pairing them with players became something of an ethical burden. On the one hand, Erin and I wanted everyone to have an equal shot—a responsibility we decided to share with the applicants by asking them to indicate their top three choices and by reassuring them that they wouldn't have to play anything against their will. But it goes both ways. Thus, someone insisted on learning Hummel's Op. 18, although we knew he'd be at a disadvantage with a Viennese-style work on a French instrument. The two most advanced players on historical pianos, in contrast, readily agreed to the challenge of Adam and Herold. Both works have an appeal in their difficulty that none of the other participants had found particularly interesting. Montgeroult, from her side, was in high demand, especially by the women. It took some convincing, finally, to ask one female participant—a highly accomplished player—to take on Adam's Variations.

Once pieces were distributed and notes learned, the experiment could begin. The first two mornings were devoted to everyone playing through their piece on the Erard for the first time—an experience we deliberately staged with everyone present. Phrased this way, it sounds cruel, but the *concours* experiment was only half the workshop: we had included a second focus on different repertoire and pianos, both Viennese and English, partly to allow participants necessary practice time and diversion from anything having to do with the competition. Access to our single Erard had to be restricted and tightly regulated. By the second week, however, everyone also started practicing their *concours* piece on any piano they could lay their hands on—a situation not unlike that for the pupils at the Paris Conservatoire, who while practicing on any harpsichord or square piano that was available, would also have needed to mentally prepare themselves for the one Erard grand piano reserved for the competition.[37]

From the first tryouts, I mostly remember that nobody commented on the quality of the Erard replica—slightly disappointing to me as the host of the event, but also quite understandable, since no reference point existed for the participants, either instrumentally or in terms of appropriate repertoire: nobody (except one) had ever played on a *piano en forme de clavecin* before, and nobody (except one) had engaged with similar repertoire before. Nobody managed to get through their pieces unscathed, and when asked what had thrown them off, the first answer invariably was: "The pedal"—in singular, in reference to the damper pedal, "no longer" positioned on the right. One person added, "the delay in the action," referring to the time between the moment when the finger strikes the keys and that of the hammer hitting the string. The advice to *listen* to the French technology, both through fingers and ears, and to adjust one's sense of timing and speed to what one feels and hears would need time to sink in. Somehow, everyone had played much faster than the instrument could handle, both mechanically and acoustically.

Over the following days, *adjustment* indeed became key. No more awkwardly twisting one's lower body in order to still operate the damper pedal with one's right foot. Steering away from constant reliance on "the pedal" to create one's tone, while at the same time drastically rethinking one's concept of tone. Some accepted a new reality where pedals are best engaged only when consciously called for and grew accustomed to leaving their feet on the ground, that is, off the pedals. Rather spectacularly, this newly grounded bodily position freed them to focus more on finger-only work, not just mechanically, but also expressively. Others did not succeed in breaking their habit of constantly keeping one's feet on the pedals, causing unnecessary tension—because, indeed, which two of the four is one to choose? During her final performance, one candidate left both feet on the middle pedals "just in case," but unnecessarily kept her legs and knees constantly tensed. While modern pianos encourage such a default *on* position—their more resistant pedals accommodating a fair amount of forefoot weight— early nineteenth-century historical pianos emphatically do not.[38]

Amid all these adjustments, one participant found clear advantage in the score of Adam's Sonata, Op. 8 No. 2. Not only did Adam's lack of prescription of any pedal in the first movement allow for sustained attention to finger playing only (revealing an important pedagogical side to the strategy we already observed in chapter 8), but also the score for the second and third movements contains detailed foot choreography with indications such as, "One has to put down the two middle pedals," followed by "Release the *jeu céleste* and leave only the *grande Pédale.*" On and off are precisely placed, furthermore, not just for musical reasons, but also for physical feasibility.[39] It was as if we were witnessing a live coaching session by Adam of his prize-winning student, polished up to a level worthy of publication. In spite of this impression of completeness, I still managed to come up with one additional suggestion. Toward the end of the final movement, for reasons of clarity and dryness ("*sec*," Adam writes in the score), I suggested using the first pedal (lute or harp) for the chromatic scale, just as Adam advises in his method.[40] This finishing touch, applied during the dress rehearsal in the acoustics of the actual space where the competition was to take place, illustrates the kind of coach Adam must have been: controlling, detailed, meticulous, but also generous and not secretive—qualities that would have made him eminently suited to write the school's piano method. By contrast, the score of Herold's Sonata, Op. 1, has no pedal indications at all. It served the young pianist-composer well, but it also hides many of the details that would have been carefully rehearsed in Adam's classroom.

Judging the Results

A few days before the competition we held a general assembly with just a single point on the agenda: the establishment of criteria for judging. In our discussions we were aided by the Conservatoire-archival knowledge of de La Grandville, who was also to serve as the president of our six-member jury—three fewer than the officially required number of nine in 1808, "appointed by the Ministry of Internal Affairs" to be the same for all vocal and instrumental disciplines.[41] On the surface, the method outlined in Adam's textbook looked rigid enough, but turning its content into some system for evaluation proved difficult. Should we (as Adam does in Article 12) distinguish between *mécanisme* and *sentiment*, with *style* combining both?[42] Or should we, in good rhetorical tradition, go for a triple division and proclaim that a good pupil must have (1) *bon mécanisme*, divisible into facility of execution (*facilité de l'exécution*), the ability of connecting well (*bien lier les sons*), and playing with equality (*jouer avec égalité*); (2) *bon style*, as evidenced by varied expression (*expression variée*) but also personality or originality (*avoir un style particulier*); and (3) good taste (*un goût délicat*), as demonstrated through an appropriate and varied use of ornaments (*agréments*) and a proper use of pedals (*manière de se servir des pédales*, i.e., when to use them, but also when not to use them)—all of these qualities amounting to what Inspector Méhul in a speech to Faculty Council referred to as *perfection d'exécution*?[43] Clearly, we found ourselves joining a debate as old as the Conservatoire itself. Thus, reflecting on his many years as a jury member, Adam's colleague, the violinist Pierre Baillot, proposed in 1835 an intricate but remarkable *Tableau à l'usage des concours du Conservatoire* ("Evaluation chart to be used during Conservatoire competitions"). It was posthumously published in 1872 as an appendix to his *Observations relatives aux concours de violon*. For our purposes it was a godsend. Adopting Baillot's dichotomy between "necessary foundation of mechanism" (*base nécessaire du mécanisme*), on the one hand, and "necessary foundation of talent" (*base nécessaire du talent*), on the other, we created a hybrid chart, infusing

Baillot's roster with terms and concepts from Adam (see table 10.2). But one term remains: Baillot's *aplomb*, which he applies to the quality of being grounded in time, undeterred by superficial emotions and measurable (yes, times had changed) by a continually beating metronome.[44]

One can perfectly well imagine the formality of the scene—jury members seated behind an impressive table, their large evaluation charts folded out in front of them. Candidates enter the room after having been asked to wait in what was cruelly known as the *passage du trac* (stage-fright passage). Without the need for elaborate prose (allowing them to keep paying attention to the unfolding performance), jury members mark their points for each of the categories by means of three quickly and easily drawn symbols: a small black circle for mediocre (*médiocre*), a slightly bigger one for good (*bien*), and a big white circle for very good (*très-bien*)—or nothing at all in "the absence of a required quality." (The other advantage here is that audience members would be left guessing as to what each jury member is writing down: there's equal effort involved in marking mediocrity as there is for excellence.) Numbers are to be added, as for example, for a ficticious second candidate in the chart, "4 mediocre, 6 good, and 3 very good," these "numbers of points gained" to be compared from one contestant to the other. In the end, though, it's not exclusively about adding points, since "[a]fter number comes *esteem*; this instinctive choice, based on forecast of some kind, can tip the balance in favor of him who, while not deprived of the first qualities, would not have as many points as another in respect to mechanism; but if he possesses intellectual qualities and expressive faculties that announce a better future, then he must be preferred."[45]

In contrast to the judgment of sixteen- to twenty-year-olds at the final stage of their formative years, our tongue-in-cheek competition was in no way meant to be career launching. Still, after we had added up the numbers in the privacy of our deliberation room, heated discussions arose, unexpectedly exposing conflicting lines taken by various jury members. "If Adam's method was to serve as our guide, then he deserves no points at all," one member opined. "But her playing is quite mannered," someone else countered, about a different candidate. Did we prove the obvious? As our president announced the results, our make-believe event suddenly felt all too real. We ended up awarding two first prizes, two second prizes, and four *accessits* ("honorable mentions"). Who won? Everyone did. Teachers,

TABLE 10.2 *Tableau à l'usage du concours de l'Institut Orpheus* (2018), after Louis Adam (1804–5) and Pierre Baillot ([1835] 1872).

	Base nécessaire du mécanisme Style Necessary foundation of mechanism		
Noms des concurrens Names of competitors	Position du corps Position of the body	Netteté, facilité Clarity, facility	Aplomb Groundedness
1			
2	◯	●	◯
3			
4			
5			
6			
7			
8			

	Style Style		
Noms des concurrens Names of competitors	Notes de goût ou d'agrément "Notes of taste" or ornaments	Nuances et sensibilité Nuances and sensitivity	Donner au morceau l'expression qui lui convient To give a piece the expression that suits it
1			
2	●	•	●
3			
4			
5			
6			
7			
8			

Doigts Fingers	
Toucher le piano et en tirer le son Striking the piano and pulling sound from it	Lier et détacher les sons Slurring and detaching sounds
●	○

[Style] [Style]		
Mesure, mouvemens et caractère Time, tempi, and character	Manière de se servir des pédales Manner of using the pedals	Variété dans les passages répétés Variety in repeated passages
●	·	●

TABLE 10.2 *Continued*

	Base nécessaire du talent Necessary foundation of talent		Vote Vote
Noms des concurrens Names of competitors	Comprendre le style de l'auteur To understand the style of the composer	Avoir un style particulier en tant qu'exécutant To have a particular style as a performer	Nombre des points obtenus Number of points gained • ● ○
1			
2	•	•	4 6 3
3			
4			
5			
6			
7			
8			

candidates, jury members—and last but not least, a repertoire of prize-winning pieces that otherwise would have remained buried in the archives of a once prestigious French institution.

Still, based purely on the results, two of the pieces proved best suited for both the occasion and the instrument. So, let's phrase the question differently: *which* won? The answer is Herold's Op. 1 and Adams's Op. 8 No. 2, two compositions linked by the vision of a highly successful teacher.

[*Vote*] [Vote]			
Premier Prix First Prize	*Second Prix* Second Prize	*Accessit* Honorable Mention	*Néant* Nil

Building a Replica

Chris Maene in conversation with Robin Blanton

It was always a dream of mine to build Beethoven's piano, and I got the chance to fulfill that dream when Tom Beghin approached me about building Beethoven's Broadwood. But I never wanted to build the Erard! As a builder, I only want to build *good* pianos. And I thought the Erard couldn't have been very good. Beethoven had received it as a gift, and he had it altered almost right away. Whoever made the alterations didn't manage to improve it. Why would anyone want to copy the butchered remains of a piano that was no good to begin with? I thought Beethoven's Broadwood was much more important to him, and much more important to music history. Most of all, I didn't want to waste my time deliberately trying to build a piano that simply wasn't good.

But Tom was persistent. He explained that Beethoven had wanted the Erard and had looked forward to it. Also that it had influenced Beethoven as a composer. He finally convinced me to take another look at it. And yes—clearly, the Erard wasn't what Beethoven was used to, and it seems he fought with it, and in the end he gave up on it. Still, the more I looked at it, the more I found to admire.

If you're going to copy an instrument, especially for a research project, there is no point in doing it unless you make a faithful copy. And you need to copy the whole thing. People take that for granted nowadays, but we used to be less sophisticated about this kind of thing. I remember the case of a builder who copied just the outside of a historical harpsichord. They had no notion of the inner construction, the bracing and so on. Of course, this so-called copy didn't work at all. It was hilarious. It simply fell to pieces. Even on a less dramatic scale, it's easy to change one aspect that seems inconsequential, and later find out that it mattered after all. It's so often true that you can't alter one aspect without worsening another. That was certainly true of the Erard, more than most instruments—and the builder in Vienna who tried to "improve" the action for Beethoven found that out, I think. But I'm getting ahead of the story.

The need to copy the whole instrument is why the 1805 Erard piano in Brussels was so important for us. This piano is one of the 1797-model grand pianos—the model Beethoven had. There are other surviving pianos of this model, and we looked at some of them. While the Brussels piano is not in the best shape overall, it had the great advantage that we could examine it with the baseboard off. That meant we could see the whole instrument. For example, we could see the system of case bracing—by this I mean all the internal struts and trusses that stop the case from imploding when you tune up the strings. We could also see how the soundboard was thicknessed and reinforced, which is very important musically, and an art in itself. Soundboards are planed to fit a specific pattern of thickness: thinner in some places, thicker in others. Then, strips of wood are glued to the underside of the soundboard, stiffening it in some areas and leaving it free to vibrate in others. We were able see the number, shape, and position of these ribs and bars. The soundboard thickness and ribbing affect the sound of the piano: its loudness, and the length of decay in different areas of the compass. All of that works together with the design of the action—the balancing of the keys, the speed of the repetition. It's an integrated system. That's why it is so important to copy the entire instrument.

I should point out, too, that maybe not all builders think this way, or are so completely in control of their work. Sébastien Erard was. He based the design of his action on the English action, the kind of action all the London builders were using, but he made substantial changes to it. He made some changes in the way you regulate the action that would have made it easier to adjust, and therefore more long-lasting. He also made changes that had more to do with the artistry of playing, with the touch of the keys, the speed of repetition, and the quality of the sound. He made thinner soundboards. And he completely rethought the design of the case and the internal construction. He used a much lighter case, and the bracing I've just been talking about is not like the bracing of a Broadwood piano at all. In that respect, Erard wiped the slate clean and started again.

You know, the English piano action didn't change much over the entire course of the nineteenth century. Broadwood kept making the same, and people kept buying it. Everyone had to have a piano! Meanwhile, Viennese pianos were often of higher quality than the English ones. The Erards could have adopted the same strategy as Broadwood, but they didn't. Instead, they kept changing what they were making, trying to improve. The first thing they did, in their 1797 model, was to try to improve on the English model. They wanted the best of both worlds: the nice, quick, responsive feel of the Viennese pianos, combined with the powerful sound and the resonance of the English piano. Then they put their own French stamp on it with the wider range of pedal registers, which offered so many new colors and combinations of sounds. And this was only their first attempt. They kept on trying. They built the 1797 model for about ten years, and then they invented a new variation on the action that they thought was even better. And they kept on in that fashion. So it's clear to me that Erard Frères cared deeply about quality and about achieving something truly excellent. And they succeeded. The 1797 model is a very skillful instrument.

So how did we go about copying it? First, we developed a very accurate drawing. We used a CAD program. This let us do more than just produce flat drawings. We actually built a three-dimensional replica of the piano inside the computer. We could animate the replica and watch the hammer action move. Building the computer model allowed us to make sure that all the parts of the piano fitted together, and it became easy for everyone to visualize the finished product. Then, from the 3D model, we could produce all the working drawings we needed to manufacture the parts of the piano on the shop floor.

To create the CAD model, we had to take a lot of measurements, and we developed a method that was quick and accurate. We first took an overall shot of the part of the instrument we were measuring with the ruler (or calipers) held in place. Then we zoomed in to take a close-up of the ruler, showing the actual measurement being taken. We were able to transfer these measurements directly from the pictures to the computer drawing, which saved us a lot of time transcribing measurements. So we have lots of photographs of what looks like just us measuring the piano! Yes, that's what we're doing—but those long shots are always paired with a close-up shot showing the reading on the ruler or calipers. We found this to be a very quick and accurate method.

It's interesting that making a drawing—on paper or in the computer—actually requires you to be more accurate than in building the instrument itself. Obviously, the Erards did not build their instruments from incredibly detailed drawings, as we did. They would have used templates, story sticks, and so on. When you make a drawing of an instrument, you have to measure things that the original builder never measured, simply to get all the corners to match up on paper. When you start building the instrument, however, you divorce yourself from some of those millimeters and tenths of millimeters. Copying an instrument is only partly about copying dimensions. Dimensions are important, but you also need to think about copying patterns.

I mentioned that we studied several of the 1797-model pianos. Obviously, they were all extremely similar (except for their decoration), but they're not completely identical. They are certainly standardized. They have the same compass; the pedals are the same; the design of the hammer action is the same; the string lengths and the keyboard dimensions are the same; the general size and shape of all the parts are consistent. We could also tell that they were manufactured in batches. This is something we learned, again, from studying the inside of the Brussels Erard. There, we could see that the case braces were marked with numbers that would have matched them up to a particular piano within that batch. But as much as this reflects a process of standardization, it also reflects a process of individual fitting and, correspondingly, some small deviations from one instrument to another.

What does all this mean for us? Well, that it is less important to copy every piece to the millimeter than it is to understand the patterns and principles behind the choices that were made. One thing you come to understand rather quickly is that you cannot copy anything exactly. There will always be things that you just do not notice and therefore do not reproduce, or some variation in your materials or tools that makes an exact reproduction impossible. This is true even if you are using period materials and tools. Inevitably, at some point you will have to fall back on your understanding of general patterns of instrument building, and your knowledge of other traditions. This knowledge is what allows you to see the things that make the instrument in front of you unique. Perhaps, paradoxically, you need a broad understanding to recognize particulars.

Let me take one small example that is intimately related to the piano sound: the hammer leathers. It is not possible to exactly replicate hammer leathers. The existing hammer leathers, if they are even original, will be worn to some degree. Your leather will be a little different than the leather the original builder used. The wood of your hammer-shanks, the alloy and precise diameters of your strings, the resonance of your soundboard and case will all be at least subtly different as well. All of those factors, and more, interact with the hammer leathering to affect the way the piano sounds. Rather than copying the exact thickness or number of leather layers on the original hammers, it is more important to understand the general principles or patterns behind the leathering. For instance, one simple pattern is that you use more layers of leather in the bass, and fewer in the treble. If you have studied Broadwood piano hammers, you might also observe something else of importance that you could otherwise have missed: namely, that the leather is wrapped around the hammer-head in a specific way. All leather has two distinct sides, a smooth side and a plush side. Broadwood applied the hammer leather with the plush side out, and Erard applied it with the smooth side out. Clearly, this has repercussions for the sound. And ultimately, the precise type and thickness of leather that you use will also be guided by your own judgment of the sound. In this regard, it was very dangerous for me to have Tom involved, as a pianist, during the voicing process! I needed to navigate by my own understanding, as a builder, of the Erard style and sound. Now, this example of the hammer leathers is just a single example, maybe an obvious one, of the problems of copying. But the same considerations apply at every level of the instrument.

While I'm on the subject of what not to copy, I should mention one of the big decisions we had to make during this project. Should we, or could we, make a replica of the hammer action as it was revised in Vienna, or the action that is preserved today? Originally, we planned to do both. The vision was to have two interchangeable actions, so that you could compare the sound and behavior of the piano between the two. After we studied both actions, however, we realized the geometry of the revised action was so different from the original action that our plan was physically infeasible. At first, we also felt that the revised action was something of a hack job, and essentially unplayable, and so it would not be worth the time and effort to re-create it. To be honest, as we have returned to the revised action over the years, our impression has changed somewhat. The revised action may be more worth exploring than we first imagined—something for a future project, maybe.

The piano we ultimately built is what I have described before as my constant goal: a historical instrument *as it was when new in the past.* You might call it Beethoven's Erard, or you might call it just the latest piano in the 1797 series by Erard Frères. And I have to say, it's a good instrument. I couldn't make it better today.

CHAPTER ELEVEN

Revisiting the Revisions

A *Glissando* That Isn't

During my graduate student years I had a colleague who, whenever he sat down at a piano, would play what we've always considered to be a *glissando*: the (in)famous octaves toward the end of Op. 53, first down in the right hand, then up in the left hand (see fig. 11.1, top). When I proudly showed him my first-ever, five-octave Walter fortepiano, freshly arrived from overseas, sure enough—he played the *glissando*. I remember cringing, and I had my reasons. Sliding across keys is a contrary way of treating a technology that is designed to move the keys down and up. When pushed sideways, the key levers make contact with the balance pins, which are meant to keep the movement of the keys nice and straight. Builders make the holes for the balance pins as tight as they can precisely to minimize any sideways movement. But during a *glissando*—the ultimate sideways maneuver—the wood inside the slanted key's balance hole starts rubbing against the metal of the pins, potentially enlarging the holes and eventually causing keys to wobble and rattle.

Apparently, Beethoven also had the habit of doodling on pianos by way of playing *glissandos*. Paraphrasing a conversation he'd had with the daughter of Moritz Lichnowsky, Thayer relates:

> When [Beethoven] did not feel in the mood it required repeated and varied urgings to get him to sit down to the pianoforte. Before he began

playing he was in the habit of hitting the keys with the flat of his hand, or running a single finger up and down the keyboard, in short, doing all manner of things to kill time and laughing heartily, as was his wont, at the folly.[1]

"Running a single finger up and down," though easy on a Viennese keyboard, would have been distinctly harder on Beethoven's as yet unrevised Erard. The same holds true for the piano that Miss Lichnowsky might have actually heard Beethoven play on—the Erard *piano en forme de clavecin*, No. 143, that her uncle, Karl Alois Lichnowsky, had bought through Breitkopf & Härtel for his estate in Grätz, Silesia. When Beethoven was a guest at Count Lichnowsky's during the summer of 1806, it may have felt bittersweet to him to have access to an instrument that represented what his own French piano had been, or (more disturbingly still) *might* have been, had it not suffered insensitive revisions but instead been properly repaired. It is reasonable to assume that the Count's instrument would still have been in fairly good condition—in any case much less worn out from intense use than Beethoven's. One imagines a complex mixture of emotions, from frustration and regret to relief and satisfaction, as Beethoven now found himself with the unexpected opportunity to finally complete his "Appassionata" Sonata in F Minor, Op. 57, and thus wrap up his long-envisioned, Erard-inspired trilogy.

But before turning our attention to Op. 57, let's continue to consider playing an alleged Op. 53 *glissando*. For it to work on an Erard (and here I mean one in its original state), we need our fingers to dig 75 percent lower into the keys than on a contemporary Walter, while pushing down with one-third more weight. These statistics (which I copy from chapter 3) confirm what I so clearly experience on my Erard replica. While a single-finger *glissando* is still achievable, playing a double-finger *glissando*, let alone one in the unforgiving shape of an octave, is nearly impossible. And doing so in each hand? *pianissimo*? Come on. That's how I'd react to Carl Czerny, who was the one in 1846 to throw down the gauntlet for subsequent generations of Beethoven-performing pianists, determining that one must "slide [*schleifen*]" the octaves in Op. 53 (see fig. 11.1, middle). Since Czerny, many a pianist has given advice on exactly how to do so, but also on how to get *around* doing so—improving on Czerny's own proposal of a solution for

The following passage *pp*   must be played by gli-

ding the fingers along the keys, in the manner we have described in the 3ʳᵈ Volume of this School, and also in the foregoing chapter in treating of the performance of *Liszt's* works.

But for persons with small hands, to whom the execution of this passage would
be impracticable, it must be played as follows:

La manière de les détacher est bien plus facile parcequ'il ne s'agit que de porter
la main d'une touche à l'autre en la relevant à chaque note; cependant, pour les faire
dans la grande vitesse, il faut encore beaucoup d'exercice pour parvenir à les exécuter correctement, et c'est ici le seul cas où l'on puisse roidir l'avant bras, le poignet
et les doigts, afin de conserver toujours l'extension nécessaire.

FIGURE 11.1 Sonata in C Major, Op. 53, final movement, mm. 456–77 (Vienna: Bureau
des arts et d'industrie, 1805) (*top*); octave *glissando* in Czerny ([1846] 1970), 57 (*middle*);
octave example in Adam (1804/5), 52 (*bottom*).

those "with smaller hands." But not even the fact that on those old and shallow *Viennese* pianos *glissando* was so much easier than it is today has stopped modern-day pianists from trying—and, remarkably, succeeding in achieving the effect.

Our perspective, however, is from the only piano that did matter when it came to Beethoven writing his "Adam" sonata, so let's take a fresh look. In m. 465 we've arrived at the traditional do-or-die moment in a multi-movement classical sonata: a 6/4 dominant chord that heralds structural-harmonic closure. It's the typical moment for a cadenza or at least some fantasy-like element, and in classical piano literature this would mean, honoring an association that goes all the way back to C. P. E. Bach in 1762, to raise the dampers.[2] But Beethoven does the exact opposite: to offset the highly pedaled (and indeed, improvisatory-sounding) sequences of pre-dominant arpeggios that have preceded it. Note especially in m. 465 the position of "O" for lifting the left foot. "O" had always appeared before the bar line (as in mm. 456, 458, and 460), but here the left foot is lifted not to clear the air before the next harmony, but to yield to an ultimate act in a long sonata that has explored a vertical/horizontal paradox (see chapters 8 and 9). Having explored many textures (single-note, five-note group, scale, tremolo, arpeggio), the pianist must be ready to execute the grandest illusion of all: to produce a *glissando* not by sliding from one pair of keys to the next, but by playing each of the octaves separately, seemingly unhindered by—yes, even embracing—the deeper and heavier touch of the Erard. And here, as Louis Adam would agree, there's only one way to do it: "this is the only case," Adam writes, "where you can stiffen the forearm, wrist, and fingers, so as to always keep the necessary extension" (see fig. 11.1, bottom).

Adam is describing the technique of playing consecutive octaves in a *forte* context, and he applied it as such in the second bar of his Op. 8 No. 2 (see ex. 10.1)—thus incorporating an element of difficulty right at the outset of a performance that is designed to impress. But Beethoven is not out to impress in a conventional way. Surprisingly too, in my experience, playing Beethoven's octaves at this late point in the sonata requires much less blind courage or sheer confidence than those at the beginning of Adam's competition piece. The amount of "practice needed to execute them correctly" (these are Adam's words) seems built into the overall Beethoven piece, especially when playing my long version of "Piano e.f.d. clavecin";

by the time I come to "O" (my left foot telling the rest of my body, "ready, set, go!"), I've mustered sufficient confidence to nail a *glissando*, employing both hands, not once, but no fewer than three times in a row. In fact, I've surprised myself when I end up pulling off what might previously have seemed impossible, as if impersonating a young Kalkbrenner without having to go through the rigors of the Adam school.

Full disclosure, though: there's careful planning involved, but at another level. Invited by Beethoven's triple *piano* a few bars before (which is the only such exceptionally quiet patch in the whole sonata), I twist my right foot (*à la* Steibelt) so as to engage not one but both my piano's soft pedals—*céleste* and *una corda*. Technology comes to the rescue of human technique, well in time for the octave passage where this kind of automated softness will significantly help compensate for the stiffening of my arms, wrists, and hands. (In this sense, the "ready" portion of the "O" command actually starts with the corresponding final "Ped." in m. 461, with the drop in dynamics from *pp* to *ppp* as a marker to shift my foot and make my soft sounds much softer still.) When I do get to play the octaves, the experience is not unlike that of practicing with a loud vacuum cleaner nearby, or while wearing noise-canceling headphones. Uninhibited by sound, I get to focus all the more sharply, through my eyes and nerves, on the sheer physiology of my hands. As I near the end of my performance, I feel I've succeeded in lifting my virtuosity to a new level, and I take pride and pleasure in having figured out a perfect symbiosis of piano technology and pianistic technique. As much as I still wanted to feel piqued and energized during the opening bars of the sonata when I deliberately "failed" to play the last of a five-note group (the one with the *staccato*), I would now, after past successful performances, be upset with myself if I didn't play my octaves perfectly. That's what the rhetorical narrative of Beethoven's "Adam" Sonata demands of the pianist.

We may now, finally, compare Adam's example and Czerny's score with Beethoven's print (fig. 11.1). Adam has the repeated 5–1 fingerings, just like Beethoven: these are indicators of perpendicular determination, no longer of the finger but of the wrist. For his part Czerny omits the obvious fingering for an octave, but keeps Beethoven's slur, prioritizing a lateral dimension. Slur and fingerings *together*, however, create the perfect graphic representation of the Erard paradox that we've been exploring. And a *glissando-like* execution, provided that it's perfect, too, both accepts and celebrates this paradox. It took Beethoven some time to figure it out (all those previous movements of Op. 53), but at the end we're witnessing a newly found symbiosis between man and machine. In his Erard-oriented explorations, Beethoven encounters difficulties, but shows himself flexible and patient enough to look for solutions, and finding these within the context of the new instrument is very much part of the sonata's narrative: human physicality adapts to mechanical affordance and hindrance.

Rounding Off the Edges

If Op. 53 operates perfectly within the box that is the Erard, then Op. 57 wants to break out of it. Its "long-drawn-out composition" (in the words of Barry Cooper) is marked, on the one hand, by Beethoven's declaration of intent to Härtel in August 1804 and, on the other, by a completed manuscript at the end of summer 1806 (see appendix B).[3] The absence of sketches or manuscripts over a long period since Beethoven's first communication to Härtel appears to confirm that summer 1806 must be taken seriously in relation to Op. 57 for more than its mere completion. Apart from an undated anecdote by Ferdinand Ries of Beethoven's "humming" what would become a theme "for the last Allegro of the sonata," there is little evidence that he did any extended work on the piece over the previous years.[4]

This period straddles the complex progress of technical revisions to Beethoven's Erard. If these affected Op. 53 when it reached the stage of publication (as argued in chapter 9), then Op. 57 might well be the artistic backdrop to the technical revisions, the before and after of the process playing an essential role in the composition itself—the former capturing the positive perspective of anticipation (things that Beethoven hoped he might accomplish once his piano was revised), the latter reflecting regret or frustration (over things forever changed or lost). As we have realized already, however, any linearity in this process is problematized by the presence of yet another piano: Lichnowsky's Erard. Rather than a "before" and "after," then (which for Op. 53 coincided with composition, on the one hand, and publication, on the other), the entire pianist-creative space of Op. 57— that is, composition *and* publication—thrives on in-between-ness: French wanting to be Viennese, but then, on encountering the Count's piano, once more pulling in the other direction.

We will soon familiarize ourselves with the details of the revisions of Beethoven's Erard, but first I want to elaborate on what it means for Op. 57 to summon up a feeling of frustration from the pianist's perspective. If there's one hummable melodic idea in the sonata, it would have to be what is popularly known as "the fate motive": the three D♭s (triple eighth notes) followed by a single C (a quarter note) that are repeated to dramatic effect in the lowest register toward the end of the first movement's opening statement. This minor-second appoggiatura, its ominous undertone shaping the first movement, returns in the third and last movement with a vengeance. The whole second movement has been in D-flat—a special tonality that reverts to its single-pitch dissonance status by the end of the slow movement and that dominates the *attaca* transition to the third. In m. 86 of the third movement, we find D♭ as the first note of a melodic turn (D♭–C–B♮–C) yet again, and here the physical challenge of playing an Erard keyboard can no longer be ignored: see example 11.1. D♭ marks the beginning and C the rupturing of a slur that starts in m. 86 and ends just before the full-on chord in m. 96. It's the length of the slur that gives me pause. At first, it looks like any other in English and French scores of the period. Beethoven, however, gives it clear shape in a distinctly Viennese manner, first by adding *sforzando*, no fewer than three times, to mark restarts of the turn; then *crescendo*, to prolong and, through the process, inflate energy; finally, *diminuendo*, to dissipate this built-up energy—all while maintaining

EXAMPLE 11.1 Beethoven, Sonata in F Minor, Op. 57, third movement, mm. 86–102; with added fingering.

the integrity of a single expanded gesture. A Viennese slur's effectiveness relies on these three components: explosion (not unlike that produced by a single strike on a Viennese piano action), prolongation (which the Erard is particularly good at), and release (like a singer who runs out of breath).[5]

But understanding turns to frustration as I evaluate my rate of success in executing this slur. The difficulties are many and complex, and range from a lack of explosiveness in the French piano (making it hard to realize the idea of an aggressively harsh dissonance) to its built-in capacity to sustain sounds (making it hard to produce a quick and sudden release to a dissonance that wasn't explosive in the first place). In order to sustain, or indeed to *shape* the long slur in the ways indicated by Beethoven, I feel I am almost fighting against what the actual sounds are telling me—well aware, furthermore, that this kind of shaping is exactly what a Viennese piano is good at. But the biggest frustration comes through what I would like my left hand to do. In the spirit of *legato*, my thumb must step as smoothly as possible from the one French key to the next—a challenge exacerbated by having to play full triads of tones instead of just single tones. (I've indicated this difficulty by adding the fingering 1 in the example.) To be sure, the sonic weight of these chords is fittingly dramatic on the Erard, and I would never want to give up it. It takes much mental power, however, to become oblivious of the physical key dip of the French piano and to shape the long line in ways suggested by the slur. Whatever I tried, I never felt quite satisfied with the result, and when I finally recorded the piece, it still took half a dozen attempts to get it right.

It was after struggling with passages like this that I went back to Linz, more than two years after our initial visit, when we had spent several days photographing and measuring every detail of Beethoven's piano. I was eager to reach a better understanding of Beethoven's revised instrument, especially those aspects that, from my growing experience on the unrevised replica, had started sending me messages of frustration. Of course, I knew the revised action model that Chris had made, but still, I wanted to try out certain things seated at a complete, revised Erard keyboard. So finally I found myself actually sitting down at Beethoven's piano, which sounds simple, but wasn't: the Linz piano is preserved on a podium with no place to sit, so we had to improvise an equally high sitting position. Then, as I sat

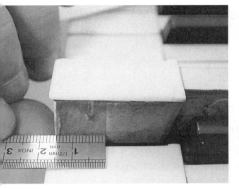

FIGURE 11.2 Beethoven's Erard: revised key (*left*); repair of the old balance points (*right*).

down behind the keyboard, something jumped out at me: hidden before, it now became completely clear.

Figure 11.2 (left) shows that the keys in Beethoven's revised keyboard have been extended with an additional piece of wood. As a result, the front bone coverings had to be replaced. This is something we'd known, and Chris had copied all of that accurately in the model-action. But what we'd never noticed before is that, through this revision process, the new tops to the keys had also been beveled at the sides, exactly like those on every Viennese piano of the day, facilitating the lateral movement that Beethoven and I had craved.

I'd been entirely satisfied with straight or nonbeveled keys in Op. 53; the fact that they weren't beveled had never occurred to me. But the desire to be able to cruise again from one key to the next became strong, not for the "*glissando*" of Op. 53 (where I quickly adopted a different solution), but for passages like the one discussed in Op. 57. Did my discovery of the beveled keys in the Linz piano confirm also Beethoven's frustrations? As the novelty of his foreign piano wore off, Beethoven's focus may unavoidably have shifted from affordance to hindrance, or from dependence to dependency. Between Op. 53 and Op. 57, or between November 1803 and October 1806, we witness Beethoven's frame of mind change from fresh excitement over all the things his new piano could do to increased frustration over things it no longer could—but also (as testified by those deep triads in the left hand

and by the long slur and continued interest in sonority) with an unwilling-
ness to simply turn back the clock.

Repair

The question of beveling or not beveling may be inconsequential from a
strictly technological point of view (nothing in the piano action behaves
differently because of it), but in a pianist's mind it is all the more symbolic
of a changed relationship between man and machine. If, during his first few
months of ownership, we witnessed Beethoven French-izing his technique
and aesthetics in relation to the new piano, then the revisions reversed this
relationship: no longer a question of man adjusting machine, but machine
being adjusted to a man, which in this case means being viennicized. The
possibility of shipping the piano back to Paris for adjustments would not
have occurred to Beethoven, nor is there any surviving correspondence
with Erard Frères in which he discussed his reservations or concerns. Instead, someone in Vienna took it upon themselves to embark on technical
revisions, which must have been instigated by Beethoven himself.

We've started empathizing with Beethoven over why the revisions took
place. But before we turn to the what and the how, I would like to bring
to the table another piece of evidence that may shed crucial light on the
context in which they were made—an insight that, exactly like the previous one regarding the beveled keys, grew in relevance only as our research
developed, particularly as we started imagining a sequence of events. From
the outset, our focus had understandably been on the more spectacular signs
of actual change. But standing alone, clearly removed from any process of
revision, is one noticeable trace of *repair*. Drawing attention to it here feels
like a vindication of my feelings regarding my colleague's compulsion to
slide across the keys and also makes Miss Lichnowsky's observation about
Beethoven's similarly playful urge highly relevant.

Overlooked in the existing organological literature on Beethoven's
Erard is the fact that the balance holes, as they existed in the still unrevised
instrument, have been repaired. In figure 11.2 (right), we can see little lines
mostly on the righthand side of the rectangular balance holes—the ones
higher up than the current ones. These are the marks of small incisions in
which tiny wooden shims have been inserted to tighten the gaps again—

indeed, to address the worst-case scenario that I described at the outset. Two major points emerge: first, Beethoven must have used the piano intensively for such a repair to be necessary after a relatively brief period of ownership, including sliding—or at least attempting to slide—way too often over the keys; second, the initial intent of the technician Beethoven turned to for help would have been to repair, rather than change, what existed.

At some point, though, the decision was made to undertake revisions to the piano. If we take Streicher's January 2, 1805, letter as the latest point at which this might have happened, it still arrived remarkably soon. Furthermore, it is reasonable to assume—as Streicher speaks of the piano "having been changed twice" in this relatively short period—that it was the same person who had the audacity to take repair to the level of revision, and, once that line had been crossed, to take the next step—and the next—with every new decision leading to yet another set of issues and solutions. "Twice," then, should be taken to mean that the piano had spent time in someone's workshop twice. All the steps together result in the peculiar piece of re-engineering that we can see today. If one thing seems certain, it is that the technician would not initially have realized the full extent of what they were getting involved with.

My research team agrees that the main purpose of revisions would have been *to reduce the key dip*. Here's the basic principle:

Take a pencil in your hand. Start with positioning one hand's index finger under the pencil so as to make it rock up and down as you hold one end between the thumb and index finger of your other hand. You've just created a model of a key-lever, your index finger functioning as its balance rail. Chances are you've put your finger roughly at the midpoint of the pencil—the point also selected by Sébastien Erard for his keys, and the kind of balance that produced the "basketball dribble" effect noted at the outset of Op. 53. In order to now reduce the key dip, you must shift your balance point in the direction of your rocking index finger and thumb. As a result, you will find yourself pushing down a pencil that now weighs significantly more than before. Once you commit to this new point of balance, a whole process of compensating and rebalancing begins.

I have systematized this process as eighteen points, each to be visualized through corresponding numbered photos in plate 9. What follows, however, is not intended as a step-by-step account of what happened. While our numbered observations systematically cover the various areas of a piano action, the reality would have been messier and more complex.

The first act of revising the piano, then, was to shift the balance of the key levers toward the front (i.e., in the direction of the player) by 45 mm.

1. The original balance rail had to be expanded to accommodate the drilling of new holes: a new strip of wood, 47 mm wide, was added to the front edge of the original rail. (This is the lighter colored strip, between ruler marks 30.5 and 35.2; the action in the photo is upside down, with the keyboard on the right.)

2. New balance holes were then drilled through keys and rail at 45 mm from the old ones (which are still visible), and the balance pins were shifted accordingly.

3. The new key mortises were reinforced with glued-on, chamfered wooden blocks or buttons in the Viennese style; also Viennese, finally, is the leather padding that was inserted inside these blocks, to avoid noise or rattling.

To fine-tune the newly obtained balance, the key levers were lengthened at the front; key covers had to be adjusted or replaced.

4. Originally 9 mm thick, the ornamented moldings at the front end of the keys were planed flat, leaving in place a plate of a mere 3 mm thickness. Annotations on a photo of a key lever from the Brussels 1805 Erard illustrate how the ornamented reliefs have been eliminated.

5a. New wooden blocks of 11 mm thickness were glued onto the front.

5b. Flat ivory plates with a thickness of 1 mm were added to these blocks, to create a smooth, ivory-covered key front in Viennese style.

6a. Head covers for the front parts of the natural keys were replaced by new ones, most likely taken from the same batch of ivory as the new front-of-key plates (see no. 5b); there's a marked difference in whiteness between the newly applied ivory and that of the long and narrow pieces in the back (which are almost certainly the original ones).

6b. The edges of these new front key plates were both rounded at the front and beveled on the sides, following Viennese custom.

6c. The original long back covers of the natural keys where shifted forward by 3 mm.

6d. Accordingly, the sharps were shifted forward as well; but to compensate
for the now empty space in front of the name board, their backs were
lengthened by glued-on blocks in black ebony of 3 mm. (The separation
line shows faintly on the first black note from the bottom; they show more
clearly in photo 10. The white back plates didn't need any extending. Since
they run under the name board, their size doesn't matter so much. They
originally overreached their black counterparts by 5 mm, which left them
with a sufficient 2 mm in the revised setup.)

When calculating the total additional length of the revised keys, one needs
to take into account both the initial shortening by 6 mm (no. 4) and the subsequent lengthening by 11 mm plus 1 mm (nos. 5a and b).[6] Six lost, twelve
gained: *the new keys are thus 6 mm longer than the original ones.*

7. The lengthened keyboard now protrudes 5 mm past the left and right key
cheeks (which are fixed into the bottom of the case and are not part of the
action). Not quite reaching the edge of the piano, the keys nonetheless
start covering the three brass plates into which the front cover slotted. Not
surprisingly, this now useless front cover board no longer exists.

Shifting the balance points created more mass at the back of the key levers,
so the keys needed to be weighted differently—or rebalanced, following
Viennese custom:

8. The original lead weights were removed from the back of the key levers,
which still show the now empty holes.
9. Wood was carved off the back of the key levers.
10. New, larger lead weights were placed in the front of the key (i.e., the now
shorter part of the key).

Aiming for a new kind of touch, the Viennese principle of key stoppage was
also implemented:

11. Instead of gently stopping the keys at their fronts (through a three-layered
cushion of woven cloth: see photo 11a, Brussels 1805 Erard), a wooden
over-rail was installed above the backs of the key levers, to set a hard upper

limit to their movement (see photo 11b, Beethoven's Erard).[7] (Some cloth is added to the over-rail but, as explained in chapter 2, this is to eliminate contact noise rather than to provide padding.)

12a. An arm was fixed to the rear of each key lever; it crooks above the over-rail and engages the damper jacks, which were previously engaged by the key levers directly.

12b. Wood was taken off the top of the rear end of the key levers, creating more space between key lever and over-rail; otherwise the dampers would have ended up sitting even higher—an issue that needed to be addressed anyway.

13. The damper jacks (now 15.6 cm long) were shortened by 22 mm to accommodate the relatively higher position of the new arms; the ones in the Brussels Erard measure 17.8 cm.

The Erard Frères hammers were replaced with hammers of a more typically Viennese construction:

14. Hammer-butt and hammer-shank are now of one piece (at the left side of photo 14a; ignore the glued-on block that engages with the escapement hopper); also the hammer-head is now of one piece: its wooden core is no longer round but has the shape of a reversed comma or quotation mark: compare photos 14a (Beethoven's Erard) and 14b (the Brussels Erard). (The unrevised Erard separates butt from shank, and has a three-part hammer-head: a tongue that is stuck into the round core from below, and a little button below to secure the hammer on the shank and to create contact with the back-check.)

15. The manner in which the hammers pivot on the hammer-rail was changed. The brass mountings used by Erard were replaced with Viennese-style *Kapseln*. The new hammers pivot on pinpoint axles (photo 15a, Beethoven's Erard), as opposed to the through axles in leather bushings used by Erard (photo 15b, Brussels Erard).

16. While the original pivot plates were screwed laterally onto the hammer-rail (see photo 15b), the new vertical *Kapsel* needed more space. Therefore, the height of the hammer-rail was reduced by 1.8 cm.

Two crucial components of the keyboard action, though technically unchanged, were adjusted to behave properly in the new setup:

17. The hoppers (*pilotes*) remained the same (photo 17 shows one from the Brussels 1805 Erard), but they're now operating a hammer apparatus that's no longer the same. Their position with respect to the pivoting axle of the hammers has changed: lower in the original, the tip of the hopper is now almost at the same height as the *Kapsel*'s pivot point.

18. The hammer back-checks are also the same, but shifting the balance point of the keys forward caused them to sit too high to catch the new hammers. Two adjustments were made: first, the back-check wires were repositioned by 9 mm (the original holes may still be seen), and then they were also bent lower.

A Re-engineered Object

After the initial bold decision to shift the balance point, the operating mode became, "let's cross that bridge when we come to it," resulting in a complex (and some might say, messy) chain of revisions, each of which may be explained as reactive or corrective. Beethoven's revamped piano takes de-scription, or the adjustment of a technical object to a new environment, to another level.[8] Madeleine Akrich lists three conditions for changes made: disagreement, negotiation, and the potential for breakdown. We've identified a "potential for breakdown" in the fixing of the old balance points, indicative of rattling keys and the wrong kind of playing ("wrong" here referring not just to Beethoven as an individual, but to a community of pianists used to beveled keys with a lower key dip). "Disagreement" between one technician and another (a Viennese vs. an absent French/English one) may have been the trigger to shift from temporary repair to drastic revision: the local technician would have empathized with Beethoven's complaints and disagreed with the French design, which in their eyes would have needed adjusting or even correcting. But what about "negotiation"? If there had been any consultation with Erard Frères, the revision process would never have gone that far, and we might now indeed have had an *adjusted* rather than a *re-engineered* object.

Yet—and this is what makes this particular case of revision so fascinating—one line was never crossed. In spite of all the revisions, we're technically still dealing with a *pushing* mechanism: a piano action that depends on the fundamental principle of an unchanged *pilote* operating a redesigned hammer. Yet in this case the Viennese *Kapsel* (a term for which there is no English equivalent in the organological literature) presents rather a grotesque sight to those familiar with Viennese actions: designed to work in combination with an escapement lever at the beak of the hammer, in Beethoven's revised action, chosen for its sheer pivoting quality, a *Kapsel* sits on the hammer bank as a lone element of metal bizarrely removed from its usual context. As one of our team members put it, "They turned a *prell*-action on its head." This makes a lot of sense: imagine turning a Viennese hammer-beak into a French hammer-butt, and a Viennese escapement lever into a French *pilote*. This transformation, within an entirely new habitat of technical parts, is all the more peculiar if one asks what stopped them from also turning everything around on a horizontal plane and reverting to a Viennese system of *pulling*.[9] But this opens up an altogether new perspective: instead of re-engineering the existing action, why did Beethoven's technician not make a second, Viennese one, to function as an alternative action made to fit in one and the same piano? The cost would have been lower, the guarantee of success much greater, and the whole enterprise with respect to the original action entirely risk-free: a win-win situation. As a bonus, if only as a souvenir, Beethoven would have been able to keep the old, French action.

All this is hindsight, of course—and historiographical nonsense. The last thing on the technician's mind would have been to offer an alternative: he simply wished to *improve* Beethoven's piano. ("Improve" is also the term used by Andreas Streicher: see below.) Bearing in mind that the resulting action is still a pushing one, it seems justified from a technical-semantic point of view to continue calling Beethoven's revised Erard a "viennicized French piano." In our organological observations above we used the term "Vienna" and derivatives of it no fewer than eight times. But as we now move to a comparison of our model actions (all three of them) and pick up where we left things in chapter 3, we ask: what in the performance of a single normal strike (neither soft nor loud) warrants us to conclude that the revised action indeed behaves in a more Viennese manner? Table 11.1 compares specifications recorded from our earlier experiments, using model actions of Walter and Erard/original, with newly generated ones on the Erard/revised.

Let's first consider those numbers that radiate success. The key dip on

TABLE 11.1 Selected specifications for single strikes on each of the three model actions

	Walter	Erard (original)	Erard (revised)
Key dip	4.33 mm	7.45 mm	4.74 mm
Hammer-throw	3.4 cm	5.2 cm	4.6 cm
Average speed of hammer, normal strike	62 cm/s or 2.23 km/h	90 cm/s or 3.24 km/h	63 cm/s or 2.27 km/h
Maximum speed of hammer, normal strike	146.1 cm/s or 5.26 km/h	202.9 cm/s or 7.30 km/h	139.7 cm/s or 5.03 km/h
Maximum speed across the board, *forte* strike	226.1 cm/s or 8.14 km/h	384.7 cm/s or 13.85 km/h	306.0 cm/s or 11.02 km/h
Time between strike and hammer/string contact (up)	54 ms (on key)	128 ms (off key) / 65 ms (on key)	73 ms (on key)
Time between hammer/string contact and back-check catch (down)	40 ms	39 ms	50 ms
Down-weight of key (c^1)	22 g	32 g	44 g
Up-weight of key (c^1)	8 g	5 g	7 g

the revised Erard comes quite close to that of the Walter: it decreases from 7.45 mm to 4.74 mm. This makes the keyboard of the revised Erard more than one-third shallower than the original Erard and almost as shallow as Walter's at 4.33 mm. Thanks to the new longer hammer-heads, the hammer-throw (or the distance between hammer-head tip and string) also becomes smaller (4.6 cm instead of the original 5.2 cm), closing in on the 3.4 cm in Walter. Both are a clear improvement from a Viennese perspective: the key dip has been drastically reduced, and the shorter hammer-throw holds a promise of more immediate sound.

But is promise being met? Do we get the more explosive strike that one associates with a Viennese action? Here the numbers start sending mixed messages. It takes 73 ms for the hammer to reach the string on the Erard/revised, compared to a mere 54 ms on Walter. This is disappointingly long, especially when compared to the 65 ms on the Erard/original. The latter is not a fair comparison, though. The Erard/original measurement is drawn from a finger strike that started half a centimeter above the key as recommended by Adam, but for the revised action, I reverted to the Viennese, Streicher-endorsed technique of touching the key before striking it.

The measurements of speed are not particularly useful, either. When we look at the average speed of Erard/revised, we find a number close to the Walter (63 cm/s and 62 cm/s, respectively). The maximum speed of the same strike, however, remains lower in Erard/revised (139.7 cm/s) than in Walter (146.1 cm/s). If we're looking for more explosiveness in Erard/revised, then the numbers are disappointing, especially when considering the longer distance for the hammer to travel in Erard/revised compared to Walter.

And yet, slow-motion video clips of a revised-action strike show a hammer trajectory that is remarkably similar to Walter. What they have in common (and what sets them apart from Erard/original) is the long pickup time for the hammer. It takes a while before the hammer gains momentum, or before it starts accelerating toward the strings. In fact, Erard/revised is overdoing it: its pickup is even longer than that for Walter. Almost in defiance of its own technical principle, it looks "flipped" rather than "thrown." Measurements confirm what the naked eye observes. During the first third of a normal strike, Erard/original increases velocity by 48 cm/s in 18 ms, leading to an average acceleration of 2.67 cm/s per ms; a Walter hammer increases velocity by 21 cm/s in 17 ms, amounting to an average of 1.27 cm/s per ms; Erard/revised, finally, increases velocity by 23.58 cm/s in 23 ms, yielding an average of 1.03 cm/s per ms.

Before we conclude that the Erard/revised piano is the most sluggish of the three, however, we must look at what exactly is being flipped or thrown, and here we hit the most problematic number of all. *My finger needs to push down much more weight* using the revised action: 44 g (for the key of c^1) or 17 g more than the 37 g in the original Erard and *twice the down-weight of a Walter key* (which measured 22 g). To make matters worse, the new up-weight (7 g) doesn't contribute much in helping the finger relax on its way up. In other words, of the three actions, the revised action requires most of my finger, both on its way down and its way up. There is no disputing it: *Erard/revised is the most sluggish of the three.*

Figure 11.3 helps us understand why, in spite of elaborate efforts to rebalance the keys, the down-weight remains high, and why fundamental

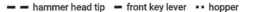

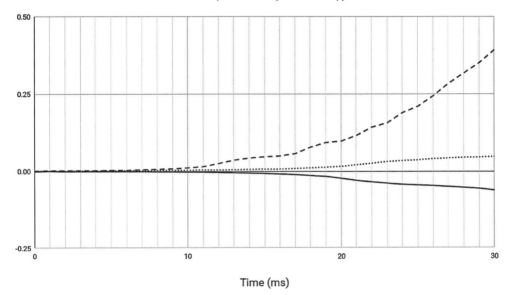

FIGURE 11.3 Beginning of "normal" strike on revised Erard action model: second run.

choices of "throw" and "flip" have proven incompatible. The way in which key, hopper, and hammer react to one another in Erard/revised at the very beginning of a strike is remarkably similar to the corresponding graphs of Walter in figure 3.4. On the Walter I prided myself on my skill in feeling the escapement lever at the beak of the hammer, so as to create a head start toward as tight and explosive a strike as possible. That we recognize the same tightness in the revised action, with hammer reacting to key and hopper instantaneously, confirms that the technician was aiming to create a similar touch. This also means, however, that my finger now carries the combined weight of those components and that I can no longer ease into the paced sequence (first key, then hopper, then hammer) that we observed in the original Erard. Why? The Viennese *Kapseln* look out of context in the French piano, yet they may well hold the answer, as the crucial connector of finger, key, and hammer. While the straight pins through leather bushings of the original French piano also provided useful resistance, maintaining the integrity of a sequentially paced movement of components, the iron points pivoting in a brass *Kapsel* allow for everything to happen at once within a relatively friction-free environment. Yes, one ends up with a more

Viennese feel (where anything having to do with hammer movement is fixed onto the key, its entire weight to be lifted by the finger), but there's a high price to pay. If Beethoven had found his Erard too heavy, he would hardly have expected his revised Erard to be significantly heavier still.

Here are some of the subjective reactions recorded during our first experimental sessions with the model-action:

"It was softer than I intended it to be." (On playing a normal single tone.)

"I'm trying to make it work with deliberately relaxed muscles, but never succeed in making the hammer really speak. The lower key dip tells me that I could play the same way as on a Viennese action, but in reality more muscle power is needed." (On playing repeated notes.)

"It's unreliable." (On playing repeated notes.)

"This is no longer fun." (On the "basketball dribble" sequence of thirds.)

"Hard to do relaxed. I have to make up with pressure, but then it sounds too intense. I feel like I have to choose between how things feel and how things sound. Gone is the effect of a pantalon, where you have to be completely loose in your technique." (On playing a tremolo.)

Have we lost the true art of playing tremolo through the revisions? The experiments strongly suggest we have. As I tried to apply the same technique that I had developed on the original Erard (moving *with* the alternating keys rather than *moving* them), my first attempt in front of the slow-motion camera resulted in failure: I barely succeeded in making thirteen notes sound at all, let alone in regular succession, and I gave up way before completing anything close to a forty-eight-note tremolo run. My disappointment is palpable on tape. Bobby Giglio politely proposes, "Do three more?" Something changed as I embarked on my second attempt at a first trial, the results of which are shown in figure 11.4, to be compared with similar graphs in chapter 7. On the video clip, determination can be seen as I lift my thumb and third finger up to a full centimeter above the keys for each strike. I play a perfect fifty-eight-note tremolo—that is, ten more than

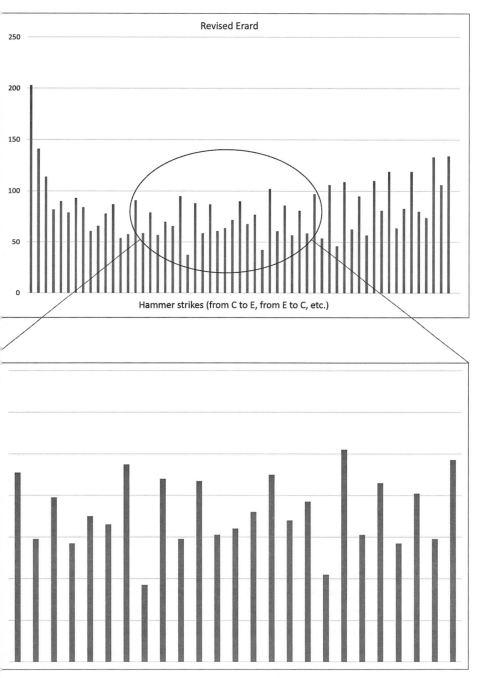

FIGURE 11.4 Revised Erard tremolo: time difference between strikes, representing the first of three runs after a preliminary failure.

strictly necessary, but more important, not missing a beat until the very last note: there's not a single failing or nonsounding strike. Not that I feel proud. The sound produced is best described as busy and tense: we hear many individual tones of C and E rather than a single C–E major third. Apparently, after my first failed attempt, I had no choice but to give up on trying to play with my ear, as Louis Adam taught. The mechanical/physiological results are impressive enough: most strikes stay under 100 milliseconds, recalling the strong performance of a Walter tremolo. But to relate my playing of the keys of C longer than the keys of E (not always but mostly) to my earlier performances on Erard/original lacks justification. In piano-technical survival mode, I have to rely on the weight of my thumb to carry me through an endurance exercise, wrist and rotating forearm coming to the aid of my hard-working fingers. The keys are simply too heavy.

"Beethoven is a strong player"

Key dip or weight: in hindsight, the revisions fought a battle that could not be won. Word of Beethoven's inevitable disappointment may have reached Andreas Streicher, prompting the often quoted assessment, "Beethoven is certainly a strong player, yet he can still not adequately treat his Fp." But how truthful or fair is this statement? Can Beethoven be blamed for the search for a solution that ended up creating an even bigger problem? Let's look at the context of the letter. Streicher resists pressure by Gottfried Härtel for Streicher *geborne* Stein to produce more powerful pianos with larger key dips. Almost certainly, Härtel's pressure reflects disparaging comments on shallow and light Viennese pianos made by international business partner Muzio Clementi, who happened to be visiting Leipzig at this time:

> Your letter contains one single remark of which I cannot approve, namely the heavier and deeper keys [*das schwerer gehen und tiefer fallen der Claviere*] as Clementi wants them. I can assure you from double experience that a keyboard player will get used more easily to a bad tone, sluggish or even stuck keys, or to any other problem than to heavy and even less so, to deep keys. I have myself made a few keyboards of this kind, but no way as extreme as H. Clementi would want them and now have all reason to regret it. Certainly the English pianos [*Claviere*] gain an advantage over

ours if we make our keyboard actions [*Claviaturen*] according to their principle, and this appears to be Clementi's intention. But also certain is that the fortepiano will then cease to be the universal instrument, since nine out of ten *Klavier* amateurs will have to give up playing.

Beethoven is certainly a strong player, yet he still is unable to treat his Fp. which he got from Erard in Paris adequately, and he has already had it changed twice without the least improvement [*ohne das mindeste daran gebessert zu haben*], since its construction does not allow for any other action.—I've chosen a middle path between light and heavy in several pianos, but have had to abandon this too, because not only local but also amateurs from abroad have protested against it.[10]

Not only the amateur player (the largest clientele for Streicher and Härtel alike) would have to give up piano playing: Streicher reinforces his argument with the example that even Beethoven, as the professional among professionals, cannot cope. Interestingly, also in Streicher's assessment, heaviness of keys is the lesser of two evils, so he implicitly agrees with the premise of the revisions: to tackle the problem of key dip first, and worry about weight later. In relation to the actual execution, however, one suspects a certain degree of *Schadenfreude*. Beethoven "has had it changed already twice, without the least improvement." Unfortunately, Streicher gives no indication of what might have been changed, and, furthermore, makes no distinction between repair and revision. Instead, he concludes (both sweepingly and objectively) that "the construction [of the Paris piano] does not allow for any other action." The latter statement may be read as a token of respect for his French colleagues, but the subtext to his German addressee must be that Streicher expects the same from Härtel: "Don't make *us* do anything that goes against *our* concept of making pianos," one hears him think. Or: "Don't listen to Clementi."

Streicher does not blame the technician for bad work, nor does he proclaim that his workshop might have done a better job. (A third possibility, which seems highly unlikely, is that the work had actually been executed in the Streicher workshop and that he wisely chose to ignore that fact.) On the contrary, there's separation between technical knowledge (which he understands, as a colleague-technician) and its practical use (the playing on it, by the foremost professional of Vienna). It was *Beethoven* who wanted the piano changed, and he should have known better: he should never have believed he could get used to a French piano in the first place. In his eagerness to criticize the object, however, Streicher ends up misrepresenting its owner. Our experience of Op. 53 tells us that Beethoven's French piano was not too deep or too heavy for Beethoven. On the contrary, Beethoven exploited these very qualities to create something entirely new. On the surface, Op. 53 has the hallmarks of the finger agility we associate with the young Beethoven (his sonatas, but mostly his variations), such as arpeggios or powerful chords in any form or shape and on any part of the keyboard, and special acrobatics, such as playing a trill and melody in one hand. But different from any piano work that came before—and different again from any work that he would write from Op. 57 onward—there's one condition: that the hands be *locked in* for maximum perpendicular finger movement. Without this constant reminder it would be impossible to survive the passagework from the final movement shown in example 11.2 (top), where broken chords return from an earlier episode and are now expanded to engage both hands, for maximum effect. This is a test of endurance, but to an Erard owner, it's also a test of know-how. In my hard-learned experience, the only way to triumph is to keep locking in one's hands from one *sforzando* to the next, trusting that finger movement (which should be well rehearsed by now) will "happen" along the way. In fact, this kind of playing—and writing—thrives on a deep-keyed piano: make the keys any shallower, and your fingers will just start running away, causing you to play much faster than you may have intended, and making for an anticlimactic and rather jarring arrival at the dominant-harmony blocks of chords in m. 378. (These comments, ironically, will be less meaningful to those playing modern instruments than to those playing their "Waldstein" on Viennese instruments; but at this juncture of Beethoven's pianism, that's exactly the point.)

Compare now example 11.2 (bottom). In this theme from the finale of Op. 57, a troubling Db keeps challenging the inside contours of an F-minor arpeggio. (Db has held a provoking presence since the beginning of the sonata.) Breaking out from the initial triad, I shift my hand sideways toward the ubiquitous consonance/dissonance pair of keys. Granted, a shallower key dip or at least a beveled key would have helped, but shifting positions on good notes that are also triadic ones (see the circles in the example) gives

EXAMPLE 11.2 Beethoven, Sonata in C Major, Op. 53, final movement, mm. 356–65 (*top*); Sonata in F Minor, Op. 57, third movement, mm. 20–39, with added fingering (*bottom*).

the theme a kind of controlled frenzy. When in m. 36 I finally get to feel the F-minor triad in a single-hand position, now undisturbed by D♭, these moments feel like respite. It is also here that Beethoven rekindles an Erard-appropriate approach to sound (the pleasure of a simple triad, even if it's a minor-third one), but the exquisitely plaintive appoggiatura two bars later, where I must glide my fifth finger from one white key to the next, makes me crave, once again, a smoothly beveled key.

These moments of frustration on my unrevised Erard leave me feel

310 · CHAPTER 11

stuck between reality and desire—or between the Walter I've kept next to the Erard and the promise of a well-revised Erard. To be sure, during more formal performance adrenaline has helped me overcome these frustrations, but there have been practice sessions where I felt like I couldn't play more than two bars without stopping because my hands just didn't manage to connect physically from one idea to the next. This emerging sense of disconnect (which is particularly surprising when juxtaposed with my never waning sense of excitement in playing Op. 53) provoked the binary thinking that we've been exploring: horizontal and vertical, square and round, French and Viennese. In either system, of course, there's room for both, but the respective tools for achieving any symbiosis are drastically different. In contrast to what Erard Frères made its regular customers believe, for Beethoven there was no perfection—at all.

Failure

Earlier in this chapter we tested the very things that I've been enthusing about throughout this book: those French affordances that I have identified in the scores of some of the best Paris-based pianist-composers. Understandably, we wished to find whether those foreign features are still realizable through an object that has been adjusted to a more familiar, Viennese way of playing the piano. But does the revised piano lend itself better to quintessentially Viennese features? In spite of the loss, is there a gain, at least? With the displacement of Erard's piano to Vienna, I had argued that the inside workings of the French object did not match the outside world of Beethoven's habitat.[11] This does not necessarily matter: foreignness was exactly the point, and we've projected onto Beethoven an open mind and a body ready for something new.

Sadly, however, the viennicized French object—with its inside now adjusted to the outside—turns out to be a mismatch as well. In fact it's a total failure, with the advantages of neither the French nor the Viennese. Though still disappointed from a research-methodological point of view (I would have loved to live those frustrations to the point of completely giving up, just like Beethoven), I also understand Chris's decision to retract his initial offer to build a second, revised action to go into the same Erard.

Just as one cannot help but empathize with Sébastien Erard, who would have been devastated to see what had happened to his piano, I had no choice but to accept Chris's professional pride in deciding not to copy something that, in his eyes, was doomed to fail. (Chris here may well represent the perspective of Andreas Streicher: the outsider-colleague who doesn't wish to get involved.)

And yet. As I pushed myself to record Beethoven's "Appassionata" Sonata on the original Erard (dragging my feet, like Beethoven when composing it), I began giving the Linz piano a second chance. During our first visit, I had had an eye only for Beethoven's French piano, and I will forever remember my disappointment when playing the opening bars of "Waldstein" on the revised Erard, the result being not at all what I had expected and much less than what I had hoped. (Somehow, the extent of the revision of Beethoven's piano hadn't registered with me yet: I was still expecting a French piano.) But now, the morning after my concert on our replica, as I sat down at Beethoven's revised piano again, I came newly prepared with two years of intensely lived, embodied knowledge.

Before traveling back to Linz, I had selected three Viennese features in "Appassionata" to check that might provide insight into the artistic context of the revisions. It was no longer the unknown but the known (including my own difficulties and frustrations with the French piano) that I now wished to conceptualize and experience, taking full advantage of the unique opportunity to move back and forth between my unrevised Erard and Beethoven's revised instrument, one piano standing next to the other. (A photo capturing this encounter is reproduced as plate 10.)

The first was the issue of an appoggiatura, that most essential phoneme of a Viennese musical language. Compared to my original Erard, could I experience the resolution of a two-note group once again as part of an overall upward gesture of hand and wrist? I made a note to check both for the *pleasure* of the lift and *confidence* that the resolution would actually sound. The second was repetition. I would need to check for *accuracy*, *speed*, and *endurance*, that is, whether repeating a note would become fatiguing after a while. The third, finally, was lateral motion, or the ability to *glide* across the keyboard.

My reactions were recorded in real time:

1. Resolution

I play two random keys, F and E, slurring the one to the other. On our replica you need a minimum of pressure to play any key at all. I'm curious to see whether I'll be able to achieve this upward kind of resolution better on the revised action. *I shift to Beethoven's piano and play a series of appoggiaturas; they sound horribly out of tune, but it's the physical sensation that matters.* It's not bad, really. In fact it's good. It works. It's easier. It passes the test. *Surprisingly, Beethoven's keyboard action is quite operative.* The revised action does restore the upward lift of a Viennese resolution.

Back to the replica, I play the appoggiatura from the first movement, m. 3, several times (see ex. 11.3). Beethoven adds an ascending trill on the dissonant part, making it thicker than it already is or should be. It's as if he makes sure that even a four-note chord like the one in m. 4 is perceived as a resolving consonant. I'm curious to see if I'm able to keep that lift even with more than one note. I try on Beethoven's piano. Yes . . . ! It's nice: more Viennese in spirit. I have to revise my expectations.

2. Repetition

At Beethoven's piano, I play a single note, E♭, and keep repeating it with one finger, as I would perform it in example 11.3. It's fine. It's easy. It's fast. I move to the replica: this is slower. Back to Beethoven's piano: so, yes, repetition works more efficiently here. And I must say, I was afraid it'd be too heavy and that I'd get tired, but I don't think that's happening. *But then I keep going for a while:* Yes, I *am* getting tired. Now I feel the heaviness of the key. Let me try to do the same over here, on the replica. I can keep doing it for much longer, only I can't do it as fast. *If the repeated notes on Beethoven's piano are triplets as in Op. 57, then those on my replica become eighth notes, more like the "basketball dribble" of Op. 53.*

3. Lateral motion

At the replica I play a sequence of diminished-seventh chords, moving my right hand down from one set of keys to the other immediately following. When I play chords like this, I always have to deliberately move down my hand for each of the chords. The question is whether, over at Beethoven's piano, I'll be able to restore a Viennese slur and do an actual *diminuendo. I try at Beethoven's piano.* It's hard to judge by the sound, but

EXAMPLE 11.3 Beethoven, Sonata in F Minor, Op. 57, first movement, mm. 1–4 and mm. 24–35.

I must say, the feeling of sliding over the keyboard is much more strongly present at this piano than at our replica.

To summarize, when I first came here and tried this Erard, my mind was very much immersed in the French piano: I was hoping to find a French sound and a French touch. And I was disappointed. Now that I've been practicing on our replica for a few years and I revisit the revised action, I must say, it's not that bad. It restores certain Viennese instincts that I had as a pianist and that Beethoven must have had. I recognize the rationale behind the revisions. There's logic to it. At the same time, there's a lot that one looses. I feel convinced that once I started practicing on the revised Erard, I'd very quickly start regretting things that I've been able to do on the other piano. It must have been the same for Beethoven.

Whodunit

While Chris had initially been quick to point out the sloppiness of the revisionary work, his admiration also grew with time, as we kept revisiting the subject and gaining insight into the motivation behind the revisions. So who might have been the anonymous technician? We've already eliminated the option of the firm Streicher *née* Stein: it's too unlikely to assume that Andreas wouldn't have owned up to it in his letter to Härtel. What about Matthäus Andreas ("André") Stein, who had parted ways with sister Nannette and brother-in-law Andreas in the fall of 1802—a suggestion first made by Huber in 1988 and uncritically copied in the literature since?[12] There was certainly opportunity: during the summer of 1804 Beethoven asked his pupil Ferdinand Ries to inquire about borrowing a Stein piano ("for money") while he stayed in Oberdöbling (near Heiligenstadt) "because I'm afraid of having mine [i.e., his Erard] moved here."[13] Did ensuing arrangements trigger a plan to finally take care of Beethoven's misgivings about his French piano? Did it end up in Stein's workshop, while Beethoven rented another? (Noteworthy here also is that Beethoven didn't risk moving his own piano, strong testimony as to how precious the Erard still was to him.) Later in Beethoven's life, as documented in the Conversation Books, André Stein was always ready to help out, as in building a hearing machine (*Gehörmaschine*) for Beethoven's Broadwood in April–September 1820. On this occasion, Beethoven's close circle described André Stein as "the more technically skilled"—and the comparison being made was to Conrad Graf, which amounts to a not insubstantial endorsement.[14]

The truth remains that we simply don't know who carried out the revisions—and it's fair to assume that Beethoven would have struggled to put the whole episode behind him. When later in life, upon the arrival of his Broadwood piano in May 1818, he stated, "They would like to tune it and spoil it, but they shall not touch it" ("they" used as a blanket reference to all Viennese piano builders), his irrational response may well have had its origin in the traumatic events of 1803–5, when he was lured into ill-guided, chauvinism-driven technical adventures.[15]

Conflicting emotions would also explain why it took Beethoven another five years to finally admit to Streicher in September 1810, "My French one is really no longer useful." He then drops what must have been a nagging question: "Maybe you can advise as to how we might still save it."[16] Streicher did not pick up on this use of "we." It seems that Beethoven was close to agreeing to sell it (a slightly unethical prospect, since he'd be transferring the problems to someone else), but he changed his mind: "As to the French one [*das französische*], which is now truly useless, I have second thoughts about selling it, because after all it is a souvenir [*Andenken*] such as nobody here has honored me with."[17] Note than Beethoven now calls it "*the* French one," and no longer "*my* French one." I dare say that Beethoven would have been spared the technical detail and that he'd be horrified to read our full analysis above, but just through touch and sound he would have understood that the Frenchness he'd loved before was lost. In hindsight, when agreeing to fateful revisions, Beethoven had in effect started bidding farewell to his beloved piano. Nobody—not even Nannette or Andreas Streicher—could do anything to save it, just as no god could help Orpheus. The laws of engineering—like those of the underworld—did not allow it.

* * *

Let's allow Miss Lichnowsky to resume her testimony:

> Once while spending a summer with a Maecenas at his (i.e., Karl Lichnowsky's) country-seat, [Beethoven] was so pestered by the guests, who wished to hear him play, that he grew angry and refused to do what he denounced as menial labor. A threat of arrest, made surely in jest, was taken seriously by him and resulted in Beethoven's walking by night to the nearest city, Troppau, whence he hurried as on the wings of the wind by the extra post to Vienna.[18]

The guests were a group of French officers, stationed in Grätz, perhaps even at the Count's estate. For Beethoven, the symbolism of it all may have been too much: the hardships of finishing Op. 57, regrets over his revised Erard back at home, resentment about being put on the spot, erstwhile worship of Napoleon Bonaparte now displaced by a new dislike of all things French—in short, an amalgam of conflicting emotions and dependencies.

But the story does not stop here. A few pages later, Thayer continues. No longer at the mercy of wannabe listeners who rely on rank and authority to hear him play, Beethoven seeks the pleasant company of Mr. and Mrs. Bigot, who became the unexpected and happy owners of Beethoven's autograph of Op. 57:

> "During his journey [back to Vienna]," wrote M. Bigot half a century afterwards on a printed copy belonging to the pianist Mortier de Fontaine, "he encountered a storm and pouring rain which penetrated the trunk into which he had put the Sonata in F minor which he had just composed. After reaching Vienna, he came to see us and laughingly showed the work, which was still wet, to my wife, who at once began

to look carefully at it. Impelled by the striking beginning she sat down at the pianoforte and began playing it. Beethoven had not expected this and was surprised to note that Madame Bigot did not hesitate at all because of the many erasures and alterations which he had made. It was the original manuscript which he was carrying to his publisher for printing. When Mme. Bigot finished playing she begged him to give it to her; he consented, and faithfully brought it to her after it had been printed."[19]

Fleeing from the French guests and returning home to Vienna, of all his pianist-friends Beethoven chose to call on a French-Alsatian pianist to try out his newest work. Paul Bigot (who was the librarian of Count Razumovsky) ascribes Beethoven's pleasure to his wife Marie's ability to play from the score in spite of the many erasures and alterations, but Beethoven must have been especially pleased (and relieved!) to hear his long-labored Sonata in F Minor played by someone familiar with French pianism and pianos. It wouldn't even have mattered whether she played a Viennese or French piano: in-between-ness was exactly what Op. 57 was about—and hearing his piece saved by a talented young pianist, the same way he had saved his "Adam" Sonata before, would have made Beethoven's day.

CHAPTER TWELVE

Mixing Sound

I like my historical instruments to be new, just as they were for the people who owned them when they were made. Once they've reached a certain age, this also means occasionally rejuvenating them. The author of a 1796 yearbook on music in Vienna and Prague wrote of the Walter fortepiano, "If one plays on it often, the tone quickly becomes sharp and iron-like, which may be improved through a fresh re-leathering of the hammers."[1] If this recommendation holds for Viennese aristocrats, whose high-ceilinged salons provided a natural acoustic buffer against oversharp hammer attacks, then it is all the more applicable to modern-day recording, in which microphones are positioned close to the piano to capture as detailed a sound of the instrument as possible.

And so it has become a ritual for me, typically a week or two before a recording session, to make a special appointment at the Maene workshop. We gather in the morning to try out various batches of leather. Once we settle on the one we like best, we remove the outer layers on each hammer and replace them with new ones—an activity that takes us well into the afternoon or evening. This is a rare occasion for me to focus on the sole issue of sound, without the context of a score or even the simplest of musical gestures. It feels like a privilege, in the presence of a builder, to contemplate how a single sound is created, how it sustains, and whether it's pleasing, round, interesting, or whatever term one decides to use. Two years into one's ownership of the instrument, this event is also a confirmation of some sort: if this is the sound I've come to expect from this instrument, can we make it fresh again? Most important, on the eve of recording, it's a statement to the outside world: "This is how we like the instrument to sound."

It was no different when we prepared to record on our Beethoven-Erard in Sint-Truiden, Belgium. We have since dubbed the recording "Beethoven and His French Piano," and it includes, as its first disc, Louis Adam's Sonata, Op. 8 No. 2, preceded by the C-major finger exercise No. 48 from his method, as well as Beethoven's "Piano e.f.d clavecin" Sonata, Op. 53, preceded by the series of C-major scales from his "Eroica" sketchbook; and as its second disc, Beethoven's Sonatas, Op. 54 and 57, followed by Steibelt's Sonata, Op. 64. We programmed a test recital a week before recording. Our releathering had been a success, and I felt invigorated, especially about Beethoven's Op. 53 Sonata, which sounded as it had when the instrument had been new, except better, given my own experience and progress. My satisfaction was in stark contrast to what I felt about Op. 57 (also the newer piece to me), which seemed to have taken a definite step backward. For that piece, I could have kicked myself for the irrevocable decision to remove layers of leather that were already a few years old.

Suddenly, the significance of the age of an instrument at the time of creation came into focus. My Erard was roughly the same age that Beethoven's (or Lichnowsky's, for that matter) had been when he was working on Op. 57. As I practiced Op. 57, I had subconsciously relied on the harshness of the hammers—their *speak*-ability rather than (or in addition to) their *sing*-ability—triggering the same desire, both in my playing and from the instrument, for the kind of viennicizing that Beethoven had craved. In contrast, rejuvenating the hammers made me love even more the luscious sonorities in Steibelt's Sonata, Op. 64, a piece I had learned alongside Beethoven's Op. 57: Steibelt's colors in the first and third movements blended better than ever, and what the pastoral-like inflections of the fourth movement lost in ebullience, they gained considerably in charm. If Steibelt excelled on any *good* French piano, then Beethoven may be said to have mapped his art *idiomatically* onto his personal instrument: his honesty, as I discovered with Op. 57, was too brutal.

We're entering an unexplored domain in object-driven artistic research. Should I have made a point of recording Op. 57 first, and only then gone back for Op. 53? Had I just undone three years of the instrument's aging that would actually have suited a piece that represents worn-off novelty and a desire for change? I tried to calm myself with the knowledge that at least I would be recording Op. 57 toward the end of an intense five days of recording. Leather changes quickly, it's true, and just a few days' wearing-in might be sufficient to deliver the artistic message I had in mind. Most important, I decided to put my trust in the microphones' ability to mimic a material process of aging: it would all come down, so I told myself, to mixing the recorded sounds and applying a different focus to Op. 57 than to Op. 53.

Bending Hammer-Shanks

This is exactly what happened, and I will analyze some of the decisions we made soon. First, however, I'd like to make a case, beyond the broad comparisons already outlined, for thinking of Beethoven's Erard as a changing object in relation to our understanding of his compositional practice. The following example mixes practicality with creation, deliberately reflecting my own experience as a fellow Erard piano owner, playing the same musical material that occupied Beethoven's mind.

It was February and cold outside, and the piano had been slightly acting up in the recording hall. Was it the dry heat of the spotlights we'd left on for simultaneous video recording, or was it our sharp focus on perfection that made me feel on high alert? The action had been regulated—escapement points had been equalized, hammers aligned, and unwanted mechanical noises eliminated—but one issue continued to bug me. When playing the third and fourth pedal (the moderator and *una corda*) together, some hammers started brushing the adjacent first string of the next note, resulting in a "double strike" of C and Db, for example, as if I was playing two keys with a single finger at the same time. Several times we had to stop for the piano technician to take out the action and check on the perpendicular motion of particular hammers. (Chris also joined us for one day; see fig. 12.1.) I wanted all sixty-eight hammers to be perfectly aligned with the strings, so as to conform to actual *tre corde*, *due corde*, and *una corda* positions: this was particularly important for the second movement of Op. 54 (see below). Adjusting meant slightly repositioning and retightening the screws of the metal pivot plates on the hammer bank, but also, rather more drastically, using a kerosene heat lamp to bend the wooden hammer-shanks.

FIGURE 12.1 Piano builder Chris Maene and technician Minh Kapek at the Akademiezaal in Sint-Truiden, February 13, 2019.

A few days into the recording, when one might expect all technical matters to have stabilized, eager to make progress within an ever tighter time frame, I got worried when playing a specific note in the last movement of Op. 53 (see ex. 12.1). Within the larger narrative of the sonata, we'd arrived at an ultimate moment of suspense: a final halt on the dominant-seventh, before a structural resolution to the tonic. Beethoven asks for triple *piano*, or the softest possible, and I used all piano-technological means at my disposal to oblige, engaging second, third, and fourth pedals together, that is, damper, *céleste*, and *una corda*. The created suspense is before a *prestissimo* Coda: *forte* and then immediately *dolce*, jubilant yet also serene and harmonious.

Prominent through the final movement has been $\hat{5}$, as the upper note of a "divine," overtone-based C-major triad (see chapters 7–9). But when playing the high g^2 key in m. 401—granted, on a dominant harmony but still precious and soft—I heard a surprising dissonance. Had my hammer just hit an adjacent string—again? By hitting g^2 more softly still and by slightly releasing my feet (leaving the keyboard and hammer somewhere in between *due corde* and *una corda*), I tried to hide the problem, deciding not to alert the piano technician and hoping it wouldn't arise anywhere else with a vengeance.

Considering the misbehavior of the hammers during the previous days, my fear was not unfounded. But in this particular case, as I realized later on when I listened to the recorded takes, it had become irrational. Not that I imagined the dissonance: it's clearly there. But rather than an A♭ (the pitch of the adjacent string), it's an A♮ that one hears (that is, no fewer than four strings farther away). As I've since verified time and again on the actual piano, the dominant chord in m. 400 (especially the combination of G and d^1) does indeed result in a clearly audible overtone of a^2. But this is an acoustic-harmonic phenomenon: *there is no malfunctioning hammer.*

I imagine Beethoven going through a similar experience and turning the idea of adjacency ("play one, and you'll hear the other, too") into a

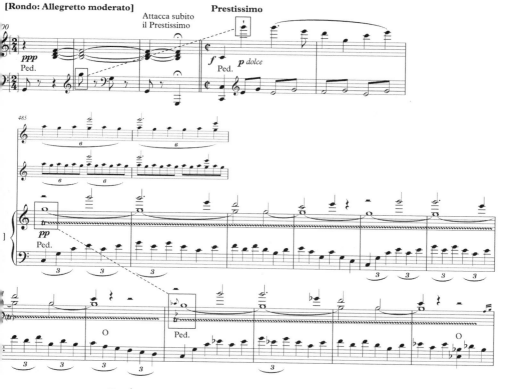

EXAMPLE 12.1 Beethoven, Sonata in C Major, Op. 53, final movement, mm. 400–404 and mm. 485–96, with Beethoven's suggestions for the trill.

compositional one, nowhere as clearly as in the extended passage shown in example 12.2. Are the boxed moments to be played as appoggiaturas (i.e., as dissonances that lean into consonances), or are they little imperfections, dirty spots on otherwise clean, triadic chords? Forced to spread the arpeggios over two octaves, where at the top my fourth finger feels like an awkward anticipation of my fifth, I'd argue the latter. (As it happens, just like those adjacent strings, ring finger and pinkie are anatomically attached to one another, through an ulnar nerve that runs along the lower elbow.) There's no room for expression, only acceptance of what mechanically is being laid out in front of me. There's also no harmonic logic except that in mm. 252–62, the next dirty spot is always one step higher than the previous. When in mm. 280 and following I revert to pure versions of triadic chords, the restored cleanness feels both striking and daunting: as awkward as it felt to play the dissonant keys just before, there's suddenly pressure to hit the right, single-string consonant keys. The same shift—from a dirty to a clean $\hat{5}$—happens on a much larger structural scale between m. 400 (the sound palette now reduced from double piano to triple piano, also the point where I add the *céleste* pedal) and m. 403 (marked by a new and final fresh start), or from dominant to tonic (see their drawn connection in ex. 12.1, top).

The double strikes return in both manifestations—major and minor—in the extended trills of mm. 485 and following, between A♮ and A♭ as the upper neighbor of $\hat{5}$: see example 12.1 (bottom). (This recalls an identical juxtaposition in mm. 287–94 of example 12.2.) The clashes are deliberate. On the last page of his autograph, Beethoven writes the following note: "N.B. Those who find the trill too difficult where it's combined with the theme can make it easier for themselves in the following manner [included in the example] or if they're up to it at double speed [also included in the example]. Two notes of these sextuplets are to be played with every quarter note in the bass. It does not matter at all whether this trill loses something of its usual speed."[2] In other words, this is a trill not to convey brilliance but to radiate sound. And as we've come to experience time and again with our Erard, such regularity pays off, whether fast as sextuplets or slow as triplets. The insiders' version of Beethoven's note would read: "Take the time to *play* the trill, including its clashes, and *listen* to the delightful cocktail of overtones that the French call *harmonie*."

EXAMPLE 12.2 Beethoven, Sonata in C Major, Op. 53, final movement, mm. 251–95.

Beethoven may have temporarily turned a technical disadvantage into a creative advantage, but those hammers would still have been misaligned. Who can fix them? Will the problem recur? Will it only get worse? Possibly this is when he started worrying about the extended life of the piano. There was no context for him to refer to, since Viennese pianos had no *una corda* pedals. But what Beethoven may not have realized is that he himself had largely been responsible for creating the problem. We remember from chapter 5 that when Sébastien Erard sold his first *piano en forme de clavecin* to Madame de St. Victor, he made sure to send a warning: "The 4th [pedal] allows one to play one, two or three chords at will; but should not be used for difficult passages, nor for the forte, because it would cause a bad effect and would put the instrument out of order."[3] Not only did Beethoven use *una corda* to fake an octave-*glissando*—an extremely difficult manoeuver that is possible only through muscular power—but the extreme dynamics in Op. 53 invite a constant switching back and forth between loud and soft, often with swells or *diminuendos* in between, and without any opportunity to stop playing in between. All this puts extraordinary stress on piano action components, as hammers keep hitting a variable amount of strings with ever changing mass and surface. In chapter 11 we talked about the need to fix balance points after keys are forced to move sideways as well as perpendicularly. We now add the necessity for hammers to keep hitting the strings nice and straight. In the case of a piano owned by Beethoven, taking care of both would have swiftly become a full-time activity.

A Model of Fittingness

If Op. 53 is linked to the *breaking in* of a new instrument and Op. 57 to its state of *revision*, then the Sonata in F Major, Op. 54 may well represent a brief period of *stability* between the two. While the Finale of Op. 53 shows signs of malfunction that led to Beethoven's interacting with the changing instrument in unusually creative ways, Op. 54 encapsulates the positive feelings one experiences when playing on a familiar instrument that has recently been put back in shape again. Chronology allows for such an interpretation. Op. 53 was sketched in November–December 1803, while Beethoven worked on Op. 54 in June–July 1804. Therefore, repairs may well have occurred just before Beethoven started work on Op. 54, which he would have completed before handing over the piano for more drastic revision later that summer—all while putting Op. 57 on hold.

Table 12.1 summarizes these shifting human–thing dependences and dependencies through Beethoven's trilogy of sonatas. At the core of them is "fittingness"—a concept that we rehearsed in chapter 1 with application to Beethoven's French project as a whole. Now we're ready to zoom

TABLE 12.1 Shifting human–thing dependences and dependencies in Beethoven's trilogy of piano sonatas

	Op. 53	Op. 54	Op. 57
Human	Ambition	Acceptance	Frustration
Human–Thing	Affordance	Fittingness	Incoherence
Thing	Novelty	Repair	Revision

in closer and acknowledge a narrower degree of fittingness in Op. 54. If Op. 53 represents ambition to explore the affordances of a new instrument, while Op. 57 exudes frustration over an instrument that has lost both its inner and outer coherence, then Op. 54 epitomizes a brief period of mutual acceptance and co-agency between human and thing.

Op. 54 was in fact the very first Beethoven piece I played on our Erard. For its inauguration event I had prepared some French music, but I thought it would be strange to unveil Beethoven's piano without playing some actual Beethoven. Within the larger research project, however, this came with a methodological problem. The plan was to create parallel tales and explore the new piano *along* with Beethoven. But saving the two bigger sonatas for later on, and substituting a relatively modest, two-movement sonata seemed like a good compromise. So I started preparing Op. 54 on a Walter fortepiano.

I plead guilty, then, for confirming a perception of Op. 54 as the little sister among Beethoven's middle-period grand sonatas. But I do not plead guilty to underestimating the piece. On the contrary, I was well aware that Op. 54 is generally feared among pianists not just because of its brevity (its back-to-back movements making for an intense twelve to thirteen minutes) but also for its content (ideas and hand positions starting off simple enough but quickly getting embroiled in a tricky pattern of diminution, in the first movement, and outright obsession, in the second).

When the instrument was finally ready, with just a few days to spare, I remember feeling both vindication and relief. The technology felt right, and this showed in aspects like tempo (a heavier keyboard keeping me in check, especially when playing those otherwise dreaded octaves in the first movement) and sheer enjoyment of the mechanical object under my hands (making me relate to Beethoven's motoric obsessiveness). I was glad to survive my first performance. It gave me the proof of concept I was hoping for. We were onto something, and I felt encouraged to embark on the artistic research that led to the preceding chapters in this book.

Having analyzed the more complex interactions and emotions in Op. 53 and Op. 57, I finally feel ready to rationalize my first moments on Beethoven's Erard. With Op. 53 and 57 it always made sense to rehearse an alternative Viennese reality (first to contextualize a transition from the familiar to the unfamiliar, then to confront the new familiar with the old again), whereas with Op. 54 I aim to explain fittingness in terms of the French piano itself. More so than its larger siblings, Op. 54 operates in a language that is to be understood on its own—at ease with the instrument that it originated from, without any traces of surprise, regret, or conflict. This does not mean, however, that the physicality of the Viennese instrument is far away. On the contrary, it's still there: I even imagine such a Walter fortepiano standing side by side with Beethoven's Erard. But the instrument has been covered and hasn't been played for months. As memory of its materiality lingers in our performing minds and bodies, we no longer need an actual physical sensation to summon its presence.

Op. 54: First Movement

"*Tempo d'un Menuetto,*" Beethoven indicates for the first movement, and the topical reference is to more than just the archaic stride of a minuet (ex. 12.3). A dotted-rhythm upbeat, an assertive downbeat followed by a second-beat lift: it's a familiar opening gesture. To illustrate, the example includes the theme of an early Haydn Sonata, his Hob. XVI:44 in G Minor, in similar minuet-style. Following custom, I put my efforts into making the second beat softer and shorter, as a release of the first. And Beethoven does, too, making sure to convey the effect of a slur by writing shorter note values for the middle voices: see the eighth-note rests in mm. 1 and 2. (The half-note top note, of course, releases at the same time: that's normal eighteenth-century practice.)

All our efforts are concentrated on realizing the quintessentially Viennese gesture of two slurred chords. Just as in the Haydn example, the slur's *raison-d'être* is a dissonance followed by a consonance, or an appoggiatura with its resolution. To reinforce this reference, I have rewritten Beethoven's opening, with a dominant harmony on the first beat, over a tonic pedal. But this rewriting exercise reveals something more drastic: Beethoven leaves behind the old language of the appoggiatura (which he himself had used not too long before in the Minuet of his Piano Sonata, Op. 31 No. 3), connecting instead one consonant chord to another—tonic to subdominant. If anything, in a hierarchy of tonal harmony, the "resolving" second beat would be the more dissonant one (ii7 chord), but this assumption is corrected by the second bar, where it is replaced by a triadic IV. All the while—and it is important to keep emphasizing this—we hang on to the *effect* of a slurred appoggiatura.

We have become familiar with the sonic apparatus of the French piano through our discussion of the theme of Andante favori WoO 57 in chapter 9, in which I discussed a similar reversal of dissonance and consonance. What would normally have been "tee-ah" (the normal pronunciation for an appoggiatura followed by its resolution) has been replaced by "tee-tee" (the deeply keyed action of an Erard requiring one's fingers to consciously strike each of the chords individually). While no longer delivering on its harmonic promise to resolve tension, the gesture still mimics the physical sensation of a lifting wrist and forearm. (I recommend rehearsing this gesture in the air. Choose two adjacent fingers—most obviously, 2 and 3. First, perform a down-and-up while pronouncing "tee-ah"; then try the same with "tee-tee." The latter contains a contradiction that's inherent to the French keyboard and part of the paradox we've tried hard to understand.)

The two chords fit the context of a moderate, beat-by-beat harmonic stride. But which is more prominent—the second beat or the first? To be clear, "prominent" here is to be understood harmonic-theoretically: it takes a preceding dissonance—the longer and louder, the better—to make the subsequent consonance shine short and sweet; and any silence afterward makes its impact all the stronger. Our embodied answer is the second beat, of course. Beethoven appears to agree, writing with those rests the equivalent of punctuation marks. Not that we have much choice: what else are we to do with a slur except to clip it? All of this is normal—and when we switch registers up the keyboard from one segment to the next, we almost overcompensate: we punctuate not just by lifting a hand, but also by shifting an arm, as segments combine to form a four-bar opening phrase.

But once we put harmonic labels to those beats, we must revise our answer and acknowledge that it is the tonic sound (F major/first beat) rather than the subdominant one (B-flat major/second beat) that reigns. As the circled notes in example 12.3 show, F-major triad-ness is omnipresent: a single arpeggio F–A–C–F reveals itself in the bass as chords progress from root, to first- and second-inversion positions, to end where we started, two octaves higher. These various triadic constellations do not present themselves easily to the ear, however: my hands certainly tell me where I am on the keyboard, but acoustically everything comes out more or less the same. Uniquely reflective of Beethoven's interaction with his French piano, this sameness in French sonority intersects with a Viennese phrase structure that is both elegant and clear. Balancing constancy with variety, we almost do not notice that the same phrase has a double function as antecedent and consequent within an eight-bar period that unfolds within the space of a single F-major triad.

Further along in the first movement, one moment always gives me pause. It involves a shift from D♮ (B-flat major) to D♭ (B-flat minor) from m. 106 to m. 107 (also shown in ex. 12.3). We're in the second *da capo*. Changing a major to a minor third is an old trick, often compared to chiaroscuro, or the contrast of light and shadow. But while as a performer I usually know very well how to handle such juxtaposition, I here fail to grasp the point. I always stop. Picking up again at the beginning of the section (only one bar back), I weigh my options. C. P. E. Bach has taught me to play harmonic deceptions louder, but this expressive certainty is no longer valid on an instrument where "louder" no longer yields the same instantaneous effect on a single, short note.[4] So what to do: play D♭ softer, shorter, longer? The end result is indecision, as there's no clear answer to be found.

Through this process of nondeciding, however, I've noticed something else. Remarkably for a *da capo*, the theme in m. 106 started not on a root-position F-major triad, but in first inversion: there's no F in the bass, but an A. (My score contains a penciled-in clarification to this effect: confused by the many ledger lines, I must have initially misread the note.) But even when I play the correct A, I don't quite hear it, failing to register the fact that we haven't started the way we did twice before. Something is up.

First, there's the question of which is more prominent: the first beat (F major) or second beat (B-flat major)? Now preceded by a less assertive

EXAMPLE 12.3 Beethoven, Sonata in F Major, Op. 54:

1st system: first movement, mm. 1–8

2nd system: compared with Haydn, Sonata in G Minor, Hob. XVI:44, second movement, mm. 1–2

3rd system: rewritten in archaic style

4th–5th systems: second movement, mm. 1–14

6th system: compared to Sonata in A-flat Major, Op. 25, final movement, mm. 1–3 version of the tonic chord, a root-position B-flat (IV) gains in prominence, replacing the more dissonant ii7 from before. Second, one wonders why Beethoven would allow the integrity of an unfolded F-major arpeggio to be broken: the newly circled notes are only a distorted version of the old ones. One cannot help being puzzled: why destroy a perfect example of Viennese appropriation? is Beethoven provoking a French-Viennese confrontation, after all? We have already explained and accepted ambiguity between gesture and content as idiomatic to the French piano. Why reinforce a question we've laid to rest already?

These questions stem from the shifting relationship between a composer and his instrument: one in which rhetoric—the art of communication between human beings—takes a backseat. In a rhetorical paradigm, I'd align myself with Beethoven as a performer who acts in front of an audience. In this particular case, my oratorical strategy would be to focus on the tonal ambiguity at the outset of the phrase, to be questioned by the D♭, only to then brush off such feigned indecision by playing the ensuing cadence in F as if it's back to business as usual. Such a detailed script, however, requires an instrument capable of projecting such fine cognitions and distinctions. At the Erard, the connection I feel with Beethoven is no longer with the listener we might both address but with the instrument we share. As I get caught in a loop between two instances that are suggestive more of what the piano cannot do than of what it can do (meaning the gesture of the appoggiatura, on the one hand, and the major/minor chiaroscuro, on the other), I surrender to the object as the most descriptive text of all. This text not only reflects the interactions of a pianist-composer in the present but also encapsulates his embodied knowledge from the past.

Op. 54: Second Movement

In the second movement (ex. 12.3, continued), compare the slur and texture of the last movement of Beethoven's Sonata in A-flat Major, Op. 26. While Op. 26 (written four years earlier on a Walter-type fortepiano) invites inflection and *diminuendo* (the melodic direction is downward), Op. 54 keeps stacking small elements of F-major-ness on top of one another (the direction is upward). Tagged onto an opening triadic arpeggio, those alternating sixths can be seen as a composed-out version of a tremolo that works its way through every step of an F-major scale. Shaping the slur is no longer possible on the French instrument, but at the same time the newly adopted paradigm of *son continu* means such transparency is no longer necessary or desirable. The instrument's inherent resonance is also the reason why, when the respective hands reach the end of their line, the *sforzandos* do not so much disrupt any continuity of sound as confirm the horizontal axes of an existing triad, defined by F at the bottom and C at the top (see the boxes in the example).

Tremolo is back—and how. On the one hand, there's the spatial aspect of sound; on the other, there's the technique of alternation. When in m. 13 dominant C takes over from tonic F, this sheer technical side claims the spotlight. We land on an octave in the left hand. But as I listen to my recording, I don't hear two pitches. I hear a double strike, as if made by a single repeated key C—and the result is most impressive. It reminds me of Erard Frères' *forte piano à son continu* (see chapter 7), which removed the challenge of repeating a key at speed and with accuracy, replacing it with a mechanical solution. But in Op. 54 there's no yielding of agency: rather, human and machine are in balance with one another, and Beethoven maximizes the robotic qualities of both.

Consider once again the opening bars of Op. 26 in example 12.3 (bottom), and play the following fingering pattern in the air: 4 and 2 followed by 5 and 1. Then add some wrist motion: there's little if no added benefit. (On the contrary, this "fingers only" technique is appropriately Viennese and more than sufficient for shallow and quickly responding keys.) The alternating sixths in Op. 54, by contrast, take their cue from the opening arpeggio. Try playing this arpeggio with your left hand: four fingers in their natural order, from left to right; chances are you've already started rotating your wrist to create a natural sweep of the hand from left to right. This next leads to a simplified version of this gesture: one simple rotation of the hand between 5 and 1, or 5 and 2, for the interval of the sixth (which is by far the most comfortable and most efficient). When, two bars later, it's the right hand's turn, Beethoven sticks to the same down-up direction, embracing the anatomical asymmetry between hands that the French had mastered. Try the hand-sweep again with the right hand, and you'll find it is easier to enact the same sweep we just rehearsed now starting from the thumb: also in pitch, "up" feels more natural than "down."

It doesn't take long to find that perfect groove—Allegretto (not too fast, not too slow)—where wrists and keys move in synchronicity with each other. Just watching this double rotation around radius bones and balance points gives pleasure. But there's another side. As momentum builds (and one doesn't want that synchronous movement to stop), we have no choice but to join the ride. "Someone" (let's call him Beethoven) has started cranking that cylinder in Erard Frères' *forte piano à son continu* and there's no end in sight. (I cannot help thinking of Charlie Chaplin at a factory assembly line in *Modern Times*: I, too, had better keep up with those rotations and keys.) The good news is that in a piece of music that revolves around motoric repetition, practicing also becomes automatic. It's not just that we're not allowed to stop, we don't want to, and through this process of continuity (in a purely mechanical sense) our hands eventually start locking in every note of Beethoven's score—as if punching holes in a piano roll that ultimately becomes repeatable and reproducible.

It has become commonplace among pianists to object to Carl Czerny's recommendation that the Finale of Op. 54 should "serve as an excellent étude."[5] András Schiff, for example, ridicules Czerny's statement and laments that it has led to renditions of this piece as a "senseless perpetuum mobile." Schiff does not object to the latter metaphor per se.[6] Rather, it is Czerny's suggestion that a Beethoven sonata movement may serve as a vehicle for practicing that irritates him. Schiff laments that the "beauty and, indeed, poetry" gets lost in a mechanical rendition.[7] But let's turn the argument around and ask: can human-machine interaction get any more beautiful or poetic? In a proto-industrial age, it may well have been the sight of rotating limbs and seesawing key levers that intrigued Beethoven. Of course, just as my comments stem from my experience with Beethoven's French piano, Schiff's reaction must be contextualized in the modern-day technology of a double-escapement piano action. One's typical *jeu perlé* performance of the opening *dolce* passage—non-*legato* and with no consideration whatsoever of Beethoven's slurs—can easily sound dull and unimaginative.

Beethoven's French piano, on the contrary, injects sense into perpetual motion. As I listen to my recorded performance, I'm fascinated by how metronomic my tempo turns out to be, contradicting my subjective experience during live performance: as my heartbeat intensifies, I would swear I'm actually speeding up. Instead, I get more and more locked into a machine-driven pace, which is hard to unlock oneself from, should one want to. From this perspective, the *più allegro* ("faster!") at the very end, when we go back to the F-major triad and scale one final time but now in overdrive, feels like the exceptional nondescriptive indication in Beethoven's score. I must accomplish Beethoven's prescription by sheer will power—a rare moment of human subversion, and the fact that this moment occurs at the very end is testament to the success of an overall script that so persistently revolves around human–machine co-agency. Not quite the eloquent peroration, these last twenty-seven bars are a man's enthusiastic thumbs-up to his cooperative machine. The opposite—a long-winded ride that finally spirals out of control—I would not wish on any colleague, despite such a scenario's comedic potential.

Our discussion of mechanical parts has so far limited itself to anything that happens above the keyboard, but one below-the-keyboard lever warrants attention as well. Contrary to Op. 53, where the use of the fourth pedal was essential but erratic, the indicated levels of dynamics in Op. 54 show remarkable restraint. They're entirely realizable, furthermore, through a controlled use of the three levels of the fourth pedal. Thus, in the second movement, I pivot my right leg up and down on my heel to materialize *due corde* for *dolce* or *piano*, *tre corde* for *forte*, and *una corda* for *pianissimo*. By reading Beethoven's dynamic markings as precise directives for fourth-pedal footwork (aided by the clever Erard-spring, discussed in chapter 4), I deliberately refrain from adding unnecessary stress on hammers and strings through fingers or wrists. Sébastien Erard would have been pleased. To maintain focus on the single pedal that counts, it helps that I don't need any other pedal at all—including the damper pedal, which I only use for the concluding thumbs-up, a final signal of human celebration and letting go.

Familiarity Transformed

One last detail in the first movement sheds intriguing light on the concept of fittingness and Op. 54. Mm. 18, 20, and 113 feature the shorthand notation of a trilled turn, or a turn that starts with a short trill. (It may be seen in ex. 12.3 as part of my archaicizing opening bars.) Beethoven may also have meant it as a snapped turn, or a turn that starts with a so-called snap or inverted mordent, which is arguably more fitting still for a minuet-style upbeat, like the one Haydn wrote in Hob. XVI:44.[8] Whether trilled or snapped, however, this ornament sounds oddly out of place on the Erard, where it can never be as crisp and lively as on any contemporary German-Austrian fortepiano, let alone on a clavichord from earlier times, which is where it really belongs. So, why this trip down memory lane?

It may be no coincidence that, of the three sonatas, Op. 54 is the only one that conforms to the conventional five-octave range, meaning that all buyers would have been able to play the entire score on their instruments. Its two-movement design may also be considered conservative. One thinks of a number of Haydn's keyboard sonatas (among others the Hob. XVI:44 we've been citing), and some of the most superb examples had again entered public consciousness in May 1802 through Breitkopf & Härtel's *Oeuvres complettes* [*sic*]: the fourth volume of Haydn's complete work for keyboard included the three 1784 "Princess Marie Esterházy" Sonatas, Hob. XVI:40–42, as well as the Sonata in C Major, Hob. XVI:48—one that Haydn had actually written for the Leipzig publisher back in 1789. It was also around this time that Griesinger communicated to Härtel Beethoven's opinion that "his keyboard sonatas are better than those of Haydn," and thus worthy of a higher fee.[9]

In a 1784 review of Haydn's Hob. XVI:40–42, Carl Friedrich Cramer made a point of praising Haydn's variations because they're so "fitting [*angemessen*] to the instrument" (whichever that was: a square piano, a clavichord, or a wing-shaped fortepiano). Yet, an anonymous reviewer of Op. 54 in *AmZ* (a journal incidentally run by Breitkopf & Härtel) did not quite know what to make of it: "This sonata only consists of a Tempo di Minuetto and an Allegretto that's not long either." But the real disappointment is that in spite of their brevity, both movements are actually "difficult to perform." By contrast, back in 1784 Cramer had expressed positive surprise at Haydn's sonatas' being "more difficult to perform than one would initially believe," since they "require utmost precision and delicacy in their delivery."[10]

It is clear that the *AmZ* reviewer was confused by Op. 54; we know that Beethoven did not make an effort to fit his composition to the German instruments, but in spite of all the "ineffective oddities and far-fetched difficulties" observed by the reviewer, he still notes that both movements are "written in original spirit and with undeniable mature, harmonic art, particularly in the way it leads to expansion." Originality and maturity—these are compliments that Beethoven should take, and he would have had his French piano to thank for it. In this sense, it is somewhat of a miracle that the reviewer does not raise the issue of fittingness; for his part, Beethoven may have thought it nobody's business how precisely he had achieved such mature and expansive harmonic language.[11]

In his Heiligenstadt Testament, Beethoven lamented being "forced already in my 28th year to become a philosopher of music."[12] Applying this statement to keyboard music (a genre that Beethoven in the wake of his health crisis was in fact planning to take a break from, before his Erard arrived), one feels tempted to contrast him to Haydn, who communicated exquisitely well with people, especially through his keyboard music. If with Op. 53 Beethoven used his French piano to settle an old score with his erstwhile rival Steibelt, then Op. 54 may be said to provide keyboard-playing Europe with a new, archetypal two-movement *Claviersonate* that on the surface looks like one of Haydn's, but that, thanks to his new French inspirational tool, actually transforms an older German-Austrian style altogether. The language remains Viennese, yet for those who understand its link with the *piano en forme de clavecin*, it sounds Austrian with a distinctly French accent. In this sense, Beethoven's perceived lack of social contact at an important juncture in his life was replaced by a private and most intense interaction with a "thing"—making Beethoven's responses to it paradoxically no less concrete and, indeed, just as "rhetorical" as Haydn's best sonata for a delightful and young princess.

Mixing a "French Beethoven" Sound

When we embarked on our recording in the Akademiezaal in Sint-Truiden, the Erard replica was to be the star.[13] "Make it sound good," was my request to Tonmeister Martha de Francisco and her recording team.[14] But the listening context I had in mind was also quite specific. "Imagine a prize-worthy performance in a hall like the one built for instrumental recital at the Paris Conservatoire." (Its *salle des concerts*, inaugurated in 1811 and still in existence, became a model for recital venues at music institutions across Europe.) The lid of the piano, centrally positioned on stage, opens up sideways toward a panel of discerning judges, seated at a privileged position in the hall. Though revolutionary back then, this mode of listening, focused on evaluating instrumental performance in the best possible acoustical and visual circumstance, also represents your typical recording environment today.

So, rather untypically for me, I ended up asking for a setup that today is considered normal.[15] This does not, however, lessen the expertise required in fulfilling what is still a highly complex assignment. A total of fifteen microphones, selected for their individuality and complementarity, were spread out over four zones (see a diagram in fig. 12.2): (A) two microphones for *close* sound, positioned next to the keyboard and directed toward the hammer striking points and the wider part of the soundboard, for definition and fine detail (No. 1: Schoeps MK4); (B) three different combinations of microphones (one set of three and two pairs) for *main* or *direct* sound, positioned at 1.5 m from the instrument (No. 2: Schoeps MK2S, No. 3: DPA 4006, and No. 4: Neumann M150); (C) two microphones at the same distance as the main microphones but higher up and pointed upward for *height* sound (No. 5: Schoeps MK2H); (D) at c. 7 m from the piano, and higher still in the room, two pairs, respectively at 4 m and 5 m above the floor, pointing backward to capture "room" sound (No. 6: Schoeps MK2, and No. 7: Schoeps MK2H). We've labeled them from A to D, but C is just as much connected to B as it is to D. If zone C focuses on how B's direct sound interacts with room sound (the latter adding important information about the former), then zone D intends to isolate the room itself, seeking information from walls and ceiling toward the definition of an ambient or reverberant sound.

This multilayered setup was designed for 3D mixing (hence the inclusion of height in addition to surround), but also our stereo mix ended up using something from every zone—but not from every type of microphone, as we ended up not using the two Neumann M150 tube microphones, whose tone-capturing characteristics proved not quite compatible with the others and/or the piano itself. This legendary microphone, promoted as capable of handling a full symphonic orchestra on its own, tends to favor the bass— too much, as it turned out, for our *piano en forme de clavecin*.[16]

Recording an instrument is one thing; recording a musician's response to the instrument is quite another. And here I do not speak of myself, but

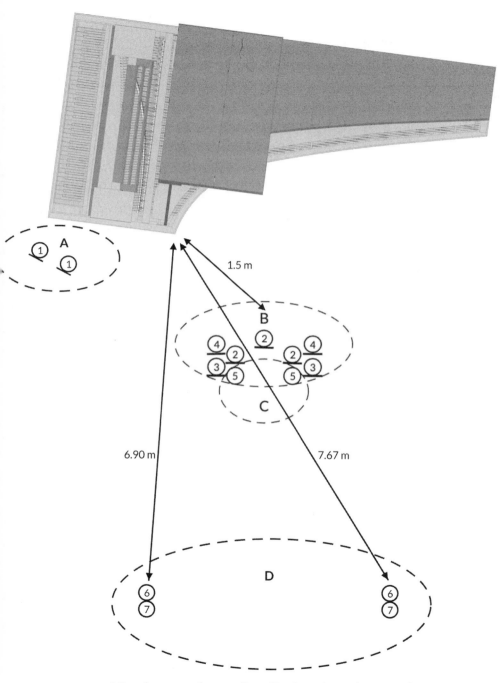

FIGURE 12.2 Microphone setup for recording of Beethoven's Erard. Drawing by Kseniya Kawko.

rather of my historical counterparts. Early on during recording, as we shifted from Adam to Beethoven, we had already repositioned the close microphones from the bent side of the piano to the position next to the keyboard. Guided by our ears, this decision may well reflect a desire to add relief to color, or gesture to *son continu*. This tendency extended itself to postproduction, where Steibelt became our point of reference. Remarkably, his was the only piece for which we felt that our recording mix (as preliminarily settled on during the recording sessions) could not be improved upon. I wasn't surprised: Steibelt had set the bar high, by mixing long stretches of changing harmonies within the reverberations of the piano, while keeping the damper pedal pushed down for a long time. If I could make it work in performance—embodying Steibelt's live mix, as it were, and allowing consonances to mingle with dissonances within the boundaries of good taste—then the recording needed to do no less, but also no more. We created a Steibelt sound by using microphones from zones A, B, and C—that is, without any need for further room sound D: all happens in or around the instrument itself.

Not so—or much less so—for Beethoven. We craved more definition, which we obtained by increasing the presence of the center microphone in the main sound (the middle one of No. 2) and by ever so slightly filtering (or equalizing) the bass, allowing the treble register to stand out just a bit more. At the same time, we wanted to experience how the instrument triggers the room by adding a few surround elements. But within the Beethoven repertoire, we again differentiated between Op. 53 and Op. 54, on the one hand, and Op. 57, on the other. While we left the additional definition we had settled on for Op. 53, we felt the need for still more room for Op. 57. As it happens, this is the only piece on our two stereo discs to use the highest microphones from zone D (No. 7). We started referring to this additional room ambient sound as a layer of "fogginess," which we deemed appropriate for a sonata that is dark and mysterious, but at times also aggressive and expansive. In hindsight, considering my fears about aged vs. fresh leather, I am surprised at how little we changed between Op. 53 and 57. Did we, by adding Viennese-like definition already to Op. 53, also anticipate Beethoven's wish to revise his piano, and conversely, did the more dramatic ambient sound we added for Op. 57 allow me to feel satisfied, after all, with the instrument's relative freshness?

These are slippery statements, though. It is wise to remind oneself that any act of sound recording, especially once reduced to a stereo image, can be no more "true" than, say, the taking of a photograph. Entering into the detail of what it means to mix a French Beethoven, then, evokes all the other "truths" explored in this book—each part of an extended process of artistic research that leads to the unavoidably final stage of capturing sound.

Beyond the documentary value of a recorded CD, it is fitting that our journey with Beethoven's Erard ends with the issue of sound—as an aspect that has gradually taken front and center in this book. Our mixing experience has taught us that Beethoven's French colleagues would have come to the recording sessions with a clear advantage: armed with years of tacit knowledge of how the piano performs, they made its aural packaging through recorded sound much easier for us. Beethoven, however, forced us to make decisions, not just in distinction to his peers, but from one of his pieces to the other. It is tempting to couch these decisions in modern-day language, such as wanting the instrument to *project* more into the room, as we did when allowing more information from the height microphones into our mix. But here we must ask: is it *we* who are listening to a Beethoven sonata, as performed on an Erard piano, or are we, through that same sonata, listening to *Beethoven* listen to his French piano? Taking into account the onset of hearing loss during exactly this period in Beethoven's life, I would suggest the latter. One thing is certain: Beethoven never wrote his piano sonatas in order for them to project in any room—and certainly not a large recital room like the one in Sint-Truiden. E. T. A. Hoffmann in 1810 famously used Beethoven's Fifth Symphony as an example to promote a new kind of listening—one, in Mark Evan Bonds's words, "in which listeners were compelled to rise to the level of the composer."[17] My recording of a French Beethoven, in contrast, may be seen as an invitation to listen to how human and thing interact in the here and now of an embodied process of performance and creation.

Time and Resonance

Today, visiting Beethoven's two foreign pianos—his 1817 Broadwood and his 1803 Erard—means traveling between Budapest and Linz. Whether you make the journey by train or car, you'll almost certainly pass through Vienna. This is the route I took, in an east-west direction, visiting the Broadwood one morning and the Erard the next. Within twenty-four hours I went from contemplating how an English piano became such a powerful and international symbol of Beethoven's genius to wondering why his French piano never quite received its due place in Beethoven biography.

The answer, I realized in hindsight, had been staring me in the face in the shape of a portrait exhibited next to each piano. In Budapest, the Broadwood is displayed in its designated room, overseen by the well-known oil portrait of Franz Liszt by Miklós Barabás (1846). The painting serves as a strong reminder of the instrument's association with the Hungarian composer, who is known to have kept the instrument in his Weimar library. Dressed in Hungarian national costume, Liszt is portrayed posing at yet another grand piano, leaning his right hand on it while standing beautifully erect, his contemplative gaze directed at some faraway point. (The way the museum designers have positioned the painting, it looks as though Liszt is following the direction of imaginary sounds emanating from under the Broadwood piano's opened lid.) By comparison, in the more spacious room in Linz where Beethoven's Erard is on display, we encounter a painting by Leopold Gross (1841), a facsimile of the original in Vienna. It's not as large and famous as Liszt's portrait, and therefore the visitor may take some time to spot it, even though, like the painting of Liszt, it is positioned to the right of and behind the instrument. It portrays Beethoven's brother, Johann van Beethoven, from his chest up: posing on a generic chair, he wears a benevolent, smiling expression. This altogether more modest image serves to explain to present-day visitors why Beethoven's French piano ended up where it did.

Each portrait marks the gift of a Beethoven instrument to a museum, but I bring up the parallel story of Beethoven and Liszt only as a backdrop to that of Johann van Beethoven, at the end of a book that has focused on a single instrument. In this epilogue we reconnect with our schematic representation of the Erard's life history outlined in table 1.1 and ask how "Johann's inheritance from Ludwig" led to the iconic "Beethoven piano" we have so painstakingly analyzed. This final story has two unlikely heroes: Johann van Beethoven, who acted both correctly and generously by finding a safe home for his brother's instrument in 1843, and the French music-journalist Charles Bannelier, who in 1875 took it upon himself to dig a little deeper into its provenance. Both deserve credit and our thanks; but both also unwittingly contributed to the confusion that has flourished around Beethoven's Erard piano during most of its reception history.

Let's start our own investigation in Linz, in the archives of the Upper Austrian Provincial Museums, where the following memorandum, dated September 16, 1843, may be found:

> Herr von Bethhoven [*sic*] donates a fortepiano in mahogany, which the city of Paris gave his late brother, the most highly praised and well-known composer, and on which he composed a lot—a gift of truly exceptional value.[1]

At the time of the donation Johann van Beethoven was sixty-six years of age and a widower of fifteen years. What better way to memorialize his own name as well as his brother's than through a museum plaque attached to a revered object? (As we shall see, such a plaque existed; today, it has been replaced by a more elaborate information board next to Johann's portrait.)[2] But there's an ethical dimension to his decision, too. More than a noble act, it was his duty to pass on to a museum the instrument Ludwig had entrusted to him. From the composer's point of view, transferring the piano to his brother rather than to his nephew Karl (who otherwise was the sole beneficiary of Beethoven's will) may even have felt like an assurance that one day it would be shared with the larger public.

These assumptions, however, betray a modern mindset. The Louvre had existed in Paris as a public museum since 1792, but it took the example of eight other states in the Habsburg monarchy (with Hungary leading the way in 1802) before Upper Austria (Oberösterreich) also requested the founding of a museum association (*Musealverein*) on February 10, 1833.[3] Johann's donation, then, must be contextualized. When Liszt bequeathed his Beethoven Broadwood to the Hungarian National Museum, it was to an established institution—the piano was transferred in 1888, a year after his death—but Johann's gesture, executed during his lifetime, was part of a pioneering and community-driven endeavor to shape local heritage and cultural identity. Furthermore, while Liszt is anointed by history as the owner of Beethoven's Broadwood piano, it was in fact the music publisher C. A. Spina who acquired the instrument, passing it on to Liszt when he was twenty-five years old and beginning to create a profile for himself as a serious interpreter of Beethoven.

The Erard's link with Johann, in contrast, was through kinship, making the donation more real than any kiss of consecration (*Weihekuss*) between Beethoven and the young boy Liszt, whether factual or imagined, could ever be.[4] Kinship, incidentally, was also on Ludwig's mind when he wrote to his notary, "Because one also has to bequeath something to relatives [*Verwandten*], even if one doesn't feel related [*verwandt*] to them, my Hr. Brother receives my French piano from Paris."[5] Beethoven's sarcasm about family obligation in this case merges with his known passion for puns. Nevertheless the impulse that made him bequeath to a close family member an instrument he had felt unable to sell and had wished to keep as a souvenir appears genuine. By contrast, Beethoven did not make any special arrangement for his Broadwood, which upon his death became part of an estate sale along with his furniture.[6]

And so Beethoven's Erard ended up in Linz, the city where Johann owned several properties and where he had practiced as a pharmacist since 1808. The board of the Museum Association, of which Johann must have known several members personally, wrote him a thank-you note, copied for the association's records by the secretary of the board on the same sheet that contained the above-quoted memorandum. (The note is dated September 18, 1843, two days later.) *Herr* van Beethoven's gift was not simply appreciated (which museum would not have liked to receive such a prestigious object?), but also explicitly understood as an act of patriotism among fellow Upper Austrians:

> The kind donation of a fortepiano, with which the city of Paris honored your brother, one of our heroes in the music world, enriches the Museum Association here with an acquisition that is all the more valuable, because per your assurance it was exactly this instrument that the glorified master of tones would use during [*bei*] the creation of his immortal compositions [lit., "tone structures"].
>
> Please accept, dear Sir, for this cherishable gift, through which your friendly share in our patriotic association revealed itself, the expression of our utmost gratitude and high esteem with which remains
>
> dVdMV [*der Vorstand des Museal Vereins,* or the Board of the Museum Association]
> Linz 18/9 1843

The value of the instrument, therefore, lay not only in the fact that the city of Paris had donated the instrument to Beethoven, but that the master had actually used it while composing. It was this "assurance"—most likely provided in a face-to-face meeting—that the Museum Board wished to record on paper. This guarantee of authenticity, offered by a respected member of the Linz community, became a liability thirty years later, when Beethoven's Erard made its entry onto the international scene. For the 1873 Vienna World Fair, Eduard Hanslick, the prominent Vienna critic, had organized a special exhibit of historical instruments. Among them were a small number of must-see "reliquaries [*Reliquien*]," a term used by August Wilhelm Ambros of the *Wiener Zeitung* to denote "instruments that have been in the possession of famous masters of music."[7] The Linz museum had "patriotically" responded to the call (the term is Hanslick's) put out to the provinces to "entrust [the organizers] with valuable and rare instruments for the duration of the World Fair."[8] Hanslick's plan had indeed been to make it an all-Austrian exhibit. But in his write-up for the *Internationale Ausstellungs-Zeitung* (International Exhibition Newspaper), which was published as a special issue of the *Neue Freie Presse* for the duration of the fair from May to September 1873, Hanslick explained that "from the principle of including only Austrian products in this exhibition we knowingly allowed ourselves three exceptions only: the Italian violins of Mozart and Beethoven, as well as the named keyboard." In his introductory article, Hanslick does not dwell on the violins, but the named keyboard was

> not Viennese, but a Paris instrument from the year 1803, by the famous Sébastien Erard. Beethoven's brother, Johann, who, as is well known, owned a pharmacy in Linz and who died there [*recte*: Johann died in Vienna on January 12, 1848], gave it to the Linz museum with the explicit declaration that it "was an honorary gift to L. v. Beethoven from the city of Paris."[9]

For Hanslick, "the heartfelt interest that we Austrians take in anything having to do with Mozart or Beethoven"[10] justified these exceptions, and in any case, the foreignness of Beethoven's piano was amply compensated for by the fame of Sébastien Erard—already a household name in piano history on a par with that of the Amati family for the much longer history of the violin. But it was the association with Beethoven that gave Hanslick pause, and as he repeated what the Linz museum had communicated to him, he gave in to a nagging thought: "I confess not to have had any knowledge of this tribute and not to have found any indication about it in the biographies of Beethoven or Erard." (Beethoven's letters, his Conversation Books, or Griesinger's letters to Härtel were not yet readily accessible.)

Among those biographical authorities, the Harvard-trained librarian and musicologist Alexander Wheelock Thayer (who in 1872–79 was at work on the third volume of his *Life of Beethoven*, covering the period up to 1816) weighed in on the matter and took the initiative of writing a letter to Hanslick, who made a point of publishing it as part of a follow-up article on September 17, 1873, under the title "W. A. Thayer on the Beethoven Piano." With the American expert and the Austrian critic in agreement, Beethoven's Erard seemed on the point of being written out of history— until a French music critic at the *Revue et gazette musicale* felt called upon to take another look. Charles Bannelier had not traveled to Vienna, but for his "posthumous visit [*visite posthume*]" to the long-closed exhibition, he used "Mr. Hanslick, the eminent Viennese critic," and his writings as a guide.[11] Bannelier published his piece on September 5, 1875. Hanslick then responded in *Die Freie Presse* on October 15, 1875.

Together, these three newspaper articles provide a fascinating read, especially after so many pieces of the Beethoven Erard puzzle have been assembled already. In them we witness the shaping of the very myth this book has tried so hard to unravel. The exchange revolved around the accuracy of the plaque then attached to the instrument, which Hanslick quotes in full in his second article on the subject. The information unveils two consecutive giftings, first from the "city of Paris" to Ludwig van Beethoven, then from Johann van Beethoven to the museum in Linz. The latter was established as fact; the former raised suspicion. Where the provincial board had taken Johann at his word (this is the "assurance" discussed above), suddenly the donor came under scrutiny and the very authenticity of the donation started hinging on *his* character. Let's listen to Hanslick and Thayer:

It's unfortunate that biographical doubts over the Beethoven piano sent by the Linz museum cannot be suppressed. As a work of the old Sebastian Erard in Paris from the year 1804 [*sic*] this piano is a rare, remarkable, and valuable object. But one cannot avoid shaking one's head when reading the plaque fixed onto it: "Fortepiano, with which the city of Paris has honored the composer L. v. Beethoven, the famed and crowned hero of instrumental music. Donor: Mr. Johann v. Beethoven, private [citizen] in Linz (his brother)." As great as the token of gratitude we owe this splendid museum for its concrete contribution to our historical exhibition [may be]—the truth must prevail. Already in my first report of June 6 of this year I expressed doubt over the accuracy of this Paris gift [*Widmung*]. After reading this essay the famed Beethoven biographer, Mr. A. W. Thayer, felt compelled to communicate his opinion through a letter; such a statement by an undisputed authority cannot be withheld from the music-loving public. The main section in Thayer's letter reads as follows in German translation [here retranslated into English]: "I saw this instrument in Linz in 1860 and have since been looking for evidence in whichever shape or form that it had indeed been in the possession of

L. v. Beethoven. What did the city of Paris know of the thirty-three-year-old composer in 1804? How many Parisians might then even have known of his existence? Was it not only in June 1805 that Cherubini came to Vienna and met Beethoven for the first time? Johann v. Beethoven sold his pharmacy in Linz in 1816 and opened another in Urfahr, on the other side of the river [the Danube], which he also sold a few years later, to buy the estate near Gneixendorf. From c. 1820 onward he spent the summer in Gneixendorf and the winter in Vienna, where after selling his country estate he spent his last years and where he also died. There exists in Johann v. Beethoven's hand a statement in which Ludwig v. Beethoven's last moments are described and where it is stated that the composer died in the arms of his brother! It is, however, widely known that nobody except Anselm Hüttenbrenner was present in Beethoven's room during his passing. If Johann v. Beethoven could make such a statement and sign it with his name, then what credence should we give him when it comes to that fortepiano? I believe that the Linz instrument has never been property of Ludwig v. Beethoven." Thus far Mr. Thayer. If this were to inspire the Linz museum to new and hopefully successful investigations, then we would welcome its victory with patriotic satisfaction.[12]

Thayer's are the words of a biographer—but of Ludwig, not of Johann. In his *Life of Beethoven*, it is easy to find a number of disparaging statements about Johann by friends of Ludwig in Vienna, variously describing him as "a fool [. . .] whose only merit is that he bears your name"; who "had neither the intellectual nor moral poise to fit him for the place which he thought he was entitled to"; as someone incapable of "command[ing] respect from a social point of view"; as an opportunist who had struck "large contracts for the supply of medicines" with the occupying French in Linz; as someone who was "fond of money"; and, last but not least, as someone "not at all musical" and whose "affectation of appreciation of his brother's works made him a fair subject for ridicule."[13] But shift the emphasis in the latter statement from "affectation" to "appreciation," and a whole new picture emerges, which may be patched together from alternative excerpts from Thayer's biography. Johann was an entrepreneurial man, who already during his early years in Vienna, "unaided by his brother," was able "to purchase and establish himself in a business of his own," who showed "magnanimity in not trying to do his brother injury and being always ready to help him when he could," who may have "lacked appreciation of his brother's real significance in art," yet was "proud of the world's appreciation of him."[14] The list of kind gestures from Johann to both Ludwig and his nephew Karl goes on and on—and all this in spite of having to put up with his brother's obsessive interference in matters of the heart and his unforgivable lack of tact, which went as far as threatening to call the police on Johann's allegedly cheating wife, Therese. Most tellingly, Thayer himself quotes Karl communicating to Ludwig in one of the Conversation Books: "But I beg of you once more not to torment me as you are doing; you might eventually regret it, for I can endure much, but too much I cannot endure. You treated your brother [Johann] in the same way today without cause; you must remember that other people are also human beings."[15] No wonder, one might argue, Johann ended up donating the instrument to the museum in Linz—far away from Vienna, with all its memories of brotherly tension and trauma.

But we're getting sidetracked. It took a Frenchman to call both Hanslick and Thayer to order. After all, it was not the character of Johann van Beethoven, but the credibility of a French gift that was under scrutiny. Bannelier's response was to simply go to the then-director of La maison Erard and ask; the fact that no one else had done so perhaps accounts for the touch of sarcasm in the opening of his piece:

> Only one [Beethoven piano] is still in existence:[16] the one of Erard, donated by the brother of the composer to the museum of Linz, which has temporarily relinquished it to the benefit of the musical division of the Exhibition. But the foolishness and vanity of the donor must have blinded him. Indeed, here's the inscription, as emphatic as it is inaccurate, that he had requested to be placed on the instrument: [same as above]. It is peculiar that the administration of the Linz museum accepted the note written as such. A tribute from the city of Paris to Beethoven! But who, in Paris in 1803, even knew that a Beethoven existed, except for a few artists? Doubts over the correctness of this fact were bound to emerge sooner or later and to lead to its negation, pure and simple. That's exactly what happened. One of the most esteemed biographers, Mr. A.-W. Thayer, taking into consideration the well-known character of *Jean de*

Beethoven, refused to believe that the piano in question, which he saw in the Linz museum in 1860, ever belonged to the composer. He reminds us that Jean de Beethoven, who, having enriched himself as a pharmacist, was in the habit of scorning the poor artist, whose name he had the honor of bearing, and the sentiments for whom as by magic changed once [this artist] was no longer alive, claimed in a declaration written and signed in his hand that his brother had died in his arms, even though it's established knowledge that *Anselme* Hüttenbrenner alone was with the master when he breathed his last. Mr. Hanslick follows the line of thinking of Mr. Thayer; and we admit that whoever possesses just a bit of a critical mind is surely tempted to agree. However, there's one very simple way to have the last word on the question. We decided to go ask where whoever had doubts on the matter should have gone first: we turned to the director of the Erard firm. Mr. [Antoine-Eugène] Schaeffer happily accepted for research to be done on our behalf in the interesting archives that his great-uncles and his father have kept. Here's his answer:

'We see in our books [*livres*] that on 18 thermidor in the year XI of the French Republic, that is, August 8, 1803 [*recte*, August 6, 1803], Sébastien Erard made the gift of a *piano forme clavecin* [*sic*] to L. van Beethoven, then living in Vienna.'

Case closed. The piano was the authentic property of Beethoven; but the city of Paris had nothing to do with it, and solely the generous and artistic initiative by Sébastien Erard may be credited with this tribute to the genius. One should not forget that Beethoven was then only thirty-three years of age.[17]

Bannelier's investigation had hinged on a simple question: was an Erard piano ever shipped to Beethoven? Yes, there was a record of the Erard firm sending a piano to Beethoven, but no, the city had not given him one: it was the legendary Sébastien Erard himself who had done so. Not only did Bannelier authenticate the claim that the French instrument had belonged to Beethoven (the only such instrument known at the time, since Liszt had not yet gifted his precious piano to the world), but the shift in agency of the gift from the city of Paris to the single figure of Sébastien allowed Bannelier to forge a powerful link between two men who by 1875 were both incontestably worthy of universal admiration. Seen in this light, Bannelier's final sentence may well be the strongest: "One should not forget that Beethoven was then only thirty-three years of age." In other words, an established piano builder in Paris (fifty-one years of age in 1803) had the remarkable foresight to acknowledge the genius of a relatively young Beethoven. In the original sales books Beethoven had been listed as a *claveciniste à Vienne* (see table V3.1)—a perfectly respectful description from a piano manufacturer, flagging an instrument for export, but one that no longer fitted the universally renowned composer in 1875, which explains why Schaeffer truncated the Erards' original classification of Beethoven to "then living in Vienna."

Meanwhile, in Vienna, it was no longer just the accuracy of an exhibition at stake, but music history itself—a point well understood by Hanslick:

> The *Revue et gazette musicale* of Paris brings in its numbers of the 5th and 12th of this month an article signed by Mr. Bannelier on the additional exhibition of historical musical instruments, which I had arranged together with state councilor Mr. Exner. In this report, whose warmly appreciatory tone pleases the Austrian reader, the author clarifies a point much contested at the time and of general music-historical interest. Apart from the entirely authentic keyboards of Haydn, Mozart, Schubert, and others, the historical exhibition also featured an Erard piano sent by the Linz Landesmuseum with the date of 1804 [*sic*] and the following inscription: "Fortepiano, with which the city of Paris honored the composer L. v. Beethoven. Donor: Mr. Johann van Beethoven, private [citizen] in Linz (his brother [*dessen Bruder*])." As painful as I felt any inconsiderateness against the Linz museum, which enriched our exhibition with many valuable relics, I still had to publicly voice my well-founded doubt over the accuracy of this inscription (coming from Beethoven's brother). A tribute by the city of Paris to Beethoven at a time when still few Parisians knew about Beethoven's existence! In addition to the well-known untrustworthiness of Johann van Beethoven, who had an elastic relationship with the truth! Mr. Bannelier now took the commendable step to have the matter researched in the trading books of the firm Erard. These reveal that "on 18. Thermidor of the Year XI of the Republic (1803) Sebastian Erard made the gift of a grand piano [*un piano forme de clavecin*] to

Mr. Ludwig van Beethoven in Vienna." Herewith the matter is solved: the Erard piano was the authentic property of Beethoven. As before, the "city of Paris" stays out of it, but the origin of the gift and the merit of the genius director of the famous piano factory, Sebastian Erard, to offer a spontaneous artistic tribute to the then thirty-three-year-old Beethoven have now been established. From now on, the Linz museum can call with absolute certainty this valuable object [*Stück*] a "gift from Sebastian Erard to Beethoven from the year 1803."[18]

Everybody wins: the nation of France, along with its "genius" piano maker, and the nation of Austria with its Viennese composers like Haydn, Mozart, Schubert, and Beethoven. And, of course, the Linz museum, which owns what is now recognized as a truly "valuable object"; Hanslick proposes that it be henceforth labeled, "a gift from Sebastian Erard to Beethoven from the year 1803." (This may well be when the initial plaque was taken off the instrument.) But there's nothing in Hanslick's prose that hints at any exoneration of the reputation of Johann, a former private citizen of Linz. Thayer, in the meantime, took note of the correction, but the Linz Erard would make its entry only in the 1921 edition of his *Life of Beethoven*, through the following paragraph added to the end of the chapter on "The Year 1803":

> As a proof of the growing appreciation of Beethoven in foreign lands it may be remarked here that in the summer of 1803 he received an Erard pianoforte as a gift from the celebrated Parisian maker. The instrument belongs to the museum at Linz and used to bear an inscription, on the authority of Beethoven's brother Johann, that it was given to the composer by the city of Paris in 1804. The archives of the Erard firm show, however, that on the 18th of Thermidor, in the XIth year of the Republic (1803), Sébastien Erard made a present of "un piano forme clavecin" to Ludwig van Beethoven in Vienna.[19]

There's no acknowledgment of Bannelier or Schaeffer, but Henry Edward Krehbiel, who edited this first English edition after Thayer's death, retained the latter's sneering comment about Johann van Beethoven.

All of this because of a plaque attached to a piano. What neither Hanslick nor Thayer got to see was the more elaborate 1843 museum memorandum and follow-up thank-you note, which were the start of our investigations. Returning to this combined document, what Johann van Beethoven may rightfully have been brought to task for was his "assurance" that it was "exactly this instrument that the glorified master of tones would use during the creation of his immortal compositions." Had Johann deliberately not told the whole truth to the museum officials, exaggerating the uniqueness of his instrument? He would have been well aware there had been other pianos in his brother's house. And what "immortal compositions" did he have in mind? The probable answer is: all and none in particular. To a nonmusician, one piano would be much like another: Broadwood, Erard, or Graf, who cares? The essential element was the genius of the composer.

But while we may cringe at this dissociation of work and instrument, chances are Hanslick & Co. would not have noticed, let alone felt insulted by, such naïve framing. In fact, the new notions of musical creation they espoused, while more sophisticated and professional, were founded on similar Platonic ideals. For them, technology, rather than acting as inspiration, is constantly playing catch-up with human creativity. This belief in progress was reflected in the design of the 1873 Vienna exhibition. The historical group of instruments was part of an entrance hall that led to the modern, "technical" group displaying the newest inventions. Every visitor would have to walk through one to go to the other, so the exhibition could not have been more imbued with the idea of evolution. Ambros, writing for the *Wiener Zeitung*, had the following to say about the experience:

> Through comparison with the new ones, the old instruments provide us with yardsticks to measure technical progress, and anyone who, for example, has seen the truly terrible honky-tonk [*Klimper- und Klapper- kasten*], on which Liszt as a boy once received the very best instruction and who then goes to an instrument of Ehrbar, Blüthner, Schröder et cetera, will rejoice in the fact that not only Liszt "eventually made it that gloriously far," but also piano building.[20]

Professional pianists hired to demonstrate the various historical instruments did nothing to change his mind. Thus, the pianist Sigismund Blumner played a *Klavierstück* by Schubert on a Graf—by Aloys, not Conrad. Clearly impressed by the sound ("What an abundance of beauty has come out from this instrument!"), the critic is willing to accept the experience as an exercise in historical imagination only and certainly not as a threat to any ideal (indeed, Platonic) version of the work. As he's quick to point out to his reader, he's not suggesting that "Schubert or Beethoven would have 'composed at the piano,' as a non-composing audience tends to believe (bless their innocence of heart)." However, "one is still free to imagine the masters leaping up from their writing desks and putting their still wet manuscript page on the piano stand, still glowing from the fire of their [creative] work, and the spirits of euphony captivated by those notes on paper obtaining sound and voice for the first time." Every word in these convoluted sentences hints at the firm belief that no historical instrument could ever have been worthy of Schubert's or Beethoven's transcendent inspiration. "Spirits of euphony [*Geister des Wohllautes*]" appear in spite of *any* instrument (whether historical or modern), and the composer's agency is simultaneously glorified and reduced to whatever happens at the writing desk.

Such nineteenth-century shifts in ideology about art and music would have mattered little to Johann van Beethoven when presenting the piano to the Linz museum. But he cared for his brother, and it may well have been fraternal pride that saved Beethoven's Erard for posterity. "If [Johann] lacked appreciation of his brother's real significance in art, he was proud of the world's appreciation of him," Thayer wrote.[21] Johann may have exaggerated when communicating to the museum that it was "exactly this instrument" that Beethoven had used to compose, but even as just one of the many pianos that Beethoven had owned, it was worthy of iconic value in the eyes of the Beethoven-appreciating world. On loan to the Kunsthistorisches Museum in Vienna between 1938 and 1987, until it was recalled to Linz because it was considered "in danger because of inadequate climate control in the Vienna collection," Beethoven's Erard, in the words of Alfons Huber (restorer-researcher at the Vienna museum), became "the oldest authentically preserved piano of one of the great musical personalities of Viennese Classicism."[22]

* * *

Let's rewind. "The oldest authentically preserved piano." Of the keyboards associated with Mozart, Haydn, and Beethoven that exist today, Beethoven's Erard is indeed the oldest that is still in the state in which its owner had left it. The two obvious points of reference are Mozart's older, 1782 fortepiano (presently in Salzburg) and Beethoven's newer, 1817 Broadwood (presently in Budapest), both of which have been subjected to restoration at repeated points during the twentieth century. (Of Haydn we have only his 1794 Johann Bohak clavichord, presently in London.) Huber is a museum scientist, and his use of the term "authentic" is intended to convey objectivity—just as the authentication of the instrument toward the end of the nineteenth century needed to be based on hard evidence alone.

At the same time, one must wonder what a restoration project of Beethoven's Erard would have looked like, since this is also the instrument that was most heavily changed during its ownership by one of the "great musical personalities of Viennese Classicism." Discussions in a hypothetical advisory committee of experts would inevitably end in an impasse. Should the restoration uphold the instrument's authenticity as envisaged by the builder, or does authenticity of this particular Beethoven instrument lie in the unique changes implemented by the player? While a reincarnated Sébastien Erard would be flattered to see his name connected with that of Beethoven, he would be horrified to find that his piano had apparently not been good enough for the youngest and most rambunctious of the Viennese triumvirate. From Beethoven's perspective, should the authentic value of his French piano be seen as relating to his prerevision enthusiasm or his postrevision disappointment? There can be one conclusion only: the documentary value of the instrument as it now stands in the Linz museum is too great, whether as an instrument reflective of Beethoven as an experimenting pianist-composer or as a battlefield of two national piano-building styles. No restoration can be allowed. To honor both player and builder, Beethoven's Erard must be left untouched.

Fortunately, our replica presented no such dilemma. Instead, it allowed us to turn back the clock in the history of an object that has taken on immense heritage value. We had the privilege of discovering the piano along with Beethoven almost in real time—with the additional advantage of hindsight. The book, in this sense, has been a collective exercise in reconstruction and reembodiment. Through a series of revisions undone then implemented again, Beethoven's French piano has helped us understand its erstwhile owner's expectations, ambitions, disappointments, and frustrations.

Beethoven's Erard gives the artistic researcher of today a lot to play with. Just as philologists look at pen strokes in centuries-old sketchbooks and manuscripts, and see in them fresh marks of intent, I like to think of the sweaty finger marks I leave on my replica's keyboard as somehow carrying Beethoven's artistic DNA. Rather than just one, Beethoven's piano contains many authenticities. Each deserves inquiry in its own right. Together, they create a web of entanglements that continues to resonate.

ACKNOWLEDGMENTS

This book started with a simple premise: let's build a replica of Beethoven's Erard piano and listen to what it has to say. The two activities—the building and the listening—were always intended to go hand in hand, so it was a privilege not only to surround myself with a team of mainly young researchers (to help me interpret what the instrument was telling us) but also to have an eminent keyboard maker (who leads his own team of artisans) as a member of our research group until long after the instrument was finished. The book could not have been written without my associate researchers: I have acknowledged their individual contributions throughout these pages.

I must thank my institute's director, Peter Dejans, for his vision and never-waning support. Peter is known for asking tough questions—especially when it comes to defining what it means to be pursuing artistic research—but they have always made us stronger, and I hope that this book will make him proud. In the same breath I thank Fund Baillet Latour and its secretary-general, Alain De Waele, for their financial support and their genuine interest in our Beethoven Erard project. I also thank our institute's Research Advisory Council for their yearly encouragements, and feel especially indebted to Jo Bury, who played an inspiring role in getting the project off the ground. Every single day at the office, I've considered myself lucky to receive the support of Daphne Ronse, Kathleen Snyers, and Heike Vermeire.

Copying an instrument of such historical value requires formal permission to do so, and for that—and so much more—I thank curator-restorer Stefan Gschwendtner of the Oberösterreichisches Landesmuseum in Linz, Austria. We are grateful also to Pascale Vandervellen (Musical Instruments Museum, Brussels) and Giovanni Paolo Di Stefano (Rijksmuseum, Amsterdam) for making their own Erard instruments available to us for study.

The following people have generously lent their expertise. Catherine Desbarats helped me transcribe a crucial Erard sales book entry and led me to Pierre Gervais, whose knowledge of eighteenth-century accounting practices proved invaluable. Michael Ladenburger's ease with German *Kurrentschrift* was remarkable. Jeffrey Kallberg alerted me to the resurfacing of an important Haydn letter, of which Armin Raab (of the Haydn Institut in Cologne) shared a diplomatic rendering. Josef Weichenberger of the Oberösterreichisches Landesarchiv in Linz tracked down some revealing documents.

As I wrote my book, Robert Adelson was preparing his *Erard: A Passion for the Piano* (published by Oxford University Press in 2021). We started exchanging ideas and facts, and I thank Robert for his collegiality and generosity. I also thank Alain Roudier and the Fonds Gaveau-Erard-Pleyel for sharing some pertinent documents.

My gratitude goes to the following individuals and their respective institutes or societies for giving me a chance to formally present on the project—occasions that invariably led to interesting discussions and new ideas: Thierry Maniguet (Musée de la musique, Paris); Thomas Drescher and Felix Wörner (Schola Cantorum Basiliensis and Universität Basel); Tiziano Manca (Conservatorio Luigi Cherubini, Florence); Geoffrey Lancaster and Genevieve Wilkins (Western Australia Academy for Performing Arts, Perth); Elissa Miller-Kay and Komsun Dilokkunanant (Princess Galyani Vadhana Institute of Music, Bangkok); Leonardo Miucci (Conservatorio della Svizzera Italiana, Lugano); Mike Lee and Annette Richards (Cornell Center for Historical Keyboards, Ithaca, New York); Sylvie Brély (La nouvelle Athènes, Paris); Anne Hyland, Barry Cooper, and Marten Noorduin (University of Manchester); Tuija Hakkila (Sibelius Academy, Helsinki); and Edgardo Salinas (The Juilliard School, New York).

Over the years, distinguished scholars came to visit us in Ghent, and for their feedback, which especially helped me frame the project in a larger context, I thank Richard Taruskin, Jonathan Sterne, Garry Hagberg, Richard Shusterman, and Ann Warde. My colleagues at the Orpheus Institute sat through countless updates of the project, making me all the more grateful for their ever-insightful advice. I thank our director of research, Jonathan Impett, for expertly steering me through some moments of crisis and for showing genuine excitement whenever I related to him what I considered the newest discovery. I also thank (among many more) Paulo de Assis, William Brooks, Nicholas Brown, Nicolas Collins, Lucia D'Errico, Bruno Forment, Seth Josel, Catherine Laws, Tiziano Manca, Luk Vaes, Joost Vanmaele, and Simon Waters.

Working with Steven Maes and Hans Bellens from Evil Penguin on the sound recording and film production components of the project has substantially shaped its scope and identity. We've been through many adventures together—filming in Linz, Paris, and Ghent, luckily mostly before COVID-19 hit. I'll treasure the memory of my Saturday-morning conversations with Stef Grondelaers, and I have admired the storytelling skills of video editor Pieter Peeters. Priceless too were the detailed discussions of how to best record and mix the sound of our Erard replica: for those I thank Martha de Francisco, Ephraim Hahn, and Kseniya Kawko.

Storytelling is a talent also of James Attlee, whom I felt fortunate to call my developmental editor. James confidently coached me through several rounds of revisions, and I'll especially remember our joint sessions (over Google Drive, taking care of some finishing touches) as master classes in writing. Copyeditor Lys Weiss instilled calm and confidence during the final stage of the process: I thank her for her keen eye and unfailing professionalism. Shanti Nachtergaele was a quick study in the art of indexing and made me appreciate the skill involved such a task, especially for a book as complex and multifaceted as this. My sincere thanks also go to my editor, Marta Tonegutti, whose hand in morphing the manuscript into this book reflected a common goal: to make it better—even if this meant making some hard choices. Her assistant, Dylan J. Montanari, was as kind and meticulous as one can hope for. Special thanks are due to the two anonymous readers, whose feedback significantly helped shape the book in its final stage.

Many thanks to production editor Caterina MacLean for expertly guiding me through the process of copyediting and typesetting, and to promotions manager Meredith Nini for her help transforming the manuscript into a marketable product. To witness the attention to detail in this production, which in many ways feels like the culmination of two others (the construction of an instrument and the release of a recording), has been a true privilege. For that I thank the entire team at the University of Chicago Press.

Finally, I thank my family, Griet, Oscar, and August. My move from Montreal, Canada, to Ghent, Belgium, as I embarked on a new chapter in my professional life, came with personal sacrifice, and I will remain forever grateful for their love and support.

I dedicate this book to Malcolm Bilson, who some thirty years ago kindled in me a love for pianos not just as music-interpreting devices, but also as machines that can be taken apart and understood silently—ultimately making us better musicians and listeners.

APPENDIX A

Beethoven's Erard: A Timeline

Making

April 12, 1797	Sébastien Erard to Madame de St. Victor: "We have only two of this kind [the new model of *piano en forme de clavecin (Pfc)*] at present, of which one is intended for my niece who is a very fine pianist, but we will provide you with what will best suit your needs."
June 24, 1797	Erard *Pfc* No. 2 sold to Mme de Saint-Victor.
February 11, 1798	Erard *Pfc* No. 1 sold to Mr Achart.
March/April 1800	Beethoven meets Steibelt twice at Count von Fries's.
Late August 1800	Steibelt brings a copy of Haydn's *Creation* to Paris and develops plans to arrange the score in French.
November 2, 1800	Erard *Pfc* No. 28 sent to Haydn.
December 19, 1800	Newspaper announcement of Steibelt's keyboard edition of *The Creation* "to be had on the day of the performance [. . .] at the Demoiselles Erard, rue du Mail No. 37."
December 24, 1800	Performance of *The Creation* directed by Steibelt at Paris Opera House.
April 15, 1801	Griesinger to Härtel (Leipzig): "The Erard Frères in Paris sent [Haydn] a beautiful grand piano in English design as a gift, in mahogany and ornamented with bronze."

November 1802   Beethoven to Zmeskall, on ordering a piano from Anton Walter "in mahogany and with the one-string register" just like Haydn's.

Ordering

August 6, 1803 [18 Therm^{dor} XI]   *Pfc* No. 133 sent to Beethoven.

October 22, 1803   Ries to Simrock (Bonn):
"The sonata with violin accompaniment [Op. 47, "Kreutzer"] you can have for 50 guilders; it will probably be dedicated to Adam and Kreutzer as the premier violinist and pianist in Paris, because Beethoven owes Adam a courtesy on account of the Paris piano, about which you can learn more from my father, to whom I wrote about all this [. . .] Beethoven recently played [his new symphony, to be called "Bonaparte "] for me and I think heaven and earth must shake underneath at its performance."

Using

December 14, 1803   Griesinger to Härtel:
"The brothers Erard of Paris have made Beethoven a present of a mahogany piano (as they did earlier to Haydn). He is so enchanted with it that he regards all the pianos made here as rubbish by comparison. Because you are dealing a lot with instruments it will [not] be uninteresting for you to hear that Beethoven even earlier always criticized the tone of the local instruments for being wooden, and that they create the habit of a small, weak touch. Beethoven being Beethoven might be right, but how many players are there like him? The keyboard action of the Parisian piano is, even by Beethoven's admission, not as supple and elastic as that of Viennese pianos. But that is a trifle to a master like Beethoven."

February 8, 1804   Erard fulfills an order by Breitkopf & Härtel's for five instruments, including *Pfc* Nos. 112, 128, and 143; No. 143 is later sold to Prince Karl von Lichnowsky.

Revising

January 2, 1805   Streicher to Härtel:
"Beethoven is certainly a strong player, yet he can still not adequately treat his Fp. [Forte piano], which he got from Érard in Paris [*sein von Erard in Paris erhaltenes Fp.*], and he has already had it changed twice without the least improvement, because its construction does not allow for any other action."

1808   Johann van Beethoven acquires a pharmacy in Linz.

September 18, 1810   Beethoven to Streicher:
"My French one [*mein französisches*] is really no longer useful: maybe you can advise me as to how we might still save it."

mid-November 1810   Beethoven to Streicher:
"As to the French one [*das französische*], which is now truly useless, I have second thoughts about selling it, [because] after all [it is] a souvenir [*Andenken*] such as nobody here has honored me with."

Discarding

August 1, 1824   Beethoven to J. B. Bach:
"Because one also has to bequeath something to relatives, even if one doesn't feel related to them, my Hr. Botheré [*mein Hr. Bruderé*] receives my French piano from Paris [*mein Französisches Klawie[r] von Paris*]."

May 21, 1825   Note of Beethoven to himself:
"Karl to judge whether a L[eschen] is as strong as mine [i.e., Beethoven's Broadwood] / One can give up [*herausgeben*] the Paris piano [*das Pariser*] and have an unleathered [one] made [from it?]."

Early July, 1825   Nephew Karl to Beethoven:
"Something you must bequeath him [i.e., Johann van Beethoven] / The Paris keyboard [*Pariserclavier*]" (*Kh,* vol. 7, 314).

April 2, 1826

Holz to Beethoven:
"Graf wants to see the French piano [*das französische Clavier*]" (*Kh*, vol. 9, 146).

January 19, 1827

Schindler to Beethoven:
"Did your brother sell his F. P. [Forte Piano]?" (*Kh*, vol. 11, 87). *Assuming that the "F. P." mentioned by Schindler is indeed the Erard, then it would have reached Ludwig's brother Johann in Linz between April 2, 1826, and January 19, 1827.*

Iconizing

1833

Founding of Musealverein (now: Oberösterreichisches Landesmuseum), Linz, Austria.

September 16, 1843

Johann van Beethoven (1776–1848) donates the piano to the Linz museum, where it becomes part of the Kunst- und Kulturhistorische Sammlungen.

1860

Thayer visits the museum in Linz.

1873

On display at the Vienna World Exhibition.

1875

Ch. Bannelier (writing a report of the exhibition) contacts Mr. Schaeffer, director of the Erard company, who confirms: "We see in our books [*livres*] that on 18 Thermidor in the year XI of the French Republic, that is, August 8, 1803 [*recte*, August 6, 1803], Sébastien Erard made the gift of a *piano forme clavecin* to L. van Beethoven, then living in Vienna."

1938

Put on loan at the Kunsthistorisches Museum, Vienna.

1987

Called back to Linz, on the allegation of insufficient climate control in Vienna.

Since then

Rumors of plans to restore the instrument, so that the "original sound" may be heard again.

Reassessing

1988

William Newman confirms the "unsolicited gift" theory and makes the piano irrelevant for the study of Beethoven.

1990	Alfons Huber pays organological attention to the least known of the three "Beethoven pianos."
2002	Tilman Skowroneck begins a musical revalorization of the piano.
2005	Maria Rose–van Epenhuysen announces the discovery of the sales books entry by the pianist Alain Roudier.

Replicating

2008	The Musée de la musique (Paris) commissions Christopher Clarke to build a facsimile of Erard No. 86 (1802) with sponsorship of the Fondation d'entreprise Hermès; after three years, the instrument is ready.
April 27, 2012	Christopher Clarke writes a letter to the prospective user: "Dear Player."
2013	A first CD (Alpha 194) is released, featuring Lubimov in works by Beethoven.
2014	A plan is hatched at the Orpheus Institute: "Let's build Beethoven's Erard."
Fall 2014	Funding awarded by Fund Baillet-Latour, Belgium.
September 15–16, 2015	Team Orpheus (Chris Maene, Tom Beghin, Michel Bernays) travels to Linz to measure the instrument.
October 10, 2016	Team Orpheus (Tilman Skowroneck, Eleanor Smith, Ellie Nimeroski, Tom Beghin) gives presentation at Cité de la musique, meeting the French team (Christopher Clarke, Thierry Maniguet, and others).
November 14, 2016	Replica by Chris Maene inaugurated during "20 Years Orpheus" Festival.
June 21, 2017	Formal presentation by Team Orpheus (Chris Maene, Tom Beghin, Robert Giglio, Michael Pecak, Eleanor Smith, Tilman Skowroneck, Prach Boondiskulchok) for the sponsors (Baillet-Latour).
July 3–12, 2018	Eight young pianists participate in a reconstruction of an early nineteenth-century Paris Conservatoire *concours*.

| February 11–15, 2019 | First recording in Sint-Truiden, Belgium, of a double CD with works by Adam, Steibelt, and Beethoven (EPR-Classic 0036). |
| April 9, 2019 | Recital on replica at Oberösterreichisches Landesmuseum, Linz, in a hall adjacent to where the original is preserved. |

APPENDIX B

Op. 53, 54, and 57:
A Timeline

Between October 22 and November 2, 1803   First idea ("basketball dribble") and // 10 scales.

December 1803   Sketching/composition of Op. 53 (first movement, Andante, final movement, minuet/trio).

[Perhaps] June–July 1804   Sketching/composition of Op. 54 (only sketches for second movement are extant).

August 26, 1804   Beethoven to Härtel:
Beethoven offers "my oratory" (Op. 85, *Christ on the Mount of Olives*); "a new grand symphony" (Op. 55, "Bonaparte"); a concerto for violin, cello and piano (Op. 56); and "three new solo sonatas." "If you'd like one of these to be with accompaniment, I will gladly comply." "I'll give them to you for 2000 (two thousand) *fl.*," knowing that I'm losing out ("one gives me 60 ducats for a single solo sonata"). "For a speedier publication of my works I'm willing to take a loss."

August 30, 1804   Härtel to Beethoven:
"Our engraving and printing facilities allow us to work fast." For economic-political reasons we're not interested

Sources: *Bw*, vol. 1, 218–19, 220–22, 225–26, 229, 236–37, 243–47, 252–56, 257–59. Cooper (2007), vol. 2, 49, 56; vol. 3, 5–6. Cooper (2017), 117–37. Dorfmüller et al. (2014), vol. 1, 288–90, 293–94, 310–12; vol. 2, 139–40. Frohlich (1991), 41–49. Thayer/Forbes (1866–79/1967), 402–3, 407. Wegeler/Ries (1838), 99. Wiesnerová (2014), 6–7.

in the oratory [Op. 85]: too costly and little demand; "but we're interested in the exclusive ownership of the other three works [*der andern 3 Werke*; namely, Op. 55, Op. 56, and the "three solo sonatas"]."

September 4, 1804   Härtel to Clementi:

"Beethoven offers us 4 new Works" [*sic*: written in English]; proposes to share costs toward shared ownership and publication.

By mid- September 1804   Anecdote of Ries, on Beethoven's humming during [or 1805? see chap. 11, note 4]   a walk near Döbling:

"To my question what it was he said: 'A theme for the last Allegro of the sonata has occurred to me' (in F minor, Opus 57). When we entered the room, he ran to the piano without taking his hat off. Now he stormed for at least an hour with the new and so beautiful finale of this sonata."

October 10, 1804   Kaspar Karl van Beethoven to Härtel:

Beethoven asks 1,100 *fl.* for "five pieces [*5 Stücke*] (*of which by virtue of their design [einrichtung] every one must be published separately [allein]*)"; "*condition* is that we must know when they can be published."

November 3, 1804   Härtel to Beethoven:

The company accepts the offer of "five works" [*5 Werke*; namely, 3 sonatas, 1 symphony, 1 concerto] at 1,100 *fl. Wiener Courant.* "The longest time in which all five works can be published by us with certainty we wish to set at 8 to 9 weeks after their receipt." "Please prepare a formal statement of ownership transfer."

November 24, 1804   Kaspar Karl van Beethoven to Härtel:

Beethoven agrees, and will send the first sonata (Op. 53), along with the concerto "within 12 or 14 days," then "in another 14 days" two sonatas (Op. 54 and Op. 57); then "again in 14 days" the symphony.

December 4, 1804   Härtel to Beethoven:

Härtel accepts that the five works "be sent successively," biweekly. He expects Beethoven to agree that his honorarium will be issued "only upon delivery of the last manuscript as well as an act of sale [or statement of ownership]."

	The latter is necessary because "it prevents German, French, and English reprints during the first six months."
Between December 4, 1804, and January 16, 1805	Fair copies sent of sonatas Op. 53 and 54, as well as the symphony; that is, not yet the concerto or Op. 57 (different to the sequence that Beethoven had announced).
December 22, 1804	Härtel to Beethoven: "After my last letter I had hoped to receive promptly the statement of ownership or [at least] some of the proposed works." (Härtel must not have received Beethoven's package yet.) He points out that, "if [the works] have not been sent yet, circumstances [. . .] do not permit me to publish them within at least 3 to 4 months."
January 16, 1805	Beethoven to Härtel: Beethoven assumes that his package [*Paquet*] with the symphony and the two piano sonatas Op. 53 and Op. 54 have not arrived yet; "the other [package, with Op. 57] will follow as soon as possible." He excuses himself for slow progress, blaming "lack of good copyists" and "poor health during winter months." "I threw in a *little song* as well." "Prince Lichnowsky will write to you concerning my *oratorium*."
January 30, 1805	Härtel to Beethoven (nonextant): Asks for two missing works (the concerto Op. 56 and the third piano sonata Op. 57), as well as the oratory Op. 85 (suggesting that Prince Lichnowsky did intervene on Beethoven's behalf); raises annoyance because of an intermediary person in the negotiations; asks for a reduction of honorarium. *If we believe what Beethoven would write in May 1805, this letter arrived with a delay of three months.*
February 12, 1805	Kaspar Karl van Beethoven to Härtel: Conveys some of Ludwig's wishes for the engraving of the symphony Op. 55; "We'll send you the other pieces soon [Op. 56 and Op. 57]."
February 20, 1805	Härtel to Beethoven (nonextant): Asks for the two missing works, namely Op. 56 and a third sonata, Op. 57; explains that the production

has been delayed because of the late receipt of fair copies.

April 18, 1805   Beethoven to Härtel:
Beethoven regrets not being able to send Op. 56 and Op. 57 quite yet; again, he blames "lack of a *trusted* copyist." He promises to do so "within 4 to 6 weeks"; in exchange he demands that engraving of the symphony and the two sonatas start immediately for publication "within two [corrected from "three"] months." He proposes to split the payment of 1,100 *fl.* into 700 *fl.* (for the three first works) and 400 *fl.* (for the two remaining ones).

[end of April/May] 1805   Beethoven to Härtel:
"I received your letter of January 30 only yesterday."
"The *honorarium* is much lower than I usually accept."
"Please send all manuscripts back" except for the oratory, for which a special arrangement exists. "There were never any intermediary persons"; "complications reside in the *nature of the matter*, which I cannot and do not want to change." Beethoven switches horses, but the fair copy for Op. 53 from Leipzig hasn't been returned yet, so he uses the manuscript as fair copy for the Viennese engraver.

[May] 1805   Beethoven to Countess Josephine Deym:
"Here is *your—your—*Andante—and the Sonata."

May 15, 1805   *Wiener Zeitung* announces the publication of Op. 53 by Bureau des arts et d'industrie (Vienna).

End of May 1805   Beethoven to Countess Josephine Deym:
"Please, send back the Andante and the two songs—I promise that you'll have all three pieces back after-tomorrow." (Beethoven needs to send some songs to the Russian Empress, Maria Feodorowna.)

June 21, 1805   Härtel to Beethoven:
"Nine months have passed since you offered us 5 new works." Gives examples of how forthcoming he has been. Demonstrates grace in terminating the agreement and expresses hope that in the future there will be no intermediary negotiator (Beethoven's brother Kaspar) and that Beethoven will agree to issue a statement of ownership.

"In a separate package, please find: the oratory, the song "Gedenke mein" [presumably "Andenken," WoO 136], the two piano sonatas [Op. 53 and Op. 54], and the symphony [Op. 55]."

[September?] 1805 Publication of WoO 57 (*Andante pour le Pianoforte*) by Bureau des arts et d'industrie, Vienna.

April 9, 1806 *Wiener Zeitung* announces the publication of Op. 54 by Bureau des arts et d'industrie (Vienna).

May, 10, 1806 *Wiener Zeitung* announces (belatedly) the edition of WoO 57 by Bureau des arts et d'industrie (Vienna).

September 10, 1806 *Wiener Zeitung* announces a second edition of WoO 57, with a new title:
Andante Favori pour Pianoforte, same publisher.

mid-July–October 1806 Beethoven resides at Prince Karl Lichnowsky's Château in Grätz, Silesia (today Hradec nad Moravicí in the Czech Republic). He has access to Lichnowsky's Erard Frères No. 143, purchased through Breitkopf & Härtel in 1803.

[late] October 1806 Beethoven refuses to play for French officers, then quartered at the castle. After a falling-out with the prince, Beethoven leaves the house "indiscreetly and suddenly," and returns to Vienna. He takes with him the autograph of Op. 57. During a storm it gets water-stained. Back in Vienna, the Alsatian pianist Marie Bigot plays from this original manuscript "which [Beethoven] was carrying to his publisher for printing."

February 18, 1807 *Wiener Zeitung* announces the publication of Op. 57 by Bureau des arts et d'industrie (Vienna).

NOTES

Introduction

1. Akrich (1997), 209.
2. For thing-theorist Bill Brown (2001, 4), one begins "to confront the thingness of objects" only when they break or become a hindrance, or when something in them makes us feel self-conscious of their thingness.
3. Walter (1970), 283.
4. Ferraguto (2019), 150.
5. Gibson (1979); and Hodder (2012, 2018).

Chapter 1

1. *Kh*, vol. 1, 31.
2. *Bw*, vol. 2, 153.
3. *Bw*, vol. 5, 377, and vol. 4, 205.
4. When Newman wrote his book, the Erard was still on loan to the Kunsthistorisches Museum, Vienna.
5. Newman (1988, 52) mistook "Kirschbaum" for the name of a builder; Carl Friedrich Hirsch remembered having his first lessons with Beethoven on "an old bichord 5-octave one in cherry [*ein 5-oktaviges Kirschbaumernes altes zweisaitiges*]"; Frimmel (1906), 63; and Rampe (2015), 20.
6. Newman (1988), 45, 50, and 63.
7. Bilson et al. (1997), 34.
8. Newman (1988), 51.
9. Wacha (1975), 107.

10. Newman (1988), 52.
11. *Bw,* vol. 1, 137.
12. Webster (1984).
13. Beethoven's piano music was typically announced in journals under the special rubric of *musique étrangère* (music from abroad) and in any case his works were considered *difficile à exécuter* (difficult to perform). Kraus (2001), 37–43.
14. Rose–van Epenhuysen (2005), 111–12; transcription corrected.
15. *Bw,* vol. 1, 176.
16. Schiffer (2004), 580.
17. *EL&D,* vol. 1, 18, 185–86, 433.
18. https://en.wikipedia.org/wiki/Ian_Hodder.
19. Hodder (2012), 88. See also Hodder (2018), 90–91.
20. Skowroneck (2014a), 401.
21. *Kh,* vol. 7, 281.
22. Fontana (1992).
23. Winston (1993), 147.
24. Watson (2010), 3–6; Winston (1993), 147.
25. Thayer/Forbes ([1866–79] 1967), 695.
26. Thayer/Forbes ([1866–79] 1967), 403.
27. Hodder (2012), 113–37.
28. A detailed report of the Paris Conservatoire appeared in *AmZ* 3, no. 24 (March 11, 1801): 411–19.
29. *Wvz,* vol. 1, 288, 311.
30. Skowroneck (2014a), 400–401.
31. Latcham (2007), 59–60.
32. Hodder (2012, 128, 130) cites both Charles Rosen's *The Romantic Generation* (Cambridge, MA: Harvard University Press, 1995) and *The Classical Style* (New York: W. W. Norton, 1997). It is surprising to see an archaeologist, of all people, engage with a kind of music criticism that is notoriously a-technological.
33. Beghin (2017, 2020).
34. Hodder (2012), 123.
35. *Bw,* vol. 2, 168.
36. Solomon (1998), 157.

Vignette 1

1. Schirlbauer (2015).
2. For instance, Beethoven's friend Carl Amenda used Zmeskall as a negotiator for an export order of several instruments by Walter; see Goebel-Streicher et al. (1999), 80.
3. Letter of November 15, 1800. Steblin (2007), 78.
4. *Bw,* vol. 1, 137, underlining Beethoven's.

5. Kopitz and Cadenbach (2009), 660.
6. According to a list that Beethoven sent to Härtel on November 23, 1803. *Bw*, vol. 1, 198.
7. Lund University Library, De la Gardieska arkivet, Släktarkiven, De la Gardie 374:1. See Skowroneck (2014b).
8. *Bw*, vol. 1, 136.
9. For these dates, see chapter 6.
10. *Bw*, vol. 1, 190.
11. Skowroneck (2010), part 1.
12. See Beethoven's Pressburg letter further below. In 1799, he recommended a Walter to Anna Brunswick (Steblin [2007], 75). He recommended a Streicher to Dorothea Krug of Frankfurt in 1809 (Goebl-Streicher et al. [1999], 126).
13. Skowroneck (2010), part 1. Audiences became more critical of his playing from about 1800 onward.
14. Letter of Griesinger to Härtel, December 14, 1803. Biba (1987), 216.
15. Junker (1791).
16. *Bw*, vol. 1, 32, 32n3. Quite in contrast to usual Viennese teaching customs, Streicher gave Beethoven's newest works to a twelve-year-old pupil. Kopitz and Cadenbach (2009), vol. 1, 59.
17. *Bw*, vol. 1, 33.

Chapter 2

1. Rose-van Epenhuysen (2005, 2006); and Skowroneck (2009, 2010).
2. Lubimov (2013), 66.
3. Lubimov (2013).
4. These words are extracted from Maniguet (2013, 31, 65), but for greater effect the exclamation point has been added in the blurb.
5. De Visscher, in Lubimov (2013), 4, 6 (emphasis added).
6. Lubimov (2013), 5, 7.
7. This letter resurfaced at auction in 2019. Previously sold in 1971 (also at auction), the letter had been known only through an abridged translation by H. C. Robbins Landon (1977b, 55). The 2019 auction catalog of J. A. Stargardt ("Catalogue 707," item 575) includes a reproduction.
8. In comparison, when addressing the cousins Artaria for the first time (together, the Artaria firm), Haydn correctly wrote *Messieurs*; Bartha (1965), 92. Undoubtedly Haydn addressed Sébastien Erard, whom he is reported to have met during one of his London residences; Mayer (n.d. [1811]), 14.
9. There's one secure way only: to remove the soundboard and reglue it. My analysis is based on a conversation with Chris Maene.
10. Landon (1977b), 55.

11. Very little is known about the Englishwoman whom Steibelt married during his trip to London in 1799, except that we owe to her skills Steibeltian titles like *Douze Bacchanales pour le forte-piano avec Accompagnement de Tambourin ad-Libitum* (Paris: M^elles Erard, 1802).

12. Also Meredith (2012, 40) highlights Op. 26 as "the first Beethoven sonata to include pedal markings" and makes a link with encountering Steibelt one year before.

13. Quintilian IX.iii.68, in Butler ([1920] 1989), 484–85.

14. *Pezzo* was the standard term for "movement." Haydn uses it too, along with its German equivalent, *Stück*.

15. Bach ([1753/62] 1994), 2:327.

16. Bettermann (2012), 14, 22.

17. Kolneder (1968), 13.

18. *Bw*, vol. 1, 85.

19. Wallace (2018), 23–24.

20. Writing to her husband, Joseph Deym, from Prague on December 11, 1803: "It just occurs to me that Julie Gucciardy [*sic*] had an excellent fortepiano: if it's still for sale, you would oblige me if you could buy it for me, because I know no better in Vienna." Steblin (2007), 82.

21. Bergé et al. (2009).

22. On a Viennese fortepiano, I play the whole transition (mm. 21–40) with raised dampers (i.e., without ever cleaning up), but on the French piano, I must change pedal every four or two bars, with every new bass.

23. Our session, moderated by Jeanne Roudet, was part of the colloquium, "Beethoven et la recherche du sensible."

Chapter 3

1. A classic example is Harding (1933).

2. Biba (1987), 216.

3. Giglio (2015) uses 3D-motion-capture technology to compare hammer- and key-in-motion in two models of a Viennese *stoss*- and *prell*-action. A pioneering study is Birkett (2010).

4. We had used Qualisys cameras with dedicated software. Giglio (2015).

5. To study our 2005-built replica of Mozart's Walter fortepiano with *prell* action (revised) and *stoss* (original). Beghin (2007) and Latcham (1997).

6. E.g., Cole (1998) and Good (2001).

7. Meaning 2b in Merriam-Webster.

8. Making a MIDI-operated *stoss*-action model is the subject of Van Gool (2014), also involving Chris, Bobby, and myself.

9. In addition to vertical movement, we also analyzed horizontal movement, but for visual clarity, we left out those data in our graphs.

10. The length of contact with the strings is similar if not identical between Erard and Walter: it's visible for a maximum of two frames.

11. The timings of those lowest points are 58 ms after initial finger impact for Walter (with the hammer strike occurring at 54 ms) vs. 68 ms for Erard (hammer striking at 65 ms).

12. I changed de Silva's translation as "supple" to match Streicher's "*elastisches*."

Chapter 4

1. Walter (1970), 283–84.

2. Reproduced in Dahl and Barnes (1997), 210.

3. *EL&D*, vol. 1, 186, 433.

4. For a demonstration, see https://www.youtube.com/watch?v=lyxuNjz5Q-o.

5. The 1798 Clementi is from the collection of Chris Maene; the 1805 Broadwood belongs to Tilman Skowroneck; the knee levers are standard for c. 1795–1800 Walter fortepianos.

6. Latcham (2009), 26.

7. Adam (1804–5), 218, 220.

8. Adam (1804–5), 219.

9. *Le Pianiste* 1, no. 6 (April 10, 1834): 83. Quoted in Goy (2009), 256, and Weitz (2015), 348–49. Weitz (332–33) corrects a widely held assumption that it was Chaulieu who delivered most of the journal's content, claiming equal share for Henry Lemoine, also the director of the journal and owner of a well-known music publishing house: it was there that the musical examples for the journal were printed. The journal was short-lived: after two years Lemoine proved too busy with his other affairs to continue it. While the use of "we" elsewhere in the article may reflect co-authorship, for the "me" in this particular anecdote I've placed my bet on Chaulieu.

10. La Grandville (2017b), 129.

11. Latour ([1993] 2000), 17.

12. *Wv*, vol. 1, 315.

13. To be dated May or June 1804. Frohlich (1999), 32–33.

14. Jander (2009), 52–53.

15. Fanny Mendelssohn and Franz Liszt are known to have performed the Andante con moto as a brief solo piece at private settings. Jander (2009), 49.

16. English translation by Kline (2001).

17. With Ensemble Caprice, Matthias Maute conducting; Montreal, June 18, 2014.

18. Latour ([1993] 2000), 17, referring to Akrich ([1992] 1997).

19. *Wv*, vol. 1, 315.

20. Letter of February 3, 1818. *Bw*, vol. 4, 173.

21. Thayer ([1866–79] 1967), 337.

22. Jander (2009); Comini (2008), 35; Clubbe (2015), 14.

23. Clubbe (2015), 27.
24. Maruyama (1987), 81; Clubbe (2015), 25. Heiligenstad Testament in *Bw*, vol. 1, 121–25; translated in Solomon (1998), 151–54.
25. Jander (2009), 171–73.
26. *AmZ* 3, no. 47 (August 19, 1801): 786.
27. Thayer's annotations of conversations with the eighty-two-year-old Mähler, Kopitz and Cadenbach (2009), 564, 566.
28. Thayer ([1866–79] 1967), 337.
29. Removing the second soundboard facilitates reaching the tuning pins.
30. Clubbe (2015), 24.

Vignette 2

1. Weber (1981), 13–16.
2. Reichardt (1804), 150–54.
3. Elsner (1957), 123–25.

Chapter 5

1. Today's address is 13 rue du Mail; back then No. 13 was No. 37.
2. Roudier (1993), 12–13.
3. Fétis (1837), 34–41.
4. Fétis (1837), 35.
5. *EL&D*, vol. 1, 49, 309.
6. *EL&D*, vol. 1, 7.
7. *EL&D*, vol. 1, 7.
8. Sébastien's surviving 1779 harpsichord in the Musée de la musique (E.979.2.5) bears his name alone, as do several surviving pianos from earlier in the 1780s. The 1791 grand piano in the same collection (E.990.11.1) is signed "Sébastien Erard et Frère" on the nameboard and "Erard Frères à Paris" on the soundboard.
9. Fétis (1837), 37.
10. Also *EL&D* (vol. 1, 5–11) is able to give several pages to the biography of Sébastien but only a brief paragraph to Jean-Baptiste.
11. Adelson (2017), 7.
12. Letter of August 1, 1791; *EL&D*, vol. 1, 84, 340.
13. Letter of January 24, 1791; *EL&D*, vol. 1, 53, 312.
14. Letter of August 2, 1791; *EL&D*, vol. 1, 85, 340.
15. Letter of March 29 [1791]; *EL&D*, vol. 1, 66, 323.
16. Pollens (2017), 337.
17. UK patent number 179402016. The documents are accessible in the British Library. The quote is from [Anonymous] (1856), No. 2016.

18. *EL&D*, vol. 1, 97, 351.

19. Letters of September 24, 1792, and September 27, 1792; *EL&D*, vol. 1, 136, 141, 387, 392.

20. *EL&D*, vol. 1, 49–50, 309–10. Recounted in more detail in Adelson (2017), 20–21.

21. *EL&D*, vol. 1, 8.

22. In a letter to Domingo Carno in Madrid, we read, "Finally, I am back in Paris for some time." *EL&D*, vol. 1, 175, 423.

23. *EL&D*, vol. 1, 185, 433.

24. *EL&D*, vol. 1, 189, 437.

25. Archives du Musée de la musique, Philharmonie de Paris, E.2009.5.98. Accessible online; see vignette 3, note 3.

26. Archives du Musée de la musique, Philharmonie de Paris, E.2009.5.100. Sébastien returned to the organ much later in his life, patenting a mechanism for creating expression through touch in 1830. *EL&D*, vol. 1, 34–35.

27. La Grandville (2017c), 67, 100; for the composer Pfeffinger, see *Grove Music Online*.

28. Letter of April 29, 1797. *EL&D*, vol. 1, 194, 442.

29. Adam (1804–5), 1.

30. Letter to Messieurs Frauscke & Rochlitz, July 16, 1797. *EL&D*, vol. 1, 198, 446.

31. Reichardt (1804), vol. 2, 93.

32. Two more, with missing serial number, are listed in Maniguet (2009), 96; another, also without serial number, is in a private collection in Bristol, England. These bring the grand total of extant old-model Erard grands to thirteen.

33. Clarke (2009) and Maniguet (2009) have been particularly useful.

34. The instrument is listed in MacSween (2014), 24, without additional information. Thomas Tomkison was active in London from 1799 to 1851.

35. Thus, for example, Ignaz Moscheles, speaking about Broadwood; Moscheles (1873), 89, 109.

36. *EL&D*, vol. 1, 196, 444; 186, 433. The translation of *"Buffle"* as "buff stop" has been adjusted to "stop of leather" to avoid confusion with the first pedal, which corresponds to the traditional buff stop on harpsichords.

37. Adam (1804–5), 218–19, also for the other pedals.

38. Steibelt (n.d. [1809]), 65.

39. Wogram (1990); Skowroneck (2010), 138–39.

40. Ollivier et al. (2012), 3984.

41. *EL&D*, vol. 1, 179.

42. Rowland (2009), 130.

43. *EL&D*, vol. 1, 183, 193, 441. Adelson (2017, 22–23) also discusses Erard's wood-buying practices.

44. Smith ([1775] 2007), 9; Aspromourgos (2013), 268.

45. *EL&D*, vol. 1, 199, 446.

46. Maniguet (2009), 86.

Chapter 6

1. In the treble, the modern piano's *una corda*, or soft pedal, makes the hammers hit two strings instead of three and in the bass, one out of two; the effect on the lowest, single-wound bass strings is no longer string-dependent, but relates to the hammer striking the string from a more fluffed-up area of its felt.

2. *AmZ* 1, nos. 8–9 (November 21 and 28, 1798): 117–22, 135–37.

3. Milchmeyer (1997), 57; translated in Rhein (1993), 136.

4. *AmZ* 1, no. 9 (November 28, 1798): 136 (original emphasis). Knecht's own two-part piano treatise (1800) carried the more modest titles of *Kleine praktische Klavierschule* and *Kleine theoretische Klavierschule*.

5. From the first letter Beethoven wrote to Härtel in Leipzig on April 22, 1801, we know that he had been reading "your *Musikalische Zeitung*." *Bw*, vol. 1, 69.

6. *AmZ* 1, no. 9 (November 28, 1798): 136.

7. *AmZ* 2, no. 35 (May 28, 1800): 622.

8. Milchmeyer (1997), *Vorrede*; translated in Rhein (1993), 2; also xiii–xvi, for scant details of his life. One remarkable achievement was his invention and construction of a three-keyboard "*mechanischer Clavier-Flügel*" with stops that in their combinations allow for "at least 250 registers" (described in C. F. Cramer, *Magazin der Musik* 1 [1783]: 1024–28). The man was clearly stop-obsessed.

9. "I confirm that [Steibelt] is German, even born and raised in Berlin, has been a soldier for some time, but that he prefers to have forgotten the German language and only spoke French—but, funnily enough, very badly." *AmZ* 2, no. 35 (May 28, 1800): 622.

10. The *Jugendfehler* are quoted from Steibelt's letter to his brother from St. Petersburg on May 9, 1823, also the year of Steibelt's death. Müller (1973), 9.

11. "Inclination to the French way of life became a true character of his identity: indeed, he went through every possible effort to forget and ignore his German roots." Translated from Müller (1973), 6.

12. Rose-van Epenhuysen (2005), 114–15.

13. Griesinger writes to Härtel on April 3, 1802: "Until now, more than 31 ducats have never been paid to [Beethoven] for any *Clavier* sonata and yet his *Clavier* sonatas are better than those by Haydn [*und doch sollen seine Claviersonaten besser als die Haydnschen seyn*]." This opinion must go back to Beethoven himself. Biba (1987), 158.

14. Biba (1987), 71.

15. The business emerged around 1799. It remains unclear at what point between 1800 and 1801 the younger niece joined the business. In the *Almanach du commerce de Paris* (the equivalent of modern times' Yellow Pages) of 1799–1800 (An VIII), the index of Parisian businesses ("*Des Commerçans*") lists "Erard, facteur d'instrumens" only (p. xli); the next issue of 1800–1801 (An IX) lists both "Erard, frères, facteurs de pianos" and "Erard (mesdemoiselles), Mdes. de musique" (p. xliv).

16. *AmZ* 3, no. 2 (October 8, 1800): 39 (emphasis added).

17. By writing in French, Haydn seems to acknowledge the French identity and status that his Austrian pupil had acquired in adult life. He addresses the letter to "Monsieur Pleyel, / Compositeur très célèbre / à Paris." Bartha (1965), 363. The Pleyel edition (consisting of a complete score with a French translation by Philippe Desriaux and another in Italian by an anonymous translator) eventually appeared later in 1801.

18. Müller (1973), 38–42.

19. *Wiener Zeitung*, December 31, 1800, 4230–31.

20. *AmZ* 3, no. 24 (March 11, 1801): 415.

21. See Landon (1977a), 619–32, for a complete list.

22. Biba (1987), 68.

23. Raab et al. (2010), 355–56.

24. Müller (1973), 40 (emphasis added).

25. At an exchange rate of 1 imperial ducat equaling 6.50 *livres*. Georgel (1818), 32.

26. Beghin (2015b), 277–78n55) and 29–32 (table 1.2).

27. Jander (1996), 592–94. The date is taken from Meredith (2012), 31. The two events (concert and private competition) are given in this order in Müller (1973), 36.

28. *AmZ* 3, no. 3 (October 15, 1800): 50.

29. Jander (1996), 593.

30. Wegeler and Ries (1838), 81–82.

31. Meredith (2012), 32–34.

32. Meredith (2012), 26. That some Steibelt–Beethoven duel happened, in whatever shape or form, is confirmed in a conversation book entry from September 9, 1825, in the words of Beethoven's nephew Karl: "*Schuppanʒich* is telling the story of what a *Triumph* you celebrated over *Steipelt* [*sic*]." *Kh*, vol. 8, 126.

33. Wegeler and Ries (1838), 94.

34. Letter of October 18, 1802. Beethoven offers them both at the single price of 50 ducats. *Bw*, vol. 1, 126.

35. *Wvʒ*, vol. 1, 199, 203.

36. *AmZ* 3, no. 22 (February 26, 1800): 398–400.

37. Maunder (1998, 161, 168, 178, 179, 183) records five English pianos for sale in the *Wiener Zeitung*, 1788–97. Of these, probably only one was a grand, but more may have been available, just not offered for sale quite yet. Another well-known Viennese owner of an English grand, of course, was Haydn.

38. Steibelt (n.d. [c. 1809]), 64.

39. Steibelt (n.d. [c. 1809]), 2.

40. The *AmZ* of November 23, 1808 (11, no. 8: 128) reports that the "gloriously famous composer and virtuoso on the *Pianoforte*, Hr. Steibelt from Paris, has arrived in Leipzig, on his way to St. Petersburg, where a highly advantageous engagement from Emperor Alexander calls him." It is then that plans for a bilingual edition

of Steibelt's *Méthode* must have been hatched: a "new, comprehensive *Pianoforte-Schule*" forthcoming from Breitkopf & Härtel is mentioned on August 30, 1809 (*AmZ* 11, no. 30: 768). Novelty may need to be qualified, however: an only-French version, presumably already existing, survives from Imbault (Paris, n.d.).

41. A perceptive Frankfurt reviewer realized how intertwined Steibelt's effects were with the particular instrument he used—"his own, from the brothers Erard in Paris [*sein eigenes, von den Brüdern Erard in Paris*]"—which he brought with him en route to St. Petersburg. But to the reviewer such symbiosis was ultimately a disadvantage: "On another instrument, however, these effects [*Effekte*] would be hard to imitate with any chance of success." *AmZ* 11, no. 11 (December 14, 1808): 171.

42. Grave and Grave (1987), 251. It is a twist of fate that Vogler would three years later also become a competitor of Beethoven's during a *soirée* at the house of Johann Sonnleithner; by all accounts that encounter remained entirely civil, "each improvising on a theme supplied by the other" (6).

43. A self-professed limerick monster, Tilman responded to mine with one of his own: "A charlatan, fresh from Parees, / Was introduced at Count von Frees': / His manners were haughty, / His *tremoli* naughty, / But his feet were a dainty surpreese."

Chapter 7

1. INPI, "Brevets français 19e siècle," http://bases-brevets19e.inpi.fr/.

2. INPI, "Brevets français 19e siècle," file 1BA650.

3. Alain Roudier, personal communication.

4. Robert Adelson, personal communication. Buying up inventions of others was part of the firm's business plan.

5. A two-manual harpsichord plus piano. Blanton (2015), 72.

6. Rose–van Epenhuysen (2006), vi, 31, 153.

7. Steibelt (n.d. [c. 1809]), 2.

8. *Le Pianiste* (April 10, 1834), 83; on the question of authorship, see Chapter Four, note 9.

9. Adam (1804–5), 220.

10. Adam (1804–5), 221.

11. Adam (1804–5), 7.

12. On the rare occasion when the hammer appeared to stay at the highest contact point for two consecutive frames, we wrote down the number of the first.

13. Gallagher (2008, 11) defines spectrum analysis as a "mathematical method for analyzing the frequencies making up a sound wave."

14. Gallagher (2008, 199) defines a spectrogram, "a.k.a. sonogram, spectral waterfall, voiceprint," as a "three-dimensional visual representation of a spectrum, displaying changes in sound energy by frequency over time."

15. Adam (1804–5), 220.

Vignette 3

1. Howard (1932), 91–94. Also Gervais (2012), 720–22. It is now agreed that Pacioli was recording a system that had in fact been in use for at least two hundred years already: Ryan (2014), 94.
2. Savary ([1723] 1742), col. 1108; translation slightly adjusted from Howard (1932), 92.
3. They have been digitized and may be viewed on the website of the Musée de la musique, Paris: https://archivesmusee.philharmoniedeparis.fr/pleyel/archives.html; follow "archives Érard" and then "registres comptables."
4. The 1797–99 volume uses a slightly different format; this book is also titled "journal," rather than "livre."
5. See Gervais (2012) for the argument that early modern account books primarily tracked not profits, but credit flows.
6. Sargentson (1996, 23, 28) describes the complex networks of credit that connected eighteenth-century Parisian merchants and artisans, and the critical role of credit in underpinning their transactions.
7. Personal communication, September 2, 2019.
8. Biba (1987), 216.
9. Rose–van Epenhuysen (2005), 119.
10. Newman (1988), 51–52.
11. Later that academic year the Erard family took the boy Ferdinand under their wing when his father grew ill: Herold senior died September 1, 1802. Pougin (1880), 139, 140, 145, 146.
12. La Grandville (2017b), 390.

Chapter 8

1. Cooper (2016), 17.
2. Cooper (2016), 16.
3. Cooper (2016), 5.
4. Cooper (2016), 17.
5. Tovey (1931), 149.
6. Taub (2002), 111, rehashing a notion that circulates through countless liner notes.
7. *Bw*, vol. 1, 190.
8. For these Hodderian terms, see the introduction.
9. Lockwood and Gosman (2013), 59; Cooper (2016), 16; *Bw*, vol. 1, 190 and 196.
10. I follow the assumption that Landsberg 6 had been bound in its entirety before Beethoven started working with it, a customary practice for Beethoven since 1798. Lockwood and Gosman (2013), 13; and Cooper (2000), 32–33.
11. Lockwood and Gosman (2013), 10.
12. Letter to Stephan von Breuning of September 20, 1826. *Bw*, vol. 6, 281.

13. Adam (1804–5), 30.

14. Adam (1804–5), 218.

15. Adam (1804–5), 61.

16. Steibelt (n.d. [1809]), 64 (emphasis added).

17. My fascination with C-sharp minor as a hypnotizing key started with Haydn's "Auenbrugger" Sonata, Hob. XVI:36. See Beghin (2015b), 199–201.

18. Also observed by Rosen (2002), 181.

19. I borrow the title of this section from Kaiser (1975, 359, 382), who calls the whole sonata "a C-major *Mysterium*."

20. Schachter (2016), 245.

21. Drake (1994), 148.

22. Czerny (1832), 324.

23. Cooper (2016), 2.

24. Schachter (2016, 252) uses the term "coda to the coda," but only to refer to mm. 293–end.

25. Montgeroult ([1820]), i.

Chapter 9

1. Wegeler and Ries (1838), 101. Corroborated by Czerny (Schünemann [1939], 65).

2. Lockwood and Gosman (2013), vol. 1, 121, 131–37.

3. Staehelin (1984).

4. *Bw*, vol. 1, 254.

5. Staehelin (1984); and *Wvz*, vol. 2, 140.

6. *Wvz*, vol. 2, 140.

7. Tovey (1931), 149–50; Uhde (1968), 584–85; Uhde ([1974] 1991), 156–59; Dahlhaus ([1987] 1991), 10–13; Rovelli (1999), 121–23; Rosen (2002), 186; Cooper (2017), 124–26.

8. See chapter 11.

9. On such "opus concept," see Sisman (2008).

10. Established in May 1801, not long after Austria's signing of the Treaty of Lunéville with France. The French name must have been "a nod to current political sensibilities"; conversely, when hostilities with the French resumed, the firm adopted Kunst- und Industrie-Comptoir as its new German name. Wyn Jones (2016), 99–100.

11. Staehelin (1984), V and VIII.

12. Beethoven had a habit of performing new works for friends at his house: "One day, when a small group was having breakfast with Prince Lichnowsky after the concert at the Augarten (in the morning at 8:00), including Beethoven and myself, the proposal was made to go to Beethoven's house and to hear his then still unperformed

opera Leonore"; this earlier version of *Fidelio* premiered on November 20, 1805. Wegeler and Ries (1838), 102–3.

13. The name appears on the title page of an edition by Magnier in Paris, c. 1880; *Wv*₇, vol. 1, 289.

14. Webster (2005).

15. Fredrik Samuel Silverstolpe, quoted and translated in Webster and Feder (2002), 40.

16. Rovelli (1999, 125–26) argues that a transitional few bars had been on Beethoven's mind early on in the creative process.

17. Cooper (2017), 123.

18. Unlike "Piano en forme de clavecin," the popular nickname "Hammerklavier" cannot refer to a single kind of instrument. Op. 106 is a *two-instrument* sonata: in the final Fugue, Beethoven introduces his new six-octave English piano (CC–c⁴) in a sonata that he had started producing on a Viennese piano, with its own six-octave range (FF–f⁴). See Beghin (2015a).

19. Cooper (2017), 123.

20. The same text is reproduced as an announcement of the published sonata of Adam in the *Journal typographique et bibliographique* 5, no. 16 (30 Nivôse, An 10 / January 20, 1802): 128. The "C." is for Chrétien or Christian (also his father's given name), which is how Kalkbrenner is referred to in the school's records.

21. *Journal de Paris*, 23 Brumaire, An 14, 2934.

22. La Grandville (2017c).

23. *AmZ* 3, no. 24 (March 11, 1801): 415.

24. Wegeler and Ries (1838), 13; Wurzbach (1885), 234.

25. Wegeler and Ries (1838), 14.

26. Emphasis in original. Reproduced at Digital Archives of Beethoven-Haus, Bonn. For a sociocultural analysis, see DeNora (1995), 83–114.

27. The term "mature" is Wegeler's. Wegeler and Ries (1838), 14.

28. *Bw*, vol. 1, 23.

29. Heer (1933), 23.

30. These abbreviated titles are rarely specified in the literature; *Wv*₇ spells them wrongly as "J. & J. R. A."

31. Heer (1933), 15.

32. Also Wegeler calls him "*Kämmerer des Kaisers von Oesterreich.*" Wegeler and Ries (1838), 13. See also Heer (1933), 13 and 17.

33. "*Ein österreichischer Patriot von reinstem Wasser.*" Wurzbach (1885), 231.

34. During these years he conducted at least one military expedition to the West Indies. Wurzbach (1885), 21.

35. Brothers Stephan and Lorenz von Breuning, childhood friends of Beethoven, knew Waldstein very well, too. That Waldstein borrowed money from the von Breunings and was unable to settle his debts makes these old Bonn friendships more complex still. Wurzbach (1885), 50.

36. Wurzbach (1885), 233.
37. Wegeler and Ries (1838), 77–79.
38. Schünemann (1939), 61.
39. As he'd done before with a method of Félix Despreaux: "You will find in the crate that has just left the first instructions for learning to play the piano, by Félix Despreaux." Letter of November 13, 1797; *EL&D*, vol. 1, 219.
40. Dumes (1842), 11; quoted in Kopitz and Cadenbach (2009), 501.
41. Adam (1804–5), 5.
42. *Wvz*, vol. 1, 69; advertised in the *Journal de Paris*, January 31, 1801.
43. *AmZ* 3, no. 24 (March 11, 1801): 413–14n.
44. *Wvz*, vol. 1, 291; the address is given in Benton (1979), 130.
45. Based on the publisher's printed address; Roudet (2005), 789.
46. Adam (1804–5), 152.

Chapter 10

1. In a review of an *exercise* (i.e., public recital or concert) of January 13, 1801, with Kalkbrenner playing the "Storm" Concerto by Daniel Steibelt. Pierre (1900), vol. 1, 461.
2. DeNora (1995), 83–114.
3. "Beethovens einziger Schüler," in *AmZ* 6, no. 46 (August 15, 1804): 777. See also "Memoir of Ferdinand Ries," *The Harmonicon* 2, no. 15 (March 1824): 34: "[Beethoven] allowed him to be the first to take the title of his pupil, and to appear in public as such."
4. The second movement of Kreutzer's own *Grande sonate pour le Pianoforte avec accompagnement de Violon* (Leipzig: Breitkopf & Härtel, 1802) is a romance by Adam ("romance de L. Adam"), which suggests that the two colleagues did perform as a duo.
5. Clive (2001), 338.
6. *Bw*, vol. 6, 182.
7. Kopitz and Cadenbach (2009), 1115.
8. Clubbe (2019), 164–67.
9. The full description reads, *le doyen des professeurs du Conservatoire*. Marmontel (1878), 238.
10. Marmontel (1878), 236.
11. Marmontel (1878), 238.
12. Choron and Fayolle (1810), 4; Pougin (1877), 22.
13. La Grandville (2014), 68; and Pierre (1900), vol. 1, 129.
14. Gautier (1873), 50–53, quoted in Dorival (2006), 101–3.
15. Duvergier (1825), 171–73.
16. Reproduced in Dorival (2006), 373–78.

17. Pierre (1900), vol. 1, 132.
18. Adam (1804–5), 1; and Montgeroult (n.d. [1820]), ii.
19. Pierre (1900), vol. 1, 140.
20. The following paragraphs draw on information in La Grandville (2017b), *passim*, and (2017c), 84, 85, 100–112.
21. La Grandville (2014), 107.
22. La Grandville (2014), 78; (2017c), 104; (2017b), 256. Jean Frédéric junior was not yet born when his father died nineteen years before.
23. La Grandville (2017b), 27; Pierre (1900), vol. 2, 384, 385, 690.
24. La Grandville (2017b), 252.
25. Pougin (1880), 139; see also vignette 3.
26. *Wvz̧*, vol. 1, 15.
27. Major secondary sources claim 1784 as Kalkbrenner's birth year, but a 1785 baptismal notice in a Kassel newspaper indicates "between 2nd and 8th November [1785]." Nautsch (1983), 1.
28. Adam (1804–5), 53.
29. La Grandville (2017b), 129, 449.
30. I reconstruct this list from extant programs of award-distributing ceremonies, where winners would normally have played their competition piece again. La Grandville (2014), 226n656.
31. At the impressionable ages of fifteen and thirteen, both Lemoine and Chaulieu had been at the Conservatoire for several years already. La Grandville (2017b), 449–50 and 128–29.
32. Pierre (1900), vol. 2, 585; see also Weitz (2016), 70.
33. Helyard (2011).
34. La Grandville (2014), 225–26.
35. Fétis (1839), vol. 5, 216.
36. Pierre (1900), vol. 1, 485.
37. On the complex question of available pianos at the Conservatoire (linked to a post-Revolution history of confiscations from private citizens and inventories), see Rose–van Epenhuysen (2006), 88–117.
38. For more on historical pedaling, see Helyard (2016) and Beghin (2007).
39. For example, the release of the *jeu de Luth* in m. 329 of the third movement, where Adam anticipates the time needed for the left foot to make it back to the second pedal.
40. Adam (1804–5), 220.
41. This number was down from twelve in 1800. Pierre (1900), vol. 1, 234, 242.
42. Adam (1804–5), 233: "We consider style in two ways: [. . .] the first has to do with mechanism and the second with sentiment."
43. Reproduced as front matter in Adam (1804–5), i. The speech was delivered "on

behalf of the special committee charged with the making of the Piano Method of the Conservatoire."

44. Baillot et al. (1802–3), 162–63.
45. Baillot ([1835] 1872), appendix (original emphasis).

Chapter 11

1. Thayer/Forbes ([1866–79] 1967), 403.
2. Bach ([1753/62] 1994), vol. 2, 327.
3. Cooper (2017), 128.
4. Because of the Ries anecdote (which he dates "by the middle of September 1804"), Cooper (2017, 132) assumes that Beethoven had begun the sonata during the weeks before; in her study of the sketches, however, Frohlich (1991, 43–47) entertains the possibility that the Ries anecdote must be dated one year later, in 1805. For more on this necessarily speculative dating of the sketches, see *Wv₇*, 311.
5. An insightful essay on the subject is Pay (1996).
6. The false notion that the "keys were lengthened in the front by 12 mm" was initiated by Huber (1990, 183), and copied by subsequent authors.
7. There is a green, single strip of felt under the front of the keys, but within the new system it has no function: it must have been gratuitously added at some later stage.
8. Akrich ([1992] 1997), 207.
9. This description applies to what happened with Mozart's Walter fortepiano; see Latcham (1997); and Beghin (2007).
10. Letter of January 2, 1805; reproduced in Skowroneck (2014a), 400–401.
11. Akrich ([1992] 1997), 206.
12. No longer "Frère et Soeur Stein" or "Geschwister Stein," André Stein started building under his own name, while Nannette's firm, with husband Andreas as its spokesperson, became Streicher *geborne* Stein. Latcham (2007, 56) speculates, "The brothers-in-law [. . .] were involved in a private battle to gain control of the company (and its illustrious name)," with Nannette "caught between her husband and her brother."
13. *Bw*, vol. 1, 172–73. The undated letter is usually dated summer 1803, but Brandenburg acknowledges that we only know for certain that Beethoven was in Oberdöbling in summer 1804; hence, "it is not to be excluded that the letter was written only in 1804." See also Skowroneck (2007), 166–67.
14. In the pen of Franz Oliva; *Kh*, vol. 2, 82.
15. Thayer ([1866–79] 1967), vol. 2, 695.
16. *Bw*, vol. 2, 153–54.
17. *Bw*, vol. 2, 168.
18. Thayer ([1866–79] 1967), 403.
19. Thayer ([1866–79] 1967), 407.

Chapter 12

1. Schönfeld ([1796] 1976), 88.
2. Staehelin (1984), VI and fol. 32v.
3. *EL&D*, vol. 1, 196 and 444.
4. Bach ([1753/62] 1994), vol. 1, 130.
5. Czerny ([1846] 1970), 58.
6. Reinecke (1895), 70; also Tovey (1931), 162; and more recently: Rosen (2002), 190; Cooper (2007), vol. 2, 57; Kinderman (2009), 107.
7. Schiff (2004–6).
8. Bach (1787), II, iv, 27–32, and 33–35.
9. Letter of April 3, 1802. Biba (1987), 158.
10. Cramer (1784), 535.
11. *AmZ* 8, no. 40 (July 2, 1806): 639–40.
12. *Bw*, vol. 1, 122.
13. This excellent performance venue was built in 1843–45.
14. Ephraim Hahn and Kseniya Kawko, then graduate students in the recording program at McGill University.
15. Martha and I had previously collaborated on two unconventional recording projects: *The Virtual Haydn* (2009–11) and *Inside the Hearing Machine* (2017).
16. https://en-de.neumann.com/m-150-tube.
17. Bonds (2006), 9.

Epilogue

1. Oberösterreichisches Landesarchiv, Musealverein, Schachtel 44, Faszikel IV.5. Two days later this identical text was entered into the museum's *Einreichprotokoll*, or acquisition register, as the description for "exhibit no. 361." Both documents may be viewed at this book's website.
2. On the other hand, a black mark "Mu 61" is still visible on the outside of the case, at the front of the spine.
3. Zibermayr (1933), 117–30. Imperial approval came nine months later.
4. Clive (2006), 210.
5. *Bw*, vol. 5, 343.
6. Gerhard von Breuning (1874, 124) expresses surprise that his father Stephan (Beethoven's neighbor, longtime friend, and attorney, who presided over the estate sale) did not purchase the piano. I elaborate on the reason ("because it went up only to C and did not meet the demands of the modern, that is Beethoven, era") in Beghin (2020), 233.
7. *Wiener Zeitung*, July 22, 1873, 1331.
8. *Internationale Ausstellungs-Zeitung: Beilage der Neuen Freien Presse*, June 6, 1873, 1.

9. *Internationale Ausstellungs-Zeitung: Beilage der Neuen Freien Presse,* June 6, 1873, 1. This is the second of a sixteen-chapter *feuilleton* between May and September 1873. Mozart's violins (identified in *Internationale Ausstellungs-Zeitung: Beilage der Neuen Freien Presse,* June 8, 1873, 3) are "Andreas Meyer [Mayr] in Salzburg [date illegible]" and "Jacob Stainer (1659)." The former is now considered authentic, the latter as being of early eighteenth-century make. Beethoven's violins are an Amati (now considered a forgery) and a Johann Georg Hellmer (Prague, 1737).

10. *Internationale Ausstellungs-Zeitung: Beilage der Neuen Freien Presse,* June 6, 1873, 2.

11. *Revue et gazette musicale de Paris,* September 5, 1875, 283.

12. *Internationale Ausstellungs-Zeitung: Beilage der Neuen Freien Presse,* September 17, 1873, 2–3.

13. Thayer/Forbes (1866–79/1967), 422, 796–97.

14. Thayer/Forbes (1866–79/1967), 181, 796–7.

15. Thayer/Forbes (1866–79/1967), 1015; translation slightly modified; original in *Kh,* vol. 10, 286.

16. The others mentioned by Hanslick/Bannelier are Schanz, Streicher, Graf, and Broadwood.

17. *Revue et gazette musicale de Paris,* September 5, 1875, 284.

18. *Neue Freie Presse,* October 15, 1875, 6

19. Thayer ([1866–79]1921), vol. 2, 21.

20. *Wiener Abendpost: Beilage zur Wiener Zeitung,* July 22, 1873, 1331.

21. Thayer/Forbes (1866–79/1967), 796.

22. Huber (1990), 18. Huber ended up defending a 2011 doctoral dissertation on the very issue of climate control and conservation.

BIBLIOGRAPHY

Adam, Louis. 1804–5. *Méthode de piano du Conservatoire*. Paris: Naderman.

Adam, Louis, and Ludwig Wenzel Lachnith. 1798. *Méthode ou principe général du doigté pour le forte-piano*. Paris: Sieber père.

———. n.d. [1813–22]. *Méthode ou principe général du doigté pour le forte-piano, adoptée par le Conservatoire de Musique de Paris, pour servir à l'instruction des élèves dans cet établissement*. Paris: Sieber père.

Adelson, Robert. 2017. "Inside an Eighteenth-Century Instrument Builder's Workshop: Erard's Letter Copy Book (1791–1797)." *Journal of the American Musical Instrument Society* 47:5–57.

Adelson, Robert, Alain Roudier, Jenny Nex, Laure Barthel, and Michel Foussard, eds. 2015. *The History of the Erard Piano and Harp in Letters and Documents 1785–1959*. 2 vols. Cambridge: Cambridge University Press.

Akrich, Madeleine. [1992] 1997. "The De-scription of Technical Objects." In *Shaping Technology / Building Society: Studies in Sociotechnical Change*, edited by Wiebe E. Bijker and John Law, 205–25. 2nd ed. Cambridge, MA: MIT Press.

[Anonymous.] 1856. *English Patents of Inventions, Specifications: 2001–2068. 1794–1795*. [London:] H.M. Stationery Office.

Aspromourgos, Tony. 2013. "Adam Smith on Labour and Capital." In *The Oxford Handbook of Adam Smith*, edited by Christopher J. Berry, Maria Pia Paganelli, and Craig Smith. Oxford: Oxford University Press.

Bach, Carl Philipp Emanuel. [1753/62] 1994. *Versuch über die wahre Art, das Klavier zu spielen*. 2 vols. Facsimile edition, 2 vols. in 1. Kassel: Bärenreiter.

———. 1787. *Versuch über die wahre Art, das Clavier zu spielen*. 3rd ed. Leipzig: im Schwickertschen Verlag.

Baillot, Pierre. [1835] 1872. *Observations relatives aux concours de violon du Conservatoire de musique.* Paris: Librairie de Firmin Didot Frères et Cie.

Baillot, Pierre; with Pierre Rode and Rodolphe Kreutzer. 1802–3. *Méthode de violon.* Paris: Magasin de Musique.

Bartha, Dénes. 1965. *Joseph Haydn: Gesammelte Briefe und Aufzeichnungen.* New York: Bärenreiter.

Beghin, Tom. 2007. "Playing Mozart's Piano: An Exercise in Reverse-Engineering." *Keyboard Perspectives* 1:1–35.

Beghin, Tom. 2017. "Beethoven's Broadwood, Stein's Hearing Machine, and a Trilogy of Sonatas." CD-booklet to *Inside the Hearing Machine: Beethoven on His Broadwood— Piano Sonatas Opus 109, 110 and 111.* EPR-Classic 0025.

———. 2015a. "Beethoven's Hammerklavier Sonata, Opus 106: Legend, Difficulty, and the Gift of a Broadwood Piano." *Keyboard Perspectives* 7:81–121.

———. 2015b. *The Virtual Haydn: Paradox of a Twenty-first-century Keyboardist.* Chicago: University of Chicago Press.

Beghin, Tom, with Mikayla Jensen-Large, trans. 2018. *Piano Method of the Conservatory Written by L. Adam . . .* Unpublished pdf document, available at this book's website.

Beghin, Tom. 2020. "Deafly Performing Beethoven's Last Three Piano Sonatas." In *Beethoven Studies 4,* edited by Keith Chapin and David Wyn Jones, 209–38. Cambridge: Cambridge University Press,

Benton, Rita. 1979. "Pleyel as Music Publisher." *Journal of the American Musicological Society* 32:125–40.

Bergé, Pieter, Jeroen D'hoe, and William Caplin, eds. 2009. *Beethoven's Tempest Sonatas: Perspectives of Analysis and Performance.* Leuven: Peeters.

Bettermann, Silke. 2012. *Beethoven im Bild: Die Darstellung des Komponisten in der bildenden Kunst vom 18. bis zum 21. Jahrhundert.* Bonn: Verlag Beethoven-Haus Bonn.

Biba, Otto, ed. 1987. *"Eben komme ich von Haydn . . ." Georg August Griesingers Korrespondenz mit Joseph Haydns Verleger Breitkopf & Härtel 1799–1819.* Kösel: Atlantis Musikbuch-Verlag.

Bilson, Malcolm, Tom Beghin, David Breitman, Ursula Dütschler, Zvi Meniker, Bart van Oort, and Andrew Willis. 1997. *Ludwig van Beethoven: The Complete Piano Sonatas on Period Instruments.* Claves Records, CD 9707–10. [10 compact discs.]

Birkett, Stephen. 2010. "Observing the 18th-century *Prellzungenmechanik* through High-speed Imaging—Pianissimo and Forte Response Compared." In *Bowed and Keyboard Instruments in the Age of Mozart: Proceedings of the Harmoniques International Congress, Lausanne 2006,* edited by Thomas Steiner, 305–25. Bern: Peter Lang.

Blanton, Robin. 2015. "Making Public: J. A. Stein's 'Funny' Keyboards and the Habermasian Public Sphere." *Keyboard Perspectives* 8:71–93.

Bonds, Mark Evan. 2006. *Music as Thought: Listening to the Symphony in the Age of Beethoven.* Princeton, NJ: Princeton University Press.

Breuning, Gerhard von. 1874. *Aus dem Schwarzspanierhause: Erinnerungen an L. van Beethoven aus meiner Jugendzeit*. Vienna: L. Rosner.

Brown, Bill. 2001. "Thing Theory." *Critical Inquiry* 28, no. 1:1–22.

Butler, H. E., trans. [1920] 1989. *The "Institutio oratoria" of Quintilian*. 4 vols. Cambridge, MA: Harvard University Press.

Choron, A., and F. Fayolle. 1810. *Dictionnaire historique des musiciens*. Vol. 1. Paris: Valade.

Clarke, Christopher. 2009. "Erard and Broadwood in the Classical Era: Two Schools of Piano Making." *Musique, images, instruments: Revue française d'organologie et d'iconographie musicale* 11:99–125.

Clive, Peter, 2001. *Beethoven and His World: A Biographical Dictionary*. Oxford: Oxford University Press.

Clubbe, John. 2015. "The *Eroica* in Its Artistic Context: Willibrord Joseph Mähler's Portrait." In *Nature, Politics, and the Arts: Essays on Romantic Culture for Carl Woodring*, edited by Hermione De Almeide, 7–36. Lanham, MD: University of Delaware Press.

———. 2019. *Beethoven: The Relentless Revolutionary*. New York: W. W. Norton.

Cole, Michael. 1998. *The Pianoforte in the Classical Era*. Oxford: Clarendon Press.

Comini, Alessandra. 2008. *The Changing Image of Beethoven: A Study in Mythmaking*. Santa Fe, NM: Sunstone Press.

Cooper, Barry. 2000. "The Compositional Act: Sketches and Autographs." In *The Cambridge Companion to Beethoven*, ed. Glenn Stanley, 32–42. Cambridge: Cambridge University Press.

———. 2007. *Beethoven: The 35 Piano Sonatas—Commentaries*. Vols. 2 and 3. London: Associated Board of the Royal Schools of Music.

———. 2016. "Beethoven's Preliminary Sketches for the 'Waldstein' Sonata." *Ad Parnassum: A Journal of Eighteenth- and Nineteenth-Century Instrumental Music* 28, no. 28:1–20.

———2017. *The Creation of Beethoven's 35 Piano Sonatas*. New York: Routledge.

Cramer, Carl Friedrich. 1784. *Magazin der Musik*. Vol. 2. Hamburg: in der Musicalischen Niederlage.

Czerny, Carl, trans. 1832. *Vollständiges Lehrbuch der musikalischen Composition [. . .] von A. Reicha*. Vienna: Anton Diabelli & Comp.

———. [1846] 1970. "On the Proper Performance of All Beethoven's Works for the Piano." Chapters 2 and 3 of *The Art of Playing the Ancient and Modern Piano Forte Works* (vol. 4 of *Complete Theoretical and Practical Piano Forte School, Op. 500*). Facsimile, edited by Paul Badura-Skoda. Vienna: Universal Edition.

Dahl, Bjarne, and John Barnes. 1997. "Changes in English Grand Piano Actions between 1787 and 1792." *Galpin Society Journal* 50 (March 1997): 208–11.

Dahlhaus, Carl. [1987] 1991. *Ludwig van Beethoven: Approaches to His Music*. Translated by Mary Whittall. Oxford: Clarendon Press.

DeNora, Tia. 1995. *Beethoven and the Construction of Genius: Musical Politics in Vienna, 1792–1803.* Berkeley: University of California Press.

de Silva, Preethi, ed. and trans. 2008. *The Fortepiano Writings of Streicher, Dieudonné, and the Schiedmayers: Two Manuals and a Notebook, Translated from the Original German, with Commentary.* Lewiston, NY: Edwin Mellen Press.

Dorival, Jérôme. 2006. *Hélène de Montgeroult: La Marquise et la Marseillaise.* Lyon: Symétrie.

Drake, Kenneth. 1994. *The Beethoven Sonatas and the Creative Experience.* Bloomington: Indiana University Press.

Dumes, Charles. 1842. *Notice biographique sur la vie et sur les travaux de Frédéric Guillaume Michel Kalkbrenner.* Paris: Aux Bureaux de La Renommée.

Duvergier, J. B., ed. 1825. *Collection complète des lois, décrets, ordonnances, réglemens et avis du conseil-d'état [. . .] du 1788 à 1824 inclusivement.* Vol. 7. Paris: Chez A. Guyot & Scribe.

Elsner, Józef. 1957. *Sumariusz moich utworów muzycznych* [A Summary of My Musical Works], edited by Alina Nowak-Romanowicz. Kraków: Polskie Wydawnictwo Muzyczne.

Ferraguto, Mark. 2019. *Beethoven 1806.* New York: Oxford University Press.

Fétis, François-Joseph. 1837 and 1839. *Biographie universelle et bibliographie générale de la musique.* Vols. 4 and 5. Brussels: Meline, Cans & Cie.

Fontana, Eszter. 1992. "Beethoven's London Piano and the Viennese Piano Makers." *New Hungarian Quarterly* 33:153–55.

Frimmel, Theodor von. *Bausteine zu einer Lebensgeschichte des Meisters. Beethoven-Studien 2.* Munich: Georg Müller, 1906.

Frohlich, Martha. 1991. *Beethoven's "Appassionata" Sonata.* Oxford: Clarendon Press.

———. 1999. "Sketches for Beethoven's Fourth and Fifth: A Long Neglected Source." *Bonner Beethoven-Studien* 1:29–48.

Gallagher, Mitch. 2008. *The Music Tech Dictionary: A Glossary of Audio-related Terms and Technologies.* Boston: Cengage Learning.

Gautier, Eugène. 1873. *Un musicien en vacances: Études et souvenirs.* Paris: Alphonse Leduc.

Georgel, M. 1818. *Voyage à Saint-Pétersbourg.* Paris: Alexis Eymery & Delaunay.

Gervais, Pierre. 2012. "Mercantile Credit and Trading Rings in the Eighteenth Century." *Annales: Histoire, Sciences Sociales* 67 no. 4:693–730.

Gibson, James. 1979. *The Ecological Approach to Visual Perception.* Boston: Houghton Mifflin.

Giglio, Robert V. 2015. "Music, Language, and Fortepianos: Testing the Speaking Qualities of *stoss* and *prell*." Master's thesis, McGill University.

Goebl-Streicher, Ute, Jutta Streicher, and Michael Ladenburger. 1999. *"Diesem Menschen hätte ich mein ganzes Leben widmen mögen": Beethoven und die Wiener Klavierbauer Nannette und Andreas Streicher.* Bonn: Beethovenhaus.

Good, Edwin. 2001. *Giraffes, Black Dragons, and Other Pianos: A Technological History from Cristofori to the Modern Concert Grand.* 2nd ed. Stanford: Stanford University Press.

Goy, Pierre. 2009. "L'Utilisation des registres dans la musique française de pianoforte au début du XIXe siècle." *Musique, Images, Instruments: Revue française d'organologie et d'iconographie musicale* 11:243–65.

Grave, Floyd K., and Margaret Grave. 1987. *In Praise of Harmony: The Teachings of Abbé Georg Joseph Vogler.* Lincoln: University of Nebraska Press.

Harding, Rosamond E. M. 1933. *The Piano-Forte: Its History Traced to The Great Exhibition of 1851.* Cambridge: Cambridge University Press.

Heer, Josef. 1933. *Der Graf von Waldstein und sein Verhältnis zu Beethoven.* Leipzig: Quelle & Meyer.

Helyard, Erin. 2011. "Muzio Clementi, Difficult Music, and Cultural Ideology in Late Eighteenth-century England." PhD diss., McGill University.

———. 2016. "'To Prevent the Abuse of the Open Pedal': Meticulous Pedal Markings from Madam Brillon to Moscheles." *Keyboard Perspectives* 9:43–66.

Hodder, Ian. 2012. *Entangled: An Archaeology of the Relationships between Humans and Things.* Malden, MA: John Wiley & Sons.

———. 2018. *Where Are We Heading? The Evolution of Humans and Things.* New Haven: Yale University Press.

Howard, Stanley E. 1932. "Public Rules for Private Accounting in France, 1673 and 1807." *Accounting Review* 7, no. 2:91–102.

Huber, Alfons. 1990. "Beethovens 'Erard'-Flügel: Überlegungen zu seiner Restaurierung." *Restauro* 3:181–88.

Jander, Owen. 1985. "Beethoven's 'Orpheus in Hades': The 'Andante con moto' of the Fourth Piano Concerto." *19th-Century Music* 8, no. 3:195–212.

———. 1995. "Orpheus Revisited: A Ten-Year Retrospect on the Andante con moto of Beethoven's Fourth Piano Concerto. *19th-Century Music* 19, no. 1:31–49.

———. 1996. "Genius in the Arena of Charlatanry: The First Movement of Beethoven's 'Tempest' Sonata in Cultural Context." In *Musica franca: Essays in Honor of Frank A. D'Accone,* edited by Irene Alm, Alyson McLamore, and Colleen Reardon. Stuyvesant, NY: Pendragon Press, 585–630.

———. 2009. *Beethoven's "Orpheus" Concerto: The Fourth Piano Concerto in Its Cultural Context.* Hillsdale, NY: Pendragon Press.

Junker, Carl Ludwig. 1791. "*Boßlers Musikalische Korrespondenz* 47 (November 23, 1791)." In *Beethoven aus der Sicht seiner Zeitgenossen in Tagebüchern, Briefen, Gedichten und Erinnerungen,* edited by Klaus Martin Kopitz and Rainer Cadenbach, 498–500. 2 vols. Munich: G. Henle Verlag.

Kaiser, Joachim. 1975. *Beethovens 32 Klaviersonaten und ihre Interpreten.* Frankfurt am Main: Fischer Taschenbuch Verlag.

Kinderman, William. 2009. *Beethoven.* 2nd ed. New York: Oxford University Press.

Kinsky, Georg, and Hans Halm. 1955. *Das Werk Beethovens: Thematisch-bibliographisches Verzeichnis seiner sämtlichen vollendeten Kompositionen.* Munich: G. Henle Verlag.

Kline, A. S., trans. 2001. *Virgil: Georgics—Book IV.* https://www.poetryintranslation.com/PITBR/Latin/VirgilGeorgicsIV.php#_Toc534524384.

Kolneder, Walter, ed. 1968. *Carl Czerny: Erinnerungen aus meinem Leben.* Collection d'études musicologiques / Sammlung musikwissenschaftlicher Abhanglungen, 46. Strasbourg: Éditions P. H. Heitz.

Komlós, Katalin. 1995. *Fortepianos and Their Music: Germany, Austria, and England, 1760–1800.* Oxford: Clarendon Press.

Kopitz, Klaus Martin, and Rainer Cadenbach, eds. 2009. *Beethoven aus der Sicht seiner Zeitgenossen in Tagebüchern, Briefen, Gedichten und Erinnerungen.* 2 vols. Munich: G. Henle Verlag.

Kraus, Beate Angelika. 2001. *Beethoven-Rezeption in Frankreich von ihren Anfängen bis zum Untergang des Second Empire.* Bonn: Verlag Beethoven-Haus.

La Grandville, Frédéric de. 2014. *Une histoire du piano au Conservatoire de musique de Paris 1795–1850.* Paris: L'Harmattan.

———. 2017a. "Le Conservatoire de musique de Paris (1795–1815): Introduction et description des sources." *Élèves et classes du Conservatoire de musique de Paris (1795–1815).* Études et documents en ligne de l'IReMus, Archives nationales de France. https://www.iremus.cnrs.fr/en/publications/eleves-et-classes-du-conservatoire-de-musique-de-paris-1795-1815.

———. 2017b. "Dictionnaire biographique des élèves et aspirants du Conservatoire du musique de Paris (1795–1815)." *Élèves et classes du Conservatoire de musique de Paris (1795–1815).* Études et documents en ligne de l'IReMus, Archives nationales de France. https://www.iremus.cnrs.fr/en/publications/eleves-et-classes-du-conservatoire-de-musique-de-paris-1795-1815.

———. 2017c. "Le Conservatoire de musique de Paris (1795–1815): Tableaux des classes." *Élèves et classes du Conservatoire de musique de Paris (1795–1815).* Études et documents en ligne de l'IReMus, Archives nationales de France. https://www.iremus.cnrs.fr/en/publications/eleves-et-classes-du-conservatoire-de-musique-de-paris-1795-1815.

Landon, H. C. Robbins. 1977a. *Haydn: The Years of 'The Creation,' 1796–1800.* Vol. 4 of *Haydn: Chronicle and Works.* Bloomington: Indiana University Press.

———. 1977b. *Haydn: The Late Years, 1801–1809.* Vol. 5 of *Haydn: Chronicle and Works.* Bloomington: Indiana University Press.

Latcham, Michael. 1997. "Mozart and the Pianos of Gabriel Anton Walter." *Early Music* 25, no. 3:382–400.

———. 2007. "The Development of the Streicher Firm of Piano Builder under the Leadership of Nannette Streicher, 1792 to 1823." In *Das Wiener Klavier bis 1850,* edited by Beatrix Darmstädter, Alfons Huber, and Rudolf Hopfner, 43–71. Tutzing: Hans Schneider.

———. 2009. "In the Shadow of the Enlightenment." *Musique, images, instruments: Revue française d'organologie et d'iconographie musicale* 11:18–45.

Latour, Bruno. [1993] 2000. "The Berlin Key or How to Do Words with Things." In *Matter, Materiality and Modern Culture*, edited by Paul Graves-Brown, 10–21. New York: Routledge.

Lockwood, Lewis, and Alan Gosman, eds. 2013. *Beethoven's "Eroica" Sketchbook: A Critical Edition.* 2 vols. Champaign: University of Illinois Press.

Lubimov, Alexei. 2013. *Ludwig van Beethoven: Moonlight—Waldstein—Storm.* CD recording. Paris: Alpha Productions (ALPHA 194).

Maniguet, Thierry. 2009. "Le piano en forme de clavecin Èrard." *Musique, images, instruments: Revue française d'organologie et d'iconographie musicale* 11:82–97.

———. 2013. "Le piano en forme de clavecin d'Érard, premier piano do concert français." Translated as "Érard's 'Harpsichord-shaped' Piano, the First True French Concert Piano." Booklet notes to Alexei Lubimov, *Ludwig van Beethoven: Moonlight—Waldstein—Storm*, CD recording (Paris: Alpha Productions) (ALPHA 194).

Marmontel, Antoine. 1878. *Les pianistes célèbres.* Paris: A. Chaix & Cᵢᵉ.

Maruyama, Keisuke. 1987. "Die Sinfonia des Prometheus." In *Beethoven: Analecta varia*, edited by Heinz-Klaus Metzger and Rainer Riehn, 46–82. Munich: Edition Text & Kritik.

Maunder, Richard. 1998. *Keyboard Instruments in Eighteenth-Century Vienna.* Oxford: Clarendon Press.

Mayer, John Baptist. n.d. [1811]. *A Complete Demonstration of the Advantages afforded by Mr Sebastian Erard's New Invented Harp with Double Action in the Pedals.* London: Willis.

Meredith, William. 2012. "The Westerby-Meredith Hypothesis: The History of the Eroica Variations and Daniel Steibelt's Fortepiano Quintet, Opus 28, no. 2." *Beethoven Journal* 27, no. 1:26–44.

Milchmeyer, J. P. 1797. *Die wahre Art, das Pianoforte zu spielen.* Dresden: beim churfürstl. Hofbuchdrucker Carl Christian Meinhold.

Montgeroult, Hélène de. n.d. [1820]. *Cours complet pour l'enseignement du Forté Piano conduisant progressivement des premiers éléments aux plus grandes difficultés.* Paris: Launer.

Moscheles, Charlotte. 1873. *Life of Moscheles, with Selections from His Diaries and Correspondence, By His Wife.* Translated and adapted by A. D. Coleridge. 2 vols. London: Hurst & Blackett.

Müller, Gottfried. 1973. *Daniel Steibelt: Sein Leben und seine Klavierwerke.* Baden-Baden: Verlag Valentin Koerner.

Nautsch, Hans. 1983. *Friedrich Kalkbrenner: Wirkung und Werk.* Hamburg: Verlag der Musikalienhandlung Karl Dieter Wagner.

Newman, William. 1988. *Beethoven on Beethoven: Playing His Piano Music His Way.* New York: W. W. Norton.

Nex, Jennifer. 2013. *The Business of Musical-Instrument Making in Early Industrial London.* Diss., Goldsmiths College, University of London.

Ollivier, François, Sylvie Le Moyne, and Sandie Leconte. 2012. "Acoustics Radiation and Modal Analysis of a Piano Forte and Its Fac-simile." In *Acoustics 2012*, 3981–85. Nantes: Société française d'acoustique.

Pay, Antony. 1996. "Phrasing in Contention." *Early Music* 24, no. 2:291–321.

Pierre, Constant. 1900. *Le Conservatoire national de musique et de déclamation: Documents historiques et administratifs.* 2 vols. Paris: Imprimerie nationale.

Pollens, Stewart. 2017. *Bartolomeo Cristofori and the Invention of the Piano.* Cambridge: Cambridge University Press.

Pougin, Arthur. 1877. *Adolphe Adam: Sa vie, sa carrière, ses mémoires artistiques.* Paris: G. Charpentier.

———. 1880. "La Jeunesse d'Herold." *Revue et gazette musicale de Paris* 47, no. 18:138–40; no. 19:145–46.

Raab, Armin, Christine Siegert, and Wolfram Steinbeck, eds. 2010. *Das Haydn Lexikon.* Laaber: Laaber-Verlag.

Rampe, Siegbert. 2015. *Beethovens Klaviere und seine Klavierimprovisation: Klangwelt und Aufführungspraxis.* Munich: Musikverlag Katzbichler.

Reichardt, Johann Friedrich. 1804. *Vertraute Briefe aus Paris geschrieben in den Jahren 1802 und 1803.* 2 vols. Hamburg: Hoffmann.

Reinecke, Carl. 1895. *Die Beethoven'schen Claviersonaten: Briefe an eine Freundin.* Leipzig: Gebrüder Reinecke.

Rhein, Robert. 1993. *Johann Peter Milchmeyer's Die wahre Art das Pianoforte zu spielen: An Annotated Translation.* Diss., University of Nebraska, Lincoln.

Rose, Maria. 2001. "Hélène de Montgeroult and the Art of Singing Well on the Piano." *Women & Music* 5:99–124.

Rose–van Epenhuysen, Maria. 2005. "Beethoven and His 'French Piano': Proof of Purchase." *Musique, images, instruments: Revue française d'organologie et d'iconographie musicale* 7:111–22.

———. 2006. "*L'Art de Bien Chanter*: French Pianos and Their Music before 1820." PhD diss., New York University.

Rosen, Charles. 2002. *Beethoven's Piano Sonatas: A Short Companion.* New Haven: Yale University Press.

Roudet, Jeanne. 2005. "Du texte à l'oeuvre: La question de l'expression dans les méthodes de piano publiées en France entre 1800 et 1840." PhD diss., Université Paris-Sorbonne (Paris IV).

Roudier, Alain. 1993. "Les origines de la famille Erard." In *Sébastien Erard (1752–1831) ou la rencontre avec le pianoforte.* Exh. cat. Luxeuil-les-Bains: Publi-Lux.

Rovelli, Federica. 1999. "The Rondos of Beethoven's Sonata Opus 53: Compositional Process and Formal Conception." *Bonner Beethoven-Studien* 10:121–38.

Rowland, David. 2009. "Piano Businesses in England and France." *Musique, images, instruments: Revue française d'organologie et d'iconographie musicale* 11:127–35.

Ryan, John. 2014. "Historical Note: Did Double-entry Bookkeeping Contribute to Economic Development, Specifically the Introduction of Capitalism?" *Australasian Accounting, Business and Finance Journal* 3, no. 3:85–97.

Sargentson, Carolyn. 1996. *Merchants and Luxury Markets: The Marchands Marciers of Eighteenth-century Paris.* London: Victoria & Albert Museum.

Savary, Philemon-Louis. [1723] 1742. *Dictionnaire universel de commerce.* Vol. 2 (D–O). Geneva: Chez les Héritiers Cramer & Frères Philibert.

Schachter, Carl. 2016. *The Art of Tonal Analysis: Twelve Lessons in Schenkerian Theory.* Edited by Joseph N. Straus. New York: Oxford University Press.

Schenker, Heinrich. [1925] 1974. "Weg mit dem Phrasierungsbogen." In *Das Meisterwerk in der Musik*, vol. 3, 43–60. Facsimile edition. Hildesheim: Georg Olms, 1974.

Schiff, András. 2004–6. "Sonata No. 22 in F, Op. 54." Part 6 of Beethoven Lecture-Recitals, Wigmore Hall, London. https://wigmore-hall.org.uk/podcasts/andras-schiff-beethoven-lecture-recitals.

Schiffer, Michael Brian. 2004. "Studying Technological Change: A Behavioral Perspective." *World Archaeology* 36, no. 4:579–85.

Schirlbauer, Anna. 2015. "Nicolaus Zmeskall (1759–1833): Zwischen Musik und Bürokratie, Österreich und Ungarn." In *Widmungen bei Haydn und Beethoven: Personen—Strategien—Praktiken*, edited by Bernhard R. Appel and Armin Raab, 245–60. Bonn: Verlag Beethoven-Haus.

Schönfeld, Johann Ferdinand von. [1796] 1976. *Jahrbuch der Tonkunst von Wien und Prag.* Facsimile edition, edited by Otto Biba. Munich: Musikverlag Emil Katzbichler.

Schünemann, Georg. 1939. "Czernys Erinnerungen an Beethoven." *Neues Beethoven-Jahrbuch* 9:47–74.

Sisman, Elaine. 2008. "Six in One: The Opus Concept in the Eighteenth Century." In *The Century of Bach and Mozart: Perspectives on Historiography, Composition, Theory, and Performance*, edited by Sean Gallagher and Thomas Forrest Kelly, 79–107. Cambridge, MA: Harvard University Press.

Skowroneck, Tilman. 2007. *Beethoven the Pianist: Biographical, Organological and Performance-practical Aspects of His Years as a Public Performer.* PhD diss., Göteborg University.

———. 2009. "Beethoven and the Orchestral Piano." *Musique, images, instruments: Revue française d'organologie et d'iconographie musicale* 11:181–89.

———. 2010. *Beethoven the Pianist.* Cambridge: Cambridge University Press.

———. 2014a. "Andreas Streichers Briefe an Gottlieb [*recte*: Gottfried] Härtel 1801–

1810." In *Unisonus: Musikinstrumente erforschen, bewahren, sammeln*, edited by Beatrix Darmstädter and Ina Hoheisel, 386–405. Vienna: Praesens.

———. 2014b. "Anton Walter and the *una corda* Shift." Blog post. https://skowroneck.wordpress.com/2014/04/24/anton-walter-and-the-una-corda-shift/.

Smith, Adam. [1775] 2007. *An Inquiry into the Nature and Causes of the Wealth of Nations.* Edited by S. M. Soares. MεταLibri Digital Library.

Solomon, Maynard. 1998. *Beethoven.* 2nd, rev. ed. New York: Schirmer Books.

Staehelin, Martin, ed. 1984. *Ludwig van Beethoven: Klaviersonate in C-Dus Op. 53 (Waldstein-Sonate). Faksimile-Ausgabe des im Beethoven-Haus Bonn befindlichen Autographs.* Bonn: Beethoven-Haus.

Steblin, Rita. 2007. "Beethovens Beziehungen zu Wiener Klavierbauern um 1800 im Licht neuer Dokumente der Familie Brunswick." In *Das Wiener Klavier bis 1850,* edited by Beatrix Darmstädter, Alfons Huber, and Rudolf Hopfner, 73–82. Tutzing: Hans Schneider.

Steibelt, Daniel. n.d. [c. 1809]. *Méthode de piano ou l'art d'enseigner cet Instrument / Pianoforte-Schule.* Leipzig: Breitkopf & Härtel.

Streicher, Johann Andreas. 1801. *Kurze Bemerkungen über das Spielen, Stimmen und Erhalten der Fortepiano, welche von Nannette Streicher, geborne Stein in Wien verfertiget werden.* Vienna: mit Albertischen Schriften.

Taub, Robert. 2002. *Playing the Beethoven Piano Sonatas.* New York: Amadeus Press.

Thayer, Alexander Wheelock. [1866–79] 1921. *The Life of Ludwig van Beethoven.* Edited, revised and amended by Henry Edward Krehbiel. 3 vols. New York: Beethoven Association.

———. [1866–79] 1967. *Thayer's Life of Beethoven.* Revised and edited by Elliot Forbes. 2 vols. Princeton, NJ: Princeton University Press.

Tovey, Donald Francis. 1931. *A Companion to Beethoven's Pianoforte Sonatas.* London: Associated Board of the Royal Schools of Music.

Uhde, Jürgen. 1968. *Beethovens 32 Klaviersonaten.* Stuttgart: Reclam.

———. [1974] 1991. *Beethovens Klaviermusik. Band III: Sonaten 16–32.* Stuttgart: Reclam.

Van Gool, Jonas. 2014. *Opname- en reproductiesysteem voor een fortepiano.* Master's thesis, Antwerp University.

Wacha, Georg. 1975. "Johann van Beethoven: Neue Quellen zur beruflichen Tätigkeit des Linzer und Urfahrer Apothekers." In *Historisches Jahrbuch der Stadt Linz 1972,* 105–53. Linz: Archiv der Stadt.

Wallace, Robin. 2018. *Hearing Beethoven: A Story of Musical Loss and Discovery.* Chicago: University of Chicago Press.

Walter, Horst. 1970. "Haydns Klaviere." *Haydn-Studien* 2, no. 4:256–88.

Watson, John R. 2010. *Artifacts in Use: The Paradox of Restoration and the Conservation of Organs.* Richmond, VA: OHS Press.

Weber, Rolf. 1981. Introduction to Johann Friedrich Reichardt, *Vertraute Briefe aus Paris 1802/03*, edited by Rolf Weber, 5–16. Berlin: Verlag der Nation.

Webster, James. 1984. "The Falling-out between Haydn and Beethoven: The Evidence of the Sources." In *Beethoven Essays: Studies in Honor of Elliot Forbes*, edited by Lewis Lockwood and Phyllis Benjamin, 3–45. Cambridge, MA: Harvard University Press.

———. 2005. "The Sublime and the Pastoral in *The Creation* and *The Seasons*." In *The Cambridge Companion to Haydn*, edited by Caryl Clark, 150–63. Cambridge: Cambridge University Press.

Webster, James, and Georg Feder. 2002. *The New Grove Haydn*. London: Macmillan.

Wegeler, Franz Gerhard, and Ferdinand Ries. 1838. *Biographische Notizen über Ludwig van Beethoven*. Coblenz: K. Bädeker.

Weitz, Shaena. 2015. "*Le Pianiste* and Its History of Pianism in Paris: 'The Corneilles and Racines of piano are not *perruques!*'" In *Piano Culture in 19th-Century Paris*, edited by Massimiliano Sala, 331–57. Turnhout: Brepols.

———. 2016. "*Le Pianiste*: Parisian Music Journalism and the Politics of the Piano, 1833–35." PhD diss., City University of New York Graduate Center.

Wiesnerová, Markéta. 2014. "Beethoven and the Musical History of the Château of Hradec nad Moravicí." *Friends of Czech Heritage Newsletter* 11 (Summer–Autumn): 6–11.

Winston, David. 1993. "The Restoration of Beethoven's 1817 Broadwood Grand Piano." *Galpin Society Journal* 46:147–51.

Wogram, Klaus. 1990. "The Strings and the Soundboard." In *Five Lectures on the Acoustics of the Piano*, edited by Anders Askenfelt, 83–98. Stockholm: Royal Swedish Academy of Music.

Wurzbach, Constant von. 1885. *Biographisches Lexikon des Kaiserthums Oesterreich, enthaltend die Lebensskizzen der denkwürdigen Personen, welche seit 1750 in den österreichischen Kronländern geboren wurden oder darin gelebt und gewirkt haben*. Vol. 52. Vienna: Druck & Verlag der k. k. Hof- und Staatsdruckerei.

Wyn Jones, David. 2016. *Music in Vienna 1700, 1800, 1900*. Woodbridge, UK: Boydell & Brewer.

Zibermayr, Ignaz. 1933. "Die Gründung des oberösterreichischen Musealvereines im Bilde der Geschichte des landeskundlichen Sammelwesens." *Jahrbuch des oberösterreichischen Musealvereines* 85:69–180.

INDEX